KU-775-555

# Singled Out

*How Two Million Women Survived Without*
*Men after the First World War*

VIRGINIA NICHOLSON

VIKING
*an imprint of*
PENGUIN BOOKS

VIKING

Published by the Penguin Group
Penguin Books Ltd, 80 Strand, London WC2R ORL, England
Penguin Group (USA) Inc., 375 Hudson Street, New York, New York 10014, USA
Penguin Group (Canada), 90 Eglinton Avenue East, Suite 700, Toronto, Ontario, Canada M4P 2Y3
(a division of Pearson Penguin Canada Inc.)
Penguin Ireland, 25 St Stephen's Green, Dublin 2, Ireland
(a division of Penguin Books Ltd)
Penguin Group (Australia), 250 Camberwell Road, Camberwell, Victoria 3124, Australia
(a division of Pearson Australia Group Pty Ltd)
Penguin Books India Pvt Ltd, 11 Community Centre, Panchsheel Park, New Delhi – 110 017, India
Penguin Group (NZ), 67 Apollo Drive, Rosedale, North Shore 0632, New Zealand
(a division of Pearson New Zealand Ltd)
Penguin Books (South Africa) (Pty) Ltd, 24 Sturdee Avenue, Rosebank, Johannesburg 2196, South Africa

Penguin Books Ltd, Registered Offices: 80 Strand, London WC2R ORL, England

www.penguin.com

First published 2007
2

Copyright © Virginia Nicholson, 2007

The moral right of the author has been asserted

All rights reserved.
Without limiting the rights under copyright
reserved above, no part of this publication may be
reproduced, stored in or introduced into a retrieval system,
or transmitted, in any form or by any means (electronic, mechanical,
photocopying, recording or otherwise), without the prior
written permission of both the copyright owner and
the above publisher of this book

Set in 11/13.75pt Monotype Bembo
Typeset by Rowland Phototypesetting Ltd, Bury St Edmunds, Suffolk
Printed in Great Britain by Clays Ltd, St Ives plc

A CIP catalogue record for this book is available from the British Library

ISBN: 978-0-670-91564-4

www.greenpenguin.co.uk

Mixed Sources
Product group from well-managed
forests and other controlled sources
www.fsc.org  Cert no. SA-COC-1592
© 1996 Forest Stewardship Council

Penguin Books is committed to a sustainable future
for our business, our readers and our planet.
The book in your hands is made from paper
certified by the Forest Stewardship Council.

# Contents

# List of Illustrations

15. The staff of the Electrical Association for Women honour their founder Caroline Haslett, awarded the DBE in June 1947 (Courtesy Institution of Engineering and Technology Archives)

16. Career woman Bessie Webster chose to be photographed leaning against her Chairman's Rolls Royce (Courtesy Isabel Raphael)

17. After thirty-seven attempts, Victoria Drummond passes her Chief Engineer's exam (from Cherry Drummond, *The Remarkable Life of Victoria Drummond, Marine Engineer*)

18. 'Gert and Daisy': Elsie and Doris Waters (Getty Images)

19. 'I thought a god was there': Richard Aldington in 1931 (National Portrait Gallery)

20. Irene Rathbone, featured in a round-up of book reviews in the weekly *Everyman*, 1933 (British Library, Newspaper Library)

21. *Private View* (1937) by Gladys Hynes. Unmistakable in the centre of the picture are Radclyffe Hall and her lover Una Troubridge (from Michael Baker, *Our Three Selves*)

22. A Universal Aunt (from Kate Herbert-Hunting, *Universal Aunts*)

23. Nannies in Hyde Park (Hulton Archive/Getty Images)

24. Mary Milne, Matron of St Mary's Hospital, Paddington. Her fiancé was killed in the war (St Mary's NHS Trust Archive)

25. In the 1920s nursing was one of the few professions seen as respectable for decent young ladies (Hulton Archive/Getty Images)

26. After her mother's death, Phyllis Bentley rediscovered a guiltless freedom (from her autobiography, *O Dreams, O Destinations*)

27. Rowena Cade, founder of the Minack Theatre, Cornwall (Courtesy Minack Theatre Trust)

28. Winifred Haward and Louis Hodgkiss (from Winifred Haward's autobiography, *Two Lives*)

29. 'I would live my life over again': lady's maid Rose Harrison (from her autobiography, *My Life in Service*)

30. Post-war, women replenished the ranks of white-collar workers killed in the trenches (Courtesy Cadbury Schweppes Plc)

## Illustrations in the Text

# Introduction

The First World War deprived Britain of nearly three-quarters of a million soldiers, slaughtered on the Western Front and elsewhere. They were known as 'the Flower of Europe', 'the Flowers of the Forest', and 'the Lost Generation'. Many of them left behind widows and orphans, but enormous numbers of these young men were unmarried when they died. Their deaths bereaved another generation: the thousands of women born, like them, between 1885 and 1905, who unquestioningly believed marriage to be their birthright, only to have it snatched from them by four of the bloodiest years in human history.

Those women started to die off in the 1970s and 80s, and now there are few left, but anyone today over the age of thirty or forty will remember them. In the 1920s when the phenomenon first arose they were known collectively as the Surplus Women, and according to the 1921 Census there were one and three-quarter million of them. I remember as a child in suburban Leeds our neighbour was one of these spinsters. Miss Pease was diminutive and self-effacing; she lived a blamelessly meek and solitary existence in a humble stone terrace house with a cat, a cottage piano and an outside lavatory. Though you couldn't pigeonhole them, these women were somehow both valiant and incongruous. Unasked questions hovered around them. Why didn't they ever marry? Did they mind? Did they harbour secret sadness? What did they do about the lack of love in their lives, and the lack of sex? Did they care that they had never had children? Did their spectacles and tweed jackets protect them from terrible vulner-abilities? One never asked the questions, because one never dared. They were private and uncomplaining, and perhaps too one hesitated to reveal answers that exposed one's own fears of loneliness. Would one end up like them, with just cats for company?

Today the word 'spinster' has all but disappeared from current vocabu-lary, but the singles are still out in force. Some statistics predict 11 million singles in Britain by 2010. Mystery surrounds the murky figures revealed by the 2001 Census, in which around a million men of marriageable age appear to have gone missing (one theory is that they have all emigrated in search of jobs abroad). In the twenty-first century women are marrying older, and they are marrying less. But while the stigma may have gone, the fears remain. Everyone now knows that marriage is not the only route to fulfilment, but the media and the internet tell of more lonely hearts and solitary singles than ever before. In this context, it is surely timely to examine a period of history when the 'problem' of the Surplus Women prompted both widespread anxiety and a wealth of solutions.

And so I set out to ask the inconvenient questions that my generation never saw fit to ask Miss Pease and her like. I wanted to find out how they coped with enforced spinsterhood and all it entailed, in a world which Ruth Adam, a now neglected writer who lived through the first half of the twentieth century, described as 'the Mutilated Society'. Learning about the women who discovered, in 1919, that there weren't enough men to go round has been at times deeply moving. They did indeed harbour secret sadnesses, and many of them yearned for the comforts forever denied them: physical intimacy, the closeness of a loving relationship and children. Many women also suffered acutely from the blame that society laid at their feet. As victims, they were often abused and marginalised. But I have also discovered many tales of individual courage in the face of a tragedy of historic proportions. Ruth Adam sang their praises in her book *A Woman's Place* (1975): 'This was the era of the spinster. At last, after so many years of being grudged the right to exist at all, she came into her own.' Like her, I am left full of admiration for the many brave women who learnt both to survive, and to triumph.

The chapters that follow trace the emotional trajectory of their subject matter from the initial plight of the Surplus Woman following the war and across the next two decades, through her experience of her own predicament and the necessity of facing life alone; they ask how she survived economically, emotionally and sexually, and they look at the advantages of spinsterhood. The final chapter reflects on, and honours, the achievements of a generation of single women. They were changed by war; in their turn they helped change society. I believe that today's women are in their debt.

My approach in writing this book has been as far as possible to tell individual stories, and to emphasise personal details that I found fascinating, however seemingly irrelevant. When we reach into the past, we look for points of contact. Few of the names in this book are remembered today, and this too is deliberate. Demographics and statistics too easily blind one to the forgotten participants who made up the numbers; and I hope my reader will forgive me for hoping that she (or he?) will find it easier to identify with the predicament of young women 'to fortune and to fame unknown'.

Many kind people wrote to me with stories of their teachers, aunts, patients and neighbours. Libraries, archives and old ladies' homes slowly but surely yielded up a wealth of telling memories. Inevitably the documents available have meant that this account may appear skewed in its emphasis on the middle classes. Where possible I have delved into accounts of their lives by working-class women. The stories of May Jones, Amy Gomm, Lizzie Rignall, Rose Harrison, Amy Langley and Florence and Annie White all testify to experiences shared with more privileged women.

There is another reason for the emphasis on middle-class case-histories. It is generally accepted that in the Great War a higher proportion of the officer class was killed than of those lower down the social scale. A hundred years ago few people married outside their tribe. Middle-class women seeking husbands after the war did not on the whole consider marrying among the blue-collar ranks, thus their chances of marriage were dispro-portionately lowered. Programmed through generations to be mere orna-ments and chattels, these genteel women's attempts to stand fast in the face of historic calamity now seem especially poignant.

There is some dispute about how real the shortage of men was, and evidence exists that women's response to the lack of 'suitable' mates was to seek them outside the usual narrow spheres, whether social or geo-graphical. Statisticians point out that the number of post-war spinsters did not in fact greatly differ from the number of pre-war spinsters (while conceding that middle- and upper-class women in particular did face reduced marriage prospects); but this is to ignore the undoubted effect of grief, loss and national trauma. As the historian David Cannadine empha-sises: 'The abiding sense of loss throughout the land was as real as it was unassuageable.' Death and bereavement were, he points out, 'a mass reality'; a pall descended over Britain.

Whatever the case, it is beyond doubt that the war had a seismic effect on marital behaviour, that all contemporary accounts take the man shortage for granted, and that many women themselves perceived the courtship arena as a competitive battleground, where defeat was perdition. The press played its usual mischievous part in this, by whipping up a frenzy over the 1921 Census figures, which revealed that there were 1,720,802 more females than males in the population: that was 1,096 women to every 1,000 men. Hysterical headlines about the 'Problem of the Surplus Woman – Two Million who can Never Become Wives . . .' were hardly conducive to morale among the husband-hunters of the day. In the event it appears that more than a million women of that generation were never to marry or bear children. This book, then, is an examination of the state of spinsterhood under the unprecedented conditions which prevailed after a cataclysmic war.

But war was not the only reason that one in four British women remained single. Under pressure from the feminists of the late nineteenth and early twentieth centuries, the patriarchal monolith was showing early signs of dissolution and that meant, above all for middle-class women, an increase in economic and employment openings. In a number of professions, medicine and teaching for example, women were usually expected to resign on marriage, but at the same time financial independence deterred many women from reverting to wifely subjection. Spinsterhood could be a choice.

Eighty years ago the world these women lived in was a very different place from ours. From the mill-girl turned political activist to the debutante turned archaeologist, from the first woman stockbroker to the 'business girls' and the Miss Jean Brodies, I have attempted to interweave their stories into the social fabric of their time. The reader may have reservations about my occasional use of that word 'girl' to describe the young women of the inter-war period; in my defence, it was universally used of unmarried women. Its patronising condescension gives, I believe, an accurate flavour of a time and a tone of voice now fading from living memory.

I myself was thirty-two when I stopped being a spinster, married and started a family. In the course of working on this book I have several times been asked what drew me to write an account of spinsterhood. The answer is both personal and, I think, universal. My mother married late because the first man she loved had been killed in the Second World War; because of this I did not grow up taking marriage for granted, and I turned thirty firmly persuaded that not yet having found Mr Right, I was unlikely to do so. In that belief I took stock, faced the fear, and counted my blessings: I had the love of friends and family, an interesting life, and some money. Barely two years later I was planning my wedding; I have been fortunate in a long and happy marriage which, along with our children, has been a wonderful, unsought and undeserved bonus. Often I look back and try to think what my life would have been like had I not had such fortune, and I conclude that the blessings I had at the age of thirty would have continued to bring me happiness, as indeed they still do. In the end we are alone. In recognising that, I also accept that marriage – even love – can never be everything in life.

The women I write about learnt out of necessity not to be reliant on husbands; in doing so many of them bravely reinvented themselves. Even if we are not, like them, forced through grief and war to learn the same lesson, it does no harm to recognise that our lives are our own to build or destroy. The following pages offer, I hope, some of their solutions, and also some of their consolations.

# 1. Where Have All the Young Men Gone?

## Two women

In 1978, when she was eighty-five years old, Margaret Jones, known as May, wrote her autobiography. The manuscript is mostly written in biro, on assorted pieces of coloured paper and the backs of circulars. It has never been published; it is not literary, sensational or revelatory. In fact there is little to single it out, for it is a story typical of thousands of women of her generation. But as you read it, a century melts away. May's story stops being a case-history and instead you catch a glimpse of the unique, transient life of a real person.

May Jones was born in 1893, the oldest daughter of a Welsh carpenter. She grew up in a small village in Cheshire not far from one of the great mill towns. Her home was a damp smoky cottage, and it was a struggle for her family to keep afloat financially. Nevertheless, writing at the end of her life, May was able to bring to mind happy pictures of her father's evening pursuits: she would hold the candle steady for him as he worked meticulously on the wood-carvings which brought in a little extra money. The child would play with the lovely curly wood-shavings, holding them up as ringlets on the side of her face. She remembered merry evenings in the village dancing to the hurdy-gurdy man, or scrambling for fistfuls of sweets thrown to them by the Squire at the annual Sunday school treat. Summer was the high spot, when she and her younger brother were carried off to stay at her grandfather's house twelve miles away, the children piled into empty potato baskets on the back of a cart drawn by a great Shire horse.

But Mother was often ill. She had three more children after May, and after each confinement she was laid up. The doctor was a frequent visitor to the Jones household. When Mother couldn't get up, ten-year-old May had to keep house and cook, look after the baby and do the washing.

May was a worry to her parents because she had an over-active imagination. She learnt to read early and loved fairy stories. The little people were real to her. There was a fairy prince who married a fairy princess and lived happily ever after; they lived in flowers. Sometimes one heard their tiny tinkling laughter, but one never saw them. The assiduous doctor wagged his head and told her parents that too much reading would damage her brain. She must be kept back, he said. On his advice she was denied books and only allowed to read at school, though she sneaked her father's carpentry manuals to bed with her at night and read whatever she could lay hands on. When she got older she managed to get hold of copies of *Jane Eyre*, *Lorna Doone* and *Kim*. But her favourite author was Marie Corelli, whose melodramatic romances imbued her with a sense that some day, somewhere, she would unite with her twin soul.

At twelve, May was taken away from school; she was old enough now to make a financial contribution to the family. Her beloved schoolmistress pleaded for her pupil to be allowed to take a scholarship, but May was sent to work in the local textile mill. At thirteen she was the works runabout, known by all in the factory as the 'Flying Angel'. She ran errands from 6.30 in the morning till eight at night, darting up and down the six-storey building from one department to another with orders, messages and samples. She was happy; the other workers were friendly, she appreciated the pretty colours of the silk bobbins, and she was earning five shillings a week. But running tired her out, and May became ill. The next three years were spent working in a tobacconist's, until at sixteen her mother set her up with a five-year apprenticeship to a milliner in town.

At the top of a new page, May Jones wrote the heading for the next episode in her young life: 'My Love Story'. This is where we meet Philip for the first time. Philip and May had been playmates from the age of six. He was a city boy from Manchester, the son of middle-class business people, but May got to know him because he would come to stay with his aunt in the village in the summer holidays. Bright and studious, in due course Philip was to win a scholarship to Cambridge. There wasn't much money around, and his parents – Quakers – were proud to make the sacrifices necessary to give their clever son a university education. He was kind and willing too, and offered to coach May's younger brother, who was studying for an exam. Mother provided a good supper in recompense for his help.

As he was leaving one evening, Mother said to me, 'Get Philip's hat off the hall stand.' We stood talking for a few minutes longer and I saw him looking at me with a smile and a twinkle in his eye, and with a great shock I realised I was hugging his hat and stroking it like I did the cat. I felt dreadful and made the excuse that I had forgotten to close the rabbit hutch up for the night, and ran off, and did not go in again until he had left.

The next day May was at work at the milliner's as usual. The apprentices were let out at 7.30. That evening there was a glorious sunset, and as she stepped out of the dark shop into the street its radiant light nearly blinded her, so that she narrowly missed bumping into Philip standing on the pavement outside: 'I thought you finished at seven,' he said. 'I've been waiting half an hour for you, and I thought I'd missed you. It is such a lovely evening – would you like to walk home Becks Lane way?' Shyly, May agreed. Though she'd known him since she was a child, she felt top-heavy and awkwardly grown-up. He teased her gently. After that, Philip met her every day and walked her home. May gave up taking her bicycle to work, and her brother started to wonder why he wasn't getting so much help with his homework. Little by little Philip and May became close, and after his return home he would cycle the twenty miles from Manchester to spend time with her on her afternoons off.

It was love's young dream . . . We walked for miles through fields, woods and country lanes. I sometimes wonder what we found to talk about. We both loved and enjoyed nature's wonderful treasures, from the tiniest flower and insect to mighty trees and hill top views of the vast Cheshire plain . . . Philip introduced me to poetry too . . . He often quoted a few lines of poetry when speaking to me, and sometimes when he kissed me good night would say, 'I could not love thee dear so much, loved I not honour more.' I was very young at that time, and wondered what he meant when he said that. In those days I must have been very innocent or very ignorant.

May knew nothing about art either; but Philip loved to talk to her about his passions. Out of the small amount of money he had, he would buy her postcard reproductions of famous pictures. The little images delighted her. One of these above all seemed to sum up the happy prospect that awaited the young lovers – a landscape entitled 'June in the Austrian Tyrol'. They would pore over it together, seeing in the picturesque setting an enchanted future. 'I love that picture too,' whispered Philip. 'So – when I am through with Cambridge and in a post, we will get married and go there for our honeymoon.'

Philip and May had been courting for nearly five years when the First World War broke out. As a Quaker Philip believed firmly in the principle, 'Thou shalt not kill.' He registered as a pacifist; nevertheless, he was imprisoned. In prison he studied first aid and care of the wounded, and on his release, felt impelled to put these skills to use. Promptly, he volunteered for active service in France as a stretcher-bearer.

Philip was notably courageous even in his non-combatant role. During battle, he was indefatigable in going over the top to pick up the wounded and carry them to the first aid post. He carried neither gun nor gas-mask.

The Tommies respected his inspirational defiance of danger, and even the German snipers, it appeared, respected Philip's impartiality in helping whoever was suffering or in pain.

May waited anxiously and patiently for his safe return. She treasured the brief letters he was able to send her – sometimes only a printed card on which he had ticked the box beside 'I am well.' At last came a letter saying he was due for leave. May was walking on air.

When she wrote her little memoir more than sixty years later, Miss Margaret Jones barely faltered in the telling of what happened next, but she didn't dwell on the details. Probably the old lady was still too pained by her memories to write more than a few sentences:

Then everything was shattered; a letter came from the War Office to say he had been killed in action. The shock and loss was terrible, I felt I had lost half of myself, or was it my twin soul. I knew then that I should die an old maid.

Miss Jones re-read what she had written, and added the next words in a light pencil script:

I was only twenty years old.

After Philip's death the impulse to continue the account of her memories leaves her. We know no more, for 'My Love Story' simply ends there, with the rest of the page left blank.

★

Fate was cruel to so many women in those forlorn years of war. Their suffering was none the less for being shared by thousands. The voices of the less articulate members of society can be hard to hear, so one can only guess at the effect of sorrow and blighted hope on the subsequent lives of innumerable May Joneses across the nation. But there were nevertheless many women who told their stories. Documents of all kinds exist which illustrate their fate. This book is an attempt to hear and understand what happened to a generation of young women who were forced, by a tragedy of historic proportions, to stop depending on men for their income, their identity and their future happiness.

★

Silent obscurity was not to be Gertrude Caton-Thompson's fate. In 1983, at the age of ninety-five, she too sat down to write her memoirs, able to look back on a long life of professional achievement and personal fulfilment. She was an eminent archaeologist, a formidable researcher and intrepid explorer. Over many decades, Gertrude had travelled and excavated extensively, making her mark on the archaeological world with far-reaching studies of African prehistory. The papers she published on her fieldwork still stand as authoritative; the academic world had dignified her, and she was garlanded with honorary fellowships.

But there was nothing in Gertrude's background or upbringing to indicate what this young Edwardian woman would one day become. Born in 1888, she was just a few years older than May Jones, but the family were a world away. The Caton-Thompsons were well-connected and well-off, cultured and sporty. When she was five and her brother nine their lawyer father died; their mother married a wealthy widowed doctor and they grew up in the Home Counties with a large family of step-siblings. A jolly girls' boarding-school in Eastbourne left Gertrude, in her own opinion, semi-educated and lacking in rigorous training of the mind. Though regularly laid up with annoying bronchitis, she was nevertheless a 'hearty' not an 'arty'. Those pre-war summers of her teens and early twenties saw her out with a group of Edwardian lovelies and young men in boaters sculling on the Thames. Sometimes the family decamped to Scotland for salmon fishing and partridge shooting. Winter often found the family in St Moritz for her mother's health; there she skied all day and danced all night. Above all Gertrude was smitten by hunting. She owned two hunters and in the seasons of 1908 and 1909 rode them alternately to hounds five days every fortnight.

What else did this energetic young woman have time for? As might be expected from a girl of her social class, her accomplishments included a little watercolour sketching and a fair ability on the violin. Concert outings were recorded with care; Gertrude's tastes ranged from Wagner to Rimsky-Korsakov, Gounod to Beethoven. The family were regular, and unquestioning, churchgoers. There were foreign holidays too, mostly with her mother, in Italy, France, Israel, Crete, Sicily, Egypt. The ruins and remains were noted appreciatively; Gertrude was interested in archaeology, and had attended some lectures at the British Museum on the subject of the early Greeks. But she was happy to get home and resume the enjoyable social whirl: golf, tennis, bridge, ten-mile walks, hockey, badminton, point-to-points, and above all an endless round of calls, race parties and dances.

Thus far, Gertrude's upbringing would be indistinguishable from that of any other upper-middle-class young woman of the Edwardian era. But she and her older brother did share one peculiarity: their intense interest in military matters. The nursery had its usual complement of lead soldiers, but to Gertrude and Arthur the toys lived and breathed. Together the children devoured tomes of military history and Army Lists. They committed to memory the battle honours of the various regiments, and knew by heart the histories of Waterloo, the Peninsular War and the Crimean War. They avidly followed the progress of the Boer War.

So it was not surprising that Gertrude found she had much in common with a family from their immediate Berkshire circle, the Mason-MacFarlanes. David MacFarlane, a soldier *manqué*, was the family doctor, and had endeared himself to the ten-year-old Gertrude when she was in bed with bronchitis by attending her in full Territorial uniform and talking 'army'. At the earliest opportunity he retired from medicine and settled down to devote himself to the training of the 4th Territorial regiment of the Seaforth Battalion in Ross-shire. His two boys, Noël and Carlyon, were destined for military careers. Dr MacFarlane sent them off to be cadets at Woolwich and Sandhurst respectively. Off-duty, the boys were the constant companions of Gertrude and her family in all that they did, from hunt balls to river parties.

Carlyon Mason-MacFarlane was a couple of years younger than Gertrude, but the bond they formed was a strong one. Military matters were for both these young people of consuming interest. The British army, its history, its exploits, its hierarchy and its achievements, was of central importance in both their lives. And why should it not be? Today such an interest may seem like a 'special subject', a blind alley. In the early years of the twentieth century, nothing could seem more relevant to the society that these people and their families lived in. In 1910 England was at peace, the Empire was at its zenith, but a major war in Europe was envisaged by anyone with an eye on the activities of the great powers. Military might was seen by the majority as the key to social stability. Soldiers fought so that debutantes could dance.

But Carlyon was no naïve jingoist. This young man was thoughtful beyond his years, incisive and bold in his judgements. Not everyone realised that his irrepressible high spirits and easy gregariousness masked a wide-ranging intellect. Leaving Sandhurst in 1910 loaded with all the honours that the institution could offer, Carlyon opted for a Cavalry commission, shrewdly exploiting the War Office's blindness to the growing obsolescence of mounted troops, and thus speeding up his promotion to a staff appointment. In 1911 he sailed for India to take up his commission with the 7th Hussars. He spent his last evening with Gertrude and her mother in their London flat.

Gertrude's life continued in the same somewhat purposeless vein after

Carlyon's departure. There were dress fittings at Bradley's and lots more hunting. There was a bout of measles, but there was also the Russian ballet. A more committed side showed when she helped to organise a meeting in the Albert Hall to raise money for the Suffragettes. In the winter there was skiing in Mürren, and in the summer there was the Chelsea Flower Show. In 1912 Gertrude read with shock of the sinking of the *Titanic*, with a loss of nearly 1,600 lives. She had a proposal of marriage too, from Montagu Luck, brother-in-law of General Sir George Pretyman, but turned him down. 'My heart was with Carlyon, though in a totally unpossessive way.'

In May 1914 Carlyon unexpectedly returned from India on sick leave; he was convalescing from rheumatic fever. By now war seemed inevitable, and Gertrude found herself mediating between him and a German friend in a heated debate on the imminence of conflict between their two nations. But a few days later the atmosphere was light-hearted as the same group motored to Epsom with an Army and Navy Stores picnic in the back of their hired vehicle for that great British carnival, Derby Day. Among her guests Gertrude had eyes only for the good-looking young officer as he perched precariously on the car roof munching game pie, 'his grey topper pushed back, as carefree as the beautiful day'. It was an image she never forgot.

With Carlyon's family in the Highlands of Scotland, Gertrude made her regular visit to the MacFarlanes at Craigdarroch in late July. In Europe the tension was building, but by Strathpeffer the river Conan teemed with salmon. Gertrude and Carlyon set up their rods on its banks and together kept the household in fish. They both knew that his hour was coming. Serbia and Austria were first to declare; Austria and Russia followed. Colonel MacFarlane and his house party motored down to see the North Sea Fleet lying at anchor in the Cromarty Firth awaiting orders. To the MacFarlanes and their guests, the orderly lines of battleships, cruisers, gun-boats and smaller vessels, all stripped and ready for action, were a majestic and heartening sight. That evening rain set in, but Gertrude and Carlyon found it impossible to stay indoors. The suspense had become intolerable, and sitting restlessly in the drawing-room at Craigdarroch waiting for news wasn't an option. They went for a long walk together; absorbed by the intensity of their companionship, Gertrude barely noticed that she was soaked to the skin. The next day German troops crossed the French frontier, and on 4 August 1914 Britain declared war on Germany.

The Craigdarroch party broke up. Carlyon awaited orders from the War Office; Gertrude went for the summer to her aunt's home near Dumfries, where she lived for the daily newspaper. She heard that Carlyon had been posted to the 15th Hussars, part of the Expeditionary Force; in the first autumn of the war he was among the troops fighting on the Marne and Aisne against the German advance. By now the lists were beginning to appear across the country. Killed, wounded, captured; the systematic destruction of a generation of young men was pitilessly getting under way.

One December evening in 1914 Carlyon arrived unannounced at the London flat where Gertrude, her mother and aunt had just finished dinner. He had been in the very thick of the Allied retreat, and was able to give a full account of his battle experiences. He had, he confessed, been terrified under fire, but he was British, and not showing his fear had been paramount. Carlyon's account of the campaign was ostensibly optimistic: the German offensive had been halted, an Allied offensive would soon follow; he too had risen in his career and was to be given a safer posting. Eventually Gertrude's mother and aunt said good-night. 'May I stay a bit longer?' he asked. When they were alone, Carlyon dropped his breezy stance and confided to Gertrude that he felt profound gloom about the way the war was going. The casualties were appalling. The German army was superior to ours in every way except for the British fighting spirit. Our commanders however were at a loss, and lacked coordination with the French. Finally, having exhausted talk of the war, the conversation turned to their shared past, and those carefree summer days now disappeared for ever. It was close on one in the morning before Carlyon left to walk back in the dark to his club.

That night Gertrude didn't sleep. She now recognised that she loved Carlyon with her whole being. But in accordance with the conventions of the time, neither of them had given each other any hint as to their feelings. As childhood friends, their manner to each other was always warmly affectionate; his letters ended 'with love'; his departures were marked with a kiss. But these were the endearments of habit, not passion. Gertrude made up her mind, in that long sleepless night, that she must never tell him of her love. 'No hint of it should distract him from his job. It must be a private affair unrevealed to anyone. And so it remained.'

After that there were a few brief occasions when they were together. She saw him in summer 1915 and again in October; he was in hospital recovering from rheumatic fever acquired in the trenches. On Christmas Eve 1915 she dined with him and his parents and heard that he was being posted as an intelligence officer to the Western Frontier Egyptian Field Force. 'I breathed the balm of his safety that Christmas.'

Relieved, Gertrude went back to her war work selling toys to raise money for refugee children. In her spare time, like women across the country, she knitted khaki socks for soldiers. Meanwhile there were still parties; still bridge, still horse-riding and concerts. To some it seemed that the worse the killing became, the gayer and madder grew the social whirl; like many young women at that time Gertrude saw no point in malingering. Early in 1916 she joined the volunteers pushing trolleys to feed the munitions workers at the Woolwich Arsenal canteen. She also managed, by skilfully dodging troop movements, to fit in an extended holiday with friends on the French Riviera; it was there that 'I made a new interest – prehistory . . .' The Palaeolithic remains of the Rochers Rouges behind Menton were being excavated by a party of French archaeologists, and while there Gertrude talked her way into helping out as a 'bottle-washer'.

But away from the Riviera sunshine the war continued to take its inexorable toll. The angel of death was abroad. Later that year the nation's resolve was tested when 420,000 British soldiers died horrible and futile deaths on the Somme between July and November, 20,000 of these on the first day alone. Barely a family in the land was unaffected, nor was Gertrude's family exempt from loss; two cousins were killed, both only sons, and she joined the weeping congregations who packed London's churches at this time. The celebrated preacher Maude Royden drew crowds to the Temple, where in her beautiful voice she told the sorrowing multitudes, 'They died consecrated lives.' Still, Carlyon was safe in Egypt. For Gertrude, the fearfulness of the casualties nearer home only served to intensify her relief that he had been posted – reluctantly – to such a comparative backwater. A bout of rheumatic fever seemed a small price to pay for staying out of the trenches.

Now she heard from him that he had recovered and had been given charge of a crack corps of racing camels, which under his command were to patrol the western edge of the Libyan desert against surprise attacks. The post required great daring and stamina; the Muslim tribes in the area were renowned for their barbarity, and the desert was notoriously inhospitable.

Everything that happened after that was reported to Gertrude via a contact at the War Office, General Creagh. In September 1916 Carlyon and a four-man patrol were sent to investigate rumours of tribal movements under Turkish command near the Baharia Oasis, an area of unmapped desert west of the Nile. The Baharia Oasis is overlooked by immense rocky cliffs; the patrol made its approach to their edge across arid, craggy terrain. Three men stayed hidden behind an outcrop to guard the camels while Carlyon and the other officer set out to reconnoitre on foot. They never returned.

Twenty-three days of agonising suspense passed before reliable reports were received as to their dreadful fate. Carlyon and his fellow officer didn't get far from the patrol. They had been stalked and shot dead by Senussi tribesmen, who then stripped and horribly mutilated the infidel corpses, leaving them exposed on the rocks. The bodies were duly recovered and Captain

Carlyon Will Mason-MacFarlane – 'an officer of the most brilliant promise'
– lies for ever in the British Army Cemetery at Minia in Middle Egypt.
With him lay buried all Gertrude's hopes, all her desires, and all her secrets.

## The crown and joy

Just as today religion, the law and economic factors combine to drive
women away from the altar, in the late nineteenth and early twentieth
century those same factors joined forces to push them firmly and unquestioningly down the aisle. The world that Gertrude Caton-Thompson grew
up in was a world that expected young women to marry. Not as a means
to an end, not as a foundation or basis for other activities, but as 'the crown
and joy of woman's life – what we were born for'. To most observers it
was self-evident that 'marriage is the normal mode of life'. In any case,
what else were all those accomplishments for? Why go to the expense of
dressmakers and milliners, balls and hunts, other than to ensure that women
like her appeared to best advantage in front of a range of potential suitors?
It is impossible to over-emphasise the fundamental importance of the
marriage market in nineteenth-century and early twentieth-century Britain.
Like some immutable law of physics, society decreed that energy expended
on females must be compensated for by suitable marriage; in due course a
further expenditure of energy went to ensure that the daughters of that
marriage, in their turn, repaid the input by suitably marrying. 'Nothing
would have enchanted me more than a pretty wedding, and a romantic
young husband, preferably a duke. I wished to do the very best for my
family . . .' one young woman growing up in the pre-war period remembered. Thus the world went round. E. M. Delafield (who went on to create
the immortal *Diary of a Provincial Lady*) drew on her own experiences as a
pre-war debutante when she wrote her novel *Thank Heaven Fasting* (1932),★
the agonising story of Monica Ingram's early years on the hamster-wheel
of fortune.

★ The title comes from Shakespeare's *As You Like It*, Act III, Scene V:

> Rosalind:  But mistress, know yourself, down on your knees,
>            And thank Heaven, fasting, for a good man's love:
>            For I must tell you friendly in your ear, –
>            Sell when you can; you are not for all markets:
>            Cry the man mercy; love him; take his offer.

E. M. Delafield, incidentally, was a pseudonym for Edmée Elizabeth *Monica* Dashwood (my
italics), which suggests that the novel has strong autobiographical undertones.

For girls of Monica Ingram's class, conformity with the ideal of maiden-liness was imperative. This meant not just the possession of accomplish-ments, but decorum and fragility, a propensity to faint and blush, modesty and reticence. Having equipped her daughter with these limiting attributes, Monica's conscientious mother has drummed into her from an early age that her only future is as the mate of a suitable man:

'My darling, never fall in love with a man who isn't quite, *quite –*' Mrs Ingram had said, at intervals, from the time Monica was fifteen.

Monica takes her mother's admonitions to heart. Every conversation with her friends boils down to the central obsession of their lives: will they capture a husband? The men they meet are 'any good' or 'no good' according to whether they are available for marriage. Their favourite fantasy topic is weddings. How will the bridesmaids be dressed? What colour will one choose for one's going-away frock? As for doing work of any kind – fainting and blushing hardly counted as qualifications in the job market. Besides, everyone knew that work was for failures, for the girls who hadn't managed to find someone suitable. Knowing about science, French verbs or mathematics did not enhance the featherbrain image that these girls so carefully cultivated. It was essential not to frighten men off.

Unfortunately Monica does just that. She gets romantically involved with a cad, whose lack of serious intentions marks him out as being very far from 'quite, *quite –*'. This transgression is catastrophic – or nearly. It soon becomes horribly, scarily apparent that society now perceives her as 'soiled' by her adventure; suitable men start to give her a wide berth. With a kind of forced desperation, Monica continues to display her wares at the familiar seasonal occasions. The high-maintenance appearances have to be kept up, but as time passes and no buyer so much as sniffs at her, the situation becomes heart-breaking. Mrs Ingram now finds it necessary to make face-saving disclaimers implying that at twenty-five her daughter doesn't wish to marry – 'She says she doesn't care about men. Well, of course, some girls are like that . . .' – or that as an only child she has renounced marriage in order to devote herself to her widowed mother. The reality, which poor Monica cries herself to sleep over nightly, is that she is a failure and men do not find her attractive. Terror strikes as she realises that the years are slipping by and life's one goal has eluded her.

Occasionally, with a close friend who is still, herself, also on the shelf, she tries to stare her future in the face:

'Why can't one have a career, or even work, like a man?' Monica asked helplessly. 'I know everybody would say that it was because we hadn't been able to get married – but they'll say that anyway.'

'There isn't any work for girls of our kind,' Frederica asserted. 'Not any that we should be allowed to do. The only way is to become religious, and go and do some kind of good works, with a whole crowd of old maids and people who don't belong to one's own class.'

And Mrs Ingram is damning:

'When all's said and done, there's only one job for any woman, whether she's stupid or clever, and that is to be a good wife to some man and the mother of his children.'

'And there aren't enough men to go round!' exclaimed Monica bitterly.

E. M. Delafield prolongs her heroine's agony for 250 pages until, like the cavalry galloping up at the last minute, she grants poor Monica a reprieve in her final chapter (ironically entitled 'The Happy Ending') in the shape of Herbert Pelham. This balding, middle-aged, bulgy-eyed suitor has been lurking inconspicuously in the Ingram orbit for some time, dismissed as being hopelessly unglamorous, but finally, in desperation, accepted as – literally – the answer to a maiden's prayer. Forget love, forget dreams of romance, forget social disgrace. Herbert Pelham may not be attractive, lovable or even very nice, but he is not a grocer or even a doctor, and he is definitely 'quite, *quite* –'. As the novel ends Monica walks down the aisle suffused with blissful relief that she has escaped shame and reproach, and with only one remaining prayer in her heart: '. . . that she might be a good wife to Herbert Pelham, and that if ever they had a child it might be a son'.

★

Angela du Maurier was an incurable romantic. Yet despite a catalogue of infatuations she was destined to remain single. It had started at childhood dancing classes, when she mooned around after a 'little boy in a sailor suit'. At ten she was sworn to a sweet little boy of eleven; they bowled their hoops together, and kissed each other good-bye. The next object of her passion was the local baker's boy in Albany Street, followed in quick succession by a village lad near their holiday home in Llanbedr, Arthur the farm labourer, who rode her around behind him on his carthorse in return for her pilfering her father's cigars, the actor Bobby Loraine ('my first big love . . .'), the Prince of Wales, her first cousin Gerald, and the head girl of her school. At the age of fourteen it was all too easy to become besotted at the sight of myriads of gorgeous officers setting off to fight for their country: 'It was wonderful, all these brilliant young men in khaki, about to be killed in action . . .' Then after the war in 1922 it was hook, line and sinker for an older man who behaved with great gallantry and gentleness to the dewy-eyed ingénue – and became her first 'Grande Passion'. He was sweet, and they parted with a tear. In her autobiography, *It's Only the Sister* (1951),★ Angela du Maurier corroborates E. M. Delafield's fictional representation of the marriage market. Now she was ready . . .

I wonder what most girls do think they are ready for, when all is said and done. In one word: marriage. I feel certain that nine girls out of ten have marriage as their goal at nineteen, whatever they may feel later. I certainly did, and Bet and I would swap ideas by the hour as to whom we'd have for our bridesmaids, where we would go for our honeymoons, what we would call our children, what sort of husbands we'd *like*. And as each young man drifted into one's life – and out of it again – one wondered.

## Deeply loved and sadly missed

Thus the women of Britain, ever-mindful that any husband is better than none at all, looked on as war took from them their future mates. Even before 1914 Monica Ingram was right – there weren't enough men to go round. In 1911 there were 664,000 more women than men in this country. This was because more boy babies died; it was also because men emigrated to the Colonies in large numbers. By 1914 nearly half a million men were leaving these shores annually to service the needs of Empire in India, Australia, Canada, Kenya . . . When war broke out many of these came back to fight for King and country, only to be shot, blown up or gassed alongside those who had stayed behind. Between 1914 and 1918 over 700,000 British men were killed:† one in eight of those who set out to

---

★ Her younger sister was the more famous Daphne, best-selling author of *Rebecca*, *Jamaica Inn* and many other novels. Their father, Gerald du Maurier, was a celebrated actor-manager.
† Though it is outside the scope of this book, the tragedy was not of course confined to Britain. 126,000 American soldiers were killed in the First World War. Of the French troops far more were killed than the British – nearly 1.5 million, as against Britain's 700,000. Germany suffered even worse, with nearly 1.8 million dead. French and German women had much more to contend with than we did, and how single women in those countries adapted and reshaped their lives in the face of such tragedy must stir up speculation.

fight, and 9 per cent of Britain's males under forty-five. A further 1,663,000 were wounded. Helpless to prevent the slaughter, a generation of women waited in vain for their boys to come home.

On Christmas Day 1915 a young nurse set out full of happy expectation to await the arrival of her fiancé on leave from his regiment. Looking out at the choppy sea from the lounge of the Grand Hotel in Brighton, she wondered what kind of a crossing he would be having. By ten o'clock that night no news had come. She was disappointed but not over-concerned. It was Sunday, and Christmas – no wonder he'd found it difficult to get a message through. News would get to her in the morning. Next day she dressed carefully; she wanted to look her best for her lover. The expected call came to say she was wanted on the telephone and she dashed joyously into the corridor. But the message brought the bitter destruction of all her hopes.

Two days earlier, the very day before he was due to go on leave, the nurse's fiancé, Roland Leighton, had set out to reconnoitre a communication trench which linked his battalion's trenches to no man's land. The wire defences were in need of repair, and Leighton wanted to be sure that the route was clear before he took a party out to do the work. Unfortunately it was a moonlit night. Unknown to him the Germans had a machine-gun trained on this path, and he had hardly gone a step into view before he was hit full in the stomach by a volley of fire. Two of his comrades risked their lives to carry him back to the British trench. At the dressing station the doctor gave him a huge dose of morphia, but nothing could save him. Twenty-four hours later Roland Leighton died.

Battered by shock and grief, it was two months before Roland's fiancée, Vera Brittain, was able to put her feelings into words:

### Perhaps –
#### (To R.A.L. Died of Wounds in France, December 23rd, 1915)

Perhaps some day the sun will shine again,
> And I shall see that still the skies are blue,
And feel once more I do not live in vain,
> Although bereft of You.

Perhaps the golden meadows at my feet
> Will make the sunny hours of Spring seem gay,
And I shall find the white May blossoms sweet,
> Though You have passed away.

Perhaps the summer woods will shimmer bright,
    And crimson roses once again be fair,
And autumn harvest fields a rich delight,
    Although You are not there.

Perhaps some day I shall not shrink in pain
    To see the passing of the dying year,
And listen to the Christmas songs again,
    Although You cannot hear.

But, though kind Time may many joys renew,
    There is one greatest joy I shall not know
Again, because my heart for loss of You
    Was broken, long ago.

Vera Brittain spoke for the thousands like her. She spoke for May Wedderburn Cannan (also a poet), whose fiancé died of pneumonia in Germany just after the end of the war early in 1919 ('Now there was no hope. It was the end of the world'). She spoke for Emily Chitticks, whose boyfriend Lieutenant Will Martin was killed by a sniper's bullet in 1917 ('My heart and love are buried in his grave in France . . .'). She spoke too for Marian Allen ('How should you leave me, having loved me so? . . . It seemed impossible that you should die . . .'), for Olive Lindsay ('Half of me died at Bapaume . . .'), for Barbara Wootton ('Her blank, shut-in face . . . told me what such a loss meant to her . . .'), for May Jones and for Gertrude Caton-Thompson.

Week after week, women across Britain waited for news from the Front. The casualty lists posted at town halls nationwide produced either temporary deliverance from the suspense of waiting, or the obliteration of all hope. Sometimes the family received the dreaded telegram 'Missing, feared killed', which only prolonged the agony. The statistics were devastating. Of the young men aged between fifteen and twenty-nine in 1911, no less than 15 per cent died. Because army policy was to place all men from the same locality in a single regiment, entire communities of young men were obliterated when that particular regiment suffered attack. A man from New Cross in Kent lost all five of his sons between 1916 and 1918, while a mother from Watford saw four out of her five killed; she lost the will to live and died soon afterwards. When young 'Pozzie' Gibson was killed, his sergeant visited his mother in the poorest part of Hunslet to break the news to her. 'I've lost my only boy,' was all she had power to say, and spoke no more, mute with grief.

In England, a mere twenty-eight 'thankful villages' eventually saw all the men who had set out to the First World War return safely. With these exceptions, not a community in the country was left unscathed by the raging slaughter of those four dreadful years. Very little helped. On 22 November 1917 Maria Gyte of Sheldon in Derbyshire recorded the deaths of 'five dear lads' from her village who had 'found graves in a foreign land'. They included her son:

> Jack Brocklehurst died of wounds on Nov. 30th 1916
> Thomas Anthony Brocklehurst killed Oct. 10th 1917
> George Bridden died Oct. 21st 1917 of wounds
> Tony Gyte died of wounds Nov. 2nd 1917
> Alfred Wildgoose died of malaria Nov. 15th 1917

That Christmas the Gyte family were unable to celebrate:

*Dec. 25th* . . . My dear lad Tony was missing from the family circle first time for 20 years. Oh Dear! What a dreadful war and what awfully sad homes there are this Xmas. The worst I have ever known. No joy. No singing Xmas hymns. No decorations.

Lieutenant Will Martin was killed in the same year. On the back of a New Testament tract a few piteous notes by his fiancée Emily Chitticks betray her attempts to make sense of his death:

> In loving Remembrance of my Dearly loved and loving fiancé, 'Will' . . .
> Who made the supreme Sacrafice [sic] on March 27th 1917
> 'Greater Love hath no man than this; in that he lay down his life for his friend.' Until we meet again before God's throne, Dearest, its [sic] only 'Goodnight'.
>
> Emily.

> Met Will August 9th 1916
> Engaged to Will Oct 27th 1916 . . .
> Killed in action March 27th 1917
> He nobly died doing his duty. Buried at Ecourt St Mein, France.
> Deeply loved & so sadly missed.

Dying nobly while doing one's duty was what was supposed to happen. The reality offered less in the way of consolation to those, like Vera Brittain, able to face it. His stomach riddled with bullets, Roland Leighton's shattering pain was only mitigated by a large dose of morphia. Nothing ever compensated Vera for the fact that, under its effects, her lover's final hours were passed in a state of oblivious stupefaction. No finer purpose appeared to have been served by his death, and he had forgotten her. As a nurse her daily life entailed tending the acute surgical cases on her ward; she was no stranger to the 'white eyes writhing . . .', the blood 'gargling from . . . froth-corrupted lungs' described so angrily in Wilfred Owen's poem 'Dulce et Decorum Est'. In spite of this it was hard for her to make allowances for 'the compelling self-absorption of extreme suffering'. The hardest thing to bear was 'the grief of having no word to cherish through the empty years'.

The men died like animals. Another nurse, Shirley Millard, recollected the undignified suffering of the soldiers in her care:

They cannot breathe lying down or sitting up. They just struggle for breath. But nothing can be done. Their lungs are gone. Some with their eyes and faces entirely eaten away by the gas and bodies covered with burns . . . One boy, today, screaming to die. The entire top layer of his skin burned from his face and body . . .

How was one to go on living with the knowledge of such violent, degraded deaths? How cruelly they corroded the human instinct for happiness. On a bright Wednesday morning only a few months after Roland's death Vera accidentally found herself rejoicing in the beauty of a watery-blue spring sky flecked with scuttling clouds. 'Suddenly I remember – Roland is dead and I am not keeping faith with him; it is mean and cruel, even for a second, to feel glad to be alive.'

The hypocrisy of the warmongers made it worse. Emily Chitticks accepted that dying for one's country was worthwhile, but not all the young women were so submissive. After the death of her fiancé the novelist Irene Rathbone rounded on the bien-pensant patriots in anguish: 'What was the use of winning the war . . . if none of the men who won it were to live? The papers were for ever quoting "Who dies if England lives?" But after all what *was* England?'

The dead infected the living with their absence, introducing a sense of annihilating guilt and insecurity. 'One recovers from the shock,' wrote Vera in her diary a year after Roland was killed, 'but one never gets over the loss, for one is never the same after it. I have got used to facing the long empty years ahead of me if I survive the War, but I have always before me the realisation of how empty they are and will be, since he will never be there again.' These men had not died as the old were supposed to die, in the fullness of time, murmuring deathbed pieties to their assembled grandchildren before being seraphically removed to a better place. Their violently truncated lives seemed against nature, unreasonable, unacceptable.

For decades after the war the fiction writers found their theme in its residue of loss and grief. Vera Brittain's *The Dark Tide* (1923), Margery Perham's *Josie Vine* (1927), Irene Rathbone's *We That Were Young* (1932) and Ruth Holland's *The Lost Generation* (1932) all traced their heroines' journey through suffering. Ruth Holland dedicated her novel 'To the memory of A.I.E. Killed in action in France, 1917'. Clearly autobiographical, a sample of Holland's thinly fictionalised experience must have expressed what many of her readers knew on their own account:

Something had snapped. Instead of a life that was like a splendid tune in her ears, with ordered sound and movement, a definite form, even though on a scale beyond her human powers to grasp, she was surrounded by a mocking terrifying jumble of discords, in which she could find no sense at all. It was that loss of contact that was so terrifying, as if she had lost the key and could no longer read the signs of life around her.

In *A World of Love* (1955),★ a later novel which describes the sabotage wrought by one soldier's death on two generations of living women, Elizabeth Bowen wrote even more eloquently of the dislocation the First World War introduced into the lives of the living:

[Guy] had had it in him to make a good end, but not soon; he would have been ready to disengage himself when the hour came, but rightfully speaking it had not . . . It was simply that these years she went on living belonged to him, his lease upon them not having run out yet. The living were living in his lifetime; and of this his contemporaries . . . never were unaware. They were incomplete.

For many of the bereaved the established Church fell short in answering the questions posed by the deaths of such a multitude. How could a beneficent God have permitted them to suffer and die? Were they now before God's throne? Large numbers of those who could not bear it at that time turned in their grief-stricken denial to psychics and clairvoyants, who in turn conjured up bogus visions of the returned dead. In those dark

---

★ An extraordinary metaphysical ghost story, in which Guy, killed in 1918, haunts the former home now inhabited by his cousin, his ex-fiancée and her daughter. Inescapably, all three women are drawn into the vortex of his non-presence. 'By striking when it did, before he had tried to see, even, whether he *could* consolidate, death made him seem a defaulter, a runner-out upon his unconsummated loves . . . His immortality was in their longings . . .' (Chapter 8).

days spiritualism flourished; by 1919 the Spiritualists' National Union had doubled the number of its pre-war affiliated societies – an estimated quarter of a million bereaved members conducting seances to reach out to their lost loved ones. 'Poor human beings . . .' mourned Beatrice Webb, when she heard that her sister Maggie was seeking to communicate with her son, killed at Ypres. And Maggie conceded that she was powerless in the face of her terrible need for him: 'How deep is the craving for extended personality beyond the limits of a mere lifetime on earth!'

## A world without men

After Roland Leighton's death, Vera Brittain went back to her job as a VAD in a hard-working London hospital. Gertrude Caton-Thompson put her hopes behind her and got a lowly job working as a filing clerk in the Ministry of Shipping. The war was a fact of life, and with the men away, Britain's women stiffened their upper lips and set to work to run the country:

### War Girls (1916) by Jessie Pope

There's the girl who clips your ticket for the train,
And the girl who speeds the lift from floor to floor,
There's the girl who does a milk-round in the rain,
    And the girl who calls for orders at your door.
        Strong, sensible, and fit,
        They're out to show their grit,
    And tackle jobs with energy and knack.
        No longer caged and penned up,
        They're going to keep their end up
    Till the khaki boys come marching back.


There's the motor girl who drives a heavy van,
There's the butcher girl who brings your joint of meat,
There's the girl who cries 'All fares, please!' like a man,
    And the girl who whistles taxis up the street.
        Beneath each uniform
        Beats a heart that's soft and warm,
    Though of canny mother-wit they show no lack;
        But a solemn statement this is,
        They've no time for love and kisses
    Till the khaki soldier boys come marching home.

But too many of the khaki boys were dead. Too many of the soft warm hearts kept themselves pure in vain. Bereavements were everyday occurrences; but there was a different kind of bereavement lying in wait for many of these strong, sensible, fit war girls. Motor girls and butcher girls, lift attendants and ticket collectors may have set their hopes on love and kisses after the Armistice, but the make-up of British society had changed irrevocably.

All over Britain the husbands, fathers and young men had gone. In churches across the country the Roll of Honour bore witness to lives cut short: sons, brothers and cousins, often half a dozen bearing the same surname, many of them wiped out in a single campaign or within a few days of each other, on the Marne, or the Somme, or at Loos. Who would the gritty war girls love and kiss now? '*But who will look for my coming? . . . Who will seek me at nightfall?*' wrote Vera Brittain. Like Gertrude, and May, like Emily, Olive and Barbara, she had lost the man she loved; but at least these women *had* loved. Countless women simply never had the chance of romance, let alone marriage or children.

★

This fact had to be faced. In 1917 the senior mistress of Bournemouth High School for Girls stood up in front of the assembled sixth form (nearly all of whom were dressed in mourning for some member of their family) and announced to them: 'I have come to tell you a terrible fact. Only one out of ten of you girls can ever hope to marry. This is not a guess of mine. It is a statistical fact. Nearly all the men who might have married you have been killed. You will have to make your way in the world as best you can. The war has made more openings for women than there were before. But there will still be a lot of prejudice. You will have to fight. You will have to struggle.' One of her pupils, seventeen-year-old Rosamund Essex, was never to forget these words. It was 'one of the most fateful statements of my life'. When Rosamund, who never married, wrote her memoirs sixty years later she accepted that her teacher's pronouncement had been prophetic:

How right she was. Only one out of every ten of my friends has ever married. Quite simply, there was no one available. We had to face the fact that our lives would be stunted in one direction. We should never have the kind of happy homes in which we ourselves had been brought up. There would be no husband, no children, no sexual outlet, no natural bond of man and woman. It was going to be a struggle indeed.

Winifred Haward was of the same generation. Born in 1898, she grew up in the village of Old Felixstowe in Suffolk, the daughter of a country solicitor. The family were not well-off, but they considered themselves 'gentry'; they were sincerely Christian, and Conservative. Despite being relatively hard-up, the Hawards sent their children to private schools, and at Ipswich High School Winifred soon began to show questionable signs of cleverness. Even then, she was aware that 'men were not supposed to like clever girls, and girls were supposed to get husbands'. She was sixteen, and still at school when war broke out. The Hawards' village was turned into an armed camp, and the family joined the war effort providing 'comforts' for the soldiers. Winifred helped, selling cheap cigarettes, tea and buns to the men; she went with her mother when the troop trains left Felixstowe station for France, giving out chocolate, tobacco and postcards to the soldiers crammed into the carriages. 'Many we never saw again.'

Winifred became head girl at her school. She was industrious, and an academic high-flyer; but ever in the background the hideous cruelty of the war tormented her like an insistent howl of pain. '[It] came when I was at a very sensitive and impressionable age. Dimly I realised that it was going to be a world without men.' Teenage boys that she knew, her contemporaries at the Ipswich schools, were sent out to the Front with commissions. On average they survived two weeks.

In 1917 Winifred Haward won the top history scholarship to Girton and went up to Cambridge. She and the other girl students went to lectures in Trinity Great Hall; they outnumbered the men four to one. Oblivious, the lecturer addressed his audience, 'Gentlemen . . .'

On a misty November morning when Winifred was in her second year at Cambridge, the war ended. She heard the pealing of bells from St Mary the Great; students had got into the church and were ringing the long-silent chimes in a wild burst of rejoicing. But she couldn't find it in her heart to join them. 'I went into my room and cried for a lost world.'

After the Armistice, Winifred buckled down to her studies. She was a talented historian, with a questioning mind. And she was ripe for conversion from her Christian Conservative background. Impelled by notions of social injustice and the meaningless suffering of the war, she joined the growing ranks of socialists and agnostics among the gifted students of her group. But when it came to finding romance, the possibilities started to close in. For a start, chaperones were still compulsory. If you couldn't get one, you couldn't go out. Going out was expensive anyway, and she was hampered by her lack of funds. On £5 a term, it was impossible to lead the kind of life that threw one in the way of eligible boyfriends. It was all very well for moneyed literati like Rosamond Lehmann and Frances Partridge (her exact contemporaries at Cambridge), but for Winifred boating and dances seemed prohibitively pricey on such a modest allowance. Back at home in Suffolk, the irony of her position was reinforced when she was invited by some of the local regimental officers (still not demobilised) to play the role of 'Mamma' to her pretty younger sister's ingénue in an amateur revue. She found herself on stage in a fright wig singing:

> 'If you ever want to marry' –
> 'And I do, dear Mamma' –
> 'It is wisest not to tarry' –
> 'Very true, dear Mamma' –

Winifred Haward came down from Girton in 1921, after beating all the men in her two-part History tripos, and staying on for an extra year to do a research studentship. (Being a woman, she wasn't eligible for a degree.) She was now in debt, having borrowed from a student loan fund; she didn't want to live in a hostel all her life, she was twenty-three, and she had reached the age where either marriage or a career would have answered her need for security. But Winifred had been born into a generation that could no longer hold to comforting certainties, and she was growing up, as she had already suspected, into a world without men – particularly suitable ones. Those brave young officers from her Ipswich schooldays had all been in front when they led their men over the top. Casualty rates among officers were roughly double those of the 'Tommies'. And so Winifred Haward joined what came to be called the Surplus Two Million.

## Surplus Two Million

The same year that Winifred came down from Cambridge, 1921, the National Census was published. The figures were devastating, confirming the worst fears of the senior mistress of Bournemouth High School. In England and Wales there were 19,803,022 females and only 18,082,220 males – a difference of a million and three-quarters. This was far worse than predicted. Already, since the end of the war, newspapers had been running scare headlines about 'Our Surplus Girls'. By February 1920 the *Manchester Evening News* was running a report on Dr Murray Leslie's alarming analysis of post-war demographics, in 'Husband Hunting – Tragedy of England's Million Surplus Women'. The *Daily Mail* caught the story, with 'A Million Women Too Many – 1920 Husband Hunt'. But with the

publication of the 1921 Census the figure doubled over-night, and the *Mail*'s proprietor, Lord Northcliffe, felt able publicly to refer to 'Britain's problem of two million superfluous women'. The phrase – with all its insinuating baggage – refused to go away.

For months the Census story was never out of the news. The *Daily Express* ran a headline: 'Problem of the Surplus Woman – Two Million who can Never Become Wives'. The *Daily Chronicle* responded, 'No such thing as a Surplus Woman'. The *Daily Mail* rejoined the debate by asserting that 'the super-fluous women are a disaster to the human race'. The *Times* edi-torial, more mea-sured but no less serious, expressed the view that 'Two millions of surplus woman-folk create a question so im-mense and so far-reaching that few have yet realized its import.' Let-ters started to fly. The issue was at the forefront of

In 1923 an issue of *Strand Magazine* caricatured the Husband Hunters in full cry

public debate. It seemed nobody knew what to do. Views ranged from: 'Learn to be useful – transform themselves into an army of workers for this country . . .' to: 'Cheerfulness is my motto . . . no need to be alarmed . . . the women probably filled in the Census forms wrong . . .' 'Leave them alone and give them equal opportunities with men' seemed like sound advice. Or, if you are set on marriage, emigration was the answer: you '. . . must go to Canada and the Colonies, where the toll of war has not been as great as it has in this country, and where men want wives'.

Poor May Wedderburn Cannan had opened the telegram from the War Office that told her of the death of her beloved Bevil. For months after the extinction of her hopes, she 'wandered in darkness', retreating into a realm of memory and poetry; she wrote of sad hearts, burials, broken dreams and the dimming of the light. But talented poet as she was, she knew that she could not keep herself on verse. May was not university-educated, and she was twenty-five. She kept afloat on temporary jobs, but the constant headlines about the surplus of women were a ceaseless reminder of the odds stacked against her and her kind. They were unnecessary and unwanted. They weren't educated, if they were under thirty they couldn't vote, and many of the professions were still closed to them. The end of the war should have revived the energies of a drained nation, but, as May sat in the tube at the end of her weary day, '. . . rocking along in the dark and looking at the white, indifferent, tired faces opposite me the wheels sang "surplus two million, surplus two million", and I was one of them'. May Wedderburn Cannan felt that she was on the scrap heap.

This tragic imbalance of the sexes was rocking society's fragile boat. During the war, an estimated two million women had replaced men in employment. All over the country women had escaped from mills and servants' halls and stepped in to fill the shortage of bus drivers, garage hands and factory workers. But now, the returning 'heroes' needed work and homes; they polished their shoes and went out looking for jobs, only to be told, 'It's the younger men we want,' or 'We've got more men and girls than we know what to do with.' With men vastly outnumbered by the 'war girls', angry accusations started to be bandied around. In 1923 Lieutenant G. Dickens (retired) of Weston-super-Mare wrote indignantly to *The Times* over the appointment of a woman to the post of assistant secretary to the Royal Astronomical Society. He had been among the applicants for this very job: '[I] was duly informed that I was unsuccessful – at which I did not "kick", until I ascertained that an unmarried woman *had been given a man's job*! Surely such an appointment, in these times, is unjustified . . .'

It was generally held that the women should give the jobs back to the boys. Most of them did so, uncomplainingly. It seemed a shabby trick to steal the men's positions while they were away fighting for their country. For married women it was not so hard to go back to home and hearth, but for single women it was different.

The anguish of the surplus two million was exacerbated by the sense that they were unwanted by men not only as wives, but also as competitors in the workplace and social stakeholders. When Asquith granted the vote to property-owning women over thirty in 1918 it was in recognition, partly, of the part they had played on the Home Front – ironical, as it was mostly much younger women who'd done the work. Now surely it was only a matter of time before all that the suffragettes had worked for would come to pass. But the prospect of a fully equal franchise was deeply disturbing to much of the male minority; fears were expressed that a vast influx of 'irresponsible' female voters would cause 'Bedlam'. With many men feeling that women trying to get parity was an unnatural state of affairs, eleven more years were to pass before women got equal voting rights with men. The feminist assault undermined their sense of who they were and, above all, they felt outnumbered. They could only deal with their fears by abusing the offending women, who were bundled into a heterogeneous mob labelled flappers, feminists, warped spinsters, man-haters, shrews, cigarette-smoking hoydens and militants. There was deep-seated anxiety among men that the battle of the sexes was being lost, and that the wrong side were winning. Hysteria, more normally expected from the opposite sex, manifested itself in smear campaigns by a number of male authors – like that of one John MacArthur, who blustered angrily against the granting of the franchise to younger women in a pamphlet entitled *Shall Flappers Rule?* (1927).

The modern feminist agitation is mainly due to disgruntled, elderly women who, having for one reason or another failed to realise their hopes, seek to revenge themselves for their fancied grievances on men. Soured and disappointed, they blame the men for all their woes . . .

Vilified in such manner, many post-war women began to feel that life had dealt them a raw deal; and when the press began to suggest that, as superfluous women, they should be shipped off to the Colonies like so many unwanted criminals, there was indignation. Miss Florence Underwood, representing the view of the Women's Freedom League, wrote angrily to the *Daily Chronicle*:

Marriage is not the only profession which women want. If there is a problem of surplus women, it will be solved not by sending women to exile in the Dominions to which they don't want to go, but by giving them in their own country equal opportunities with men to work. If more professions and industries were opened out to women, and if the tops of such professions were not reserved for men by men, we should hear little of the surplus woman problem.

If it is a problem, it is a problem created by men, which should be solved by men.

To call any woman 'surplus' simply because she is not married is sheer impertinence.

★

So what did the world have to offer a surplus young woman in the aftermath of the First World War? For Winifred Haward, now twenty-three, the answer was staring her in the face. It was the job that any educated woman like her would automatically qualify for: teaching. As many as 80 per cent of female graduates from Oxford and Cambridge colleges in the 1920s got jobs in the classroom. But Winifred was determined not to become a teacher:

All our mistresses at the High School were spinsters and that seemed the predestined fate of anyone who entered the profession. I liked men's company, I wanted to marry, and had romantic ideas of love. I knew very well that it was almost impossible because hardly any men of my own age had survived. Also I was short and rather plump, with dark hair and dark blue eyes, strongly marked brows and a fair but not very good complexion. People's opinion varied from 'plain' to 'attractive'. I think I was attractive only when I ceased to be shy and was at ease.

For lack of other options, Winifred took a post as history lecturer at the University of London, and started work on a tedious doctorate about fifteenth-century merchants. It wasn't what she wanted; she wanted a love affair, a grand passion: '"Great love survives the night and climbs the stars" ... That was what I wanted and felt I could give, if there were someone to take it.'

★

Like Winifred Haward, Vera Brittain felt nothing but heartache and anger when the war ended; she was still only twenty-two and she had lost everything she had ever cared about. Roland had died at the beginning of the war, but its subsequent course had also taken from her her two best friends and her beloved brother Edward. On Armistice Day the streets were full of jubilant crowds, waving flags and shaking rattles. But Vera blocked her ears; she felt there was no place for her in this 'brightly-lit, alien world . . .' and the future seemed empty.

The war had interrupted Vera's Oxford education after only one year; now, more from inertia than from any sense of purpose, she decided to return and finish what she had started. Numb and passive, at that point her only aim was to fill the blankness of her future with as little exertion as possible. She did not then foresee that the war, and Oxford, were ultimately to shape her political commitments. For now, she pinned what little hope she had left on the university. It would, she trusted, offer balm to her sore and bitter soul; she would make friendships; her fellow-students, though not of her generation, would be kind to her, they would listen to her with respect for having survived the greatest event of history. Pity would mingle with admiration, there would be tranquillity to write and study – and maybe time would do the rest.

*

Gertrude Caton-Thompson continued to work for the Ministry of Shipping, first as a filing clerk, then as a secretary. In 1918, when she was thirty, her previous suitor, Montagu Luck, tried again to persuade her to marry him – unsuccessfully. 'Carlyon's death had left me with the feeling that nothing much mattered,' she later recalled. After the Armistice she stayed on as personal assistant to the Ministry head, with whom she attended the Paris Peace Conference. Gertrude and her friends took a day off at the Longchamp races, where she won 3,000 francs backing an outsider. With the war over, there was every indication that she would resume the aimless social round that her upbringing had accustomed her to. She had no money worries, and life had much to offer in the way of visits to friends, hunting, golf, and foreign holidays. But now the door stood open. In 1921 Gertrude returned to her earlier interest – archaeology. She enrolled for classes at University College London, took a course in prehistoric archaeology, learnt surveying, studied Arabic and museum collections, and immersed herself in reading. 'I allowed myself few social engagements unconnected with archaeology.' As soon as she could, she signed up to join an excavation at Abydos in Upper Egypt.

Mysteriously and inexorably, the bones and shards of remotest African prehistory had become of prime importance in Gertrude's life. She had learnt the hard way that death is the end, and that those who are gone are irreplaceable, but her career was to be spent in reverently resurrecting and understanding the past. Here, she found meaning. For her, the dead were as real as the living, and through archaeology she rediscovered them. It was to absorb her for a lifetime.

Gertrude was not alone in seeking to make sense of a future without marriage, even if her solution was an uncommon one. War had stolen the hopes of a generation, but they were still young. And little by little, the Surplus Women began to find that life had not come to an end after all. The blank page was not the last page of the book.

## 2. 'A world that doesn't want me . . .'

### The twilight state

War killed a generation of husbands; it also stole the future from those who would have become their wives. Wives kept house, cooked dinners with love, bore babies and nurtured them. Wives had companionship, homes and respectability; they had smelt the orange blossom, walked down the aisle, attracted and possessed a man. It seemed wives had the secret of happiness. Where did that leave the women who were not wives, who would never be wives? What could they do, and who could they be? Were they to spend their remaining days consumed with sick envy? Were their lives to be defined by their failure in the eyes of the world?

May Jones, Gertrude Caton-Thompson, Vera Brittain and Winifred Haward were Victorians. When they were born, between 1888 and 1898, the old Queen still sat on the throne, festooned in black, symbol of a society which revered her as submissive wife, fecund mother, loyal widow. That was a society in which the single woman knew her place. The rare exceptions – travellers like Marianne North or Mary Kingsley, social reformers like Octavia Hill or Florence Nightingale – only served by their striking independence to prove the rule.

And that rule was unambiguous. The status quo demanded that male members of the family support their female relatives, so genteel women learnt French and fancy needlework rather than a trade or skill that could earn money. The world of employment did not offer opportunities for single women to become self-sufficient, so they were reduced to dependency. The demands of gentility were cruel. If you wanted to stay respectable you could be a governess or a ladies' companion but you couldn't enter any form of commerce. Normally, an unmarried middle-class daughter would live at home and care for her fractious and ailing parents until their death. Then, if she was lucky, she would be left just enough to live on; late in life, she might find freedom of a sort. But if not, she moved on down the line and went to live with whichever male relative felt morally obliged to have her. Her status was lowly. If the male relative was married, the spinster yielded precedence to his wife.

Gradually, the majority of such women sank into what Jessica Mitford described in her memoirs as 'the twilight state of aunthood . . .' Jessica's Maiden Aunts were gentle and wispy, their lives suffused with an aura of tragic legend. 'Why didn't she ever marry?' Jessica would ask. The stories were mysterious, awful, and incomplete. One of the aunts had got ill and her teeth had started to fall out; despite panic-stricken attempts to shore them up with bits of bread her looks, and chances, were ruined. Another one was dancing at her first ball when a young man stepped on her foot. 'She was laid up for some time, and by the time she recovered it was too late for marriage.' The Maiden Aunts lived parsimonious lives in small London flats with one maid, their distressing existence a baleful warning to avoid such a fate.

The twilight deepened into night for single women who took the veil as a refuge from the hostility of the outer world. The Church had also for centuries been an institution which gave sanctuary to society's outcasts, and these of course included unmarried women. In the Middle Ages families cast off their surplus females into convents. Imprisoned behind grilles, nuns may have wondered which was worse, the alienation and hardship dealt out to single woman by uncomprehending society, or the privations of poverty, chastity and obedience. Their fate, whether chosen or imposed, only deepened the pall of prejudice against the spinster. It was the general view (as Monica Baldwin discovered when she re-entered the world after twenty-eight years in an enclosed order) that nunneries '. . . were filled with herds of semi-demented spinsters whose repressed and abnormal existences induced a warped unhealthy attitude towards life . . . [they were] unhinged old maids . . . who had shuffled off their responsibilities in order to live lives of soured virginity'.

Prejudice prevailed across the social classes. In the nineteenth century some single women in rural areas still endured the stigma of being regarded as witches. Contemporary accounts told of bands of unruly spinsters creating mayhem around the countryside – a threat to order and decency. But old maids who persevered in facing their responsibilities still had to endure the often blatant contempt of their neighbours. Robert Roberts, who grew up in a Manchester slum at the turn of the century, remembered how the old maids' best efforts to stay respectable were derailed and undermined by the backstreet housewives and their wild children. It was common round Roberts's neighbourhood to find a couple of spinsters sharing a home. They were house-proud, as he recalled, and generally kept their steps, doors and windows scrupulously clean, but the married women were merciless. The unfortunate spinsters were vilified as 'old faggots'; they had 'nothing better to do'. And the smug wives turned a blind eye when their children played evil tricks on the single women and taunted them. 'Their lives could be made a misery – a sort of cruelty that would not be tolerated today.'

But as Victoria's influence glimmered dim, a new world for single women was flickering into life. Gibson girls, bicycles, Bohemians, the Bloomsbury group, *The Woman Who Did*, shirtwaisters, divorce, H. G. Wells and Olive Schreiner were among the heralds of change. Each confrontation with censorious Victorian society sent shock waves through Kensington and the suburbs, but little by little the prison doors were creaking open. As May, Gertrude, Vera, Winifred and their contemporaries grew up, the language of equality, suffrage, emancipation, pacifism, socialism and agnosticism was starting to filter into the vocabulary.

For Vera Brittain, brought up in bourgeois Buxton, the new horizons on offer made its limitations seem doubly stifling. Vera was 'mentally voracious' and, as soon as she made the discovery that women's colleges actually existed, set her heart on a university education; she got into Oxford in 1914, but it was not what her parents had planned for her. Their clever daughter had been brought up by them to be an 'entirely ornamental young lady'. As usual, marriage was the be-all and end-all of their ambitions for her. 'It feels sad to be a woman!' she wrote in 1913. 'Men seem to have so much more choice as to what they are intended for.'

Twenty years into the twentieth century an unmarried woman had possibilities undreamed-of by her spinster aunts. But the aunts, with their wispy buns and ruined hopes, were still there to haunt her. The contempt and humiliation suffered by maiden ladies were an ever-present reminder of the spinster's predicament. And what made things harder still for Vera Brittain and the Surplus Two Million was the feeling that, having lived through 'history's cruellest catastrophe', they were now irrelevant, isolated, and figures of fun in the eyes of a rising generation who had sat out the war in schoolrooms. 'I'm nothing but a piece of wartime wreckage living on ingloriously in a world that doesn't want me!' wept Vera.

She was desperately lonely. Having opted to live away from her family, Vera now had only the ghosts of her dead brother and dead lover for companionship. She returned to Oxford after the war, but steered clear of the other students, instead spending the grey October evenings wandering alone on Boar's Hill, before returning to her chilly room 'at whose door nobody ever knocked'.

In this morose and de-socialised condition, she found herself sharing history tutorials with a blonde Valkyrie, strong-featured with intelligent blue eyes and an athletic figure: Winifred Holtby. The pair got off to an uneasy start. Vera was prickly and critical and adopted superior airs. There was a particularly awkward episode when Winifred invited Vera to speak against her at the Somerville College debating society. She agreed, her sufferings during the war having made her angry at the limitations of academe. She made a passionate speech attacking the narrowness of university life, and recommending the 'school of hard knocks' as against cloistered insularity. Unfortunately Winifred wittily opposed the criticism in such a way as to make Vera feel even more superfluous than she already did, and persuaded the audience to defeat the motion decisively. The incident left Vera feeling embittered and misunderstood. But from such inauspicious beginnings friendship grew. Out of the ashes a relationship was born which was to become for both of them the most intimate and affectionate of their lives.

★

Winifred Holtby was born in Yorkshire. She was sixteen when war was declared. Unlike Vera Brittain she neither lost anyone close to her, nor endured the groans, pain and bandages that constituted Vera's daily life as a nurse. But Vera was eventually to marry; Winifred died a spinster.

Winifred's family had always half-expected her to marry her childhood friend Harry Pearson. Harry had written poetry to her, and they shared a love of their Yorkshire roots. Educated, good-looking and patriotic, typical of the public-school officer class, he survived the war and emerged wounded. But then he did nothing. The promising writer who had won the school prize for English verse quit his Cambridge place and started on a lifelong career as a drifter, aimlessly travelling, always short of money, a disaffected loner and vagabond. When he turned up, which he did from time to time, Winifred would sympathise and try to help him, but her vigorous self-sufficiency crushed Harry's fragile pride. The relationship was on-off; at one point, to her anguish, he got engaged to a pretty pianist, but it was short-lived. Later he and Winifred may have had a brief sexual relationship. She struggled to be non-possessive, but there were days when she was powerless against his old charm and physical presence. 'I love every tone of his voice, every movement of his hands. And I wouldn't *not* love him for anything,' she wrote to Vera. Though she knew it would never work – she described him to another friend as 'my-young-man-who-will-never-be-more-than-my-young-man' – he was the only man who ever held any attraction for her. But Harry was not to be had. The poetry he had written to her back in 1916 withered, and after the war he was never there for her again. Vera Brittain described Harry Pearson as 'a war casualty of the spirit'.

In Harry's long absences, Winifred Holtby refused to languish. She was committed to the cause of internationalism, and lectured widely; she was a prolific journalist. In many of her writings, but above all in her fiction, Winifred wrestled with the question of what it meant to be an unmarried woman, and with her own unresolved and unsatisfactory singleness. Characteristically unshrinking, she harnessed that sense of incompleteness to the cause of her novels. In *The Crowded Street* (1924), her heroine, Muriel Hammond, grows up in the oppressive small town of Marshington where 'the only thing that mattered was marriage . . .' Muriel's long lonely path in coming to terms with singleness must have mirrored her author's own dark nights of the soul, when dread of the twilight state of aunthood could bring her to the brink of despair:

'Nobody wants me – I'm like Aunt Beatrice, living in fear of an unloved old age. I must have some reason for living. I must, I must. I can't bear to live without. I just can't bear it. Oh, what am I going to do with myself?'

A later novel, *South Riding* (1936), tells the story of an enterprising headmistress, Sarah Burton, who falls stormily in love with an unavailable man who is also her political opponent. But Sarah's love affair with Robert Carne is thwarted, her hungry longing violently disrupted at the point when it is about to be consummated. Robert comes to her bed, but before anything can happen suffers a terrifying heart attack; shortly afterwards his horse rears on a clifftop and he is killed in the fall. The great question of Holtby's story is, how will Sarah herself survive? Despair threatens to engulf her:

I cannot bear it, she repeated to herself. I do not want to live . . .
She suffered not only sorrow; she suffered shame. If he had loved me, even for an hour, she sometimes thought, this would not have been unendurable.

Winifred Holtby never pretended it was easy. In an essay she wrote in 1934* she stared her own prospects as a spinster in the face:

What am I missing? What experience is this without which I must – for I am told so – walk frustrated? Am I growing embittered, narrow, prudish? Are my nerves giving way, deprived of natural relaxation? Shall I suffer horribly in middle age? At the moment, life seems very pleasant; but I am an uncomplete frustrated virgin

* 'Are Spinsters Frustrated?' in *Women and a Changing Civilization* (1934).

woman. Therefore some time, somewhere, pain and regret will overwhelm me. The psychologists, lecturers and journalists all tell me so. I live under the shadow of a curse.

Holtby's books are about coming to terms with being alone – but they are also about community, about personal serenity, and about refusal to compromise. She herself was courageous and unflinching, and her spinster heroines travel beyond the confines of a quest for personal happiness. For many 'surplus' readers in the 1920s and 1930s remembering their own anguish and frustration, her writings must have brought a sense that this author was their champion.

## Odd women and Ann Veronicas

And a champion was needed for the single woman, whose image, by the 1920s, had become stuck in a literary time-warp. The aunts – 'living in fear of an unloved old age . . .' – haunt the pages of Holtby's novels, but they are strewn across British fiction. There is Miss Matty, lace-capped, genteel and economical in Mrs Gaskell's *Cranford*; there are the Miss Maddens, faded, plain and poor in George Gissing's *The Odd Women*; then Miss Miniver, dingy, pinched and petulant in H. G. Wells's *Ann Veronica*; or Rachel Vinrace's twittering, unimaginative spinster aunts in Virginia Woolf's *The Voyage Out*. Sad, prudish Miss Prism and her three-volume novel are objects of ridicule in Oscar Wilde's *The Importance of Being Earnest*. Charles Dickens specialised in spinsters. There is Miss Havisham in her cobwebbed wedding dress, wreaking eternal vengeance on mankind for her wrecked hopes, and the lunatic Miss Flite in *Bleak House*. In *David Copperfield* there is the tyrannical Miss Murdstone and in *Dombey and Son* the obsequious Miss Tox – all of them grotesque, laughable and lonely. Yet more bloodless specimens haunt the pages of Trollope, Henry James and E. M. Forster. As a breed these spinsters are shabby, sallow, petty, sour and queer. Their lives are dominated by hopeless longing and hard struggle. They knit, read improving books and drink cocoa. They are content with little.

Some fictional spinsters are endowed with more sympathetic qualities, but then they get married, which lets them off the hook. Jane Austen's Emma (who swears she never will) is sprightly and life-enhancing, despite being a thoroughly meddlesome nuisance. But Mr Knightley is more than equal to her, and their marriage provides both control and contentment. The lowly Jane Eyre has bravely endured loneliness, grief and poverty with her self-respect intact. For Jane, plain though she is, love triumphs and

Charlotte Brontë rewards her heroine with the most cathartic of fairytale endings. 'Reader, I married him . . .' is the biggest sigh of relief in English literature. These earlier novels fed the notion that only marriage offered true happiness; they did not dispel the overwhelmingly negative and distorted image that was accepted as a portrayal of the single woman in literature.

Even as the horizons for women started to broaden, the pervasive stereotypes barely shifted. The audience at Gilbert and Sullivan's *The Mikado* (1885) would have been doubled up at their outrageous portrayal of mad old bat Katisha, a raucous harridan ensnaring the younger Ko-Ko:

> KO-KO:      Is a maiden all the better when she's tough?
> KATISHA:            Throughout this wide dominion
>                     It's the general opinion
>                     That she'll last a good deal longer when she's tough.
> KO-KO:      Are you old enough to marry do you think?
>                     Won't you wait till you are eighty in the shade?
>                     There's a fascination frantic
>                     In a ruin that's romantic
>                     Do you think you are sufficiently decayed?

Light verse, popular fiction and children's books found a wealth of material for caricature in the unfortunate image of the maiden lady. Hilaire Belloc's Aunt Jane was 'a gorgon who ought to be shot'. Hideous and interfering, Aunt Jane is visited only by irreproachable clergymen, has a lady companion, bullies her servants and generally behaves like a disapproving rhinoceros. Disappointed spinsters were fair game too for Noël Coward:

> We must all be very kind to Auntie Jessie,
> For she's never been a Mother or a Wife,
> You mustn't throw your toys at her
> Or make a vulgar noise at her,
> She hasn't led a very happy life.

Richmal Crompton (herself unmarried) wrote in her *William* books of sniffy boy-hating maiden aunts with piles of darning to do; their function is to dampen and impede the irrepressible William in his exploits. Dorothy L. Sayers fixed the image of the academic spinster forever as a round-shouldered woman in a yellow djibbah, with hair coiled in shells round her ears and a face like the back of a cab. Agatha Christie's knitting detective

Hilaire Belloc's 'gorgon' Aunt Jane settling up with her maiden
lady companion

Miss Marple incarnated the spinster sleuth, while shrill scheming old maids
likened to hyenas and birds of prey stalked the pages of E. F. Benson.

★

Being reviled as a bossy, warped, cat-loving virgin with thick legs was
hurtful, but one could live it down. It would be po-faced and humourless
to object to a spot of harmless comedy; after all, nobody thought the
demonic Miss Elizabeth Mapp was *real*. But unmarried women had to
contend with attacks by writers who failed to disguise their venom under
the mask of fiction.

In 1913 Walter M. Gallichan wrote *Modern Woman and How to Manage
Her*, followed a few years later by *The Great Unmarried* (1916). Gallichan
was what we would probably now describe as a sexual psychologist, though
he also wrote books on travel and trout fishing. In these two works Gallichan
set out to make sense of what he saw as the growing alienation of women
from their natural role – that of marriage. It was in those early years of the
twentieth century that the 'spinster problem' had started to make itself felt.
Hitherto the maiden ladies had appeared content to knit passively in the
chimney corner. Now, as men like Gallichan observed, 'The present is the

era of the man-contemning, man-hating woman'. It worried him, for he had begun to observe that not all these man-haters ran true to type:

She is not always an ugly woman, with an unpleasing voice, and dressed like a dowdy. On the contrary, she is sometimes beautiful and very attractive to men, though sexually abnormal.

Gallichan became preoccupied with trying to define and 'manage' the modern woman. What was to be done with these 'Ann Veronicas'?★ Who

The literate spinster, with her 'busy little brain', was an easy target for caricaturists like Nicolas Bentley

was to blame for their thrusting moves towards independence? Gallichan had the grace to concede guilt on the part of the British patriarchy '. . . who have kept their womenfolk under lock and key . . .' and therefore had only themselves to blame, but he was also himself deeply patronising, raining blame on the rampancy, defiance and fanaticism of modern woman:

Ideas are seething in her busy little brain. She is desperately intellectual. One day she tells you that she is prepared to die for the cause of Women's Suffrage. Next week she will be immersed in economics, or vegetarianism, or free love . . .

★ The eponymous heroine of H. G. Wells's shocking novel *Ann Veronica* (1909) readily gave her name to independent-minded women like her who ran away from home, experimented with emancipation and broke the moral taboos of the day.

'I don't mean to marry,' she says, with a ring of disdain. 'I want to live my own life.' . . . She tries to disguise her sex attractions by dressing dowdily, neglecting her hair, wearing square-toed boots, and assuming inelegant poses.

Inelegant poses were one rebellion too many for this concerned but conventional observer. His next book was published during the war, when men were already dying in great numbers. Reflecting the nervousness felt by men like him, it was much more unforgiving in tone. In *The Great Unmarried*, Gallichan solemnly noted that the increase in spinsters would end in tears. He prophesied a calamitous post-war fall in the birth-rate, and the swamping of the labour market by working women; he also issued a stern warning against spinster teachers who, he said, would disseminate 'false views of life . . . oblique and distorted conceptions of love . . . and intellectual insincerities . . .' Such women, because they had not known 'conjugal love', would be tyrannical, domineering and censorious. He went on to diagnose 'psychic sclerosis', and produced a damning range of statistics proving that ill-health, crime, lunacy, early death and suicide were vastly more prevalent among the unmarried than the married.

Men's fear of unmarried women grew as the numbers multiplied after the war, and as their potential for wage-earning increased. The anxiety produced by the feeling that they were in a minority took curious forms. In the press it was, for instance, felt necessary to emphasise the scientific aspects of housewifery; this might help to deflect women from careers and independence. In the 1920s, propaganda in the dailies urged women back to re-dedicate themselves to the home, which more than ever must be dainty and spotless. Wonderful labour-saving devices and convenience food conspired to lure women back to the hearth, the shops and the kitchen sink. One advertisement for floor wax portrayed a row of beautiful brides driven to become 'scrubwomen' at forty, because they didn't use the Johnson Electric Polisher. Those brides could have stayed 'fresh and lovely' for so little . . .

Then there was the frightening reality that women had emerged into the post-war world physically superior to their damaged men. How can Harry Pearson have felt, with his smashed shoulder and bullet wound, when confronted by Winifred Holtby's lithe greyhound beauty? Castrated, no doubt. The sad remnants of men who returned from the war maimed, gassed and psychologically scarred were subjected to the spectacle of jolly Jazz Age flappers dancing, golfing, motoring and mountaineering. Women like the svelte and shapely Mollie Stack, who began teaching keep-fit in 1920 to support the family after her husband was killed in the first months of the war, going on to found the Women's League of Health and Beauty, can only have exacerbated men's feelings of emasculation.

After the 1921 Census there was no disputing the figures, and a relatively moderate disquiet about the Surplus Women was replaced by open consternation and intolerance. Society itself was in peril. In *Lysistrata, or Woman's Future and Future Woman* (1927) by Anthony M. Ludovici,* the author's fear and hostility are audible.

Ludovici was English, born in 1882 of Italian ancestry; the son of an artist, he himself abandoned art for literature and became enthralled by the German philosopher Nietzsche, six of whose works he translated. Ludovici's own beliefs are now so shockingly unfashionable and misogynistic that they are almost entirely neglected; he opposed modern art, democracy, liberalism, miscegenation, birth control and feminism. His polemic against women was published in 1927. Ludovici held an unshakeable conviction that women must mate. Their 'bodily destiny . . .' was sexual – leading to maternal – satisfaction; women were born from women whose grandmothers and great-grandmothers before that had known 'the ardent embrace of a lover, the ecstasy of consummated love, and the clinging adoration of adoring offspring'. It was against nature to rupture this time-honoured lineage of love. And now . . . ? Two million women, condemned to bitter sub-normality, the arts and virtues of the home lost; sewing, cooking and the nurture of the young forgotten; young women, reft from the home, withered and broken by long years of secretarial work . . . Ludovici mourned their fate, but he also blamed and cursed the victims. Like an enraged animal who feels himself to be under attack, he lunged and charged at his wounded enemy. The spinsters are 'malign . . . thwarted . . . jealous . . . bitter . . . deficient . . . wretched . . .' And society will live to repent the appalling feminist tendencies that have led to the disastrous desertion by women of their natural place:

A large body of disgruntled women, mostly unmarried, who having turned away from Life and Love either through lack of mates or the nausea acquired in modern matrimony, are prepared to slander not only Life, but also motherhood, domesticity and Man . . .

* The book draws its title from Aristophanes' drama about the Peloponnesian War, in which the heroine, Lysistrata, attempts to bring an end to the conflict. She does this by persuading the women on both sides to withdraw their sexual favours from the men until they agree to peace.

Now Ludovici waxes apocalyptic. These disgruntled women will rise up, he cries, and take over the world. They will slander and destroy their married sisters and all mankind. They will try to prove to the world that they can live without mates, and war will break out between the sexes.

But, paranoid as they seemed, some of Ludovici's prophecies were not so far out. Next, he raved, the feminists will call for 'extra-corporeal gestation − science will be allowed no rest until a technique is discovered that will meet the public demand . . . a means will be discovered by which the fertilized ovum will be matured outside the female body . . . Legislation will now be passed, which will make it a felony for a man to give a woman a child in the old corporeal sense, and any man found guilty of such an offence will be sentenced to death or else to a long term of hard labour.'

Now 'triumphant feminism will reach its zenith'. And the form of that triumph? Evolution will bring about a de-sexed woman, with only her hairlessness and genitalia to show that she was once − a wife.

Men will then be frankly regarded as quite superfluous.

Fortunately, Ludovici's proto-fascist views represent an extreme which would have been better received in Nazi Germany than it actually was in twentieth-century Britain. Nevertheless he was widely published, and *Lysistrata* articulates the widely-felt threat that unmarried women seemed to pose to men, and to society as a whole.

★

Arch-critics of the spinster like Gallichan and Ludovici were not Victorian throwbacks. The language had changed; the lid was off sex now, and bottling it up was simply passé. Between them, Freud, Havelock Ellis, Marie Stopes and D. H. Lawrence had seen to that. Nineteen-twenties Britain was in a ferment of candid debate about free love, contraception and permissiveness. This didn't make it any easier for the singles. Dark tides of passion were bringing orgasmic bliss and maternal fulfilment to liberated women, but only so long as they had men with the loins and vigour to provide it for them. In a world whose male population seemed composed of amputees and trauma victims, the dominant and often overt female fantasy was of the athletic super-stud, be it gamekeeper, black boxing champion or smouldering-eyed sheik. The picture palaces had typists queuing up for their next hit of Rudolph Valentino's romantic virility.

Where did that leave the Surplus Woman? Too often sitting quaking in her cold lodgings, wondering yet again how she had managed to get left out. The nineteenth century ignored women's sexuality; yet that ignorance had been a form of salvation for the spinster. Probably, if she thought about sex at all, the gorgon Aunt Jane would have counted herself deeply fortunate at not having to go through all that nasty messy stuff endured with clenched teeth by her married sister-in-law.

But now it looked as if the married sister-in-laws were having all the fun. They not only had respectability and babies; they had gorgeous sex too. The novel *Treasure in Heaven* (1937) by Rosalind Wade (herself married with children) tells the cruel story of Fanny Manningfield, a lively, contented and busy single woman aged fifty who has filled her life with useful activity – until events force her to confront the devastating fact that she has been repressing her 'natural' instincts all along. Fanny's zest for life, her enthusiastic energy and useful occupations have, it turns out, been nothing but substitutes and compensations for love, home, protection and babies – 'happy, natural things'. The psychologist she goes to see forces her to face the awful truth; she is a 'sex-starved spinster'. Wade's bleak and sadistic book ends with its heroine in tears, staring at her lined face and dumpy figure in the mirror, recognising that life has failed her: '. . . it was too late. No matter the agility of her spirit, she saw that she was too old. She had missed something that could never now be claimed on this side of death.'

It seemed as if the more women sought freedom and self-determination the more they must be suppressed. Nowhere is the anger and insecurity of men faced with independent women more evident than in D. H. Lawrence's punitive novella *The Fox* (1920). Here, Jill and Nellie live lovingly and tranquilly together on their farm, until the appearance of a returning soldier who wreaks havoc in their lives. Characteristically, a red mist seems to descend over Lawrence at the thought of two women managing self-sufficiently without male mastery. They must not be allowed their contentment, and this violent and bitter little story tells how the soldier forces Nellie to marry him and kills her friend Jill.

Fiction even managed to present sexually liberated single women as the losers. All too often the 1920s heroine is independent but brash, bitter and indifferent, 'hard as nails' or, like the women in T. S. Eliot's *The Waste Land*, pretentious and cold:

> When lovely woman stoops to folly and
> Paces about her room again, alone,
> She smoothes her hair with automatic hand,
> And puts a record on the gramophone.

More than ever, society as a whole, not just men, held single women responsible for their own predicament. Their detractors included women like journalist and novelist Charlotte Haldane, who took it upon herself to attack spinsters for fanaticism, crankiness and deviancy. She herself was married, and might be excused some prejudices. But it took an unusually sadistic turn of mind for a spinster to censure other spinsters for not being married, which was exactly what the virulent anti-feminist Miss Charlotte Cowdroy did in her book *Wasted Womanhood* (1933). Wasted, as she explained, because so many women were perverted away from their natural destiny of marriage and motherhood by Gallichan's tyrannical spinster teachers and their false intellectual creed. Wasted – on university, on the vote, on independence and on the hockey field. Miss Cowdroy's book is a bitter lament for the army of women who 'deliberately' put aside marriage in favour of being 'clever' and earning their living. She grieves at the spectacle of 'beautiful young girls . . . [who] gradually wither as the years pass them by and they lose their bloom . . .'

A few years ago such girls would have had mind and heart satisfied with the multitudinous duties of home and little ones. Instead of withering, their cheeks would have bloomed anew under the kisses of their children . . .

And, according to Miss Cowdroy (whose own cheeks, one trusts, were round and rosy), they had only themselves to blame. Frustrated, unhappy and queer: Britain had two million barren, dowdy, pathetic women, growing old alone.

★

Not surprisingly, with such a stereotypical reflection staring at them from the mirror, single women found it hard to avoid presenting an equally stereotypical image. Cicely Hamilton, a powerful advocate of women's rights and equality, and a later friend of Winifred Holtby's, started out persuaded by her family that being attractive to the opposite sex was essential if she was not to be a failure. But as time passed and other activities left no space in her life for marriage, she relapsed gratefully into being an Aunt Jane – living alone with just her cat Peterkin for company, like a witch. No, it was not how she had envisaged her life turning out, but it suited her and she had no regrets.

The war destroyed novelist Ivy Compton-Burnett's private and family life. Five of her sisters and half-sisters survived the war; none of them married. Beset by personal loss and moral confusion, the almost exaggeratedly 'spinsterish' appearance and habits which Ivy rigidly adopted for the rest of her life seem to have been in some way a reaction to sorrow and doubt. She was painstakingly correct in her dress and in the way she arranged her hair, yet she remained stuck in a time warp, holding on to past certainties. Her skirt lengths never changed; the eccentric coiffure was from a bygone era. She looked like one of her own fictional governesses.

Enid Starkie was of another type. Wild, intense and Irish, she was an outsider whose fragmented, emotional character made it hard for her to make relationships. She adored men and it was a permanent sadness to this brilliant French scholar that lasting love eluded her. However, she lacked the self-effacing qualities expected of the average meek spinster, adopting instead an uninhibited and eccentric appearance that startled her colleagues in the senior common rooms of Oxford. Actressy, with her vividly dyed hair and chalk-white face powder, Enid loved to make an entrance. She bought cheap, colourful clothes off-the-peg, and there was something of the mad bag lady about her, decked out in blue trousers, scarlet coat, quantities of imitation costume jewellery and broken-down umbrellas.

## The spinster problem

No doubt about it, single women were conspicuous in the 1920s and 30s. Conspicuous by their numbers, by their manner and appearance, and by what they represented, statistics were on their side. Today, singles are increasingly prominent and powerful: since 1975 single-occupant house-holds have risen 31 per cent. But in the 1920s they were a lost generation, an ever-present reminder of what the country had suffered in the war, and many of the Surplus Women had become impatient with knitting in the chimney corner – in other words, they were a problem, a talking point. Society could no longer afford to ignore or marginalise them.

Fortunately there were plenty of writers more sympathetic to the situation of unmarried women than Gallichan, Ludovici, Cowdroy and their like. Among these were feminist doctors, psychologists and preachers – like Maude Royden, who published *Sex and Commonsense* in 1921, Dame Mary Scharlieb, author of *The Bachelor Woman and Her Problems* (1929), Esther Harding, who wrote *The Way of All Women: A Psychological Interpretation* (1933), and Laura Hutton, who wrote *The Single Woman and Her Emotional Problems* (1935). The authors of these works spoke to women who, like the Muriels and Sarahs in Winifred Holtby's novels, were full of despair and darkness. They acknowledged the 'bitter grief' of loss, and the 'dull, deadly days when one realises at last that youth has passed without granting fulfilment of any of one's dreams', and tried to offer consolation along with solutions.

Though opinions varied among these pundits, the gist of all of them was that single women need not sit in chill rooms waiting for a knock at the door, that society was much to blame for the common perception of the spinster, and that there were practical remedies for their problems. Their books redressed the balance towards insight and support. Though they adopted the vocabulary of sublimation and repression, they were also full of sympathy and ready advice.

Maude Royden – a remarkable orator and preacher – had taken up the suffragettes' cause before the war; in the 1920s she was quick to speak again on behalf of women who had been left single as a result. Royden's Christianity gave her pity for their plight a compassionate intensity; she sided adamantly with the individual, refusing to belittle the suffering of women who endured enforced celibacy. 'The idea that they . . . do not suffer if their sex instincts are repressed or starved is a convenient but most cruel illusion,' she wrote, and she pointed to the evidence of repression: thwarted emotions expended on poodles and parrots, lachrymose religiosity. The way forward was painful but, she insisted, it could be glorious; the sexual and maternal impulses might be diverted Christ-like to the greater good of humanity:

We too can transmute the power of sex and 'create' in other ways. He did it supremely for the world. You and I can do it for our village, our city, for England, for the world, for anything you like.

More down-to-earth, Mary Scharlieb, a pioneer gynaecologist from an earlier generation (she was born in 1845), offered words of sympathy and caution. *The Bachelor Woman and Her Problems* addressed itself very directly to the multitude of post-war women who outnumbered their male counter-parts. We were living in abnormal times, according to Scharlieb, citing the population statistics of one London borough, Marylebone, as evidence. In this one London neighbourhood there were no fewer than 21,567 more women than men in 1921, and more than half of the borough's female population were unmarried. In her book Scharlieb set out to deal with the practical problems arising from singledom on this scale, ranging from what she saw as its less desirable side-effects like 'unwholesome' female friend-ships, to the solitary bad habits which so easily tempted the weary, despon-dent woman worker – like a whisky and soda at the end of a tiring day, rather than a restorative cup of tea. But she too eulogised the spinster, seeing her as having a universal role to play in society; she was '. . . essential to the welfare of the nation'.

All this helped. When Geraldine Aves, who was born in 1898, was at Newnham just after the war, a distinguished woman doctor came to lecture to the students there on the subject of relationships between men and women. 'The thing that deeply impressed me was her description of how young women had to face the fact that many of them would not get married. She talked about sublimation and how you can, in fact, have a very worthwhile and interesting and happy life if you somehow adjust to that.' Geraldine, like many highly educated women whose cheeks were never to bloom anew under the kisses of her children, turned her attention to her studies and became in due course a most eminent civil servant and social reformer.

In the mid 1930s two other writers, Esther Harding and Laura Hutton, sympathetically considered the predicament of the single woman. By that time, any young woman who might have hoped against hope for a husband in the post-war period had either got one or was having to come to terms with the fact that she probably never would. If she was born in, say, 1888, like Gertrude Caton-Thompson, she would have been forty-seven in 1935. May Jones was forty-two that year; nearly half her life had gone by since she lost Philip. Both Winifred Haward and Winifred Holtby would have been thirty-seven in 1935. These women would have felt the clock ticking; they would be having to come to terms with the future as singles. And whether or not the psychologists and medics consoled them with their words of faith and encouragement, there must have been days when they were depressed, days when they felt that, however essential they were to Jesus Christ or the welfare of the nation, they themselves were plain, dull, queer and unnecessary.

\*

All too often it seemed that the world just wasn't designed around their needs. Single women in the first half of the twentieth century had an image problem, which they and their defenders were struggling to redress; but survival was about more than persuading a hostile world to tolerate cat-lovers and cranky maiden aunts with pince-nez. Post-war society wasn't ready for the influx of Surplus Women, and the spinster population felt acutely the uncertainty of their social position.

Victorian conventions lingered on beyond the point where they were obsolete. One evening in the mid 1920s, when she was about twenty-seven years old, Winifred Holtby took a family friend to the theatre. This lady was middle-aged, and worked as the matron of a celebrated boys' public school. As Winifred described her:

I doubt if there is among my whole acquaintance a more admirable and respectable person or one whose looks inspire more confidence in her tact, wisdom, moderation and morality. Her face, her bearing, even her hats emphasize the strong sense of responsibility towards the young which has developed during her life's work. She has also, mercifully, a sense of humour, a knowledge of human nature, and many other pleasant qualities.

The play was a long one. When they reached the station Winifred and her friend found that they had missed their train, which left them with an hour to wait until the next one, at midnight. It was cold and rainy, the ladies' waiting-room fire had gone out, and the café had closed. Fortunately, Winifred recalled that the Station Hotel, right opposite the platform, had a comfortable lounge where they would be able to spend an hour in the warmth with a cup of tea. She had often been there and the staff knew her by sight. It would be a relief to have a hot drink sitting in their deep sofas on such a miserable night. They went in.

Winifred beckoned the waiter and ordered. In return she got a puzzled look; embarrassed, he shuffled off and brought back with him the manager, who now made cautious enquiries. 'I'm sorry – but are you residents?' No, Winifred explained, they were waiting for their train. 'I'm sorry,' he responded, 'I'm afraid you can't stop here. We can't serve you. You must go.'

Protest was in vain. It turned out that there were quite unequivocal rules: 'Ladies not admitted unless accompanied by a Gentleman'. These rules had been made to safeguard public morality. Winifred and her respectable friend were females, they were not residents, and they were entering the hotel without a man after a certain hour. So they must go out.

And out we went. We walked up and down the bleak, chill, draughty platform until our train arrived – twenty minutes late. Next day my companion was in bed with a bad cold and acute rheumatism . . .

Later, Winifred was furious with herself for not marching straight on to the platform and borrowing the first friendly porter she could find to play his part, but at least she had made her point in print. The assumption that she and her nice middle-aged friend in her matronly hat, entering a café unaccompanied after ten o'clock, were prostitutes was, in the circumstances, laughable. But it was insulting and damaging too.

Life for the single woman was full of such grey areas. Should she entertain, travel alone, be seen in public? What should she wear? If she was not a housewife, could she be a house-spinster? And if she could not find a man to support her, how could she support herself? Job possibilities were very limited, and after the war unemployment was high; between 1914 and 1918 the female workforce increased by nearly a million, most of the uneducated ones going into munitions factories or domestic service, while higher up the social ladder they became nurses or teachers. Friendships, whether with men or women, were cast into doubt by post-Freudian society's heightened awareness of sex ('. . . Do they? . . . Don't they?'), while sexual appetites themselves, ravenous and urgent as they might be, were virtually taboo in polite society. All these topics have their place later in this book; here, I want simply to establish that the Surplus Woman had many problems, not just of grief and loss, but of closed minds, of male (and female) hostility, of archaic expectations and the law stacked against her. A single woman's life in the 1920s and 30s often felt like a gritty struggle against prejudice, poverty and exclusion.

## Destiny and the devil

When she was nearly ninety, Miss Amy Gomm wrote a book of memories, *Water Under the Bridge*, for her nieces. She wanted to tell them about their grandparents, about the Cotswold countryside she'd grown up in; about how the family were always singing hymns and ballads because there was no radio; about eating raw walnuts from the hedgerows on the way to school; about seeing the grand folk at Oxford in Eights Week ('. . . Such hats! Such dresses!'); about how she shared a bed with her six cousins when they came to visit; about her father's charm and her mother's quiet strength. The memories brought back tears and smiles: '. . . you'll think me an emotional old biddy . . .'

Aunt Amy was born in 1899 in Charlbury, a small town in rural Oxfordshire. She left school when she was fourteen and went to work in her mother's home-based laundry business. Obsessively puritanical, the Gomm parents brought up their daughters in fear of 'disgrace'. They were heavily protected and not allowed to get work outside the home. There was a saying then among mothers of big families: 'Give me boys every time. They don't bring the trouble home.' But after their mother died in 1916 the laundry business disbanded, and Amy and her two elder sisters struggled to get through the hard war years. Food was scarce and un-nutritious; as a result, Amy was blighted by an ugly rash on her face which defied all remedies. The three girls kept house together; Dorothy continued with laundry work, and Laurie helped out at the local Liberal Club.

Amy, who was bright and motivated, yearned to get an office job: '. . . that was for me. It was pretty high-flying in those days.' Despite her lack of qualifications, Sainsbury's offered her a post as a junior clerk and cashier, but her father wouldn't let her take it. Finally she insisted on taking a job at the haberdashery counter of the local Co-op, where she managed to hang on till 1920:

[One day] I opened my wages bag and found myself with only one week to go. The respite I'd enjoyed was explained by the fact that there was no man home from the war with an actual claim on a job in our shop. Those who had left didn't return to it. Tragically, in some cases they couldn't.

So the decision makers had let it ride. Mass unemployment now forced their hands. There were men – married men with family responsibilities – begging for work. They couldn't justify keeping girls on. The job was, always had been, a man's.

Every cloud has a silver lining. We no longer had to spend our evenings and weekends doing the chores. We had a domestic help living in. Me.

Getting food on the table for her sisters cheered Amy up, but the cloud of unemployment was dispiriting. Jobs were snatched up as soon as word of them got out, usually by people 'in the know'. None of them were for 'young ladies'. So Amy joined the queue at the Labour Exchange. In the second week she was sent for a waitressing job at an unwholesome café where the manager offered her a pitiful half-a-crown a week's wages which, he implied, would be supplemented by earnings from demobbed soldiers looking for pleasure. Tormented by her inflamed complexion, Amy was morbidly conscious that no man had ever taken a second look at her. 'With my spotty face . . . ? I'd have to put my head in a bag, then. But it wasn't my face he was looking at.' Desperate for work, unlovely and unhappy as she was, she wasn't yet ready to sell her body. After she turned the job down, the Labour Exchange lost interest in her.

I had my twenty-first birthday that year. There must have been girls around unhappier, more ill-used than I was. I wasn't the only one who was living on her family . . . I wasn't the <u>only</u> one with a stagnating brain and frustrated ambitions. I wasn't the <u>only</u> one with a spotty face.

But I <u>was</u> the only one among the folks we knew . . . who suffered all these miseries at once. So I had a lovely wallow in my woe; took time off from the shopping and the chores and the futile job-hunting, to have a 'good birthday cry' while the others were at work.

Determination, and her supportive sisters, came to Amy's rescue. With the last twelve pounds in the kitty – four years' savings – the girls clubbed together to send her for a term to secretarial school. On the first day she was mortified by her spots, but after that she was too busy, and too optimistic, to care. Bubbling over with excitement and happiness, she was intent on her future, which now seemed full of hope and promise. Between September and November Amy crammed in a year's worth of shorthand and typing. Every evening after work Dorothy and Laurie would spend hours drilling her with dictation. She was driven on by their faith in her. By Christmas she'd landed a job with a multiple tailoring shop in Ealing. London!

I'd have gone anywhere, slept rough if need be . . . Now, at last, I'd got what I'd always wanted. I was <u>in</u>. Now there was nothing to stop me.

I was off to conquer the world. Now I'd got my foot on the ladder, I'd show 'em. The sky was the limit!

Amy's robust good spirits helped her brave the bad times. Aside from the occasional 'lovely wallow' she was not self-pitying. *Water Under the Bridge* ends as its author sets off for a brave new secretarial career – book-keeping, tea-making and logging measurements for a chain of outfitters in West London. For a young single woman in 1921 this represented independence and victory. And in old age, with sister Laurie and her husband close neighbours in Oxford, life was still '. . . wonderful – I'm staying the course.'

★

For all the hardships, for all the obstacles, frustrations and stigma, it is not hard to find examples of single women setting out, like Amy Gomm, to rescue the image of the 'old maid' from the pitiable and grotesque model so readily communicated by her enemies. Perhaps it came naturally to her. Certainly women who scorned to fall into the 'queer spinster' trap shared an innately optimistic outlook which upends the stereotype. Not all the aunts were submissive or dowdy or bitter.

Bessie Webster, for example, was the most beloved of female relatives to her niece, Isabel. This vital, adventurous, life-enhancing, maverick lady had loved her university tutor Jimmy Brown; he died in the war. She didn't get over it, and always wore his ring; but her spirits were irrepressible. 'There was always laughter when Bessie was around.'

Or take the writer Elizabeth Jenkins, whose avowed role model (and namesake?) was Queen Elizabeth the First, the Virgin Queen ('. . . she refused to marry'). Despite her mother's hopes and expectations, Elizabeth Jenkins simply regarded herself from the outset as unmarriageable, and never attempted to behave in any kind of way that would get her a husband. Instead she concentrated her energies on teaching, writing and falling in love. Pretty, high-spirited, self-centred and talented, she saw herself as a gift from providence to any man lucky enough to gain her fleeting attentions or get her into bed. Marriage was never in her sights.

Similarly 'Rani' Cartwright, a well-known model, described herself as 'free-range'. Rani, daughter of a Siamese mother and an English father, escaped from her convent education and came to Britain in the 1920s, where she discovered a world hungry for her exotic beauty. Success came easily. She sat for Epstein, and was taken up by a top agency to model clothes for Chanel, Lanvin and Molyneux, while her alluring glance was soon on display advertising eye treatments as one of 'The Optrex Girls'. Travel, glamour, money and high society were there for the taking; in comparison, marriage held little attraction. The thought of losing her free-dom, of having to compromise with somebody else's needs and habits, repelled her. Even in her nineties, reminiscing in the bedroom of her comfortable residential home in suburban Suffolk, Miss Cartwright was adamant: 'I couldn't bear to be with one person, so I'd much rather not marry than have this to face; anyway, I'd seen so many unhappy marriages that started out happy in the beginning. Until you live with a person you don't know their habits, do you? I didn't want to know, so consequently I didn't want to get married. I don't want to be tied down in anything.'

This was not sub-normality, or man-contemning, or 'psychic sclerosis'. These were women controlling their own destinies. Now that there were too many of her to ignore, the time had come to give the single woman not just a voice, but an image makeover. Though warped virgins still outnumbered free-range singles in literature, the fictional model of the spinster began to explore more rounded, complex portrayals.

★

One of the most extraordinary spinsters to come out of the 1920s is Sylvia Townsend Warner's *Lolly Willowes* (1926). Laura – Lolly – starts out as a

classic aunt, sallow, plain and pointy-faced. Aged twenty-eight when the
novel starts, she is starting to look perilously unmarriageable. Lolly, who
lives according to the Victorian model under her brother Henry's roof
in London, along with her conventional sister-in-law Caroline and their
children, seems to be an unobtrusive member of the family. It is true she is
rather erudite and has shown an early interest in herbalism, but she does
her fancy needlework conscientiously. However, she is also given to making
unexpected pronouncements. The one and only suitor to come calling is
rapidly deterred by Lolly's blithe hint that he may, entirely without knowing
it, be a werewolf. 'This settled it. Henry and Caroline made no more
attempts to marry off Laura.'

Lolly's perceived eccentricities gradually accumulate. She roams London
secretly haunting second-hand bookshops and furtively feasting off marrons
glacés. One late afternoon she strays into a greengrocer's shop in Moscow
Road, where she purchases a bunch of russet-coloured chrysanthemums.
The flowers come with a generous spray of beech fronds:

They smelt of woods, of dark rustling woods like the wood to whose edge she
came so often in the country of her autumn imagination. She stood very still to
make quite sure of her sensations. Then: 'Where do they come from?' she asked.

Buckinghamshire, comes the answer.

Lolly moves out. Deaf to her family's indignant protests, she takes a
cottage in the remote and secluded village of Great Mop, in the heart of
the Buckinghamshire Chilterns. Gradually she learns her new landscape by
heart; it is full of cooing pigeons and rustling beechwoods, and the nights
are lovely and serene. Every evening after supper she chats with her friendly
landlady over a glass of home-made dandelion and mangold wine. In the
village the neighbours are unconcerned by her ways, for theirs are just as
odd: the clergyman keeps a tame owl, Misses Minnie and Jane Larpent
cook stewed rabbit for the Bishop, Mr Gurdon the parish clerk has a curly
red beard and bullies the choirboys. Slowly, Lolly takes on the life of this
curious village, and then one day a small kitten comes into her room.
Surprised by the uninvited guest, Lolly bends to stroke it; it bites and claws
her ferociously, streaking her hand with red scratches. And now she knows
for certain what she has always guessed:

She, Laura Willowes, in England, in the year 1922, had entered into a compact
with the Devil. The compact was made, and affirmed, and sealed with the round
red seal of her blood.

Laura is a witch.

She joins the Great Mop coven. Unerringly, her Master has led her to his place. She has come home. And finally, in a graveyard, she meets him. Lolly's evolution is complete, and yet she is what she always was: adventurous, independent, odd and unsafe. Sylvia Townsend Warner – herself unmarried – challenged propriety in her own life. She loved women, not men. Her impatience with the conventions that governed single women's lives takes form in *Lolly Willowes*, a triumphant vindication of the spinster. Lolly refuses to be patronised, to be 'Poor Lolly' or 'Dear Lolly'. She will not submit to being the kind of maiden aunt who gets given hot water bottles for birthdays. What does she care if men disdain her body as unattractive, when the Devil himself has sought out her soul? Satan offers secrecy, charm, danger, and immunity from judgement:

That's why we become witches: to show our scorn of pretending that life's a safe business, to satisfy our passion for adventure . . . One doesn't become a witch to run round being harmful, or to run round being helpful either, a district visitor on a broomstick. It's to escape all that – to have a life of one's own, not an existence doled out to you by others . . .

*Lolly Willowes* is witty, lyrical and affirmative, not agitprop in the war of the sexes, but a profound *cri de cœur*: 'Leave me alone, and let me be what I am.'

There were other novels whose heroines, though they did not go so far as to sell their souls to Satan, still resolutely turned their backs on hot water bottles and knitting needles. As an apologist for despairing, embattled singles fighting for identity and independence in hostile territory, Winifred Holtby was unequalled. Her heroines Muriel Hammond and Sarah Burton emerge from setbacks strong and self-sufficient. Muriel's sick terror at being unwanted, of never becoming a wife, has evolved into a determination not to compromise with an unhappy marriage. She has been taught that there are other things in life, has glimpsed ideals that may be even more significant for her than marriage; and though a lover eventually comes to Muriel, she turns him away: ' "I can't be a good wife until I've learnt to be a person," said Muriel, "and perhaps in the end I'll never be a wife at all." '

Sarah Burton's shame, sorrow and loss of hope after Robert Carne's death are finally tested when the pilot of the light aircraft she is in momentarily loses control; at that moment she knows she wants to live. 'Comforted by death, she faced the future.' And Sarah's future will see her finishing the task before her. It is school speech day. Bandaged from her near-miss, she stands before her pupils and delivers an eloquent address on anti–authoritarianism: ' ". . . Question your government's policy, question the arms race, question the Kingsport slums, and the rule that makes women have to renounce their jobs on marriage, and why the derelict areas still are derelict . . . Questioning does not mean the end of loving . . ." '

Even F. M. Mayor's melancholy spinster Mary Jocelyn in *The Rector's Daughter* (1924) makes a heartfelt case for the single woman, delving deep into the inner life of its heroine. Mary *is* the kind of aunt who gets given hot water bottles; dutiful to her demanding father, humble and 'nice', her unassertive, indoor nature is the antithesis of the witch. Not for Mary the freedom of sleeping in a leafy ditch like Lolly Willowes. She will never orate from a platform like Sarah Burton, nor seek political fulfilment like Muriel Hammond. Her father squashes her literary ambitions, and after losing the one man she loves to a rival, Mary's romantic hopes are blighted too. Her life is not entirely empty; in late middle age she finds gentle happiness with a group of other spinsters like her, who invite her to lectures, matinées and philanthropic meetings. She dies quietly, resignedly, lovable to the last. But Mary's creator F. M. Mayor, herself a bereaved, thwarted single, unflinchingly lays bare the quiet torments of her heroine. Anguish always lies close to the surface, breaking through even at the end, when she has a meeting with her rival, now married to the man she once loved. Despite Mary's 'busy, happy life', she suffers bitter pangs:

She was seized with jealousy of him and Kathy – the primal jealousy of an unsuccessful rival. Kathy had him, had children, had everything.

F. M Mayor's tale of a woman's buried, intense emotions, its detailing of the loneliness, the crushed passions and the fear, is deeply true. The courage of this novel is in its recognition of individual hopes and fears. *The Rector's Daughter* is not palliative, it is not comforting. 'Don't be deluded,' is its message, 'life is hard for single women, so don't expect other people to be kind or understanding. Make your own way in life. Seek integrity.' Where Mary wins is in her painful honesty, disconcerting as that may be to her few friends – like Dora:

'To love and be loved,' said Mary musingly. 'Did you feel it like a key, Dora, to let you out of prison, and open a treasure-house to you?'

'Is that a pretty bit out of your writings?' said Dora with a kindness that would have checked the flow, but Mary was not listening. 'I have *longed* for it,' she went on.

She spoke with an intensity that startled Dora . . . [her] eyes burnt too, with a fire which made Dora uncomfortable . . .

'I have sometimes thought –' Mary said with feeling, 'the kisses –'

The gorgon Aunt Jane, the tweed-clad figures of fun and the wispy-bunned virgins of popular fiction never smouldered with longing. They weren't even allowed to. F. M. Mayor never denies how hard it could be.

THE SUPERFLUOUS WOMAN: A HOLIDAY TRAGEDY.

*Punch*, August Bank Holiday weekend, 1927: the caption 'A Holiday Tragedy' seems barely an exaggeration

## The more of us the merrier

When Vera Brittain first met her, Winifred Holtby was wearing a boldly striped costume, topped with an emerald green hat; as she was exceptionally tall and well-built, the effect was astonishing. Winifred, throughout her tragically short life (she died of an incurable disease aged thirty-eight★), made a career out of her refusal to be pigeonholed, denounced or ignored.

★ Vera Brittain and her husband Gordon Catlin persuaded Harry Pearson to come to Winifred's deathbed, and in her diary Vera recorded that the pair had there come to an understanding that they would marry. However, Winifred's biographer has no doubt that Harry Pearson was under pressure from Gordon to show compassion to a dying woman and would never have agreed to this on his own account.

And in the same spirit as F. M. Mayor, she publicly confronted frustration.

Winifred was eventually so goaded by the attacks on spinsters (Oswald Mosley had publicly referred to them as 'this distressing type') that she sat down to write a robust defence of the millions like herself. The single woman was in need of social rehabilitation, and Winifred was not one to shirk the task. Her essay 'Are Spinsters Frustrated?' is a war-cry, challenging the assumption that sex is the only channel for fulfilment. Yes, she conceded, frustration was bad; but we have to get our terms sorted out. Popular psychologists were wrong that marital sex was the only alleviation for frustration; this was a misconception based on the Protestant emphasis on women as primarily wives. It was dismaying to see Mosley and the others so fixated on the idea that women without sex lives would 'become riddled with complexes like a rotting fruit'. Holtby refuted the notion that pleasure, ecstasy, happiness, achievement and a full life were dependent on this one circumstance. Many wives were utterly miserable, yet society had taught girls to dread the fate of the 'old maid'. The muddled thinking that made spinsterhood seem so unenviable prevented the world from recognising the reality:

The spinster may have work which delights her, personal intimacies which comfort her, power which satisfies her. She may have known that rare light of ecstasy.

Funny, intelligent and courageous, Winifred Holtby was herself a powerful embodiment of her own creation Sarah Burton's compressed philosophy: 'I was born to be a spinster, and by God, I'm going to spin.' Thus armed with courage, humour and pride, Sarah Burton/Winifred Holtby looked to the future. The war was past. It had taken the husbands from two million potential wives, but along with it, it had removed the shame. Being one of two million felt less blameworthy than in the past, when the spinster suffered from the shame of being unable to attract a man. Now, being unmarried could be regarded as a misfortune rather than a fault, and with this recovery came a renewed sense of their own power and importance. 'I was off to conquer the world,' wrote Amy Gomm, '. . . the sky was the limit.' 'I was a high-flyer, and I was too much interested in what I was doing in the way of writing to think at all about marriage . . .' remembered Elizabeth Jenkins. And Rani Cartwright's 'no-ties' approach brought her travel and a hectic social life: 'I was never lonely, never bored. You're too busy, living out of a suitcase, always with different people. I want my freedom, I still do!' Conviction and solidarity gave these women their momentum.

There was so much that still needed to be achieved for unmarried women in the wide world, not just in dispelling prejudice (hot water bottles, tweed suits and sex-starved old maids), but also in righting the balance for single women economically and socially. The men were dead who might have led Britain, but they had left behind them women who felt there was much that needed changing. Winifred Holtby made the point that wives were hampered by the responsibilities of husband and children, whereas the unmarried had liberty to make progress in many fields – education, medicine, politics, art and exploration. This remains true. Provided they were prepared to make the break from their families, and turn their backs on the expectation that they would live unmarried under the parental roof as unpaid – and often unthanked – carers, the 1920s and 30s were full of openings for talented ambitious women.

Those glimmerings of change from the turn of the century were becoming brighter, steadier. Slowly but surely, the barricades were being dismantled from traditional male preserves – the law, medicine, politics, journalism, academe and finance. It could be uphill, but if you were prepared to work hard and fight your corner, there were rewards. After she left Oxford in 1921 Vera Brittain, with Winifred Holtby, removed her 'disappointing spinsterhood' to Bloomsbury and took up a career as journalist, writer and political activist. She lectured for the League of Nations and travelled widely. Her parents tolerated their breakaway daughter: 'They understood now that freedom, however uncomfortable, and self-support, however hard to achieve, were the only conditions in which a feminist of the War generation . . . could do her work and maintain self-respect.'

Vera Brittain's father generously made over to her a small private income – not enough to live on, but enough to save her from penury. With this, her Oxford education and her middle-class confidence, Vera was in a good position to follow her star. But there were also women who had never studied medieval economics or Greek verbs who were beginning to realise that lack of a husband might be a beginning and not an end.

★

In 1886 and 1889 two daughters, Florence and Annie, were born to an illegitimate vaudeville singer and an illiterate mill-worker in Bradford. James White, their father, was talented, politically minded and unstable. Before Annie's birth, James abandoned the family, and before long found himself imprisoned on a petty charge; he died in jail of pneumonia aged fifty. Though they weren't on the bottom rung, the girls and their brother Albert grew up in poverty. They lived in a back-to-back house, and Caroline, their mother, took in washing and baking. Florence went to school in clogs, but she wasn't barefooted like many of the backstreet children who lived around them. The lesson Florence learnt from her childhood was one of self-reliance. Men couldn't be depended upon.

At twelve, Florence White left school and went to work at Tankard's Mill, the biggest employer in that area of Bradford. For the next six years she spent ten and a half hours a day weighing skeins of wool in the deafeningly noisy, grim and dangerous factory. She never forgot those years, nor the friends she made then: Polly, Rose, Martha . . . poor women whose jobs required them to stand all day at a machine, whose calloused feet had worn holes in their shoes, who worked at Tankard's all their lives, who never married, and who died young. The injustice of their lot affected Florence for the rest of her life.

But their lot was not hers. Florence had inherited her father's mercurial streak; bossy and driven, all her life she was given to temper tantrums and excesses, though her nieces were also to remember her as deeply thoughtful and generous, funny and warm-hearted. When she was eighteen, in 1904, something gave way, and she broke down. She never went back to the mill. The family now managed to move to a slightly larger house belonging to an uncle, where Florence and Annie started dressmaking and giving piano lessons. This was a step up the social ladder, and the moderate success of their business gave the sisters a new-found freedom. Leaving their uneducated mother to mind the house, Florence and Annie would gad off on outings to Blackpool and Ilkley; they took an interest in local politics and the suffrage movement. Their relationship was quarrelsome but deeply affectionate.

Florence White had a wartime love affair, but the information on it is scanty. She was already thirty when she and Albert Whitehead became engaged in 1916. Any hopes she had for wifehood or motherhood must have rested on this relationship, but he and Florence were doomed to join the grievous statistics. Albert was sent home from France to a military hospital, presumably to recover from wounds. There he died from pneumonia in 1917.

Florence's sister Annie had a boyfriend too, a plumber called Charles. But Florence had become used to having things her own way in the White household, where, as eldest daughter, she ruled the roost. Charles was seen as unacceptable and Florence jealously did everything in her power to kill off the romance. Despite engineering secret assignations with Charles, Annie's will failed her, and the unfortunate young man was left to languish.*

---

* Annie got her revenge years later when Florence, in her fifties, showed signs of fancying a train driver from Bournemouth. Annie wasn't going to let her get away with it, and this time it was Florence who caved in.

Thus the pair settled in for long-term spinsterhood. Florence was stout with gig-lamp glasses; she certainly neglected her hair and most probably she adopted inelegant poses. Annie and she were well into their thirties now, and marriage hopes had waned. In the early 1920s their mother died. Their nieces, the daughters of their brother, were living with them, and the dressmaking business was keeping them modestly. Florence and Annie might have drifted into the twilight zone of aunthood had it not been for Florence's restless nature, which drove her to seek out causes. Ideas were seething in her busy little brain.

She did not have far to look. On her doorstep, at Tankard's Mill, were many women unluckier than her, unmarried and living in poverty – women like her friends, the three sisters Polly, Rose and Martha Jackson. Worn out, all three of them died before they were sixty-five, before they were eligible for a retirement pension.★ It was their deaths that galvanised Florence. Already working for the Liberal Party, in the early 1930s she set up a sub-committee to look at women's pensions: Florence had finally found her life's work. Stop feeling sorry for the widows and orphans, was her message. Think about the spinsters! In 1935, in a church hall in Bradford, more than 600 single working-class women attended a public meeting addressed by Florence. By the end of the evening the National Spinsters Pensions Association was born to fight for their rights, with rules, membership, officials and subscriptions, and Miss Florence White at its head.

★

In 1961 when Muriel Spark wrote *The Prime of Miss Jean Brodie* she was able to look back twenty-five years and finally give the image of the inter-war spinster her most enduring, if retrospective, incarnation. The character of Miss Brodie is the antithesis of the maiden aunt. She is sexy, romantic and subversive; wrong and ruthless, but inescapably influential. Her 'set', five schoolgirls growing into young women, are mesmerised by their liberated schoolmistress. Far from looking on her as a pathetic specimen, Rose, Eunice, Sandy, Jenny and Mary are enraptured by Jean Brodie's exhilaratingly different approach to lessons. An English grammar session is replaced by Miss Brodie's stirring reminiscences of her dead lover, one of the 'Flowers of the Forest', who 'fell like an autumn leaf, though he was only twenty-two years of age'. They are equally obsessed by their

★ Lloyd George first introduced old age pensions for those over seventy in 1909; in 1925 this was updated to entitle anyone earning less than £250 a year to ten shillings a week from the age of sixty-five, provided they had paid their contributions.

teacher's sex life, by her bosom – sometimes flat and straight, on other days 'breast-shaped and large, very noticeable' – and by her talk of Shakespeare, Cimabue and Mussolini. Inevitably, Miss Brodie's seditious educational methods bring her into conflict with the school's principal; while her amours provoke jealousy and, eventually, betrayal. But in her prime, Miss Jean Brodie is irresistibly dangerous and different: 'Safety does not come first,' she tells the girls. 'Goodness, Truth and Beauty come first. Follow me.' And they do.

Though Muriel Spark asserts in *The Prime of Miss Jean Brodie* that her heroine was by no means unique as a type of 'war-bereaved spinster', and that there were indeed 'legions of her kind during the nineteen-thirties', still it took time and distance to turn the thwarted spinster into such an icon. A few decades on, Helen Fielding has given us urban über-singleton Bridget Jones as a role model for our own times – drunk, nicotine-addicted, modern, funny and, along with her angry-young-woman friend Sharon, determined not to be squashed by the Smug Marrieds:

'. . . I'm not married because I'm a *Singleton*, you smug, prematurely ageing, narrow-minded morons,' Shazzer ranted. 'And because there's more than one bloody way to live: one in four households are single, the nation's young men have been proved by surveys to be completely unmarriageable, and as a result there's a whole generation of single girls like me with their own incomes and homes who have lots of fun and don't need to wash anyone else's socks. We'd be as happy as sandboys if people like you didn't conspire to make us feel stupid just because you're jealous.'

'Singletons!' I shouted happily. 'Hurrah for the Singletons!'

The Surplus Woman has come a long way – but Ms Bridget Jones only echoes the anonymous correspondent who wrote to the editor of the *Daily Mail* back in February 1920, remonstrating with the author of that alarming article entitled A MILLION WOMEN TOO MANY:

Sir, – A million women too many; it is indeed a bombshell that Dr Murray Leslie has hurled among the women who are so valiantly striving to take and hold 'a place in the sun'.

But there are consolations. No girl, anyway, until she is well past girlhood, considers that *she* is one of those excess females.

All the same, if a woman would definitely decide to be 'in excess' then she should enter a profession or business with no fear that marriage would ruin her career. She could help in the world's work in another sphere.

Why should not some of us bury our hopes and form a Union of Surplus Women who mean to succeed? Why should we be downcast? The more of us the merrier – and we are a goodly company.

ONE OF THE MILLION

# 3. On the Shelf

## Husbands

A MILLION WOMEN TOO MANY – 1920 HUSBAND HUNT, proclaimed the *Daily Mail* headline reporting Dr Murray Leslie's lecture to the London Institute of Hygiene on 4 February 1920. The report stood alongside other stories – Princess Alice had visited the Ideal Homes Exhibition, Brinsmead's famous piano factory in Kentish Town had closed, and the price of petrol had increased by 8d a gallon.

The *Daily Mail*'s story covered the main points of Dr Leslie's lecture, and reported his grave concerns regarding the disturbing excess of women over men (which, as the Census was to show the following year, was an underestimate of almost a million).

Dr Leslie could see no redeeming features; on the contrary, he observed only the disadvantages. Social stability was threatened by female discontent. The disproportion led to young women having greater freedom, and failures in discipline and parental supervision permitted sexual licence. 'The old ethical standards' were crumbling, he noted; there was 'a lowered standard of morality', and a collapse of marriage and family life brought about by infidelity among married men, who readily availed themselves of the numerous unattached women. Economically, inflation meant that single daughters were forced out of the home and into the workplace, where market competition ensured that our most able women got jobs, leaving only the unskilled lower orders to breed for the nation. Meanwhile 'jazzing flappers' with their claws out, desperately displaying their nubile bodies in over-revealing garments, fought like cats over 'the scarce and elusive male'. Spellbound by the availability of sex, young men 'with dance invitations four and five deep' were becoming jaded and spoiled. In short, the country was going to the dogs. Reassuringly, there was still space at the foot of the column for a comforting advertisement placed there by a convenience food manufacturer: 'In these days of changing and uncertain values, there is one article which has remained standardised in quality – Symington's Soups.'

The *Daily Mail*'s correspondents, however, took Dr Leslie's comments to heart. The majority of them were women; over the next few days they wrote in with their reactions to this calamitous state of affairs, and recounted their own experiences: 'Most of us are looking for husbands, and the competition is keen . . .'; 'To attract men, girls will dress daringly, and generally try to appear very bold and dashing and knowing . . .'; 'I want to get married, but my chances do not seem very bright . . .'; 'There are just not enough men to go round . . .' Never mind the effect on the nation, Dr Leslie's lecture had clearly touched a sore nerve with Britain's 'matchless maidens'. The letters told of their blighted hopes, their sense of having been cheated of a prize owed to all. Marriage was woman's crown, her glory and her birthright. If there were a few dissenting voices whispering that a husband represented anything other than a happy ending, the *Daily Mail* did not think fit to report them.

★

And yet in the early years of the twentieth century marriage was being scrutinised and redefined as never before. Plainly, for the majority of women, wifehood fell short of the joyful ideal. All too often, once the confetti had settled, the new bride had little to look forward to beyond a life of drudgery, oppression and ennui. No matter what their social class, women found themselves condemned to a kind of house-arrest, sentenced to a lifetime of food preparation, needlework and childcare. There was no escape.

When young Frances Graham set up home in County Durham with her miner husband Jim in 1919 she had no hot water, no electricity and no bathroom. She had been trained by her mother for a lifetime of housework: 'I don't know what made us like this but when I was married, that day I swept the confetti out of the lobby myself.' Frances generally worked from 6.30 in the morning till 10.30 at night, on her feet. Scrubbing, washing and fetching hot water were back-breaking tasks; life was a permanent battle with soot, bugs and coal-dust. If you had only a distant outside toilet, there was the necessity of emptying chamber-pots; sanitary towels, too, had to be soaked and washed by hand. Cooking, laundry, dusting and scrubbing were the tyrannical, never-ending reality of the housewife's day. The unlucky ones also had to endure drunkenness, savagery, abuse and infidelity by their husbands.

Even by 1939, when the birth control campaigner Margery Spring Rice published *Working-Class Wives: Their Health and Conditions*, little had improved for the sample of over 1,000 wives interviewed:

My life for many years consisted of being penned in a kitchen 9 feet square, every fourteen months a baby, as I had five babies in five years at first, until what with the struggle to live and no leisure I used to feel I was just a machine . . . Our men think we should not go out until the children are grown up . . . It isn't the men are unkind. It is the old idea we should always be at home.

I pay 7s 6d for two rooms I have a sheet board ceiling when it rains it runs halfway along this ceiling and then drips on the floor we have a bath in the middle of the room to catch the rain . . . the council people offered us a flat at 19/7 per week . . . how they think we could pay that out of 33/3 when my husband is out of work I don't know. I have just had my 8th baby . . .

Working-class wives were not the only ones condemned to cramped and narrow horizons. Though not burdened with poverty, middle-class and upper-class wives were, like their poorer sisters, expected to confine their activities to the domestic sphere. Nobody ever thought to ask a married woman what she did, since everybody knew: her fate was to endure a life of endless and pointless leisure. 'If the fire required poking, one rang for a maid to fulfil this duty. No lady made any effort,' remembered one young lady who had grown up in Edwardian England. Flowers had to be arranged, of course, the canary fed, and calls paid. Embroidery must be done and bridge played. Daughters might also have to be taken to dancing classes, and books changed at libraries, but generally speaking drawing-room life was far from arduous. Henrietta (Etty) Litchfield, the daughter of Charles Darwin, led a life of exemplary futility. Etty had been delicate as a child and, having been advised by her doctor to have breakfast in bed for a while, never got up for breakfast again for the rest of her life. She did not have children, and had nothing to do except rest, and worry about her health. Her niece, the artist Gwen Raverat, related that Etty had never ever sewn on a button, posted a letter, made a pot of tea or been out alone after dark. 'Ladies were ladies in those days; they did not do things themselves, they told other people what to do and how to do it.' Gwen's mother, Maud, made a profession of telling other people how to do things, despite her total lack of knowledge. Of course, as Gwen noted, their housekeeper 'really ran the house completely, but appearances were always preserved'.

These women's husbands inherited a Victorian ideal of wifehood which was marvellously encapsulated in 1837 by Charles Darwin himself, as he considered the pros and cons of marriage with Emma Wedgwood. In methodical fashion, the great scientist listed his arguments in favour of matrimony as follows:

Children – (if it Please God) – Constant
companion, (& friend in old age) who
will feel interested in one, – object *to be*
*beloved* and played with. – better than a
dog anyhow. – Home, & someone to
take care of house – Charms of music
& female chit-chat. – These things
good for one's health. – *but terrible*
*loss of time . . .*
Only picture to yourself a nice soft
wife on a sofa with good fire, & books
& music perhaps – Compare this vision
with the dingy reality of Grt. Marlbro'
St.
Marry – Marry – Marry Q.E.D.

Emma was highly intelligent, graceful and a brilliant musician; she spoke three languages well, and was well informed on politics and literature. But she accepted Darwin's unspoken assumption that she was essentially a comfortably upholstered appendage, secure in the knowledge that she was doing her duty. She had no choice. Marriage had the weight of centuries

An illustration to Daisy Ashford's
romance *The Young Visiters* places
the nineteenth-century wife firmly
in context

of custom behind it. And for the rest of the nineteenth century, that was the deal. Security, economic maintenance, social respect, status and companionship in return for, in Emma's case, lifelong devotion and the production of ten babies. It appears that most Victorian men regarded marriage as a state of semi-captivity for their wives in which they bore numerous children, were financially dependent on their husbands, and at the same time embodied the feminine ideal of mother-goddess. Their wives were both Madonnas and martyrs. They must be beautiful and virtuous, but they must also be younger, shorter and stupider than their husbands. And yet whatever the drawbacks and expectations of 'female chit-chat', never would it have crossed Emma Darwin's mind to trade wifehood with such a man for the single state. The same probably applied to her daughter Etty and her daughter-in-law Maud.

This then was the catch. Marriage was patently unfair to women – until the Married Women's Property Act was passed in 1882 all their belongings and wealth passed automatically to their husbands – but it represented their only chance of security, of having children, of attaining social status. Happiness was neither here nor there. A late nineteenth-century vaudeville song summed up the options:

> I think we would all prefer
> marriage with strife
> Than to be on the shelf
> and be nobody's wife.

But lest they rebel, there was also the entrancing prospect of true love – a vision indulged in to the full by artists, poets and romantic balladeers throughout the nineteenth century. Blue-eyed Mary the dairy-maid gets her ruby lips kissed before becoming the Captain's bride; Phoebe, Nancy and Polly all end up at the church with their dark-eyed sailors or plough-boys.

The poetic fantasy exerted a powerful pull. Despite all the manifest disadvantages for married women, to the unmarried the grass almost invariably looked greener on the other side of the fence. 'There is nothing so incorrigibly and loftily romantic as a spinster's idea of matrimony . . .' wrote one retired headmistress in the 1930s. One of Ivy Compton-Burnett's spinster schoolmistresses confessed to the sense of awe it inspired in her: ' ". . . They are elemental things, the love between man and woman, marriage, motherhood," said Miss Luke . . . "The things untouched by civilization, primitive, immune from what is called progress." ' For the spinster, it was very hard not to idealise the married state and it would have taken a strong-minded woman to resist that commandment: 'Marry – Marry – Marry Q.E.D.'

Thus romance, social expectation and money all played their part in weighing down the nineteenth-century woman with the millstone of marriage – a heavy burden. The few who challenged it were conspicuous, like Florence Nightingale, who only by standing aside and remaining single was able to fulfil her ambitions. Married women 'must sacrifice all their life . . . behind *his* destiny woman must annihilate herself . . .' she declared. This she refused to do. But by the end of that century the institution of marriage was being subjected to scrutiny as never before. Women began to ask what was in it for them; they questioned the Victorian notion of duty which hitherto had anchored both happy and unhappy marriages; they began to look for personal happiness, beyond the orange blossom and the church door. If marriage fell short in this respect, then what was the point? By the 1890s a new breed were emerging who, collectively, were strong-minded enough to defy marriage.

This breed came to be called the New Women. Mutiny was in the air, and to the consternation and alarm of reactionaries, the New Women took a cool look at wifehood and decided to reject the mess, the boredom, the misery and the exhaustion. They left their families, not to get married, but to live in lodgings, to occupy a kind of nether-Bohemia, writing poetry and novels, discussing ideas and earning their own living. Their mantras were independence, equality, freedom and, of course, the vote. In 1913 over 60 per cent of the membership of the Pankhursts' Women's Social and Political Union were spinsters. These women were both influential and threatening. Grant Allen, Ibsen, H. G. Wells and Shaw observed them with fascination and created heroines out of them. Walter Gallichan lay awake at night worrying about the problem of *Modern Woman and How to Manage Her.*

Social advances of many kinds contributed to the anti-marriage revolution: the Married Women's Property Act, the divorce laws, contraception, improved health care, labour-saving devices, female emancipation all played their part in giving women the freedom to marry or not to marry. Plainly as a vocation marriage left much to desire, and the modern world was starting to provide women with alternatives. Thrilling to the idealistic vision of Walt Whitman, the young shop assistant Margaret Bondfield looked to fulfil herself through service to humanity and, above all, through her involvement in the National Union of Shop Assistants, her co-workers. 'This concentration was undisturbed by love affairs. I had seen too much – too early – to have the least desire to join in the pitiful scramble of my workmates . . . I had no vocation for wifehood or motherhood, but an urge to serve the Union.' In 1923 Miss Bondfield became one of the first three women Labour MPs. Spinsterhood could be a conscious choice, not a failure.

By 1920 Dr Leslie's assumptions, and those of the *Daily Mail*, were already – in advanced circles at least – starting to look out of date. It was evident to most people that with the war history's tide had turned. The time when every Jill got her Jack was past, and the Surplus Women would have to look elsewhere for fulfilment. For them, the New Women had gone before, like John the Baptist, pointing the way to salvation and release from bondage. And though the *Daily Mail* continued to print only letters from women who longed to be wives, that tide had turned for ever.

## Mr Wrong

British women were all too aware that the war had cheated them, not just of marriage but of marriage with Mr Right. Even women who in time married continued firmly to believe that the cream of their generation had all died. Rosamond Lehmann, born in 1901, grew up convinced that the alternatives were all second best. 'I had it lodged in my subconscious mind . . . that the wonderful unknown young man whom I should have married had been killed in France, along with all the other wonderful young men; so that any suitor – and quite a few uprose – would be a secondary substitute, a kind of simulacrum.' Vera Brittain's suitors were just as inadequate. In *Testament of Youth* she tells how in the early 1920s she was importuned by cynical married men, sugar-daddies, 'fussy and futile' middle-aged men, lechers, wimps and drippy poetic types who 'hadn't the brains of an earwig'. They were 'insufferably second-rate'. How desperate did one have to be? When Vera finally met Gordon Catlin, the man whom she was to marry, she was tortured with doubts. Shortly before agreeing to be his wife she had a terrible dream that Roland Leighton had never really died, but had gone missing with amnesia, and after terrible suffering had returned to England 'anxious to marry me'. She woke racked with anguish.

But for most, the cruel statistics remained: in the 1920s British women had lower chances of getting a husband than at any time since records were kept. Winifred Haward was one of them. In 1921 she was starting out in the world aged twenty-three, with a history degree and a short plump figure, stubbornly resisting the compulsion to become a teacher. Teachers were spinsters. Undeterred by the obvious deficiencies of matrimony, Winifred was yearning for a great love, and she wanted to marry, but with the Husband Hunt in full cry, her prospects weren't looking too good. Instead she got a job as lecturer at Bedford College in London, which was unlikely to improve her chances, since the college was women-only, and she lodged in a segregated hostel in the Euston Road. However, she was earning nearly £400 a year, which made it easier for her to indulge – 'I tried to dress well. It was useless trying to look smart and sophisticated but I could wear well-cut clothes and bright colours . . .' Over the next couple of years she holidayed in Brittany, Italy and Austria; there were no boyfriends, but she was seeing something of life.

Winifred's best friend was Muriel, a fellow lecturer at Bedford College, and in 1925 they decided to share digs together. Part of the attraction for Winifred was that Muriel was attractive, rather 'fast', and had a foreign admirer called Gustav (he was married, but Muriel thought he would soon divorce and marry her); she also had a stylish widowed mother who saw her daughter's friend as a challenge. On the widow's advice, the dowdy history lecturer was got up to look bold and dashing and knowing. She had her hair shingled, started using make-up and was persuaded to have all her skirts shortened. Winifred marvelled as Muriel's mamma transformed her into a 20s flapper. ' "Don't waste your legs," she said – "Think of Mistinguett" – Mistinguett being an actress famous for her nether limbs . . . I felt quite encouraged.' Thus with her not-so-nubile body suitably revealed, she and Muriel set up home together in Hampstead, Winifred hoping that her friend's honey-pot good looks would lure some of Gustav's male friends into their little circle, and that with luck, one of them would spare a look for her nether limbs, and might even want to marry her . . .

Muriel was quick to disillusion her on this front:

You and Gustav wouldn't get on. You wouldn't get on with his friends. You're too virginal, Winifred, too 'good'. If you haven't had a man by the time you're thirty, it will be too late. You'll get more frustrated and unhappy. Husbands are scarce but lovers grow on every tree . . .

Muriel was persuasive, and though Winifred was initially plagued with doubt, she now allowed herself to be talked round. 'Life wasn't very kind to women like me. Wasn't one entitled to warmth and happiness? I was twenty-seven and my chances were going. So many nicely brought-up girls were withering into virginity.' She agreed to meet an acquaintance of Muriel's called Martin, a married man. There was a good rapport between them from the start. Martin was intellectual, friendly and kind, and soon afterwards he gently and considerately relieved her of her burdensome virginity. 'I hadn't any feelings of guilt. I thought, "I have become a woman."' Though not in love, they continued to meet for some time, but Winifred still wanted marriage.

Miraculously, from somewhere, George appeared. George had survived the war. George was unmarried. Best of all, George seemed to want Winifred as much as she wanted him. He worked in the Ministry of Health, and he just seemed so suitable. Could this be it? For two years they went out together:

[We] went dancing, played tennis, and took long walks in the countryside . . . I thought it would have a happy ending. Suddenly, he fell for a young widow, and married her out of hand. I heard he said of me, 'She's too high class. I want someone commoner.'

This morale-shattering rejection left Winifred crushed, feeling she couldn't win. She was too clever and too 'good', and now she was too 'high class', plus she was not pretty, she was spoiled goods, and she was nearly thirty into the bargain. What did men want? Whatever they wanted, it wasn't her.

Her work began to suffer, but fortunately Winifred's PhD supervisor was an understanding woman; an opening had come up for a lecturer to exchange posts with their New Zealand counterpart in Christchurch for a year, and this she tactfully proposed to her pupil. Fight or flight? Winifred unhesitatingly chose the latter; she booked her passage and did her best to face the lonely future stoically. 'I left London at the end of the summer term in 1928 and spent my thirtieth birthday on board. The worst birthday in a woman's life didn't seem too grim!'

★

Staring at the Pacific Ocean on 31 July 1928, Winifred Haward felt angered at the accident of being born into a generation of women denied their natural mates. Though she knew a successful career could be hers, she wanted more, and she felt the war had cheated her of it.

Despite fearing that she would never meet Mr Right, Winifred could nevertheless look back on her twenties as a period of financial independence, sexual freedom and experimentation. Phyllis Bentley was not so lucky. Phyllis, who was born in 1894, grew up in Halifax in an irreproachably conservative middle-class home. As a child, she daydreamed vividly. The heroines of these dreams were beautiful Brontë-esque young women called Ellen, with Titian hair, who danced and ran wild on the moors; the Ellens all married young, for love, to men like Heathcliff or Mr Rochester – 'outwardly rather difficult and dominant, inwardly very loving and protective'. Later, Phyllis recognised that the daydreams 'released precisely those desires which I consciously knew I should not fulfil'.

Unlike Winifred Haward's parents, Phyllis's did not support her in wishing to study at university, and when she left her boarding school, she returned to Halifax where, as the only girl of the family, she fell into the role of daughter at home. Despite pressure to remain there, she managed to get a teaching job in a boys' grammar school in 1915. It didn't last; shy and inhibited, she was a disastrous teacher. So she went back to look after her mother. But Phyllis had an ambition: what she longed to do was write.

Phyllis Bentley's autobiography, *O Dreams, O Destinations*, was published in 1962. This book barely mentions any hopes she may have had in her youth of boyfriends, husbands, or babies. An early hatred of housework had determined her that domesticity was not her thing. However, she makes it very clear that she felt herself to be among the Surplus Women. 'Surplus! Rather a bitter word. The reason for the surplus was even more bitter: a million dead men. Still, it was depressing to think we had no value save as mates . . .' Phyllis considered that she had much of value to offer without being a mate. She retained a strong belief in 'the brotherhood of man', and a passionate desire to make the world a better place through her books, which would concern themselves with nothing less than the reform of humanity. Her struggle to achieve these noble aims – against the odds, for her family always made first claim – forms the substance of her memoir.

But Phyllis did long for a husband. Pulsing beneath the surface of her elevated literary ambitions were dreams never to be realised, destinations never to be reached. Tenuous and evanescent, the dream was so unthinkably intense that Phyllis's account of the one profoundly hurtful romantic episode of her life occupies barely a paragraph of her autobiography.

It happened like this: after the war dancing was the rage. In cities and towns across the country anyone not actually crippled went out and joined a dance class. In hotels, homes and clubs there were people charlestoning and quickstepping as if their lives depended on it. In a sense that was true – young women certainly saw dance halls as the best place to meet and mate. So Phyllis went along, often with a group of half a dozen of her girlfriends as partners, for until demobilisation was complete it was quite acceptable for women to dance together. But gradually the men came back, some in uniform, some in lounge suits. For the men the lure of the dance was great: they could take their pick from the prettiest of the bunch. For the girls, there was the agony of waiting to be asked.

Lack of men meant feminine charm and looks were at a premium. Phyllis was not pretty and the competition for partners was fierce, so all too often there were awkward gaps when she was unclaimed. It was hard for nicely brought-up girls to push themselves forward for fear of being thought 'cheap'. However, Phyllis made sure to go prepared – with a book. Rather than be a wallflower, she would retreat to the cloakroom and retrieve whatever small volume she had brought with her – Burke, Gibbon or Benvenuto Cellini – and read unobserved for the duration. Then one day a man who seemed different from the others asked her to dance. He was 'large [and] agreeably ugly . . .'; he also seemed kind, warm-hearted and well-read. Phyllis's heart quickened. And yet that one foxtrot when her dream took shape was so fleeting, so painfully insubstantial:

. . . for the space of a dance I thought my destiny was settled . . .

she remembered. For that was all it was. Minutes later, Phyllis's partner rejoined his group, '. . . [and] I perceived that he was already deeply in love with an old High School schoolfellow of mine, a more than pretty, intelligent, unconventional, altogether delightful girl whom I greatly liked; I perceived also that she was deeply in love with him.'

And so it ended. Phyllis's ugly dream man married the pretty school-friend within the year.

In retrospect one smiles at this episode, so extremely brief, but that it was not trivial is shown by the fact that the man in question (modified suitably) descended into my daydream world and played the hero's part for years . . .

Not long afterwards, in 1919, Phyllis had her second, and final, brush with romance. It lasted a little longer; this time the man quite visibly paid court to her over several months, but then abruptly got engaged to another girl. Just as well, reflected Phyllis, though being rejected was painful. She was dreadfully immature and not really in love. To be married to him would have been a disaster. 'It is significant, however, that this fickle swain never entered my daydream world.'

Phyllis Bentley: just one of the sober statistics of the 1921 Census, which showed the imbalance of the sexes hitting her exact age-group harder than any other. She was twenty-seven at the time of this episode. The figures revealed that the proportion of women to men was higher for twenty-five-to twenty-nine-year-olds than for any other group: so, for every 1,000 men of the same cohort there were 1,209 desperate twenty-something women. When the next Census was taken ten years later, in 1931, 50 per cent of those women were still single, and longer-term statistics showed that 35 per cent of them failed to marry during their reproductive years. Phyllis was never to marry, but the bigger dream that drove her did come true. Books poured out of her – novels, short stories, criticism and articles. *Inheritance* (1932) was the first in a series of historical-regional novels set in her home county of Yorkshire, chronicling 150 years of the Oldroyd family and their mill. The books brought her critical and popular acclaim, and were eventually made into a television serial. Phyllis became famous both here and in the United States, found acceptance in London's literary circles, and late in life was recognised with an honorary degree, an FRSL and an OBE.

★

Botched affairs, dashed hopes, the prospect of loneliness: two million women now saw their dreams slipping away from them. For many, isolation and longing replaced the cosy fantasy of home, hearth and adoring little ones. 'On the shelf', 'old maid', 'sex-starved spinster' – these were the fearful labels attached to the Surplus Women. Terror loomed around the prospect of spinsterhood. On her twenty-sixth birthday, Alix Kilroy (later a senior civil servant) felt life was passing her by. She was full of 'secret longings'; 'I seem to want very badly to see some chance of matrimony in the future – for children and the physical side too . . .' she confided to her diary. Walking in France that summer Alix became consumed with anxiety about a remembered mountain stream which had been her favourite bathing place the previous year. Would it have dried up? 'My thoughts dwelt on minimised matrimonial chances and the passing years. My throat was tight and I couldn't have trusted myself to speak . . . When I got to the place and found only a dry stream bed I sat down and wept.'

The novelist Christina Stead (born 1902) was tormented as a young woman by her father, who told her she was too plain to find a husband. The taunts found their way into her books; in *For Love Alone* (1945) the heroine spends her youth anguished by the passing of time:

Teresa suffered for herself and for the other girls; each year now counted against them; nineteen, and has she a boy-friend? Twenty, and does she like anyone particularly? Twenty-one, now she has the key of the door; she ought to be looking round! Twenty-two already! Twenty-three and not engaged yet? Twenty-four and not even a nibble?

But maybe it wasn't too late? At what point does the single woman abandon hope of marriage? The agony was protracted as time ticked inexorably by: twenty-five, twenty-six. 'A girl of twenty-seven is lost . . . The long night of spinsterhood will come down. What's to be done?'* Twenty-eight, twenty-nine . . . The Tommies in France used to sing – '*Hug me, kiss me, call me Gertie,/Marry me quick, I'm nearly thirty!*' For Rosamond Lehmann and her readers the assumption was that thirty was the upper limit. The ill-bred dressmaker in *Invitation to the Waltz* (1932), though warm-hearted and musical, is definitively past her sell-by date: '. . . she wouldn't get a husband: she hadn't a chance now. She was thirty. Letting I dare not wait upon I would, youth had gone by; and now the candour of her desires was muddied, her spark of spirit spent.' With reduced opportunities should she have settled for second-best rather than hold out for a prince? ' "Good husbands don't igzackly grow like blackberries, do they? No." ' But a survey of single women done in the 1950s showed that over a third of those over fifty years old still believed that marriage would bring them complete happiness. Did one ever give up wishing and wanting? Must life for the spinster always be provisional, a transit lounge between birth and death, no ground beneath your feet? This was not life, but an interminable holding pattern.

Novels like those of Christina Stead and Rosamond Lehmann, and memoirs – like those of Winifred Haward and Phyllis Bentley – give a close-up picture of what it felt like for middle-class women to be 'on the shelf' in the 1920s; Phyllis wanted to tell the world about her life because by the time she was in her late sixties she had become a successful writer. Winifred had another, odder story to tell. But it is harder to disinter the emotional reality of singleness for the less literate members of society. One way to get close to the experience of working-class singles is by looking at the papers they read, the sixpenny magazines like *Woman's Friend*, *Woman's Weekly* and *Woman's World*, which printed romances, knitting patterns and advice on the complexion for servants and factory hands. For such women, the agony aunts gave important moral support. Through their replies to correspondents we get close to the poignant distress of the Surplus working girl, with no lofty ambitions, and doomed to disappointment.

* Jane Austen laughs at Marianne, the heroine of *Sense and Sensibility*, when she has her declare: 'A Woman of seven and twenty can never hope to feel or inspire affection again.' But perhaps the obvious hyperbole also insulates the author – in her thirties when the book was published – against her own feelings of spinster exclusion.

## Heart-to-heart chats

In the 1920s the magazine problem pages didn't usually differentiate between emotional questions and queries about how to wash corsets, renovate the bathtub or remove superfluous hair. But in the face of evident need, they now began to publish replies to a barrage of letters from women desperate to fill the gap in their lives. From a sense of delicacy and privacy lacking in today's agony columns, the letters themselves were not usually printed, and one is left reading the loneliness and unhappiness from between the lines of the replies. Take the following example from the 'Fireside Friends' page in *Woman's Friend* of 1926, addressed to 'A LONELY GIRL':

I am very sorry that I cannot put you in touch with a young man, my dear, but it is against our rules to give private addresses. If you write to the Salvation Army they will let you have particulars about their emigration scheme . . .

Or Mary Marryat's advice to 'LONELY DOROTHY' on her page in *Woman's Weekly*, published in 1920:

I do not know of a whole book on how to make paper flowers, although we have published separate articles at various times. I am so sorry for all you tell me, Dorothy. I do hope and trust that 'home of your own' will come along soon . . .

It is hard not to conjure up a picture of poor Dorothy assuaging her sad longings with attempts to fashion garlands of paper roses – phantom bouquets for the never-to-be bride.

'TIRED OF LIFE' also wrote to Mary Marryat in great distress at her inability to find a 'nice young man' to marry. She felt her 'young life was all wasted', and worried that loneliness was driving her down the road to ruin. Marryat agreed:

By all means join a girls' club. Your friends are quite right. It is very wrong, and running a terrible risk, to 'pick up' men 'friends' in the street. If you do so you may rue it very bitterly one of these days.

Meanwhile in her 'Heart-to-Heart chats' page the 'Editress' of *Woman's World* was at pains weekly to provide the balm of Christian consolation to her broken-hearted or lonely readers:

Not 'broken-hearted', sister dear – very, very sad, and very lonely, but with a heart too brave and true to break because the boy you loved has passed over to join the glorious army of God's heroes . . .

Cheer up, sister. Twenty-seven is many years too soon to give up hope that love will come into your life . . . We cannot all be married, but we can all make the world the better that we have lived in it . . .

Cheer up, dears, the right men will come along your way sooner or later . . . And if it is not your destiny to meet and mate, then never worry. Marriage is not everything in life dears. There is work for all, and in work we find our true content.

Did it help, being told to 'Cheer up'? Probably not much, though reading of others' experiences might have consoled the readers of *Woman's World* in feeling that there were others like them.

But while *Woman's Weekly* and its like doled out sympathy with one hand, their editorial slant told another story. Men may have been in short supply, but the housemaids, typists and mill-girls who read such papers were never discouraged from dreaming. Even if marriage was not 'everything in life dears', the ideal of the 'wee wifie' who snares Mr Right pervades the sixpenny magazines, from their romantic fiction to their advice columns. In the midst of a man-shortage (August 1920), *Woman's Life* ran a column directed at pickers and choosers ridiculing all the Mr Wrongs for their defects: cranks, mean men, know-alls, flirts, golf-freaks and grumblers (though it didn't include the shell-shocked, the disabled or the stretcher cases). The author was 'the kind of nice ordinary girl who always DOES get married'. Beggars can't be choosers, but a girl can dream.

The same year *Woman's Weekly* contributor Rosalie Neish published *How to Attract Him*. The stakes were high, she wrote, but the prize was great. There were so many things a girl must do: '. . . keep a man on tenter-hooks . . . let him *feel* you think him a super man . . . let him see you are a home-maker and a home-lover . . . be careful about your appearance . . . if you use a henna shampoo, don't overdo it, and *don't let him know* . . . Listen to him . . . above all be cheerful and gay and sunny-tempered . . . put him in a holy and sacred niche in your heart . . . Finale! The Wedding March and orange-blossom and that "little grey home in the West" – matrimonial heaven.'

If the girl played her cards right, she would catch her man, provided she satisfied his conditions. And it appears from the pages of the women's magazines that his conditions hadn't changed much since the days of Charles Darwin. Women's magazine editors gave men plenty of column space. In

August 1920 *Woman's Life* ran a page written 'by the ordinary kind of nice young man who lives in every street' headed: 'The Girl I'd Hate to Marry!' This was a cautionary reckoning of the negative attributes to be shunned by any woman hoping for a husband. The 'nice young man' had no time for jazzing flappers. The wearing of 'extreme fashions' came top of his list of Don'ts; sartorial extravagance would scupper your chances without a doubt (but '. . . the home-made girl often marries before the Bond Street Girl – men admire her clever fingers . . .'). Being 'self-centred' was out too: 'I mean to pet and make much of my little wife when I marry, but I shall want her to make much of me in return.' Like Charles Darwin, the nice young man was perhaps finding that dogs didn't quite measure up. And nice as he was, the young man came down even harder on 'the insane craze for "independence" and "equal rights" . . . Preserve me from a girl like this . . . a woman's true happiness comes with a husband, a home, and children of her own . . .', and he followed this with a tirade against girls who chose to live in digs rather than houses, girls who insisted on earning their own living after marriage, girls who were 'clever' but couldn't dish up a decent dinner, and girls who talked loudly in public. What hope for a hard-up young woman who just wanted to make her own way?

The same message can be heard in *Woman's Weekly*. 'A Bachelor' writes that 'although there are at least three eligible females to every bachelor, it is more difficult than ever to find a nice modest girl'. What he is after, he explains in a subsequent article, is reserve, decorousness, and that subtle, exquisite and indefinable quality, 'Womanliness'. We are back in fainting and blushing territory. Though not enamoured of the blue-stocking or highbrow, 'the feather-brained thoughtless girl sooner or later has to join the surplus million . . .' Perhaps Winifred Haward should have paid more attention before George ditched her.

Perhaps George simply felt frightened off by Winifred's neediness. There were plenty of instances of attractive young men afraid that every woman who approached them, however innocently, was trying to hijack them into marriage. After her brother Edward was killed in June 1918, Vera Brittain, desperate to learn the particulars of his fate, relentlessly pursued his injured colonel, who as it happened had not only been awarded a VC but was also tall and good-looking. Despite this, Vera had no interest in him but for his knowledge of Edward's last hours; to this end she haunted his hospital bedside and took every opportunity to get him to talk, but the young colonel was vain, cold and reluctant. He seemed 'nervously afraid that every young woman he met might want to marry him'. The more she pursued him, the more he avoided her. In the end she was never able to get him to divulge what he knew, and 'lost sight of him altogether'.

By the late 1930s single women were so numerous that men went on the offensive. In their February 1938 issue *Woman's Fair* commissioned American psychologist Bertram Pollens to attack the breakaways in an article entitled 'Running Away from Marriage'. Marshalling a number of spurious premises, and summoning some ill-digested Freudian psycho-jargon to his aid ('the career woman who unconsciously wishes to be a man . . .', the victim of 'neurotic ailments . . . repression . . . inferiority complexes'), Pollens presented the case that '. . . any girl who declares she prefers to stay single is only fooling herself ':

If you are still clinging to single blessedness, the chances are that there is something wrong with your emotional make-up or your attitude or that you are the victim of false ideas . . . Knowledge and guidance on the subject may help you to change your attitude and outlook.

These editors knew their readership. Throughout the inter-war period the magazines continued to offer advice on how best to sell yourself in the marriage market. The scarcity of buyers made it all the more important to undercut the competition by whatever means. In a July 1920 interview with Phyllis Dare, *Woman's Life* asked the popular musical comedy actress for her secret of how to charm men – 'We may pretend we don't care, but we do!' the article opened, '– specially in these days of "surplusness", when the race is to the fair, and the battle to the guileful!' Miss Dare confessed herself a traditionalist who still believed in the power of women to enchant through mystery: 'A woman should be different – alluring . . . like a delicate piece of porcelain . . .'

In October the same magazine ran yet another piece on how to charm men, entitled 'Cupid's Bow and Arrow'. How come, its writer asked, men married plain girls like 'Gwen' while some of the prettier ones were left on the shelf? Gwen, it turned out, was hideous, dumpy and had a dreadful complexion. She had no conversation at all, but just sat and smiled and listened . . . ' "Exactly!" I said, "she listens! Most men love a good listener." ' How reassuring such articles must have been for its more unlovely or tongue-tied readers – for it went on to assert that '. . . in nine cases out of every ten, it's the plainer girls who get married before their prettier sisters . . . the pretty girls can pick and choose . . . but the plain girl hasn't so many chances, and so she knows right away when the One Man appears on the scene, and she grasps her happiness when it is offered to her.' So, Never say Die:

An old maid is only an old maid when she makes up her mind that she *is* one and gets upon her shelf unaided. Girls get married so late in life sometimes that no one can really be called an 'old maid'.

Cupid's bow and arrow are waiting for everyone . . .

Other writers dwelt on such issues as shyness ('. . . the shy girl seldom marries easily . . .'), loneliness ('. . . for every lonely girl there is a lonely man . . .'), and ageing ('. . . you can keep your heart young!').

## A buyers' market

Articles like these kept hope alive for the working-class girls who read them. 'Marriage was the goal of every woman servant . . .' Rose Harrison remembered in her autobiography *Rose: My Life in Service* (1975):

It wasn't easy for them. After the war men were scarce, the demand far outweighed the supply and a maid's limited and irregular time off was an added disadvantage. Then there was the having to be back by ten o'clock which made every date like Cinderella's ball, only you didn't lose your slipper, you could lose your job. There was no status in being a servant, you were a nobody; marriage was the way out of it.

Early in her career, Rose Harrison worked in London for Lady Tufton; but at Christmas the family and staff all decamped for the festive season to Appleby Castle in Westmorland, where the female staff locked horns with the local girls over the available male talent. Any dance within ten miles, and the four parlourmaids, three housemaids and two ladies' maids would descend on it with the one aim of enticing the village boys away from the rural maidens. It was locals versus city slickers – and the locals, it appeared, didn't stand a chance against the perceived sophistication of Gladys, Miss Emms, Rose and the others. 'We were an attractive set, although I say it . . .' Rose remembered. Gladys, the second parlourmaid, snared the Mayor of Appleby's son – 'a big coup in the servants' hall'.

Rose spoke for her contemporaries, but her own case was different. She described herself as 'partial to the boys', and it seems – though she is extremely discreet about her romantic life – that they were partial to her too, for she managed to go as far as being engaged. It got no further, however, for Rose, a stubborn, outspoken and ambitious Yorkshire lass from a poor background, was a career girl, determined to see the world, and for her service was the ladder to a wider experience. It was plain to Rose that kitchen work would never take her abroad or provide opportunities to meet interesting people. She could also see that if you wanted the world to open up to you, you had to become lady's maid to someone sufficiently rich and cosmopolitan. Rose had set her heart on securing such a position, and marriage just wasn't compatible with the hard work and long hours required of a personal maid. Her engagement endured, in name only, for nine years. 'All right, in those days long engagements were normal, but this got ridiculous. We hardly ever saw each other, so it was severed by mutual agreement.' That ended Rose's love life; she never married.

She fulfilled her ambition, however, becoming lady's maid to the formidable Nancy Astor, whom she served for thirty-five years. With Lady Astor she travelled the world, met the cream of international high society, and made herself indispensable to the doyenne of one of the first families in the land. Lady Astor's life was her life, eighteen hours a day, seven days a week; she had none of her own. That was the deal.

★

Rose Harrison opted not to spend her life penned in a nine-foot-square kitchen with five babies and a leaky ceiling. She preferred to see America, meet George Bernard Shaw and visit the great European cities in return for being at the beck and call of a spoilt aristocrat, but for too many there was no choice. Girls like Irene Angell, who had prayed during the war years for their brothers and fathers to come home safely, now faced the shortage of boyfriends for themselves. Irene mourned the loss of a score of her pre-war schoolfellows, cadets killed at Mons and Ypres. 'I knew every one of those boys. I used to play tennis with them and go to school with them. But there were no more.' Irene's sister was luckier than she was; she managed to get the brother of a friend. 'He was twelve years older than she was. You really had to work hard to get a husband, I think, in those days. It wasn't the kind of work I was looking for.' Like Rose Harrison, Irene was not well-off. She was forced to make her own way in life, and she never married.

The social balance in the 1920s was skewed by the lack of men, and in the new world some of the old niceties had to give way. The dance boom of that decade was a symptom of the need among young, mainly working-class women to exert themselves in finding partners. Night after night you put on your warpaint and went down to the Locarno or the Palais with your girlfriends. Girls danced together or stood on the side waiting to be asked by a boy. It didn't matter if you didn't know them; formalities like being introduced were dispensed with. But only if it was a

'Ladies Excuse Me' or a 'Buzz Off' did the girl get a chance to ask the boy to dance. The fittest, and fairest, survived. Postal worker Evelyn Symonds shot up after the age of seventeen and felt crippled with embarrassment by her height. 'I used to tower over all the men I ever met, and it was silly but I was *so* self-conscious. I used to think to myself, Oh, I hope people don't think you belong to me.' So she stopped dancing.

In some ways the upper classes had the worst of it, for they had most to lose. The mating game had given their lives meaning. The haunting story of Isie Russell Stephenson gives a glimpse of what it felt like after the bottom dropped out of their once dizzy social world. Although Isie, who married, never had to experience the depredations of spinsterhood, nevertheless her story vividly communicates the sense of social distortion that all her class of women seem to have felt.

Towards the end of the war in 1918 Isie got a message to say that her husband, Hamilton, who was at the Front, would be arriving home. In high excitement Isie prepared for the long-awaited reunion. She decked herself out in her prettiest dress and headed for the docks to await his boat. But the dreamed-of moment turned suddenly to nightmare: Hamilton appeared on a stretcher, mangled and bandaged; he was appallingly wounded and clearly dying. There had been no warning. She had not even known he was injured. Isie took him home and nursed him, and not long afterwards he died. Isie mourned; nevertheless she was young, she could not mourn for ever.

The following year, during the Season of 1919, Isie was invited to a ball in London. She willed herself into the mood, did her hair, and put on her ballgown. One had to keep going. But when she arrived and walked into the ballroom, she thought she must have made a mistake. The party seemed to be women-only – a hen party. 'But if it's a hen party,' she thought to herself, mystified, 'why is every woman in full evening dress?' At last, through the crowd, she spotted a man in tails . . . and again through the crowd another . . . and then a couple more. And gradually she realized that this pathetic clutch of males, this speckling of survivors, were the men who were left. There were about ten women to every man. Isie never forgot that overwhelming experience of the way in which war had laid waste to her class. 'It's hard to explain,' she remembered, years later. 'It was as if every man you had ever danced with was dead.'*

---

* I am indebted to Julian Fellowes for telling me this story about his Aunt Isie (born a Fellowes), whom he later immortalised as the formidable Lady Trentham in his screenplay for the film *Gosford Park* (2001).

If being in a majority of ten to one was hard work for the young women, pity the middle-aged hostess trying to achieve the right 'mix' at her parties. Before the war the Season had gone with a swing; every mother kept a list of eligible men who were automatically invited to her match-making balls

*Punch*'s solution to the lack of dancing partners (October 1923)

– with a few spare men thrown in for luck. After the Battle of the Somme there was a huge hole in the guest list that was never again filled. Hostesses gave up the unequal struggle, and sent out invitations to 'Miss — and Partner'.

When the invitations came Miss — was then faced with the responsibility of finding somebody to escort her. You had to beg, borrow or steal them; blind dates were the norm, and one couldn't afford to be choosy. Barbara Cartland had to negotiate with a schoolfriend for her first dance partner. As she remarked in her memoirs, such unorthodox arrangements contributed signally to the breakdown of class distinctions in the 20s: '. . . Society had ceased to have any meaning.' Beatrice Brown, who, like Barbara Cartland, was born in 1901, noted how the lack of men aged precisely two to five years older than herself – men killed at the ages of between eighteen and twenty-one – now left her awkwardly stranded. It was not so much that there were no men at all, it was just that the few there were 'were not for us'. The older men in their late twenties – the 'war graduates' as she called them – didn't want greenhorn youngsters like Beatrice who had been schoolgirls in 1917. They were looking for women who had been out in the world as they had. Men in their late twenties wanted to experience the gaiety of post-war London with the young women who had been VADs and Wrens – women who had danced in nightclubs during the war, used the latest slang, and could match them drink for drink.

They were not for the likes of her. 'It was like trying to jump on to a merry-go-round that has already got into its stride.' With heavy heart Beatrice would get out her address book and start the wearisome task of trying to pin down an acceptable partner. This was not how things were supposed to be: having to make a nuisance of yourself by ringing up second-rate young men, in the dim hope that 'Were they doing anything, perhaps they would like to . . . ?'

I was not the only one, I suspect, who after trying this out for three or four dances, swore that I would never again accept an invitation for which I had to supply my share of the party. One went to parties to meet young men, not to wear out those one had by importuning them.

It was a buyers' market, though not all the young men appreciated their popularity. One of the hapless male victims even wrote to the editor of the *Daily Mail* in 1920 complaining that he felt squeezed. 'As one of these unfortunates I suggest that the worst thing any young man can do is to learn to dance. Once he does so he becomes a slave to dancing, he spends all his money on it, and he never has a moment of his own from dancing. His life becomes a constant round of pressing invitations that he is unable to refuse.'

Even if you were lucky, and did find a man willing to spare you a quickstep, he would be in such demand that more often than not you'd get abandoned halfway through the evening when he saw someone he liked better. But the chances were that all the popular ones had already been snapped up, leaving behind only the dull ones – 'what, later, we would have called "wet" . . .' – so one spent the evening dancing with a drip. Meanwhile the glamorous 'war graduates' found themselves equally glamorous dancing partners who were sophisticated and could understand them: 'their steps fitted'. Beatrice Brown and her friends watched these smug couples with mortification.

With no proper balls to go to, she got her entertainment where she could. You were fortunate if you happened to be on the list of one of the hostesses who connected with Americans, because these ladies were known

to 'get up' little 'gramophone dances' to which they invited respectable
American officers who had not yet been repatriated, or were working for
embassies, depots and the like. The American officers Beatrice Brown
danced with were decent, sober and boring, and they conversed respectfully
about English cathedrals. At least they could dance. But they were not
husband material.

It didn't help that Beatrice had, in her own view, a lumpy figure and a
muddy complexion. The race was to the fair. Another of her contemporaries, Mary de Bunsen, daughter of a senior diplomat, was handicapped
both by her parents' narrow-minded assumption that women's natural
destiny was marriage as well as by her misfortune in being physically disabled
from an attack of childhood polio; she was also short-sighted. Mary sat out
dance after dance, struggling to endure until her party finally went home
'at some unearthly hour'. Her too easy compliance with her parents' expectations wasted five years of her life: 'I was far too innocent to recognize
this life as the marriage-market which, indeed, it still is, or to realise the
fact that with a lame leg and horn-rimmed spectacles I stood no chance in
it whatever . . . A debutante born with the proper equipment saw, and still
sees, a very different side of the picture. All it gave me was a hatred of
dance music and a horror of hunt balls.' In later life Mary overcame her
disabilities to become an accomplished aviator. She never married.

★

The battle for husbands left defeated girls lining the walls of dance halls
across the country, wondering where to go next. Sooner or later, the
Surplus Women had to acknowledge that they were part of a demographic
crisis, and must face the fact that a large proportion of them were not likely
to find husbands in this country. Sooner, as it happened, for the war was
barely over before concern started to be voiced as to where to put that
surplus. To many of the great and the good, it seemed self-evident that
now was the time for our Empire Overseas to do its bit and take up the
slack. This had, after all, long been the accepted route for debutantes
'*refusées*', who, after failing to find a husband over the course of three or
four seasons, used to get packed off on the aptly-named 'fishing fleet' to
find one in Rawalpindi. The Countess of Dudley wrote promptly to the
*Daily Mail* urging us to 'distribute our material' among the Colonies. Louise
Field, the Hon. Secretary of the National Council of Women's Emigration
Committee, added her voice to the *Times* correspondence columns, with
figures demonstrating a total excess of over 430,000 men in Canada, Australia, South Africa and New Zealand combined. Public-spirited ladies like

these saw the sending of thousands of single women to the far-flung reaches of Empire as essentially a make-weight, an adjustment of supply to demand. A *Mail* editorial reacted by urging the government to legislate to prevent 'too heavy a flow of foreign virgins into the country . . .' And Dame Mary Scharlieb, responding to the news of the 1921 Census, penned a letter to the editor of the *Daily Express* recommending that '. . . girls who want to

Master of Ceremonies (at village dance). "MAY I INTRODUCE MR. JONES, MISS SMITH?"
Miss Smith. "OF COURSE YOU MAY. WHAT DO YOU THINK I'M HERE FOR?"

Meeting and mating (*Punch*, December 1921)

get married must go to Canada and the Colonies, where the toll of war has not been as great as it has in this country, and where men want wives . . .' Not slow to pick up a theme, the lower-class weeklies now started to run articles for 'the girl who thinks of emigrating'. In 'What Australia Wants' (June 1920), *Woman's Weekly* gave practical advice on wages for cooks, waitresses and companion-helps, while not forgetting to emphasise the romantic opportunities: 'No matter what your work is, there is time for pleasure, and the pleasures in Australia, though mostly simple ones, are enjoyable. There are moonlight river trips and rides, impromptu dances etc.'

Many women readers responded. Like Winifred Haward on her slow boat to New Zealand, the failure to get husbands at home propelled them overseas. In 1920 the number of British emigrants (male and female) to all countries peaked at nearly 300,000. In Census year the figure dropped again, but by 1923 the numbers were back up to over 250,000. Despite attempts by the overstretched Women's Migration Societies to play down the matrimonial opportunities of the Colonies, and to make it very clear just how hard a life women were letting themselves in for, applications for passage soared in the early 1920s.

And sometimes it worked. The description of her life by a young woman who wrote home from Vancouver Island in the 1920s might well have sounded enticing to a grimy, exhausted kitchen-maid waiting for Cupid's bow and arrow to penetrate her Birmingham basement:

I am now a companion help to Mrs O.; though I work hard I have never had such a time in my life. I have been to hundreds of dances and dinners and tennis teas and out for picnics on the lake. In the Autumn we got snowed up and I put on breeches and worked shoulder to shoulder with the Colonel and another man . . .

Mrs O. said I dropped from heaven. I got up early, got breakfast, dressed the children, skipped round the rooms and then went out sawing till about 11.30 am. Then, knocked up a savoury mess for lunch, washed up and went in the Wagon with the Colonel to the meadow and there stacked logs, great big ones, into the wagon till it was piled high . . .

Mrs O. had supper ready when we came in and I put the baby to bed, then bathed and went out to dances and anything that was going, in anything that could move in the snow. It was Life . . .

And now for *the* news. I'm engaged to be married to—. He is 29 years old and is just like one of Vachell's\* heroes, only nicer.

For one happy young woman, the risk had paid off.

But the hope that once you set foot on foreign soil, the male–female ratio would be miraculously reversed – that suddenly any half-presentable female would find herself besieged by glamorous colonial officials hell-bent on leading a wee wifie to the altar – was not solidly founded. W. A. Carrothers, author of *Emigration from the British Isles* (1929), pointed out that in most of the Dominions the excess of males was restricted to the outlying rural districts. 'In the towns of the Dominions the surplus male population is negligible, and in some cases there is an actual surplus of females . . .' he said. Lumberjacks and ranchers might be there for the taking, but in his view most ordinary women of marriageable age would be unlikely to choose the hardship of life in the bush or the jungle. Moreover, once you settled for a posting on one of the remote farms, distances were prohibitive, and you were perhaps even lonelier than back in the old country. A children's nurse who took a job in Nyasaland in the late 1920s described

---

\* Horace Annesley Vachell, 1861–1955, author of *A Woman in Exile* (1926).

her life in a cottage on the Zomba mountain looking after two small children with five native house-servants:

It was dreadfully lonely at night when the boys went to their kraals . . . I always slept with a six-chambered revolver under my pillow, since leopards abound here.

Marriage prospects were nil, but there was a different kind of romance about living in such a wild spot:

It's a wonderful feeling being out in the blue alone. Last night the hyenas made a fearful noise and occasionally we see lions, plenty of baboons too . . . It really makes me sad when I think of the girls in England who spend their lives going to Town in the mornings with a little Bridge or Tennis in the afternoons, why *don't* they get out and come out to these wide open spaces?

★

Settled in to her new life in Christchurch, New Zealand, Winifred Haward too began to discover the glories of the natural world, and to pit herself against them. Every vacation she had, she spent in the mountains. She took up climbing and hiking, and with a group of her students set out on the challenging cross-country route to Milford Sound. Trekking, ice-picking, skiing and on horseback, they tackled extremes of terrain, from glaciers to fjords, and semi-tropical bush. 'I enjoyed myself immensely [and] discovered what I had not realised before, that I was uncommonly tough.' If only she could meet a man whose vigour and guts matched hers, but for some reason the only men in New Zealand who seemed to be attracted to her were puny little things to whom she just couldn't respond. 'The right man hadn't appeared. It looked as if he never would.'

Winifred now began to realise that New Zealand was far from fulfilling the promise that she had half-hoped for. In 1929 she returned to England and her old job as history lecturer at Bedford College, but couldn't settle. The PhD wasn't getting finished, and the cautious approach didn't seem to be getting her anywhere. She returned to New Zealand in 1930, not to resume her lectureship but to look for a job; 'I was sure I could find other work.'

This hit-and-miss attitude immediately landed her in difficulties. New Zealand society had a long way to go in its attitude to women. If you weren't a wife you were nobody: '. . . the highest praise was for a woman to be singled out as "the best housewife in the location"'. In 1930, with the slump hitting worldwide, it was impossible for an educated woman like

Winifred to compete in the career field. Thus for the next three years she was forced to stick it out in low-status jobs: home help, shop assistant, live-in nanny. Back in Christchurch she took a job helping an old lady to write a dubious book proving the truth of astrology; later she managed to scrape by on bits of journalism. And still there was no romance on the horizon – unless you can describe her unobtrusive relationship with an elderly widowed Englishman as love. It held out no prospects for Winifred, but it gave modest and undemanding pleasure to both.

Finally she caved in and accepted employment in the one area where she had sworn never to work – teaching. For a year she taught English, history and scripture at a girls' boarding school, hating it. At the end of the year she had saved enough for a tourist-class ticket home.

I had gone all out for adventure, and failed . . . I hadn't failed in anything that called for my own kind of ability but in mean little jobs that no one else wanted . . .

I think that, thereafter, I was instinctively on the side of the underdog.

In 1933, when she returned to England, Winifred Haward was thirty-five years old.

★

Winifred's wilderness years lasted until 1939. In her memoir she is characteristically stoical about her single state, while never disguising the fact that she would have liked to be married. For respectable educated middle-class women it was hard. What could she do, where could she go?

Winifred had pride; perhaps she was not desperate enough, perhaps she was too romantic, or simply too poor. Although there were men willing to hire themselves out as 'taxi-dancers' in the dance halls, she didn't take advantage of their services. These were the original 'gigolos'; they cost six-pence a dance, and were available from a corral at the end of the dance-floor. Women who had less to lose – divorcées or rich widows – were content to buy the 'Super-Lizards' in return for flattery, company and sometimes sex. Black gigolos had a particular cachet – like 'Chokey', Mrs Beste-Chetwynde's 'irreproachably-dressed' companion in Evelyn Waugh's *Decline and Fall*. A gossip column in *Woman's Life* (1920) complained bitterly about the way these suave studs were skewing the market:

No Men for the Girls!
Fearful complaints from the 'debs' this season that the few young men the war has spared us are monopolised by middle-aged women, mostly those with private

incomes; if it's a true complaint – well, it's not *entirely* a new one. Only – well, one does sympathise with the poor forsaken 'buds'.

Even supposing she did spot a respectable man she liked the look of, for the woman to approach the man was taboo. Dorothy Marshall, a Cambridge contemporary of Winifred Haward's, lost the chance of romance with a fellow student because they were never introduced. She would see him in her history lectures; no beauty, he had a red face and walked with two sticks as both his knees had been shot away. 'He rejoiced in the name of Smellie; I lost my heart to him completely.' For three whole years the pair eyed each other across lecture theatres, but there was no socially acceptable way of bridging the gap. Later they were close friends and colleagues at the London School of Economics, but Dorothy's career took her to South Africa before anything could materialise '. . . and somebody else had married him by the time I came back.' Dorothy never married. 'If I had married anyone, it should have been Smellie.'

Social taboos also prevailed against women hoping for a second chance with a divorcé. Irene Angell's office boss would have liked her to become his second wife but, brought up in a strictly conventional lower-middle-class family, Irene preferred to remain single rather than marry a man whose 'scandalous' past would have stigmatised her for life as a home-breaker. Thus the cruel conventions of the day condemned her to spinsterhood. Looking back nearly seventy years later, Miss Angell clung gratefully to the meagre morsel of true love she felt to have been briefly hers: 'You can always tell a person who has loved – the way they approach things is quite different. I feel sorry for the women who never really loved somebody, because at least I've got that. And there are a lot of women who have never loved . . . I'm very romantic – stupid aren't I? Being romantic ends you up like me with two cats and a house.'

When the dance halls failed, when the agony aunts were sympathetic but inadequate, and when New Zealand fell short of its promise, where did you turn? The sex psychologist Walter Gallichan urged single women to check the local population statistics when deciding where to go husband-hunting: Sussex, Bournemouth and Leicester, he pointed out unhelpfully, were particularly unpromising areas to look for spare men, as they already had a disproportion of married men or Surplus Women, so don't go there. Bad luck if that was where you happened to live.

But when geography, good intentions and advice fell short, lonely hearts had recourse to a final alternative. Vera Brittain was extremely struck by an advertisement that she had seen placed in the press during the war:

Lady, *fiancé* killed, will gladly marry officer totally blinded or otherwise incapacitated by the War.

There were no preconditions, like 'Good Sense of Humour' or 'Fun-loving'. This lady was not proud; she had lost the one person she loved, so rather than die an old maid, she might as well marry someone who needed her. By 1921 the editor of the monthly *Matrimonial Times* (founded in 1904) was claiming to bring about twenty weddings a week, 1,000 every year. Based in Holborn, this magazine set out to be a 'bona fide medium for introductions', business-like and confidential. Along with its predecessor the *Matrimonial Post and Fashionable Marriage Advertiser* (founded 1860) these papers published the sparingly worded advertisements of spinsters, widows and bachelors who no longer knew where else to turn.

Today, leafing through their pages, it is tempting to imagine 'BUSINESS WOMAN, 43' pairing up with 'WIDOWER, 50' – but presumably nothing came of it, since the Business Woman's advertisement, along with many others like it, was still running in the paper six months later . . . An issue from 1921 makes revealing reading:

MATRIMONY – Spinster, 38, loving disposition, fond of children, entertaining and country life, is anxious to correspond with a wounded officer of cultured tastes, with view to a matrimonial alliance; one with some means.

LADY, aged 49, spinster, cultured, bright temperament, small capital . . . would like to meet officer or civilian age 45–60 and good position . . . could be very happy with disabled officer needing a cheerful companion and pal.

SPINSTER, well-educated and of good family, aged 41, is desirous of marrying either bachelor or widower, aged about 48. Wounded officer for preference, receiving an income of about £400 a year.

The above, well past the usual age for marriage, seem no longer to have rated their chances of marriage with the fit and healthy males now in such short supply and, like the lady whose case had so struck Vera Brittain, were prepared to settle for cripples and invalids. Such realism may have worked in their favour, though one wonders whether 'Spinster, 31 . . . not painfully plain' was well-advised to be quite so brutally honest about her looks. These women's stark neediness is often pitiably transparent: 'Dressmaker, 5 ft 4 in' was only twenty-one, 'but so lonely . . .' A Lady aged forty didn't want to damage any chances she might have of marrying a 'good-tempered sailor'; she spelled out that she was 'gay and cheerful . . . and [had] no new-woman ideas'. In the majority of cases the advertisers give their real age, but are at pains to point out that they look younger: 'Tailoress . . . 24 years old, and told I do not look 16'; 'Spinster, 31, looks 25'; '50, but pass as 40'. And it must have taken real courage for a thirty-seven-year-old spinster, hoping to meet a bachelor or widower aged thirty-seven to sixty, to confess to having a six-year-old child.

Most significantly, nearly all the advertisers stress their desire to marry someone socially and financially compatible. As an indicator of the stranglehold class had on British society in the early twentieth century, the advertisements are telling. 'Would prefer introductions to men in really good social position only'; 'Public school man preferred'; 'He must be refined, domesticated and well-connected' – are typical stipulations; similarly, a 'superior domestic servant' aged forty-one very much hoped to marry a 'superior working man', preferably a non-smoking Baptist under forty-six years of age. However desperate these women were to marry, they were not, it seems, desperate enough to marry outside their class. And, understandably perhaps, in almost all cases the advertisers emphasise economic security alongside the wish for companionship, from '£2 to £3 a week . . .', to 'must possess not less than £500 a year'. For spinsters in their thirties and forties, it would appear that two cats and a house didn't add up to happiness; and that the romantic dream had been replaced by the simple wish to stop struggling on alone.

★

It wasn't Winifred Haward's style to place an ad in the *Matrimonial Times*, nor to write to the Editress at Heart-to-Heart Chats for comfort, but women whose hopes were dwindling might well have found sympathy and advice in some of the self-help books for 'bachelor girls' that started to fill bookshops in the 1920s and 30s. There was a very real gap in the market for psychologists like Mary Scharlieb, Esther Harding, Laura Hutton (all mentioned in the last chapter) and a number of other journalists and commentators writing for single women.

The term 'bachelor girl' has an unmistakably jaunty and modern tone. It seems to have been coined in America in the 1890s, when the 'American Bachelor Girls' Club' set out to challenge the received notion of the spinster. 'Old maids no longer exist!' declared the Club's constitution. 'Unmarried women, until they reach the age of thirty, shall be known as bachelor "girls", and after that they shall be known as "bachelor women".' Like many American neologisms, the term successfully filtered over time into British vocabulary. By the 1920s it was current here, and British readers of American authors like Clara Amy Burgess, who wrote *The Sex Philosophy of a Bachelor Girl* (1920), would have recognised themselves in her target readership.

Burgess's book, and *Live Alone and Like It – A Guide for the Extra Woman* (1936) by Marjorie Hillis (another American), were unambiguous and direct in their approach in a way that would have been unthinkable twenty years earlier. Both authors adopted a bracing, no-nonsense tone aimed at rallying the spinsters out of their gloom and passivity.

*The Sex Philosophy* invoked God's aid and the psychology of substitution in helping the Bachelor Girl to 'change and revise her whole mental attitude toward sex'. But Burgess's theory that physical longings could be sublimated through healthful exercise and fresh air, folk dancing, callisthenics, long walks, swimming and camping out seem not to have applied in Winifred's case – the hiking trips across the New Zealand fjords seem, if anything, to have sharpened her sexual appetites.

Marjorie Hillis's book was much more earthy. The knowing tone of *Live Alone and Like It* is captured in chapter headings such as 'A Lady and her Liquor', 'Pleasures of a Single Bed', and 'Setting for a Solo Act'. The text combined bossiness with intimacy:

It is probably true that most people have more fun in bed than anywhere else. We are not being vulgar. Even going to bed alone can be alluring. There are many times, in fact, when it's by far the most alluring way to go.

. . . If even the most respectable spinsters would regard their bedrooms as places where anything might happen, the resulting effects would be extremely beneficial.

There was plenty more in this vein, along the lines of keeping your end up, putting on a brave face and jolly well enjoying yourself. Though much of Hillis's advice was sound, she aimed to provoke rather than to console. Nor was her book aimed wholly at women who were likely to remain single for ever, so although she extolled living alone, her readers were assumed, probably rightly, to prefer marriage. There were many hints on how to make yourself attractive. Some of these were not so sound. Take up astrology, numerology, palmistry, graphology and tarot, she advised. Use them to intrigue and waylay men . . .

Another book which made no attempt to be anything other than a husband-catching manual was *The Technique of the Love Affair* by A Gentle-woman (1928). Its real author, the fashion historian Doris Langley Moore, had already caught hers (though she later divorced) and aimed her instructions at chic socialites like herself, who were likely to have met their suitably suave Englishmen in a hotel or at a party. As usual, it was most important

not to appear clever, but to play the game of artful coquetry. 'Be sophisticated and wonderfully feminine. Be elegant and a little spoiled, but not
bored. Be light, amiable, quite dissociated from care and all the common

*The Technique of the Love Affair* by 'A Gentlewoman' gave tips on how to make your
dreams come true

things of life . . .' An intellectual looking for love, like Winifred Haward,
might have found such directions hard to follow. But maybe the 'graceful
attitudes and airy ripostes' recommended in this early version of *The Rules*
worked for some.

Probably Winifred Haward would have gained more from authors like
Esther Harding, who reminded her readers how much value could be had
from friendships with women. Don't look, she counselled, for emotional
satisfaction from men; it is not in their power to give, nor do they want it.
Only women are capable of the kind of psychic connections that give true
richness to life. Laura Hutton too was firmly realistic; recognizing that the
basic problem of the single woman was loneliness, she urged her readers to
be courageous and make efforts of will:

It is possible . . . to take steps to join a ramblers' club . . . spend an evening at the
ballet . . . accept an invitation to a Church Social. These things lie within everyone's
power to say 'Yes' or 'No' to.

In *The Bachelor Woman and Her Problems* Mary Scharlieb pondered the
psychological implications of marriage-deprivation and concluded that a

husband could never meet the longings of a large number of single women, precisely because, deep down, it was not a husband that they wanted:

... it is not this: very often the unfulfilled desire is for motherhood. There is an incessant aching longing for the fulfilment of that primary feminine instinct . . .

## 'But who will give me my children?'

This was surely true. Here is part of a letter written by the otherwise unidentified Miss R. Williams of Dorking, Surrey. It was sent in 1927 to Marie Stopes, whose books and views on birth control had by then made her a household name:

Dear Madam,

I sincerely trust that you will pardon the liberty I am taking in writing to you . . .

My love of little babies has prompted this action, as I must tell you I am passionately fond of Babies. I would so love to have one of my own, but I have given up hope of getting married, as I intend to stay with my Mother as long as God spares her to me, as it was my only Brother's last wish, who was killed in the great war.

My mother is a widow . . . She has a small income and we let 'Apartments' by which means we get our livelihood. My Mother and I simply adore babies, and would love to take one of the dear little unwanted ones into our Home and hearts for love only. But as you will quite understand we are not in a position to do so. Please forgive me if I am inclined to be bold in what I am about to ask you, but I have been wondering if you would care to sacrifice say about £250 so that I could adopt a Darling little baby Boy about 9 months old (perhaps you might know of some dear little unwanted one) if you could only realise what joy it would give me, what pleasure, how we would both love, & cherish it, words would fail to express my gratitude to you . . .

The £250 was not forthcoming. Marie Stopes's secretary was brief in her reply to this *cri de cœur*, indicating merely that Miss Williams should approach the main adoption societies, and giving addresses.

A survey of elderly spinsters carried out in the 1960s confirmed that two-thirds of them felt that they had missed out on having children. Examples of the responses included: 'Married life's not much without a child. They're handy for you when you're older' (Boot and shoe machinist, Northampton); 'Yes. I like children. And when I see women with their grown-up children around them, I regret it' (Dressmaker, Harrow). These women felt that society reproached them too: 'They look at you as if you've never lived. You haven't had children and haven't had a man about the house, but you're no different' (Cotton worker, Oldham). Deep feelings of deprivation were equalled by a dual sense of failure: failure to do their social duty by bringing the next generation into the world, and failure to fulfil themselves as women.

Never having thought too hard about marriage, Irene Angell's sense of inadequacy was reinforced when she became an aunt. 'My sister had her first baby and I changed then.' (When they grew up Ruby's children didn't help by rubbing it in: 'Aunty, you know you've never married because you never worked hard enough to get a husband.') But something in her drove her to seek contact with children. When her sister asked for help looking after her growing family Irene was the ever-available aunt. Realising when she was thirty that she was unlikely to attain the dreamed-of husband and family, she trained in social work and got a job looking after prostitutes and their homeless children in the East End of London: it was tough, thankless work, trying to dissuade the girls from having more babies, stitching knickers for the little ones and then trying to dissuade their mothers from pawning them, but it didn't put her off. 'I'd have loved to have had a child. I think every woman should be allowed to have a child – married or not married. It's not a right thing to say, but I think one should have been allowed that. I have a dream son who's very good to me. I'd rather have a son than a daughter . . . I think every woman wants a son, you know, more than a daughter.'

Almost as much as by marriage, the nineteenth-century woman was defined by her capacity to breed the next generation of sons – and daughters. Her contribution to the human race was the bearing of children, while government, science, the arts, industry and empire-building were the preserve of the male. Rosy little faces rewarded the wee wifie for her devotion. Worried by the poor physical condition of our young men, particularly army recruits, the patriarchy determined that more and better breeding was the answer. They took a poor view of women who couldn't or didn't contribute to the upgrading of the population. After the destruction of young men in the war, society continued to look to its women to replenish the losses. What good was a woman who couldn't procreate? For the Surplus Woman, barren and unproductive, feelings of waste and worthlessness went very deep.

Women's magazines, too, did their best to persuade their readers that being hit by Cupid's bow and arrow was only the beginning. The sixpennies venerated the Victorian ideal of motherhood as much as they venerated marriage, and too bad if it wasn't likely to come your way. Beside the romantic fiction and features on the latest diet, their columns gave space to articles on layettes, perambulators and knitting baby bonnets. *Woman's Life* argued the case for motherhood through the voice of the lovely 'Ann', a fictionalised archetype of dutiful womanliness. Ann concludes that it is inconceivable for any woman to choose work in preference to being married, the clincher being woman's infallible instinct for motherhood. Her own shiny-eyed certainty of this stems from the fact that she herself is knitting 'a tiny woollen shoe'. And because of this she gets the last word: '. . . the highest service a woman can render mankind is only *through* love – and *through* marriage'.

Babies had never featured prominently in Vera Brittain's dreams of love, until she heard that her fiancé Roland Leighton was due home from the Front in December 1915. In the long dark watches of night-duty at the 1st London General Hospital, Camberwell, Vera Brittain now pictured their reunion and allowed herself to hope. While he was on leave they might get married. And then – if only he would survive the war . . . Maybe after it ended they could both earn a living as writers or lecturers, '. . . even though – oh, devastating, sweet speculation! – I might have had a baby.' As Christmas approached she found herself close to prayer: 'Oh, God . . . do let us get married and let me have a baby – something that is Roland's very own, something of himself to remember him by if he goes . . . *do* let me have a baby, dear God!' Within weeks, her hopes and prayers came crashing down around her.

Convinced in the early 1920s that she was doomed to permanent spinster-hood, Vera was eloquent about her regrets: the powerfully physical long-ing for babies – 'sweet anticipated comfort of warm responsive flesh . . . visionary children for whom, during strange dark nights in Camberwell, I had planned to work and achieve . . .' – and forced herself to suppress them. Her poetic lament *The Superfluous Woman* (1920) concludes with the image of rows of black crosses silhouetted against an angry sunset, and the bitter questioning refrain –

> *But who will give me my children?*

There was no answer.

*The Single Woman* (1953), by Margery Fry, though written too late to help the Surplus generation, contains a wealth of wisdom and insight from one who had lived through it and was well-positioned to offer it. She was then nearly eighty and long retired from her job as the much-loved principal of Somerville College, Oxford. Margery herself had never married; she had lived a life surrounded by spinsters and wryly compared herself to Saint Ursula, '. . . who, you will remember, went about with 11,000 virgins . . .' Her short book tells us at first hand much of what the author's generation experienced. She herself knew what it was like to be belittled by her own mother for not producing grandchildren; and she had had to hide her frustration from the outside world while she missed out on marriage. She felt for the women whose love affairs had 'come up against hopeless obstacles . . .' or just fizzled out. 'There are the friendships which just don't ripen as love affairs. The possible husbands who are just impossible. And perhaps the worst pain of all – simply watching the things taken for granted in other lives passing you by.'

Margery Fry also shared Mary Scharlieb's view that for many women the desire for children was 'an instinct at least as profound as that of sex'. The short poem she quotes to illustrate this is harrowing in its sense of pain and incompleteness, but also offers healing:

### Old Maid's Child

Child of my body whom I never bore
Dear fruit of all a woman's fruitless pain
Come, nestle in these empty arms again,
Come, nuzzle at my milkless breasts once more.

You cannot feel, and yet I hear your cries.
You seem to weep because, since you are blind,
You cannot even see if I am kind.
Hush, darling! Look through other children's eyes.

The other children's eyes, as Margery then explained, looked to the childless woman for comfort and love of a kind that only she could give. 'She came when the new babies arrived, or when the scarlet fever children wanted nursing . . . one associated her with sweets and presents . . . she remained a beloved figure to the end.'

Meanwhile women who couldn't have children but were 'passionately fond of babies' must be discouraged from falling into despair. Margery Fry's book speaks of the importance of friendship, of social utility, of independence, realism and training for the single life.

Mary Scharlieb also urged women who wanted children to care for but couldn't have their own to divert their energy into childcare. They should become nurses, governesses or teachers. The preacher Maude Royden delivered a clarion call to the childless to sublimate their creative and maternal talents into bettering society – 'I tell you what I know when I say that the power of sex can be transmuted into a power that will make your lives as rich, as fruitful, as creative as that of any father or mother in the world . . . those of you who have never borne a child may some day bear the new world.'

★

Nobody would judge Miss Olive Wakeham tragic or despairing because of her childlessness. Born in 1907, Miss Wakeham now occupies a bed-sitting-room in an old people's home in Exeter. Aged nearly 100, she is very lame, but enormously cheerful, and happy to chat volubly in her attractive West Country accent over a cup of tea. The memories of her childhood in Plymouth nearly a century ago come flooding back: they include watching the First Battalion of the Devonshire Regiment with all their artillery, marching away to the First World War – 'I was stood outside St Luke's College, and they entrained at Queen Street – but hardly one came back! They were just massacred.' Two of Olive's aunts lost their husbands. She herself remembered that as she grew up there was a definite shortage of men. Taken to Italy at the age of twenty while working as nurse-companion for an elderly lady, Olive visited Sorrento. 'It was lovely. I always said I'd go back for my honeymoon, but I never had one, so I didn't go back!' she says, laughing, and remarks with the same blithe sense of distance: 'I would have loved to have had lots of children, and married, but I've got over that!'

What helped Olive 'get over it' was her immersion in childcare. Her earliest memory was coming home to view her new baby sister – 'She was so beautiful! She had little auburn curls tight all over her head – oh, she was so pretty!' From then on, she loved small children. Teaching would have been her first choice of career, but the family couldn't afford to pay for her training, so instead she took up nursery nursing. The Plymouth Day Nursery, where she worked, took in the babies of the local fisherwomen – 'wonderful mothers' – and she soon learnt to change the babies' nappies and get them breastfeeding when the mothers came in. 'I loved those children, all of them . . . and I'm an expert on washing nappies!' Often, she recalled, she would 'borrow' one of the poorer infants for the weekend, bring it back to her parents' home, and dress it in her little sister's donated cast-offs.

On top of that Olive had no fewer than twenty-eight first cousins. Whenever the clan got together, Olive was in charge. Keen on acting, she would marshal the entire crowd and make them learn a play by heart, 'every word'; then they'd cut costumes out of coloured paper, rig up a sheet for a curtain in her aunt's sitting-room and charge the local children a halfpenny to come and watch. 'It was lovely – I *did* enjoy it!'

Much later, 'Auntie Olive' became the mainstay of the family, especially after her married sister was widowed. The nephews and nieces would come to stay with her in Exeter, where she used her mothering skills with tact and ingenuity, persuading the children off to bed with a wily combination of bribes and firm discipline. 'Aunts can do this . . . I would put their milk in the hall on a little shelf – somehow or other this appealed to them – and some biscuits, and at 8 o'clock they could take this milk and the biscuits and go to bed. And they'd always say, 'Oh, we love going to stay with Auntie Olive – she and her biscuits!'

The beautiful curly-headed little sister died at sixty-two, leaving Olive as the stable centre of her extended family. By then she had done well for herself, and greatly bettered her world into the bargain. Childcare had occupied the first half of her working life; the remainder she spent employed by the Devon County Association for the Blind, ending as their President, with MBE to her name. 'I've been so lucky. It would have been very nice to have been married, but I've had to make the best of things and I have. Above all, I've got all my nieces' children, my great-greats; I'm so lucky!'

Giving love was the main thing, not giving birth, as Rose Harrison pointed out in *My Life in Service*. Rose was a devoted daughter who never cut herself off from her humble family and, despite the elevated circles she attended, provided for her mother all her life. After long experience of the upper classes, she felt qualified to comment on their neglectful attitude towards their children. The children were given everything that money could buy, but to Rose it was evident that all too often the grandes dames of high society were uncaring mothers, spoilt by privilege. Poignantly, though she is careful to exempt her employer, Rose juxtaposes these comments with an account of her own adoring relationship with Michael, the baby son of Lord and Lady Cranborne. Charged with his care on a long train journey to Switzerland, Rose spent a sleepless night consumed with anxiety lest the infant should fall out of his bunk. Michael loved Rose in return. 'We had a lovely time together. Little boys are always so appreciative of what you do for them and he was a great companion. It was tragic that he should have died so unexpectedly while playing football at Eton when he was only sixteen. Richard, the youngest, was killed during the war.'

Rose felt these tragedies almost as personally as if the boys had been her own sons; their presence in her life pulled on her maternal heart-strings. In the end one of the greatest rewards of servitude was, for Rose, her inclusion as 'a member of a wonderful family'.

Maternal instincts, the need to be needed, found outlets for women like Rose Harrison or Olive Wakeham who became part of a larger family. Aunthood could go some way to compensate for lack of motherhood. This appears to have been the case with the author Richmal Crompton, a much-loved aunt who was strongly drawn to the younger generation. Her home was well provided with toys for any child visitors who happened to drop in, and she was always happy to join in games and romps with her numerous nieces and nephews – not easy, for Richmal could only walk with a stick. The hugely successful books she wrote – *Just William, More William, William Again, William the Fourth* and so on for another forty-odd volumes – are glorious proof of her ability to communicate with children.

Richmal Crompton's biographer insists that the author's anarchic, well-intentioned but disaster-prone boy hero 'was in no way a substitute for any real-life son that she might have liked to have'. This is doubtless true, but the invention of William Brown shows a childless woman transmuting her creativity into the richest, most fruitful of channels.

Born in 1890, the educated daughter of a clergyman, Richmal's career as a teacher was curtailed in 1923 owing to an attack of poliomyelitis. This lost her the use of her right leg; in the thirties she developed breast cancer and had a mastectomy. Thus disabled, she turned entirely to writing. Marriage, it would seem, was never on the cards. Rather than persuade oneself that William was Richmal's notional child, it would be safer to speculate that he represented her own alter ego. The boy speaks as the small shrill voice of the misunderstood individual against the vast chaos of society. In the *William* books, the grown-up world, with its rules, conventions and conformity, is oppressive and incomprehensible. It is tempting to think that Richmal Crompton, ruled out of the 'natural order of things' by her handicaps and failures, took refuge in a child-centric universe. William, like his creator, feels excluded from the middle-class normalities so convincingly described in the books – a world of conventional suburban marriages with subservient mothers and wives; adult mysteries like Women's Guild meetings, family gatherings and vicarage tea parties – in short, all the adjuncts of the wife and mother.

Something inside Richmal Crompton rebelled against the bourgeois orthodoxy of it all, and took shape in William Brown. To imagine Miss Crompton, who described herself as 'the last surviving example of the

Victorian professional aunt', dressed in odd shoes and a borrowed policeman's helmet, with pockets full of woodlice, innocently sliding down coal
heaps, painting cats green, putting frogs in teacups, and aiding and abetting
the local burglars, is a liberating vision. The spirit of a dirty, lawless child
with a pea-shooter lived within her; no wonder her nieces and nephews
adored her, and no wonder the *William* books continue to reach out to
thousands of children, even today.

In the end, maiden-aunting was what you made it, for the aunts of the
1920s and 30s were no longer expected to sink into the twilight zone.
Winifred Holtby was robust about her childlessness. She did not deny her
strong maternal feelings towards small children, but neither did she indulge
in sentimental regrets for the babies she would never bear. It must have
been hard for her when in 1925 her best friend Vera Brittain found a
husband, Gordon Catlin, and harder still when their first child was born
two years later. But Winifred was simply fascinated gazing at Vera's new-
born: 'His head's just like a pussy-willow,' she observed. One might have
supposed that Winifred's jumble of feelings would have driven her to avoid
contact with the baby, but far from it. According to Vera, she became John
Edward's 'discreet but devoted slave . . .', deeply loving to him, often
pushing him in his perambulator to the Chelsea Babies' Club clinic, and
even taking charge of Vera's entire family of five under-sevens when she
and Gordon went to America on a lecture tour. Thus she was forthright
and realistic about children. Babies were 'a nuisance', and boring, and
anyone considering having one should contemplate seriously the prospect
of a great deal of laundry. At the same time she sought contact with them;
according to Vera children were, for her, an 'essential part of experience'.
After his Auntie Winifred's untimely death, seven-year-old John Edward
was silent and miserable for weeks, heartbroken.

Manacled by small children, Vera Brittain at times envied Winifred
Holtby's freedom and confidence. Wisely, the childless creamed off, when
they could, the joyful aspects of childcare, leaving the chores to the mothers.
Here is a snapshot from the 1937 diary of Harriet Warrack, a single laboratory worker from Kent, in her mid-thirties, well-read and educated, living
independently, with a wide circle of friends. It describes an afternoon spent
with her sister's family:

Sunday September 12th
2.15 . . . the boy aged 2¾ immediately asked to get out of his go-cart and rushed
to me and insisted on accompanying me . . . he would insist on climbing banks –
which I let him do – and also on pushing the go-cart violently along. After a time

with a little tact I got him to get into the cart and ran along pushing it much to his joy . . .

5.45 Played game of make-believe in the garden with Michael.

5.45–6.30 Went to my sister's house, gave Michael a bath – He would drink the bath water – I let him, felt flattered as he would not let his mother bath him – I suppose because I let him do what he likes ie spit, and splash.

6.30–7 Sat by his cot and looked at books with him.

Harriet's relationship with her little nephew is fun, loving, and joyfully irresponsible; she gets all the pleasure and none of the burden. At the end of the day she can walk away.

Harriet Warrack may have felt the 'incessant aching longing' for babies, but she could see for herself that children were hard work. Michael's mother mustn't let him spit in the bath; she can, and in return he adores her. Harriet may have consoled herself in thinking she had the best of both worlds with her sister's boy. Angela du Maurier would have concurred. She had planned to have six children; by the age of eighteen she had chosen all their names: Domini, Julian, Sonia, Michael and twins David and Deirdre . . . until she had to face the fact it wasn't going to happen. Sunny-tempered by nature, Angela looked for the compensations, and found them in godchildren, nieces and nephews. 'There is nothing I enjoy more than taking a collection of children for beach picnics to climb rocks and splash and swim, unhampered by their adult relatives.' Not having become a mother herself, she felt that the child in her was still alive. One eleven-year-old godson, firmly persuaded of Angela's playfully youthful qualities, made up his mind that at thirty-five his single godmother would make the perfect wife. 'How dearly I loved him.' And when regrets got the better of her she would try to recall her own father's favourite maxim when she and her sisters were being troublesome: 'Blessed are the Barren.'

Cicely Hamilton reasoned that not having a future generation to fear for in this troubled world was compensation enough for being childless, but other women looked on childlessness as positively liberating. Realistic and level-headed, the model Rani Cartwright weighed up the pros and cons of motherhood and made her choice in favour of freedom. No children meant no conflict on that front. Anyway, as she explained, not only were the majority of children nasty spoilt brats as far as she was concerned, but they were unpredictable: 'You just don't know what they're going to grow into.' Rani wanted to be in control of her own life. The author Elizabeth

Jenkins also shrank from the prospect of having babies; they were the last thing she wanted. If marriage was off the menu because it was far too boring, having children was an equally unpalatable prospect to this high-spirited and mercurial young woman: 'I never thought it would have been nice to have children, and I will tell you why: whenever I thought about it I had an absolute horror of the idea of childbirth. My mother used to say "That's what you think now, but when you've got the baby you'll be surprised – you'll believe that you never didn't want her, or him" – but I'm extremely cowardly. I can't endure the idea of physical pain. I was born absolutely without a spark of courage. So, anyway, I just shuddered at the idea of childbirth and then went on to something else.'

★

Women like Rani Cartwright, Rose Harrison and Elizabeth Jenkins toppled the pedestal on which men had once idolised their wives. For far more – Olive Wakeham, Winifred Haward, Winifred Holtby, Amy Gomm, Phyllis Bentley, Gertrude Caton-Thompson, May Jones, Miss R. Williams – the pedestal was violently and forcibly kicked from beneath them. Most of these Surplus Women no more chose their unmated futures than their mothers had chosen to remain pointlessly penned in the kitchen or parlour, compelled by a patriarchal society to produce eight babies and delight their husbands with female chit-chat. The singles had no real alternative to making their own way in the world, but in the post-war era that way was now broader and brighter than it had ever been before. You weren't condemned to captivity in the twilight zone.

'We are not going to pity the Surplus Woman after all,' wrote a columnist in *The Woman's Leader* (5 August 1921). 'So far are we from pitying her that sometimes we think she has the best of it.' Picking their way among the shattered plinths that once supported the matrimonial temple, many individuals found the courage to abandon the wreckage of their hopes and start anew. If you could ride over the reproach and disappointment, your own and others', life could be good listening to the lions under an African sky, or writing about the brotherhood of man, or just seeing the children's faces as they munched their milk and biscuits at bedtime. Women like this were not machines; they might well feel smug at avoiding the daily grind of washing, scolding and scrubbing which fell to their married sisters.

Gertrude Caton-Thompson turned to archaeology with the enthusiasm of one who had found her life's consummation. Amy Gomm set out with invincible optimism to take up a clerical job with a tailoring firm in Ealing: '. . . I'd show 'em. The sky was the limit . . .' Vera Brittain remembered

Winifred Holtby, a childless spinster who died young, as '. . . the most brilliant journalist in London . . .', and as one whose 'zest for life had a physical as well as a spiritual quality . . .' And Margery Fry, looking back at her generation at Oxford University, while noting that only seven of the twenty-four who had entered Somerville College with her had married, and between them had produced a mere fourteen children, felt an intense pride in their achievement:

You will find that in transforming nursing and education, in changing the whole status of women, in bettering the position of children, they have supplied, not only the leaders, but the rank and file and the enthusiasm. They have addressed the meetings and they have addressed the envelopes.

Perhaps the Editress of Heart-to-Heart Chats was right when she counselled, '. . . never worry. Marriage is not everything in life dears. There is work for all, and in work we find our true content.'

But for innumerable women destined to face life without men, work was an economic necessity.

# 4. Business Girls

## War, work and wives

Today nearly one million women in the UK own their own businesses. Women make up nearly half the workforce of this country; they can take their pick from the full range of professions and occupations, and the number of women directors and managers is steadily increasing. We have had a woman prime minister, and in January 2001 Clara Furse was appointed the first woman Chief Executive of one of the oldest Gentlemen's Clubs in Britain, the London Stock Exchange. The term 'career woman' no longer contains any element of shock.

More than sixty years ago when Beatrice Gordon Holmes\* published her autobiography, *In Love with Life – A Pioneer Career Woman's Story* (1944), she knew that the tale she had to tell was one of success against the odds, of triumphant breakthrough. In the 1920s it was almost unthinkable for a woman to work in stockbroking. Gordon's rise from £1-a-week typist at the age of nineteen to affluent director of the leading 'outside house' in the City of London would barely excite notice today. But in early twentieth-century Britain this woman's energy, acumen and perform-ance were virtually unprecedented. Beatrice Gordon Holmes showed it could be done.

She came from an unpromising background. Born in London in 1884, Gordon was the daughter of an indigent doctor and a possessive, house-proud mother who ran everything on thirty shillings a week. The family lived in City Road, within striking distance of that hub of metropolitan finance which was later to become Gordon's adult territory. Until she was eleven years old she stayed at home, schooled in the basics by her mother. Gordon developed an appetite for books, and the house was full of reading matter: Dickens, Kingsley, Scott, and endless copies of the *British Medical Journal*. She described her childhood as 'serene and repressed . . . I never knew the glow of real happiness until I got out of the home and was earning my own living – and then the happiness lasted for the rest of my life.'

Schooling was erratic. Gordon had no formal education until the age of

***

\* Like many lesbian women, Beatrice Gordon Holmes adopted a masculine sobriquet. All her friends knew her as Gordon; I will follow suit.

eleven. She excelled at lessons, but only went to school when her father could afford to send her, which wasn't always. He chose the cheapest he could find, and his daughter was expected to economise by walking the four miles there and back, doing without lunch, and submitting to wearing her mother's horrible home-made clothes. Her father took her away at the age of fourteen, but was persuaded to part with four guineas for a ten-month course at Cusack's Secretarial College, where she absorbed shorthand, typing, the basics of commerce and a miscellany of instruction on Greek history, music appreciation and essay-writing. Thus equipped, she landed her first job as a typist at the glorious sum of twenty shillings a week. It was 1903, and to her this seemed 'incredible wealth'. Not for another three years did Gordon have her eyes opened to the world of ideas, science, culture, mathematics and philosophy – by a visiting uncle who took her under his wing and told her she had a brilliant mathematical mind.

Gordon's first proper employer ran the London office of a Danish egg-exporting firm:

Business interested me from the word 'Go.' We imported millions of Danish eggs into the British Isles, most of them sold before landing through a team of agents all over the United Kingdom . . . The great thing was to sell consignments at top speed. Eggs won't keep and cold storage charges were heavy . . . We were the premier firm and the premier brand. [We] ruled the market.

Eight years of egg-selling made Gordon familiar with the world of capitalism. The business had taught her all about deliveries, prices, concessions, bills of lading, the rise and fall of markets and trade etiquette; about accounts, consignments, shipping documents, branding and packing, commissions and sales, loss and profit. Meanwhile, outside the office, she had become involved with the Suffragette movement, helped found the new Association of Shorthand Writers and Typists, and immersed herself in music, literature, philosophy and theatre. When she left in 1911, having saved enough money to take her mother on a trip to America, Gordon had transformed herself from the gauche, dowdy maid of her teenage years and, determined to increase her salary from £2 to £2 5s a week, was ready to take on the world.

I answered dozens of advertisements for several months, quite without result. My ambitious demand for £2 5s put me out of court as a typist, and there were hardly any other jobs for women in the business world in 1911.

Interviewers regarded her ambitions with astonishment. Even when she
had the necessary qualifications, she was told that under no circumstances
could such and such a firm employ a woman. She was unwanted. Finally,
under threat of a deadline, she railroaded Mr Thorold, the Canadian chairman of a Lombard Street stockbrokers, into offering her a three months'
trial. 'I knew nothing of finance.' Thorold however plied her with reading
matter, '. . . including Hartley Withers's fascinating and amusing "Stocks
and Shares" . . .', and thus armed, in August 1912, Gordon Holmes began
her financial career.

Thorold was a hard taskmaster, brilliant, maverick and mercurial.
'Women are incapable of understanding financial matters,' he asserted,
following up with, 'Your only limitations are the limitations of the female
mind.' Tetchy and prejudiced though he was, Gordon impressed him. She
unearthed an irrational system being used for client recruitment, overhauled
it, and in doing so quadrupled the company's client base. Thorold's approval
was enhanced when one of his top clients spotted Gordon's talent and
pronounced: 'No price can be placed on a woman like that! She is invaluable
to the firm that gets her!' From then on her abilities were established, if
precariously, in her employer's eyes.

Those first years in the City! Those for me were the romantic years, the golden
years in which everything was new and fascinating . . .
  I liked the atmosphere of the City. I liked the excitement of negotiating what
to me then were large deals. The first large amount I handled alone was $80,000
of City of Westmount bonds . . . I resolutely found a buyer, pushed the whole
transaction through in a few hours, took 1½ per cent commission for my
Company, and felt thrilled – never was sky so blue or sunshine so golden as on
that day . . .

When war broke out in 1914 Thorold went back to Canada, and the
other directors joined up, leaving Gordon in sole charge of the office.
She was then at the peak of her energies, aged thirty, without family
commitments. Her work in that wartime office honed and perfected her
abilities; she was there fourteen hours a day, seven days a week. When the
men came back in 1918 the ship was in better shape than when they had
left, and every single man had a job waiting for him, at an increased salary.
Characteristically, Thorold picked a fight with her immediately on his
return; the storm broke over a disagreement on profit-sharing. Minutes
before he sacked her, Gordon resigned. She came down with appendicitis
and retreated into a nursing-home – paid for by Thorold. And it was there,

while having her stitches removed, that she met the woman who was to share her life, Dr Helen Boyle.

The year 1921 was the next turning point in Gordon's career; which now became meteoric. Years in the City had bought her much goodwill; her closest friend in Thorold's company was Sefton Turner, and together they now managed to find backing to launch their own financial company. 'Of course we were an "outside House," because the Stock Exchange, like the Church – God and Mammon – refuses to admit women.' Seven years later their Corporation bought out Thorold himself.

[Starting] in two rooms with two typists, by 1929 it employed 140 people. It has lived to see three of its largest and long-established competitors all collapse in the 1929–31 slump and after, while it still modestly flourished. We emerged from the slump with our modest capital and reserves intact, while others wrote wads off their balance sheets.

Gordon's venture flourished. She travelled extensively, building up her business interests on the Continent, seeing South America, Africa, the East. Money became plentiful. After the years of scrimping and saving, she took herself off to Bradley's and indulged her latent love of clothes: soft beige, cream and silver-grey outfits draped in fox furs gave her tall, handsome figure resonance and sophistication. After purchasing a capacious residence in Bedford Park, she spent thousands on having it fitted with luxuries: central heating, hot and cold running water in every room, a state-of-the-art bathroom with a heated towel rail, and rose-coloured carpets. 'Rose-coloured carpets, that was another dream of mine . . . Where does one pick up these notions of ultimate luxury? Anyway, rose-coloured carpets were mine.' And there she lived with her Siamese cat and kittens, enjoying each spring the happiness of seeing the early almond blossom bloom in her suburban street. In the opening lines of her memoirs, written aged fifty-nine in the middle of a second world war, Gordon felt able to reflect:

I've had a glamorous, romantic life since I was twenty. I've travelled over half the world. I've had a career that has seemed to me incredibly lucky. My income, and I've never had a sixpence I haven't earned, has risen from £1 a week to – at its height – a steady £4,000 or £5,000 a year. Have I ever been in love? Always. In love with life, people, projects, things, thought. Always in love, always some star on the horizon.

★

Gordon Holmes had many setbacks on the road to achieving her ambitions. Determination and self-belief were her allies; her lack of interest in marriage and motherhood cleared the path towards her goals. And the timing of the 1914–18 war was critical in giving her the opportunity to display her abilities, single-handedly running Thorold's office. In this respect Gordon was able to look back on that great convulsion of international conflict and see it as a time of radical change in the fortunes of women. As the leading feminist Millicent Fawcett pronounced in 1918: 'The war revolutionised the industrial position of women – it found them serfs and left them free.'

At the beginning of the twentieth century less than 30 per cent of women had jobs. It is important to understand how alien and unpalatable the general public found women in the workplace – unless that workplace was the scullery, kitchen, laundry, nursery or, of course, that romantic cul-de-sac, the teaching profession. The generally held view was that a woman earning her living was doing so as a temporary shift while waiting for a husband to turn up. Since women's work was not seen as permanent, no efforts were made to reform pay or conditions. The unlucky ones who never married and had to spend their lives working in ill-paid and exploitative jobs were to be pitied or ignored.

Women like Gordon Holmes carving out careers for themselves were so unusual that they excited astonishment, baffled admiration or blank condemnation. Ambitious women like her were anomalous, deviant, unloved: 'A woman who is loved has no need for ambition. She leaves that to her sisters whom fate has cheated of their due . . .' wrote a lady commentator in the *Daily Mail* in 1922. Not that there were many openings for the ambitious woman at that time; broadly speaking, the range of acceptable jobs a woman could do was limited to domestic service, factory work, retail, teaching, nursing, clerical work. Few women trained for any sort of job, taking up occupations they had learnt at their mother's knee, such as needlework or laundry-work. Upper- and middle-class women did not work at all. They were trained in accomplishments that could never earn them a living: speaking Italian, embroidering dressing-table sets, playing the harp. It was a point of honour for a husband to be able to keep his wife as a useless ornament. Working-class women aspired to become supported wives like them, and to keep house. When they married, 90 per cent of women gave up work.

★

Victoria Alexandrina Drummond was born into the kind of privileged background in which she would have been expected to stay under her parents' roof until her wedding day. Her father, Captain Malcolm Drummond, was a high-ranking retainer in the Royal Household and Victoria, born in 1894, was named after her godmother, the Queen. Like Gordon Holmes, she was ambitious and talented. She was also lucky in reaching adulthood at exactly the point when she could turn Britain's shortage of skilled workers to her own advantage.

October 14th 1915 was Victoria's twenty-first brithday, and her family showered her with presents. From her mother she received a silver-mounted umbrella, a pound note, four packets of socks, three books on how to do conjuring tricks, and a writing block. Helped by their parents, her brother and sisters clubbed together to give her a matching fox fur boa and muff, a box of chocolates and a book. But the best gift of all was from her father, who, after presenting her with a paintbox and two diamanté shoe buckles, took her aside and said, 'Victoria, now you are twenty-one, you can choose your own career.' ' "I'm going to be a marine engineer," I said, but I don't think he took me seriously.'

It was, however, wartime. For a brief period it was acceptable for women to do men's work while the boys were at the Front, so the Drummonds tolerated what they saw as their daughter's patriotic willingness to do her bit, and didn't stand in her way. By the following October Victoria, clad in overalls, was ready to take up her apprenticeship at a garage in Perth, where she was to spend the remainder of the war years cleaning out gearboxes, dismantling engine parts and sweeping down the shop floor awash with paraffin. But Victoria had no intention of dropping her career when peace returned. In 1918 she continued her training at the Caledon Ship Works in Dundee, before taking her first on-board post as tenth engineer on SS *Anchises*, Blue Funnel Line.

Almost everything about this short account of Victoria Drummond's early life is extraordinary, because ninety years ago for a young woman of her background to propose pursuing a career as a marine engineer would have been like calmly suggesting she earn her daily bread as a prostitute. No wonder her father didn't take her seriously. Had he foreseen that his daughter would never marry, would spend her life with engine oil under her fingernails, sailing the world on freighters, convoy ships and tankers, working in shipbuilding and winning medals for bravery at sea, he would surely have been speechless.

But the war took away the prospect of a wedding day and wifehood from two million women and replaced it with a different model of female existence. The housemaids and shop girls became stokers, tool-setters, ticket clippers, van drivers, landgirls and butchers. The factory workers turned from making silk stockings and tableware to making munitions and vehicle parts. These women were better paid and better nourished than they had ever been before. Government departments and committees provided thousands of jobs for typists and clerks. With decent earnings these women workers could for the first time afford to live away from the parental roof, in hostels and lodgings. Stay-at-home middle-class young ladies like Victoria Drummond discovered new-found abilities as VADs, volunteers, garage hands, mechanics. Nearly a million extra women were in employment by 1918. During the war the female workforce was applauded and valued for its patriotism and can-do attitude. The serfs were liberated.

Temporarily. In 1918 and 1919, when the 'khaki boys' came marching home, the market was flooded with men wanting their pre-war jobs back again. By autumn 1919 three-quarters of a million of those women had been handed their cards. It was back to the kitchen sink for bus conductors, insurance clerks, landgirls and electricians alike. Voices were now raised against the 'limpets', 'bloodsuckers' and 'bread snatchers' who tried help-lessly to hang on to their jobs. Public opinion was still stuck in the past. With the war over, it was time these lazy scroungers returned from their paid 'holiday', rolled their sleeves up and got back to the laundry and the scullery. If they worked at all, women were supposed to be employed in low-status jobs, or be supported by men. Married women workers were reviled for taking men's jobs while they should be 'kept' by their husbands, but single women also bore the brunt of much abuse. They had no depend-ants, therefore their earnings could only be for 'pin money', selfish indul-gences, rose-coloured carpets even. These were the 'superfluous' women. It was inconceivable that such women could have financial needs, desires for independence, ambitions, goals, or imperatives outside the home.

This was, of course, a fallacy. The war had given thousands of women their first taste of financial autonomy and personal freedom; they were not going to give it up in a hurry. Nor was it a matter of affording fox furs and central heating. Women on their own had to afford bread and butter, footwear, and a roof over their heads.

## Palaces of commerce

During the war, white-collar workers volunteered for the army in greater numbers than from any other sector. Thus, inevitably, it was bank tellers, clerks and book-keepers who made up the highest proportion of casualties in the trenches. Office employers looked to women to replenish their ranks, and so it was that the business girls multiplied in city offices. For every Victoria Drummond or Beatrice Gordon Holmes there were a thousand typists, insurance clerks, lowly civil servants and underpaid secretaries, looking in vain perhaps for the congruent partners who lay buried in military graves, but more or less reconciled to their nine-to-five lives,

*Weldon's Ladies' Journal* (1930) targeted women employees with economical dress-making advice

strap-hanging their way to work, strumming away at their Remingtons in the 'palaces of commerce', making do on thirty shillings a week. By 1921 there were half a million female clerks and typists working in the United Kingdom, and by 1931 another 150,000 had joined their ranks; the numbers of women were fast catching up with those of the men.

To begin with, a job in an office had seemed to offer undreamed-of liberation, and at the end of the nineteenth century girls took up clerical work in vast numbers; by 1911 there were 400 times as many women clerks as there had been in 1861.

George Gissing's melancholy 'New Woman' novel of 1893, *The Odd Women*, revolves around the idea of office work as the route to female deliverance. It tells the story of the Madden sisters, who have come hopelessly down in the world. Virginia and Alice are two entrenched old maids eking out their pitiful existence in Battersea on boiled rice and brandy. With scrupulous detail, Gissing describes how they almost break under the strain. Virginia and Alice are starving, trying to live on fourteen shillings and twopence a week between them. With the rent costing half of that, they have only a shilling a day for food between them. They pin their hopes of betterment on their youngest sister, Monica, who is ruining her health working as a shop girl. Monica is paid six shillings a week for her job at a draper's, where, as was commonly the practice, she was a resident employee, expected to do thirteen-hour days six days a week in return for board and lodging and this small sum. Atrocious hours, under-nourishment and prolonged standing have brought Monica to the verge of physical collapse. But their friend Rhoda Nunn appears to offer salvation.

Miss Nunn (portentous name), who has escaped from the treadmill of teaching by acquiring secretarial training, has now joined her friend Miss Barfoot in establishing a benevolent school to teach shorthand, typing, book-keeping and commercial skills. Virginia sets out to persuade Monica to leave her job at the draper's and train at Miss Nunn's school:

'She will be the most valuable friend to us. Oh, her strength, her resolution! . . . You are to call upon her as soon as possible. This very afternoon you had better go. She will relieve you from all your troubles, darling. Her friend Miss Barfoot will teach you type-writing, and put you in the way of earning an easy and pleasant livelihood. She will, indeed!'

In the event Monica's fate is very different; she becomes trapped in a deeply unhappy marriage, and dies in childbirth. The spinster sisters survive and start a school; but Rhoda Nunn is the real heroine of the book. She has a tumultuous love affair, loving passionately and entirely, and yet Gissing leaves her at the end unshackled, carefree and optimistic. She will remain heart-whole and independent, she will start a journal, she will educate women to become free. Office work has shown her the way.

Shorthand typing was new and fashionable, it was feminine – tinkling away on a keyboard had maidenly charm – but it also had status. Being in an office increased your chances of meeting a husband too, and when that happened, you left. So if marriage was part of your grand plan, you could rule out any ambitions around getting a 'top job'. Most offices had a rule not to employ married women. Of course the flip side of this was the independence conferred on the 'business girls'. If you had a decent job, you didn't have to get married.

★

That was certainly how Miss Evelyn Symonds saw it. Now nearly 100 years old, Evelyn got her first job in 1922; she was only fourteen at the time. Her family had taken its share of buffeting by the war; her mother died when she was ten, her cancer untreated because so many doctors were laid low by the 1918 influenza epidemic. Her father made a loveless second marriage to a war widow, and the family of six lived in three rooms in

Tottenham. For Evelyn work was an escape from unhappiness and domestic claustrophobia. It was also a source of pride, for Evelyn was employed by the Post Office, and this made her a Civil Servant. She had no training – 'just the ordinary three R's you know' – but took exams at the age of sixteen to become a sorting assistant. In essence the job consisted of nothing more than filing. Gradually promoted – she passed her clerical exams second time around, which enabled her to take up a vacancy – she next progressed to the money order department.

Today Evelyn's job would be replaced by computerised systems; in those days the qualities needed by workers like her were the patience and passivity of an automaton. Each day's work consisted of a stack of postal orders tied into a bundle, which had to be sorted before you could go home. Each postal order was numbered; the numbers had to be coded and posted accordingly into a big board with slots. Next door was another room full of the slots to be pulled out, packed, and re-sorted into numerical order. If you didn't complete your stack, you didn't go home.

After thirty years, Evelyn ended up as executive officer in the Accountant General's Department; this entitled her to six weeks' holiday. She retired at sixty after forty-five years in the Post Office. 'I never had to worry about having someone to keep me, because I had a job for life, and a pension. I stayed in that job, and all the people I worked with, we none of us got married, and we all stayed friends . . . It didn't occur to any of us that we needed to get married – it didn't to me anyway. As for boyfriends – there weren't many around in those days, not of our age group, they'd all disappeared in the war. But I don't remember being bothered about it at all. We used to go on holidays and please ourselves. We had good money, and I loved my job. I've thoroughly enjoyed life, I must admit . . .'

Miss Doreen Potts was another clerical worker of that generation who spent all her working life in the same job. She lived at home with her mother and went daily to the offices of Prudential Insurance. 'It was a good place to work, a solid place. You didn't have to be particularly clever or anything, so long as you behaved yourself and got on with it. And you weren't afraid that you were going to go to bed Saturday night and wake up Monday morning and find yourself without a job.' Doreen missed the boat on marriage, but wasn't especially troubled by it; she accepted her mother's view that her fate was 'in the stars, dear'. Doreen's priority in life was enjoyment. She liked to go out with the girls for a few drinks, and she loved dancing – 'We used to go to the Streatham Locarno . . . My mother always said to me, "You don't want to get married, because you're enjoying yourself too much as you are." It was true, I was.'

In some ways the 1920s and 30s offered a brave new world to respectable single women like Evelyn Symonds and Doreen Potts. In her late nineties Miss Symonds felt that her generation, despite living through a cataclysmic century, had had the best of everything. 'We had gracious living, which you never get now . . .' She would go walking in the great London parks with her friends, and end up with a copious tea at Lyons Corner House: '. . . a great big plateful of bacon and eggs, a glass of orange juice and a roll and butter, with a waitress, a cloth and a live orchestra – all for two-and-sixpence. People now have nothing like that!' Such sufficiency and sense of worth inspire more admiration than pity. And yet her daily life must have been hard and monotonous at times. What was the everyday reality? Evelyn and Doreen's memories, and those of other working women of their generation, supplemented by the descriptions of contemporary journalists and authors, help to paint an unvarnished picture of what life was like for the business girls.

★

Salaries were tight in the 1920s; even more so after the 1929 Crash. Thirty shillings a week was considered a good wage for a female clerical worker in an office. That meant making decisions about where to live. The girl who stayed under the parental roof would contribute to the family budget, but would have to be within walking distance of her job or find fares. Flats might be more convenient, but were expensive and often lonely; tenancies for single women were hard to come by – they weren't supposed to live alone, it wasn't thought respectable, and some landladies clearly suspected that if they did, it must be on immoral earnings. In 1930, prompted by the rise in the number of single women, the Women's National Liberal Federation called upon government to recognise that spinsters had special needs in this area. Their secretary, Miss Aline Mackinnon, spoke up for many like herself: 'I am an incorrigible spinster, and I think it would bring an enormous amount of happiness to a great many spinsters if they could have their own little homes. I know of dressmakers, cooks, elementary school-teachers, and all kinds of people who live in lodgings and who, if they had a little house of their own and a little bit of garden where they could get dirty in the evenings, would have an entirely different outlook.' The government was dilatory, but various utopian bodies, like the Women's Pioneer Housing Company, did look out for their needs and started a programme of converting old houses into groups of apartments for independent singles; however, the rents were expensive.

Many working women preferred to live in hostels, because they were much cheaper, centrally located, provided breakfast, dinner, laundry facilities and ready company, yet gave one the feeling of independence. Nineteen-year-old Mary Margaret Grieve felt herself to be reasonably well-off when she started her first London-based job as a trainee journalist on *Nursing Mirror* in 1925. She had £2 15s a week, and her family supplemented this with another ten shillings, yet even so it was essential to economise. The Grieve parents lived in Glasgow, so staying at home was not an option.

Mary lodged in a hostel in Earls Court. It was a great gloomy mansion block, but from her minute first-floor cubicle she could just see stars between the chimney-pots. Hostel life was full of shifts and expedients. The mean manageress charged threepence for a bath; for this sum the geyser produced a barely tepid puddle at the bottom of the tub, so the girls clubbed together and bought a length of red hosepipe. This they attached to the hot water tap on the landing, diverting the water supply from a little basin which was normally used for washing stockings and underwear, to just reach the bath at the other end of the corridor.

Stingy rules also prevailed over breakfast. Mary would join the queue and receive her permitted portion of half a slice of toast, one pat of butter, one minute portion of marmalade and a cup of tea. Seconds were allowed, but nobody had time to queue twice before dashing off to catch the underground from Knightsbridge. 'I was slightly hungry all the time I was on *Nursing Mirror* . . .' she remembered.

Affording enough to eat is the constant refrain of the business girls. 'By far my biggest financial strain was lunch,' remembered Mary. Normally, fivepence for a sustaining cheese roll, a glass of milk and a slice of fruit cake at a dairy in Maiden Lane kept hunger at bay, but every so often when finances were very low she would go a little further afield to an unusual free canteen hidden away on the upper floor of an office block in Kingsway. Mary suspected that the business girls who frequented this 'unique feeding place' came from 'an older profession than mine'. Nobody else she knew seemed aware of its existence, so she was probably right. The procedure was as follows: as you went in the lady at the entrance handed you a paper on which was written a biblical text. You seated yourself at a long trestle with all the other young women, then bowls of a good substantial stew were passed down the row:

One ate one's lunch in silence. On finishing each luncher stood up, recited from memory the text on her slip of paper, handed in her paper at the desk and left. No payment was asked.

1. 1914–18: the pitiless destruction of a generation of young men.

2. Wartime munitions workers: in those same four years the female workforce increased by nearly a million.

3. In the late nineteenth century a new world for single women was flickering into life. Bicycles were among the heralds of change.

4. Somerville students in 1917. Winifred Holtby, seated, on the far right.

5. Margery Fry was Principal of Somerville College, Oxford from 1926 to 1931; she was also a noted penal reformer

6-7. Celebrating physical vigour, the Women's League of Health and Beauty may not have done much to comfort men scarred and crippled by a remorseless conflict.

8. Richmal Crompton: 'the last surviving example of the Victorian professional aunt'.

9. Society belle Isie Russell-Stevenson was fortunate in experiencing marriage and motherhood, but the war was to change her elite social scene for ever.

10. Rani Cartwright, a celebrated catwalk model who described herself as 'free range'.

11. Joan Evans lost the man she loved in 1915, and by the age of twenty-two had given up hope of marriage.

12. Cicely Hamilton lived 'like the traditional spinster, with a cat for company'.

13. With the help of Jessie Monroe and her dogs, Elizabeth Goudge (right) learned to 'deeply prize the blessings of a single life'.

14. 'Rose-coloured carpets were mine'; stockbroker Beatrice Gordon Holmes photographed in the 1940s.

15. The staff of the Electrical Association for Women honour their founder Caroline Haslett, awarded the DBE in June 1947.

16. Career woman Bessie Webster chose to be photographed leaning against her Chairman's Rolls Royce.

17. After thirty-seven attempts, Victoria Drummond passes her Chief Engineer's exam.

18. 'Gert and Daisy': Elsie and Doris Waters.

19. 'I thought a god was there': Richard Aldington in 1931, the year Irene Rathbone first met him.

20. Irene Rathbone, featured in a round-up of book reviews in the weekly *Everyman*, 1933.

I have no idea who ran this admirable enterprise, nor do I know if I was strictly entitled to the hospitality offered . . .

The free stews for fallen women might have been a godsend to Beatrice Brown and her sister Enid, who worked as typists in central London and grew to know every nasty tea-shop in the Strand, from the 'Busy Bee' to the 'Chintz Teacloth', in their search for cheaper and better lunches. In vain – 'they all smelt of sugar and fat and dusty curtains', and the tables were so uncomfortably low that you hit your knees when you pulled your chair in.

Like Mary Grieve and the Brown sisters, Ethel Mannin, who started as a typist for a big advertising company in London on twenty-three shillings a week, was always ravenous, always watchful of her purse, making up for inadequate cheap lunches with sweets and chocolates at her desk. With an upper limit of ninepence for lunch, she too became a reluctant habituée of tea-shops. 'Through constant usage you grow to hate them all.' There were the big noisy popular ones, the quiet arty ones, the cinema tea-lounges and the risqué basements appointed with screens and couches for courting couples. Ethel had been to them all. And always the question was, what could you 'run to'? Usually, tea and sardines on toast, a sausage or a Scotch egg; when what you longed for was fruit compote and tinned peach melba at prohibitive prices. Dare you treat yourself? Would the pert waitresses despise you if you went cheap? Arty 'Copper Kettle'-style tea-shops were exorbitant, their decayed gentlewomen owners charging as much as one-and-sixpence for their 'home-made' jams, cakes and cress sandwiches, but cinema lounges were reasonably priced, the tea good and the ambience cosy.

Ethel Mannin observes everyday life in the 1920s from the inside, and her detailed accounts of aspects of British society, from clothes to contraceptives, air travel, education, Bright Young Things and the Chelsea Arts Ball, have the ring of truth. One of her essays, 'Palaces of Commerce', complains tellingly of the tedium, vexations and frustrations endured by thousands of female wage-slaves like her, compelled daily to be swallowed up behind the pitiless glass and concrete façades of the modern office.

Mannin lamented the 'Americanisation' of office life. Open-plan systems, electric lifts, buttons to summon office-boys, coloured lights to indicate 'In' or 'Out' on office doors, all contributed to the worker's sense that she was forever under surveillance. There was no hiding place – except one: the lavatory.

'Going up to wash' is the boon and blessing of every office-worker, and the curse of every employer.

'Where is Miss So-and-So? I want her to take some letters . . .'

But Miss So-and-So has 'gone up to wash'.

Of course, Mannin points out, Miss So-and-So has really gone up to fix her lipstick or spend a little time gossiping with Miss Something-or-Other, but the 'Chief' is powerless to object. 'Going up to wash' was the salvation of the work-dodger, the avoider, the late-comer, the plain bored. Mannin herself lived her office days in a state of fear and hate:

. . . the sick dread of having to take down shorthand and being required to read portions of it back to the Chief whilst he sat and waited, 'Read me what I've just dictated,' whereupon the pages of hieroglyphics would mean nothing to me, and I would stumble and falter, rely on memory, or stare blankly at the page of my notebook, feeling myself growing crimson, and tears of sheer panic rushing to my eyes . . .

and impotent anger:

. . . hurrying along the same road six days a week, and back again at night . . . strap-hanging in hot crowded carriages . . . having to go into an office on a sunny day . . . jealousy of [the other girls] because they earned more money and were more efficient than I was; and then, when I earned more money than they did, hatred of their jealousy of me . . .

O palaces of commerce, how hatefully ye stand . . . prisons of youth, machines that swallow up human beings, turning them into Robots, work-slaves . . . thirty bob a week, and never enough to eat . . .

Ethel Mannin escaped captivity; she turned her skill to copy-writing in the advertising firm, married, and became a journalist and successful novelist. But she would have sympathised with the 'Business Girl' who wrote a piece for *Woman's Life* in September 1920 itemising the 'Things That Make Me Grouse'. The Business Girl's day was consumed with petty annoyances:

. . . the girls who work with me keep on borrowing my pencils and paper and rubbers and pens, and anything else they can think of . . .

. . . my typewriter wants seeing to every half minute, and, because it won't work properly, I waste letter after letter, and of course there are more letters than ever to do –!

Illustration from 'Things That
Make Me Grouse', *Woman's Life*,
September 1920

... I'm poked away in a smutty room, about six feet square, that never sees the
sun and gets its air from a passage, and I see other girls, in my lunch-hour, who
can spend all day in the sun if they choose. I wish then that I need not earn my
living!

Rainy mornings on crowded buses, temperamental bosses, short lunch-
hours, hunger, overtime, the expense of shoe-leather and the price of fares,
all combined to crush and break the spirit of the working girl. Miss Marjorie
Skrine, born in 1896, was still imprisoned as a hard-up typist for a Temple
law firm in her forties. She journeyed there from Tulse Hill and back again
every day. Miss Skrine's short account of her working day refers to the
'dull strain' of work as a legal secretary. Marjorie was thoughtful and
perceptive, but notes of cynicism and accidie tinge her tone of voice, which
is that of a wry, unhappy woman. As a female in the office she was in the
minority: 'There are many male typists, but not many women, as they
cannot stand the long and irregular hours.' But the men she worked with
were, according to her, unmarriageable, the lawyers vain and stagy, the
shorthand writers mad, drunk and improvident.

On 13 December 1937 Marjorie recorded that she had written to thank
her wealthy aunt for her 'munificence' in sending her a five-shilling postal
order for Christmas. 'I put it more politely than that ... I am regarded
as the lost sheep of the family because I work for my living. I suggested
the obvious remedy years ago, but the general whip-round was not

forthcoming . . .' Later that afternoon, about half past six, Marjorie went out for a break with another of the typists, a man, and over tea they commiserated over their poverty, and discussed the attitude of men to wives and mistresses. Englishmen, Marjorie claimed, are good to their mistresses and show the worse side of their nature to their wives, '. . . though it is also true that many a wife would be put through the hoop much more than she is if her husband didn't have a secret mistress to keep him in something like a good temper'. Marjorie was certainly not a wife, and from her diary it would seem that she was not a mistress either. Towards seven, they were back at their desks, working late again. The 'Chief' was in a bad mood. Marjorie checked her diary and noted that it was nearly full moon. 'The effect of the moon on unbalanced nature is very true of men quite as much as of women . . .'

Who can say, from these glimpses, whether the single woman worker suffered more than her stay-at-home married counterpart? The journalist Leonora Eyles was certain that she did. Unmarried career women, according to her, were certain to suffer from nasty disorders of the (unused) reproductive organs in middle age. You surrendered motherhood in favour of a job at your peril. 'Neuritis' – a catch-all word used then to describe mental instability – was also, according to her, a risk for such women. In *Lysistrata*, his lament for the unmarried, Anthony Ludovici railed against those who defended the business girls; how, he asked, could 'a girl withered and broken by long years of typing' be anything but a tragic figure? Just because the spectacle of innumerable unmarried female workers crowded on to the trams and omnibuses each morning had become a familiar one in the inter-war period did not mean that these wretched commuters were fulfilled and happy. John Betjeman wrote 'Business Girls' in 1954, but his 'thousand business women/Having baths in Camden Town' could just as well have been the typists and clerks remembered by the poet from his twenties. In any case the poem is worth quoting for its compassionate sense of the fragility and waste of those enslaved lives:

> Rest you there, poor unbelov'd ones,
>     Lap your loneliness in heat.
> All too soon the tiny breakfast,
>     Trolley-bus and windy street!

Evelyn Symonds and Doreen Potts would have been amazed to have been so pitied. The unavoidable reality was, however, that unbelov'd women now had to earn a living. And there were some authors, less angry than

Ludovici, less wistful than Betjeman, who believed that the best way forward was a little practical advice.

★

Agnes Miall, no-nonsense author of *The Bachelor Girl's Guide to Everything – or The Girl on Her Own* (1916), was one of these. Her book was written in wartime, but was as applicable to the 'bach'★ – as she was often called – of the 1920s and 30s. Then there was May Henry and her co-author Jeanette Halford, two cookery writers who set out to fill a much-needed gap in the market with *The Bachelor Girls' Cookery Book* (2nd edition 1931). Little guides such as these were addressed directly to the 'girls who . . . are forced to re-arrange their lives at a distance from home and friends', and girls who 'live independent lives'. Many of these found themselves unexpectedly cast into the world of employment, and the *Bachelor Girl* books offered hints and solutions to all their everyday problems. Chapter headings in Agnes Miall's book included Furnishing, Household Duties, Etiquette and Income for the Woman Worker. She explains how to keep accounts, draw cheques, and gives an example of the budget of a typical 'girl office worker, who earns 35/- a week and lives in a London hostel, within walking distance of her work':

Salary: £1 15s

| | |
|---|---|
| Partial board and bedroom | 19s |
| Working expenses (lunches) | 5s |
| Laundry | 1s |
| Dress (£15 yearly) | 5s 9d |
| Amusements and literature | 1s 3d |
| Savings | 1s |
| Presents, charity, extras | 2s |
| Total | £1 15s 0d |

This is twelve shillings more than Ethel Mannin earned, and most bachelor girls, as we have seen, had to catch a tube or omnibus twice a day; at a penny-halfpenny a fare that would have reduced lunch money to ninepence. Indeed Agnes Miall's estimate was in many cases wildly overgenerous. In the 1930s some typists were on twenty-five shillings a week. At a conference of women clerks in 1938 a delegate blamed office

---

★ Pronounced 'batch' to rhyme with 'catch', rather than 'Bach', the German composer.

inefficiency on low wages; junior typists who had only had a sandwich and an apple for lunch lacked the stamina to deal with the work load. Provincial city offices paid clerical workers even less, sometimes as little as ten shillings a week; on that you could afford a penny bun or, on good days, a three-penny bowl of soup for your lunch. Cheese rolls and fruit cake would have been unthought-of extravagances. A budget like this left no space for impulse buys, hairdressers, restaurants, alcohol, holidays or any of the things the credit-card-carrying office worker of today takes for granted. (It also, as one office worker remembered, left no spare income for soap or extra sets of underwear. The typing pool on a hot day could be suffocatingly smelly.)

*The Bachelor Girl's Guide* goes on to provide a wealth of invaluable information and advice which, in its ingenuity and judgements, tells us much about the humble standards of the day. Take Agnes Miall's words of wisdom on the furnishing of bed-sitting rooms: 'Soft art green and a dull brown are a good basis in almost any room. A dark bedcover is always preferable to a white in a bed-sitting room. Artistic washstand china often tempts girls to spend a good deal of money, but considering its fragility this is hardly worth while.' And on store-cupboards: 'The store cupboard should always contain a tin of condensed milk . . . a quarter of a pound of plain biscuits, packets of jelly, blancmange and custard powders, cubes of soup, a pot of jam, a tin of shortbread (in case a friend drops in to tea on Sunday), tinned salmon and sardines and a tin of apricots, peaches or pineapple chunks; also . . .' (presumably to assist in the preparation of that forgotten dish, junket) '. . . a bottle of rennet'.

May Henry and Jeanette Halford come to the rescue here with a wide range of catering solutions. Their cookery book gives recipes calculated in small quantities, many of which could be performed easily on a spirit or oil stove, with minimal *batterie de cuisine*. The aim was to encourage: 'We hope this book will continue to be considered one from which any fool can cook.' Thus heartened, the trusting 'bach' might turn to sustaining recipes for Fried Sprats, Boiled Sole, or Baked Pigeons. But if that seemed too daunting, May and Jeanette had helpful instructions on how to make Sandwiches ('The slices should be thin and the crusts neatly trimmed off . . .') or, failing that, Toast.

Agnes Miall saw herself *in loco parentis* to the unwary woman worker, proffering warnings of the 'mother-knows-best' variety: every bachelor girl 'should make it a rule to wear pure wool combinations, with fairly high neck and sleeves to the elbow, next to the skin in winter . . . cotton should never be worn next to the skin. It is liable to cause severe chills.' Not content with such mundane practicalities, she took the plight of the single girl to heart in her tips on etiquette. At work, it was important not to permit fellow employees to single her out 'on account of her sex', the assumption being that women were often treated with undue deference. *'Try to forget that you are a woman'* was her advice. Social life could be tricky too: 'Bachelor girls are too apt to fall into free and easy ways . . .' Don't imagine that the formalities can be ditched, she cautions: 'This is a very serious mistake that may lead to terrible trouble . . . People who are willing to waive introductions are rarely desirable companions and should be sternly discouraged.' She worried too about their solitariness:

Girls who go about much alone in big towns (especially in certain parts of London) sometimes complain of being spoken to by strange men. This will rarely, if ever, happen, if you walk along briskly and purposefully, not staring at anyone. It is loitering and aimless strolling that are to be avoided. If spoken to in spite of precautions, a decided answer or a cold stare will usually end the annoyance.

The reality that emerges from the *Bachelor Girl* books is one of economic stringency and drab loneliness, of lunches on trays – a Marmite sandwich and a cigarette – of washing your hair under the tap and using the leftover shampoo to clean out the basin, of sitting in the park on Sundays. In this context, dreaming of rose-coloured carpets was the nearest one could get to having them. Agnes Miall even has a chapter with tips to the Bachelor Girl on how to fit and lay her own carpets (assuming she could afford them), probably art green or dull brown ones at that. Perhaps being a business girl wasn't such an 'easy and pleasant livelihood' as it at first appeared. For many thousands the name of the game was, simply, survival – surviving fear and hate and poverty, hunger, cold, tedium and sexual harassment. But what else could a Surplus Woman do?

## A rotten hard life

Right up to the Second World War it seemed plain to many that marriage was still a better option for a woman than trying to support herself. 'The average woman worker has a rotten hard life,' wrote the scholar and political pundit Margaret Cole in 1938, 'and a pretty poor chance at the end of it of maintaining herself in her old age on anything like a decent scale. This is the fact.'

Cole advised parents of single daughters to concentrate on finding husbands for them 'while they are still of an age to get one easily'. If only it had been so easy. But Cole was right in assessing prospects in the majority of women's occupations as meagre.

There was shop work, often the only option for girls who, like Sue Quinell, couldn't afford secretarial training. Miss Quinell had dreamed of a job as a shorthand typist, earning enough to rent her own flat. Instead she spent her working life living over the shop at the Bon Marché in Gravesend; when after twenty-five years they made her redundant she was homeless and penniless.

A 1920 issue of *Woman's Weekly* ran a cheering article aimed at retail employees like her entitled 'The Charm of the Shop Girl'. Its male author praised the taste, calm, dignity, good humour and civility of the shop girl, which he claimed to find inspiring. 'I have heard of many of them who have made good matches, and thoroughly deservedly so; for a woman who has the patience of a shop girl would make an excellent wife.' This susceptible gentleman probably thought that a girl with flat feet, varicose veins, anaemia and menstrual troubles would be delighted to trade her job standing all day behind the counter of a department store for seventy hours a week slaving in the home. But probably the 346,774 women who worked in the retail sector in Britain in 1921, 90 per cent of whom were single, didn't object to a bit of sentimental build-up.

Some of them looked on the work as more glamorous and genteel than manual work. Miss Doris Warburton, who was born in 1901 and grew up in a small village in Lancashire, saw her job in a Rochdale shoe shop as an escape from the petty narrow-mindedness of village life. In Doris's village the local employer was the slipper factory, and every morning the slipper workers got the early bus to work at eight o'clock. Doris left home for a later bus at nine. But it was impossible to avoid the taunts of her neighbour, who was out with her broom on the pavement each morning as she passed and never failed to remind her that the factory girls felt looked down on by the shop workers: 'We'll sweep the road for *the nine o'clock people*,' she would sneer as Doris walked by. Despite her gradual promotion through sales lady to manageress in the Bacup branch of 'K' Shoes, and eventually to running her own sweet shop, Doris Warburton failed to catch a man. Perhaps her manners were too blunt. When she moved to the Bacup branch two of her lady customers noticed the ring on her finger (which had accidentally got turned round) and cross-questioned her:

'You're new aren't you?'

So I said, 'Yes. I've been sent on from Rochdale.'

'Oh – are you divorced?'

I said, 'No.'

'Are you a widow?'

I said, 'No.'

'Oh,' I said, 'look, my ring's turned round,' I said. 'Look, my name is Miss Warburton. I'm here in Bacup now to manage this shop, I'm here to do just what I can for you to make you happy – I've never apologised for being Miss Warburton and I'm not going to start now.'

And they laughed. And I sold them a right damn good pair of 'K' shoes.

Shop work was certainly less abject than domestic service, but despite contact with affluent consumers, conditions for shop assistants themselves in the 1920s hadn't improved so very greatly since Gissing described Monica Madden's life in the 1890s.

Marjorie Gardiner worked a mere sixty-hour week at a smart Brighton milliner's from 1925 to 1945. The merchandise ranged from five-shilling felts to ostentatious confections trimmed with mink, ermine tails and birds of paradise. But there was no luxury for the girls who worked there. Rules were strict, and they suffered. In theory they worked ten- or twelve-hour days, but often it was more. The temperature inside the shop was kept pitilessly low, the door being left open for customers all day long summer and winter. Marjorie and all the other girls had terrible chilblains. Warming one's perishing fingers on the one tiny radiator was not permitted, and at lunchtime the girls took it in turns to use the kitchen gas stove: 'Hygiene or no hygiene – we often used to put our feet in the oven to unfreeze them!' There were no tea or coffee breaks. Nine times out of ten, if you nipped out to the back to grab a warming cup of tea in the kitchen, a customer would demand attention and it would have to be abandoned. 'Madam', who ran the shop, and arrived in a chauffeur-driven car, was a dragon who often dismissed girls on scanty pretexts when they displeased her. 'No wonder they sometimes ended up on the streets.'

Domestic servants and factory workers made up by far the largest proportion of women workers in the country. These soul-destroying and largely dead-end jobs had, like clerical and secretarial work, the Civil Service and retail, only one escape route: marriage. If you didn't find a husband, growing old as a mill-worker could be unutterably hard. In 1938, 229 ageing spinsters surveyed in the factory town of Huddersfield were found to be earning an average wage of £1 2s 6d. On this wage, nearly half of them were helping to support elderly relatives. It was also found that seventy of these women were physically infirm, that all of them were regular attendants at their doctor's, but that few were claiming more than a couple of days off per year for illness. They could not afford to.★ Yet sociologists looking at conditions for single women factory workers in the inter-war period were struck by the way their job was, as one described it, 'the last anchor of life. If that is taken from them, nothing much remains.' Many interviewees surveyed pointed at the war as having taken away their chances. One woman born around the turn of the century was still bitterly resentful: 'About two million girls in this country have little chance of marriage, so they should be given an equal status with men in everything. Anyway, they will have to make a living of their own and the country may as well face the problem squarely. I don't know whether this country is fair to its womenfolk.'

Researchers looking at the plight of domestic servants found worse hardship: writing in 1937, the sociologist Joan Beauchamp described them angrily as 'the Cinderellas of the labour market . . . obliged to slave from dawn till dark for a miserable pittance'. Her statistics showed over 1.6 million indoor domestic servants working in Britain in 1931. Among these Beauchamp picked out a daily maid (live-out) being paid seven shillings a week; more typically, she gives the instance of fourteen shillings paid to a resident servant, expected to do all the work of a small house, including washing and ironing, from 6.30 in the morning till nine at night. At the top of the scale, wages rose to as much as £65 a year for cooks, housekeepers and parlourmaids.

For unemployed or lower-paid single women the world could be a very hostile place. The war had left them particularly vulnerable. Investigating the housing problem of this particular class in 1936, the sociologist Rosamund Tweedy found instances of fear, loneliness, hunger, squalor, debt and prejudice. Tweedy's findings were published by the Over Thirty Association in a campaigning pamphlet; its accusing title employing a biblical quotation: *Consider Her Palaces*. One typical case interviewed was an Irishwoman, a fifty-seven-year-old skilled tailoress who had been made redundant by modern technologies after twenty-seven years in the same job:

I havna' a job and I havna' a reference. A've kept masel' since I was twelve years of age an' always paid ma way, but now the work's not regular for my eyes are bad, and I canna see the black stuff. If I had a room about 6s. I could manage, but I'm that afraid o' bugs, I'd drown masel' sooner nor go in the slums.

---

★ The 1911 Health Insurance Act provided contributors with money when they fell ill; however, on reduced wages such as this, and with dependants to look after, the sums remained inadequate.

Women were not supposed to spend a lifetime in employment; they were supposed to get married. The state had no safety net for people like her, ageing and poor.

Another respondent described her 'home' in Norwood:

I want a room nearer into Central London as fares run into such a lot of money. We lodge in a workman's cottage in Norwood, very old, no bath or other conveniences. There are bugs in the house. We pay 10/- for the room and share the bed, but while my friend, Miss X, is out of work, she only charges us 8/-. The landlady feeds us for 10/- a week each, but mostly it is not fit to eat.

Masquerading as a potential landlady interested in letting unfurnished rooms as a business proposition, Rosamund Tweedy went spying on a number of houses in north London inhabited by waitresses, shop assistants and other lower-paid workers. She was appalled by what she saw: 'A twelve and sixpenny camp bed, a flock mattress with hardly any coverings, a bare floor, the food exposed to dust in an upturned orange box, hardly any crockery, the washing-up bowl under the bed, towels and washing on lines; that is what lay concealed behind many of those Yale locks.' Palatial indeed. Such was 'the price of freedom'. Tweedy called upon society to shoulder the burden of help for the single, lower-paid woman worker. Surplus to requirements, dependent upon the whims of landladies (who frequently favoured male tenants – 'I'd rather have a man any day, they're less trouble and have more money . . .') and the vagaries of rents, these women 'must choose between hunger and squalor, and, in fact, often must suffer both'.

No wonder, if it came to a choice between bug-infested palaces and commercial palaces, business girls like Evelyn Symonds and Doreen Potts felt lucky to be in the commercial ones, soulless and robotic as they may have been. In a world of political and economic uncertainty, they clung gratefully to their precarious independence, their latch-keys, their 'thirty-bob a week, and never enough to eat . . .'

## Miss All-Alone in the classroom

Unvarnished, colourless, dull brown lives in dull brown rooms. But there was a rosier picture for single working women. A commonly-held view was that marriage consisted of a life of drudgery and privations, while remaining single pushed one up the economic ladder. Post-war, there was even – despite the competition with men for jobs – a perception that single girls were becoming scarily independent and brazen. 'Dressy Mill Girls.

Saturday Afternoon House Parties. Money to Burn. Chocolates, Cinema
and the Hesitation Waltz . . .' carped one disapproving headline. This was
certainly Puritanism carried to extremes.

It took frugal economies for a clever girl to work her way into the trades
or professions and get her own flat, but it could be done. 'Miss All-Alone',
interviewed by a reporter from the *Westminster Gazette* in 1925, found she
could just afford a top-floor studio in St John's Wood. She was busy picking
up second-hand items to furnish it – 'great fun, building up a flat bit by
bit . . .' – and with the help of a woman friend who was an electrical
engineer had entirely rewired it, installing light, heating and a geyser: 'Yes,
it was a bit of a job running the leads up all those stairs . . .' Was she lonely?
'Not a bit of it. There's a gramophone . . . Friends come in. We just take
this out of the way, and this, and dance to it on the stained floor. I have
friends coming to dinner tonight . . .'

Beyond that, the evidence of women like Miss Symonds and Miss Potts
points to feelings of pride and autonomy in their jobs; in their late nineties
neither of these ladies seems to have felt crushed or unfulfilled. Their
memories were full of the good times, the dancing years, of getting a
one-and-sixpenny to see Ivor Novello in a show, of sallying out to Kensington Gardens on a Sunday, going to watch Gary Cooper in the talkies, or
curling up with a good adventure story: simple, satisfying pleasures. And,
at the last, until Evelyn couldn't walk any more, a maisonette in Walton-on-
Thames – 'That's where my heart is still.'

Where circumstances allowed, making a living could be better than just
survival. Education was the key; Mary Gulland's father made sure that she
was well taught, and during the war she had reason to feel grateful to him,
as it gradually dawned on her and her fellow pupils that there would be
nobody for them to marry:

Every morning in school we had read out to us the list of those who had disappeared,
as they did through the war. We had the spirits of the young, at the same time, we
did have this awful feeling of all our boy friends disappearing . . .

Mary's good qualifications ensured that she got a teaching post, first at
Westonbirt and then at Cheltenham Ladies' College. As she suspected, she
was never to marry.

Schoolmistresses had been long defined by their spinsterhood; it was
what deterred Winifred Haward from working in a school till she could
avoid it no longer. The figures tell their own story. In 1911 there were
180,000 women teachers; during the war 13,000 more women joined the

profession and by 1931 the number had risen to nearly 210,000. By that time, the average woman teacher's pay was £254 a year. True enough, that was £80 less than the average male teacher; nevertheless, though life might not consist of rose-coloured carpets on five pounds a week, it could be a lot better than starvation and bed bugs.

The unequal pay levels were the product of an ironic kind of double-think by the powers that be. Men must be paid more in order to support their families, ran the argument, and a single woman has only herself to support; but at the same time women must be deterred from breaking free of motherhood and the home. High remuneration would encourage the bachelor girl to escape her destiny as breeder of the race, so the differentials must be maintained in the interests of demographic stability.

This manipulative attitude to pay prevailed for decades; nevertheless teaching remained, *par excellence*, the profession for middle-class single women – 85 per cent of women teachers in the 1920s and 30s were un-married. Servants, typists, mill-girls and shop-assistants might view their employment as a way of marking time till they married, but teaching carried the heavy stigma of spinsterhood.

So, if you hoped for a man, you would go to great lengths to avoid admitting you were a teacher. 'That would put off every man in sight,' lamented one of them, '. . . so young teachers . . . said they were secretaries or something like that.' Magazine editors did nothing to dispel the negative image of the schoolmarm. 'What a pity Mrs Brown has allowed her daughter to go in for teaching! She will *never* get married!' was the view aired in an article in *Woman's Weekly* in 1920 entitled 'Do Teachers Make Good Wives?' Men viewed intellectual women with alarm, and teachers were inevitably labelled 'clever', 'blue-stockings'.* *Woman's Weekly* deplored their narrow minds, their domineering manners, their dowdy and frumpy appearance. The accompanying illustration showed them in high-buttoned blouses, long skirts and scraped-back hairstyles. If they couldn't find a husband, they had only themselves to blame.

Worse, in an increasingly sexualised society, there was actual hostility towards the spinster teacher, who was seen as sex-starved and sour, and therefore ill-equipped to have charge of small children and adolescents. Many schoolmasters suspected the schoolmarms of conspiracy to take over the schools, and in the process harming the boys. A generation of young

---

* Clever women still have to put up with this kind of prejudice. A 2005 survey reported a 40 per cent drop in women's marital prospects for every increase of sixteen points in their IQ.

men had fought for their country imbued with patriotic ideals impressed
on them by their classroom mentors – all male. 'It would be a national
disaster if the education of our boys were delivered entirely into the hands
of "jaundiced spinsters."' At a schoolmasters' conference in 1924 one
of the delegates fulminated that feminist teachers were hell-bent on 'the

Not sexy: the 'scholastic woman' as depicted by *Woman's Weekly*, October 1920

canonisation of the spinster'. 'The virile boy had a right to a teacher of his
own sex, and the effeminate boy required it no less.' (One assumes his
remarks were taken at face value, in those days before the spectre of
paedophilia stalked the nation.) Walter Gallichan joined the chorus of
disapproval, denouncing the spinster teacher as intellectually insincere,
censorious and unbalanced, and the 'progressive' educationist A. S. Neill
(who should have known better) criticised her for her anger, shrillness and
vindictiveness, while strongly advising her to go out and get herself a sex
life – not exactly a practical proposal for a hard-working schoolmistress
with the next day's lessons to prepare.

Teachers often felt defenceless against such onslaughts. A 1930 article
quoted a teacher in despair at her nun-like existence: 'I know I'm becoming
thwarted and spinsterly and my pupils despise me secretly for it . . . I would
rather be married to a drunken collier who beat me every week-end than
live as I am doing at present.' But in the world of the Surplus Woman,

becoming a schoolmarm was as good as abandoning all hope of catching a husband.

However, if by some miracle, despite being frumpy, frigid and domineering, you did find someone to marry you, you lost your job. In the inter-war years, most local authorities imposed a marriage bar on teachers. The argument was that married women did not need to work, and if they chose to do so, they were depriving necessitous single women who needed the money. In this, the Education Boards' ruling reinforced the traditional assumption that the man's role was to provide, the woman's to keep house for him and bear his babies. The sad case of Elizabeth Rignall testifies to the unfairness of these assumptions. It also testifies to the way in which teachers were often condemned to single lives by their profession. A woman like her, from a poor background, could advance socially and better herself financially if she took up teaching – but often only at the expense of marriage.

Lizzie Rignall probably never expected her autobiography to see the light of day. She wrote it at the age of seventy-nine, her memory for the past still crystal clear, though her body was by then crippled with arthritis. She had been a teacher all her life. Lizzie was born in 1894 into a hard-up, hard-working family; her father was a painter and decorator who frequently found himself out of work. Her mother, a forthright Yorkshirewoman, let lodgings in their house in south London. Looking back from 1973, her childhood seemed to have taken place in a different world: the happy pre-war days on her grandparents' farm in Haworth, her father playing the euphonium in the Salvation Army band, the street hawkers of Lavender Hill and the itinerant Italian with a dancing bear.

Lizzie was a very pretty child: petite, flaxen-haired and blue-eyed. She had admirers from the age of five: 'Mummy, Jackie Brown kissed me in the playground this afternoon!' Later, when a magic lantern projector was set up on the common near their home, Lizzie and her current heart-throb would find a back-row seat to watch the flickering screen; they held hands, and willed the projector to break down so that they would be plunged into the thrilling darkness. Her 'god' was the dashing star of Putney's roller-skating rink: dark, handsome dreamboat Leslie Stephens, the elder son of a major-general. 'There was nothing he could not do on a pair of skates.' It never occurred to Lizzie that someone as glamorous as Leslie might be attracted to someone as humble as her, but later it struck her that this was indeed the case. With hindsight, his habit of escorting her and her brother home after skating, and his manner of farewell, were signs of obvious partiality.

Lizzie was ambitious, however. She knew she was clever, and by the age of sixteen had set her sights on a scholarship to Girton. Letting lodgings like her mother was not her idea of a bright future: 'You see, I had not yet resigned myself to lesser things.' Unfortunately, French let her down in the exam and Cambridge eluded her. In 1913 Lizzie, 'nothing daunted', took her place at St Katharine's Church of England Teacher Training College, and by the age of twenty-one was teaching slum children at an elementary school in the Walworth Road for a wage of £1 16s 5d a week. This was 1916. On so little, work at the Ministry of Munitions seemed both a more patriotic and a better-paid option, so for the duration Lizzie became a little cog in the great war effort; then after the war it was back to the classroom.

Her family now relied heavily on Lizzie's financial contributions; it was essential for her to stay in paid employment. In the early 1920s she moved to Buckinghamshire and took a job at a village school. For four years the diminutive Miss Rignall was a familiar sight on the country lanes astride her Velocette motorcycle, got up in government surplus cord breeches, black leather knee boots, a brown leather helmet and a pair of goggles. Every evening, the headmaster would come and help her shove the bike to start it – tiny, at only four feet eleven-and-a-half, Lizzie just couldn't manage to get it going. But four years of village life was enough; in 1925 she was ready to move back to London, and applied to be interviewed for a post at a school in Kensington.

And it was here and then that I found the great love of my life. I was one of six chosen to be interviewed. I had reached Campden Hill Gardens and was searching for the meeting-place. As I hesitated, scanning the numbers that were visible, 'Can I help you?' asked a pleasant voice, and I turned to see a tall, slim, red-gold giant, with intensely blue eyes and an immense hooked nose . . . my heart missed several beats as I gave him the number.

'I'm going there myself, so perhaps you will allow me to escort you?'

Long, long afterwards he told me that he too fell at that moment, as I did.

Lizzie got the job, and the giant, Bob, turned out to be her headmaster. But not for another four years did either of them dare to confess their feelings to the other. For Bob, the strain was finally too great. A large upstairs classroom doubled as his office and storeroom. One day, when the room was empty, Lizzie had to fetch an item of stationery from the cupboard. Turning to leave, she saw Bob entering; he held the door open for her. As she passed, he put his arms around her from behind, and bent his lips tenderly to the nape of her neck.

We stood thus, quite still, for a long moment, then his arms fell away and I darted out of the room like a frightened rabbit. Down the stairs I scuttled and into my own classroom, breathless, my heart thumping. When school ended that afternoon and as I donned my outdoor clothes he came into the room.

'Thank-you for not raising the alarm, my dearest. You know now, don't you?'

Speechlessly I nodded.

In love, and loved, life should have given Lizzie more than it did. She was now thirty-five. But the London County Council had strict rules and, under them, women teachers had to leave the service if they married. If Lizzie gave up work, her parents would have to 'go on the Parish'. Bob, too, had heavy commitments to his family. It was impossible for them both to live on his salary and support their dependants.

And so for six years the affair was secret. It was difficult, as initially Lizzie was still living at home. Even after she managed to afford a flat nearer to her work, there was the constant fear that they would be found out. Weekday rendezvous were risky, so their time together was confined to weekends. After a year they both felt it would be better for her to leave the school in Kensington, and she reluctantly got a post at a school in Wandsworth. For five years they continued seeing each other, yet always knowing that they could not be married. Looking back at the end of her life, Lizzie was more puzzled than bitter – 'I have often wondered since how widespread in the profession was the immorality this led to. Nowadays of course it is no longer considered "Immorality" and premarital relations are not frowned upon . . . But at that time things were very difficult for such as we were.'

It came to an end in 1935. After six years of this provisional, unblessed, furtive arrangement, Bob got cancer and died. She neither gives details, nor refers to her own altered prospects. There was to be no husband, no babies, no home of her own. Lizzie was now in her forties, and life had to go on. In the Second World War she went to live with her brother and sister-in-law. She got a job in Scunthorpe, then a headship in Avebury. In her fifties she moved to Sussex and ran a secondary modern school in Heathfield. The last couple of decades after her retirement get scanty treatment, but at nearly eighty Miss Rignall continued to hold her own in the educational field: 'They still call on me for part-time teaching, for coaching, and even for home tuition.' There was no anger or resentment at the unjust hand life had dealt her. Nearly forty years had passed since Bob had died, and perhaps the passage of time had blurred regret. Patient, modest and discreet as ever, she concluded her memoir of the past in 1973, giving it the title 'All So Long Ago':

I have had a good life. It has been really varied if undistinguished and I can look back now in unalloyed pleasure at both the failures and small successes I have had . . .

I can say, with complete honesty, that I think the life I have had was right for me.

And yet how much more fulfilled it might have been.

★

A closer, and more distinct picture of the emotional reality of a teacher's life emerges from Ruth Adam's novel *I'm Not Complaining* (1938). Ruth Adam wrote this unsentimental portrayal of the schoolmarm's life after she herself emerged from five years of teaching miners' children in a Nottinghamshire school in the late 1920s and early 30s. So frank and authentic is her account that nobody could dispute the author's mastery of her subject. *I'm Not Complaining* is drawn from life.

Madge Brigson tells the story. Funny, honest and spirited, she observes and participates in the lives of the other spinster teachers who are her fellow-sufferers at Bronton Elementary. The waifs they teach are slum children; their parents are unemployed, their big sisters turn to prostitution, their community is given over to ignorance, thieving, copulating, breeding and brawling. Madge's daily descent by tram from her mean little flat in thinly respectable Upper Bronton to the seething, verminous disorder of Lower Bronton is like a descent into hell. The reality of the 1930s school was that, all too often, it was draughty, dirty and ill-equipped. Classes might have as many as sixty pupils. Working conditions for teachers were often shocking; at night the classrooms had to do duty as community centres, so the local whist drive or rabbit show would take over and the space was never properly cleaned.

Against this backdrop, the virginal schoolmarms of *I'm Not Complaining* must survive through stealth, stubborn resolve, wits, and industry – or make their escape. And escape is, as usual, only through marriage. Miss Harford the headmistress will never marry; her fiancé didn't die in the war, but he had both his arms and both his legs shot off and lives in 'one of those homes'; as a result she is touchy and difficult to work for. Frumpy Miss Jones – a middle-aged old maid – dyes her white hair and nurtures hopes of marriage with a sailor. Miss Simpson, despite her ardent socialism, burns for the local curate, but Miss Lambert, beautiful, carnal and provokingly unreliable, has hooked him. And Madge? She too is jealous of Jenny Lambert:

Hardworking, contented women like me get this longing, from time to time, for all the experiences that have passed us by. We do not go mad over it, as women do in psychological books, nor even get a little bit queer. It goes off after a few days and we are ourselves again.

Ruth Adam gives convincing substance to her heroine's daily life; this must have been the reality for many teachers in the 1930s – a shared bungalow with two other spinster teachers, frugal, hasty meals of boiled eggs, ready-cooked meat pies, and baked beans. On about five pounds a week, they can afford a charwoman to 'do' for them, cinemas and inexpensive holidays, but they count the pennies. Work consists of toiling over endless registers, fear of inspectors, and sick, screaming, primitive children. Madge is aware of drinking too many cups of tea and gossiping too much. The painful consciousness of the spinster's lot recurs with humiliating insistence. Now thirty, she knows that people regard her as a 'nervy old maid', comical and barren. She knows too that she is nothing special to look at: 'My jaw was too heavy. My eyebrows were too thick. My nose was too large . . . I looked exactly like a schoolmarm . . .' Sexy Jenny describes her as 'the kind of emotion-starved old maid who gets her only sex-satisfaction by poking her nose into the details of other women's affairs'.

And yet Madge is not fixated on marriage, or sex. Her work matters to her. And she feels true despair only when one of her pupils is run over and killed in a chance accident. Moira was her monitor, an obedient, affectionate child. Now she is 'a broken, crushed, red mass at the feet of the crowd'. Madge tries to sleep that night, but cannot; she walks down to the dingy town canal, and overwhelming thoughts of her own uselessness come close to defeating her:

My work was all that I had. No personal ties counted with me. And now I felt I would never care to work again. For if my work led to this, then children would be better leading their uncertain lives in happy anarchy, untroubled by weary preparation for the future. I wondered how Moira's mother was spending this black night . . . Was she suffering so much more? Then I knew that of course she was . . . Outcast and barren virgin that I was, even my sorrow did not belong to me. I was only her school-teacher, and my loss, in the calculation of the world, was nothing at all.

I felt too humiliated, too broken to take any action at all . . .

This is not the end for Madge, however. She looks on as dowdy little Miss Jones is granted the ultimate reprieve: the sailor returns from the sea and she packs in teaching to become a wife. But not to find happiness: the sailor is a cranky, sexist old boor, who pours cold water on his new wife's enthusiasms and criticises her domestic failings; like so many teachers, she is amateurish at the 'complicated business of hot meals and clean sheets and managing gas-cookers . . . But he could not understand it.' To Madge the message is plain: Miss Jones misses teaching.

And then, unexpectedly, Madge's turn comes. Love is finally offered to her, a deep, comforting love that has grown out of friendship and familiarity. It is as if the dark stinking canal of her despair has transformed itself into a clean sparkling torrent tumbling joyously down a rocky hillside. They will marry; it will be the end of her spinsterhood. Once more at night-time she cannot sleep but this time, gradually, joy, tumult, and delirium give way to chill certainty. No, it cannot happen. She cannot be his wife. She can be nobody's wife. Madge now faces up to who and what she is, and knows that no 'tinsel-trimmed fairy-tale' or romantic façade can replace her hard-won sense of identity and purpose:

I, if I did not grasp at illusion, could go on steadily with my task and know that, however the world mocked, I was doing the part that I could to heal the sickness of the world. This was reality . . .

So Madge rejects marriage, and so the novel concludes, with the cathartic if not entirely satisfying feeling that a good schoolteacher with energy and commitment can make a difference. What she can accomplish as a teacher can never be accomplished as a wife.

★

It would be heartening to think that the stoical message of *I'm Not Complaining* helped real teachers in similar circumstances to endure their lot. Miss Hewson, an infant teacher working at a school in Prestwich, Lancashire, was a real-life Madge Brigson, whose 1937 diary seems to echo the defiance and clear-sightedness of the fictional schoolmistress:

Monday morning – I do not know if I am glad or sorry, but I find it annoying to have to get up to a dictated time: nevertheless it seems more pleasing to me to be facing a day where I shall be away from home earning my own living than if circumstances were such that I should have to be attending to the breakfasts of a husband and family. No, I do not want my mother's life, or the life of any one of the women in our avenue, to cook dinners with love in them. I'd rather be in the gutter than grubbing around the slopstone.

Yes, I'd rather be padding to school than living in a red brick box called a sunshine house, with the appellation of Mrs. Their married conceits make me laugh. I want to do what I want to do, when I know what that want is, and their conceits are a burden . . . which isn't to say I don't want a love affair . . .

I love youth because it looks lovely. Yes, I'm really sorry to be 37 and not 27 . . .

Other than having to get up at a dictated time and the obvious trials of a teacher's working life, we do not know what adversity Miss Hewson faced on a daily basis. Evidently she was finding ways of persuading herself that the single state was a positive one.

But there were cases where this took more control than an individual possessed. Miss Dudley's story is one. This most poignant recognition of a teacher's fortitude came to me in the recollections of a small boy in her school, John Edge. John was the son of a vicar, and he grew up in his father's parish of St Jude's in Stoke-on-Trent in the 1940s. This close-knit community encompassed poor factory workers and their ragged barefooted children; shop assistants, railwaymen and clerks lived in a slightly better area of scrubbed steps and brick terraced house fronts. Respectable as it was, this was also the 'area of the Misses'. The Misses would come to Evensong at St Jude's: Miss Stevenson and Miss Cobden, Miss Hall, Miss Burden and Miss Dearing, Miss Gladys Eason and her sister Doris. And Miss Dudley. They came, 'most faithfully, wearing their sensible hats, their grey or fawn coats, their sensible shoes'. Miss Dudley taught at John's school; she was one of the best teachers, quiet and self-controlled, always dressed in grey; she never had problems with discipline, but she never smiled. John never thought to wonder why.

Every November on Armistice Day the congregation listened when the names on the War Memorial were read out; to young John the list seemed never-ending. There must have been 150 deaths in that one parish. His mother told him that after the Battle of the Somme whole streets in Stoke had gone into mourning. The churchwarden, Billy Gimbert, was one of the lucky few from Stoke who had come back unharmed from the war. Billy was a kind, likeable man, 'one of us', but he had a sharp-tongued wife.

And then one day scandal broke. The tragic news came that Billy Gimbert had been found hanging in the office where he worked. John never found out why; there had been whispers of infidelity, disagreements with his wife; eventually he had resigned his churchwardenship and shortly afterwards took his life. Not long after it came out, John, sitting quietly in the kitchen reading, heard the vicarage doorbell ring. His father had so many parishioners dropping in seeking help that this was not unusual. A little while later the vicar came back into the kitchen and there, unaware of his young son's attentive presence, disclosed to his wife an awful tale of thirty years of disappointment:

It was Miss Dudley. She asked if she could speak to me. I took her into the study, and she sat down and just burst into tears. I have never seen anything like it. You see, she and Billy had been engaged before the War, and when he came back safe and sound Mrs Gimbert, who had lost her boyfriend, stole him. He was never happy, ever. She brushed away her tears and said she was alright and as she walked down the street no one would have been able to tell.

And John never told either, until he himself was an old man. Miss Dudley was probably in her fifties when she saw the man she had loved for so long destroyed by an unhappy marriage. How had she borne the betrayal, the loss, the agonizing sense of waste? One can only hope that her religion, her composure, and the acceptance of her own value as a highly-regarded teacher, 'one of the best', eventually brought peace in her despair.

★

Acceptance must have been hard faced with so many bitter regrets, but teachers like Lizzie Rignall and Madge Brigson were able to find meaning and self-worth through their professional achievements. D. F. P. Hiley, the author of *Pedagogue Pie* (1936), an advice book for the teaching profession, was open-eyed about the futility of struggling against one's fate. 'What a waste of force, what a wearing of the spirit, all this kicking against the pricks!' Yet Hiley also recognised that ageing spinster teachers were liable to stagnate, to become sluggish, bitter and bad-tempered. This, she was quick to point out, was not necessarily due to frustration, but middle age observably brought with it a sense of regret and finality. 'That decision of twenty, thirty, years ago, was it the wrong one? Ought we to have been doing something else all these years?' Hiley had a remedy for this:

It is a good plan . . . at about the age of forty to do something strange and new, such as beginning golf, or buying a car, or writing a detective story. There is nothing very wild-oaty that a respectable, professional female can do, but do let the free part of your personality flap in the wind. Madness is so vitalising. Keep your sense of wonder fresh, and your interests active, especially human, artistic, spiritual interests. Travel to strange and beautiful places.

In this respect, of course, a reasonable salary helped. Muriel Spark's fictional creation Miss Jean Brodie holidays in Italy, visits the great cathedrals, goes to art galleries and concerts. And the reality was equivalent: women teachers frequently shared a home for reasons of companionship and economy, and then found they could afford to spend their summer holidays like Miss Brodie admiring masterpieces in the Louvre and the Uffizi. They took what they learned back to the classroom with them.

Such a high-minded and idealistic approach to life bore fruit. Now nearly eighty, author and documentary-maker June Goodfield remembers being taught at a state grammar school in Solihull in the 1930s. Her teachers, she said, were all from 'the bereaved generation'. June felt immense gratitude to these teachers for having instilled in her a lifelong sense of civic responsibility. 'It was a terrific privilege to have been taught by them. They in their turn taught us that it was a privilege to be alive, and that it was our job to feed something back into society. I owe it to them that I can't pass a piece of litter without wanting to pick it up. They were gifted, educated and cultured, and they had exacting standards. They also taught us that it was our civic duty to vote; they were from the generation that had fought for that right, and we had it drummed into us that you betray it if you don't exercise it.'

Another woman who looked back on the spinster teachers who taught her at the local council school from 1923, when she was five, also paid tribute to them: 'I did not realise till much later how fortunate we children were to be taught by so dedicated a group of teachers. It was as though we were their surrogate children that they never bore . . . Our classes averaged about 60 pupils, but there was no difficulty in keeping order . . . We respected them and they were highly educated and well-read people. These cultured ladies led us into the world of art and music. I am glad to acknowledge my debt to them.'

The old idea that education for girls was one of those things that 'nice' people didn't discuss had failed to survive the post-war climate. Miss Lilian Faithfull, Principal of Cheltenham Ladies' College between 1906 and 1922, remarked that whereas before the war 70 per cent of her pupils returned to their families on leaving school, after the war that figure reversed: '. . . certainly seventy per cent wished to have a career.' The curriculum quickly adapted, becoming increasingly oriented towards qualifications as opposed to accomplishments.

A virtuous circle was created, whereby young women educated of necessity grew up to become the teachers of the next generation of girls. By the second half of the twentieth century illiterate women, or women who could only faint, blush and play the piano, had become the exception. In all this the 'Surplus Women' schoolmarms had a deeply formative influence, and one might argue that their independent approach to life bucked a trend that was to evolve into the fully-fledged feminist movement advanced by many of their one-time pupils thirty years later. Stay-at-home wives and mothers could never have provided the role model of these valiant mathematics and history mistresses.

## Miss All-Alone on the wards

Compared to the teaching profession, hospitals could be seen as good husband-hunting territory. During the war this was probably true. If, like Vera Brittain's 'Lady, *fiancé* killed . . .', you were only too glad to marry anyone, even if 'totally blinded or otherwise incapacitated by the War . . .', then the wartime hospitals were a rich source of grateful, submissive and sex-starved young men.

When nineteen-year-old Stuart Cloete's shoulder-blade was smashed by a German bullet at the battle of the Somme he was taken back to recover in hospital in Reading. Watching the VADs in their starched uniforms as they bustled busily around the ward, his mind was on their bodies underneath, and with nothing else to do but recover, Cloete's sex fantasies took hold of him. After his discharge, shell-shock kicked in and he had to be hospitalised again, this time in London. Emerging from an amnesiac coma, he looked up to see a tall dark-haired nurse standing in the doorway:

> Her uniform was pale blue with a white starched apron, belt, collar, cuffs and cap. I stared at her – or so she said afterwards – and instantly fell in love . . .
>
> My nurse-wounded-soldier pattern was one with a thousand precedents. Gratitude on the part of the man, a reversion to infancy and a desire to be taken care of by a woman. On the woman's part, her sympathy for pain, an effort to make up to the soldier for what he had gone through, and a kind of almost incestuous maternal feeling for this man-baby. A whole galaxy of instincts, feelings, thoughts and passions on both sides. All in all an atmosphere of war urgency.

War, Cloete explained, has an aphrodisiac effect. Boys were forced more quickly into manhood; the losses on the field stimulated the natural impulse to regenerate. It was all part of the survival of the race. 'As far as nature was concerned I was not a boy or a man. I was an organ of reproduction to be used before it was destroyed.' He guessed that the young nurse, Eileen, may have felt something of the same sexual pressure. Her fiancé had been killed on the Somme only a few months earlier, and Stuart in some way filled his place. Cloete returned to the front and in 1918 was wounded again. This time his groin and spine were damaged, and both his buttocks were half blown off; he nearly died. Five operations later, and a couple of months before the Armistice, Eileen agreed to sleep with him. In October 1918 they were married.

The awful injuries of returning soldiers were the inspiration for many a starry-eyed young woman to offer herself up to a life of service to the sick. After the First World War, there were more nurses than there were jobs for them; 20,000 nurses joined the profession between 1914 and 1921. One of them was seventeen-year-old Gladys Hardy:

Mother [was] anxious about my future. She had the idea that nurses were similar to nuns, that there was no possible chance for a nurse to get married, and that eventually I would become 'queer' and have to be kept by my family. I had no such doubts . . . I dreamed of wearing a smart uniform and a snowy cap; of appearing as a ministering angel to the sick, and of being a very important person.

Gladys was in for a shock: she found on her first day on the ward that she was expected to be not a ministering angel but a charwoman. There were floors to sweep, baths and lavatories to clean, and brass to be polished. 'By 9.30 a.m. that morning, I was tired and dusty . . . my feet ached in their new black shoes and stockings, and I felt, and looked, untidy and miserable.' Nevertheless, Gladys felt privileged, and buckled down obediently. Though menial, nursing was one of the few professions seen as respectable for decent young ladies, and eligible doctors were an attraction if you aspired to marriage with a man of status; but Gladys soon found out that the reality was not as romantic as the sixpenny fiction papers would have their readers believe.

As in so many cases, there weren't enough men to go round. Nursing had much to offer as a career, but this didn't alter the fact that it was, like teaching, a job for single women, and in most hospitals a nurse would be dismissed or expected to resign on marriage. Only the determinedly – or terminally – single could reach Sister or Matron level. By the age of thirty Gladys Hardy was a Sister Tutor; at thirty-five she was a Matron. In a job like this the responsibilities were all-consuming, and she marvelled that any professional nurses ever managed to get married, for there was simply no time to meet anyone 'outside'; 'Indeed I never even had the wish to get married; for life was complicated enough as it was.'

Her mother's anxieties were borne out by the facts, for the truth was

A 1930s careers manual for girls conjures the familiar stereotype of the nurse as a ministering angel in smart uniform and snowy cap

that life in a hospital was more like life in a nunnery, and stretched employers quite cynically exploited the desire of young nurses to regard their job as a vocation. There was the iron discipline, the monastic rules, the compulsory daily prayers and intricate uniform, but with the addition of strenuous physical labour, exhaustion and often repellent conditions. Although board, lodging and uniform were provided, self-abnegation extended to the pay, which was a pittance; a probationer started on £25 a year. While women were finding new freedoms in other professions, the life of a nurse had become increasingly enclosed. Dedication, obedience and irreproachability: these were the qualities expected of the band of aspiring Florence Nightingales who staffed our hospitals – virtues more suited to a company of Vestal Virgins than to the healthy red-blooded young women in their late teens and early twenties who actually worked there. It was well-known at Gladys Hardy's hospital that quite a few nurses would break out to meet boyfriends, but the offenders could have expected no sympathy, and probably instant dismissal. One enlightened Matron, however, took a different view.

Mary Milne, who was to become Matron of St Mary's Hospital, Paddington, was born in 1891. As a young woman she had tried secretarial and teaching work before opting for nursing in 1915. Mary had a fiancé; at some point during the war the fiancé was killed in action. Nothing else is known about him, nor about their relationship. Did she decide to become a nurse to honour his memory, filled perhaps with compassion and fellow-feeling for others who must suffer? This is pure speculation. Whatever her motives, Miss Milne seems to have developed an unusual sympathy for her staff when she later rose to the top of her career. Matrons were lofty, remote and usually fearsome people. In those days the private life of such an august personage would normally have been off limits to the junior staff. But at St Mary's it was common knowledge that Miss Milne had borne great personal tragedy. She was also renowned for her humanity and kindliness.

Mary grew up in a medical family, so it was not surprising that she turned to nursing at a point in history when care for the wounded and sick seemed imperative. As a student she was exceptionally able, winning medals and scholarships, and after working as a nursing tutor both here and in South Africa, she gained her appointment at St Mary's on merit, without an interview, in 1928. She was then thirty-seven, a well-travelled, self-sufficient, modern woman, with advanced views on the hierarchies so prevalent in the hospital world. As such, she had the old guard to contend with. Summoned for briefing by her predecessor at St Mary's, she was kept waiting for half an hour before being looked up and down and advised that she would do well to disguise her fashionable bob with an artificial hairpiece.

The comfort and happiness of her staff were Mary Milne's priority. The majority of matrons ruled over their nurses with despotic and petty discipline. Julie Mullard,★ a probationer nurse at the Radcliffe Infirmary in the 1930s, remembered the awful dread of being summoned to Matron for having committed some unknown misdemeanour. After a nerve-racking wait, she was severely rebuked for her transgression: she and a friend had been seen leaving the hospital '*without wearing hats!*' Julie stammered excuses. 'I am disgusted with you,' said the Matron, and sent her packing.

But Mary Milne was different. From the start she insisted her staff have one off-duty day a week. She made improvements to accommodation and diet. She was hands-on and kept in touch with problems. But the most memorable difference she made was in her sympathetic stance towards the nurses' love lives. Nurses had of course always been prohibited from having any contact with the (predominantly male) medical students at St Mary's; Miss Milne lifted the ban. Instead there were to be joint musical and dramatic ventures, and St Mary's Matron's Ball was her invention. The nurses were encouraged to bring their boyfriends, if they had them, and Matron would invite the couples to tea in her flat before the dance. During the Blitz St Mary's staff remembered her coming across male students who had penetrated the hitherto monastic sanctum of the nurses' home. 'I suppose you are all busy firewatching, gentlemen,' was her only comment.

When you are a spinster who has been deprived by fate of your natural mate, it takes a generous spirit to show benevolence towards youthful romances. It is tempting to interpret Mary Milne's humanity as an expression of solidarity with girls many of whom were also heading, inexorably,

★ Mullard (born 1911) became the lifelong companion of the novelist Mary Renault (pseudonym of Mary Challans, 1905–83); they met while training as nurses at the Radcliffe Infirmary, Oxford.

for spinsterhood. As if that wasn't enough, their profession locked them up in impenetrable nunneries. When a second war broke out, likely to rob the next generation of their fiancés, just as she had been robbed of hers, the reaction of this remarkable woman was one of enlightened compassion. She was admired, and blessed.

★

It would be hard to describe Mary Milne as a 'Surplus Woman', though after she lost her sweetheart in the Great War she never married. Perhaps in some way this made it simpler for her; love had died back in 1915, and she was to live another fifty-seven years. She had the gift of finding meaning in a fulfilling occupation. In 1945 she was made OBE, and to the end of her life was active in charities and on nursing and governmental committees.

But Matron Cassy Harker's story is one that may well speak to our own times, when the choices faced by women are in some regards more complex. Her story – told in her autobiography, *Call Me Matron* (1980) – is illuminating because, although Cassy never felt herself to be a 'Surplus Woman' either, her choice of nursing as a career demonstrates how hospital life in the 1930s could effectively scupper marriage prospects. Working in a hospital was, and is, a stressful, emotionally fraught occupation and, as Cassy discovered, its demands and rewards can be comparable to those of a marriage. For some, that made the job a satisfying replacement for marriage, but for Cassy – a strong, passionate, intelligent woman who both loved her work and loved to enjoy herself – it took a lifetime to come to terms with the wrecked hopes that her success as a nurse had imposed on her.

Cassy started as a probationer in Leeds in 1932; like Gladys Hardy, the hard domestic labour came as a shock to her. The girls woke at six, dressed in their regulation corset, vest, bloomers, long dress, white cuffs, starched pinafore, bib, black lace-ups and peaked cap, and started work scrubbing the wards at seven. '[It] was quite mindless . . . but it certainly did teach you how to clean. I reckoned to be the best lavatory cleaner in the world in late 1932,' remembered Cassy. At eight there was half an hour's chapel. After this they did an eleven-hour day of bedpans, cleaning, lectures, bed-baths, studying, and more chapel before bed. There were long lists of *Don'ts*. Don't smoke, don't take off your stockings while sitting in hospital grounds, don't call each other by Christian names, don't communicate with the outside world, don't go off the premises without permission. And despite knowing how to give enemas and how babies were born, the probationers were given a total of one quarter of an hour's instruction about human reproduction.

When Cassy started work on the wards any stars she may have had in her eyes were, in those pre-penicillin days, quickly dispelled. She encountered oozing pus, rotting flesh and peritonitis; her stomach turned when she was required to wipe off the maggots that were applied to cure wounds. Leeches to draw blood were in common use. And despite all the cleaning the hospital was crawling with insects – black beetles, cockroaches and ants.

Somehow Cassy survived (two out of five probationers didn't), and by the age of twenty-five, as a qualified staff nurse, had started belatedly to discover that there was more to life than gangrene and sick babies. There were after-hours parties in the doctors' quarters: 'I became a regular party-goer and generally started to let my hair down.' For a girl with a Methodist background this was a breakthrough, though initially she didn't touch the demon alcohol and contented herself with soft drinks. But one night a young doctor decided that her elementary sex education was in need of updating:

. . . my orange juice was liberally laced with gin or vodka. I naturally drank it like an orange juice – with the expected results. It knocked me out and I was put to bed upstairs.

When I came round the young doctor who had brought me the 'orange juice' was still beside me. I learned about more than just drinking that night.

Having notched up his conquest, Cassy's seducer lost interest in his victim; for her part she was consumed with guilt and remorse. But Cassy was not disenchanted; rather this shabby episode awakened her dormant interest in the opposite sex.

Harry appeared on the scene a year later, in 1939: he was a young, good-looking Canadian registrar, working for his surgery qualification, and they fell in love. Now she was an operating theatre nurse, they spent much of their working lives together, and there was plenty of opportunity to pursue the affair. Had the Second World War not intervened, the relationship might have ended happily, but it was not to be. Harry could not serve as a doctor in Europe, since the British army would not recognise his Canadian qualifications; he was forced to return to Canada, and they did not see each other for three more years. His career there flourished, and when he came back for her, it was to ask her to make a choice:

There are decisions which stay with you for the rest of your life – and a decision on Harry would obviously be one of those . . . It is still far from easy for women to choose between marriage and career, despite the great improvement in women's rights and conditions. For nurses, this can be an especial problem because they are facing a choice between two sets of emotional demands. In many careers emotional involvement is not required, but nursing is not one of them: the emotional demands of a working day in a hospital can be the equal of any marriage, so you want to get it right. In the more cloistered conditions of nursing up to 1946 this emotional link with work was perhaps even stronger and it seemed crazy to throw it all away when I was on the verge of having a satisfying career. It would take ages to get a similar position in Canada. On the other hand, it seemed crazy to say goodbye to the man who meant more to me than any other.

The decision was torture, for both of them. Eventually Harry went back to Canada alone: 'The affair was not called off, just put on ice for the time being. Again we parted not knowing if we would ever see each other again.'

By 1950 Cassy Harker was a matron. Sometimes her choice gnawed at her; she was into her forties now and the chance of having children was slipping away, but she did her best to count her blessings. She had never liked housework, and didn't feel she'd missed out on having a marital home to look after. Irregularly, Harry kept in touch and meantime, if boyfriends offered, she was available – though nothing stable materialised. But by the time she hit her fifties Cassy realized that intermittent companionship was not giving her what she wanted or needed. She had no trouble in diagnosing her own disease, for it was one that she had come to recognise as common to matrons: isolation. And now the regrets started to close in over her. 'Was the real benefit of marriage companionship in later years? Should I have gone to Canada with Harry? What might have been?' But he was now married with children, and it was too late.

There was one final meeting. In the mid 1960s Cassy's commitments took her almost by chance to Canada, and for two dreamlike days they were able to make up for the lost past. 'This was the mental and emotional climax we both felt had been missing over the years. In those few hours of completeness neither of us doubted that we could have made a happy life together. But we had not taken our chance and we knew that it was too late to start a life together now.' When she returned to England, Cassy broke down. Loneliness overwhelmed her; the empty house echoed with misery and menace. She began to depend on sleeping pills. After receiving a letter from Harry's daughter to say that her father had died of a heart attack, Cassy drank half a bottle of whisky, and was found the next morning lying collapsed in the garden in her dressing-gown.

It was to be another six years before Cassy was able to fight free of the results of her depression. Psychiatric treatment helped, and she was well-placed to secure the best, but even that failed to exorcise the demons that tormented her. Crazed with loneliness, and desperate to alleviate it by any means, Cassy rushed headlong into an ill-advised marriage with an elderly man she had met through a match-making service; it was, of course, a disaster. They had nothing in common, but unstitching her rash action was tortuous; this was a time of strain and heartache. At long last, at the age of sixty, and coinciding with the date of her retirement, she was free.

The last few years had taught me, painfully, that there was in fact more to be feared from living with the wrong companion than from living with your own company. By early 1972 I was installed in a small terraced house in Darlington – alone, save for my dog Sally, and happy to be so. The phobias about living by myself were behind me and I had come to terms with life. From then on everything got better.

★

How hard it could be. Millicent Fawcett was right when she declared in 1918 that the great convulsion of the First World War had revolutionised the industrial position of women; unquestionably the absence of men released women from their state as captive wives and childbearers to become earners. When, after it ended, the Surplus Women had to support themselves, it helped to feel that they had something of value to offer as workers, that they were doing their part 'to heal the sickness of the world'. On the bad days, sometimes just the brutal fact of having to earn a living held them together. As Miss Irene Angell told an interviewer years later: 'With no one to go home to, unless you like your work, you'd put yourself under an electric train.' But on the good days, there was the satisfaction of knowing that one could survive without a man. And there was always the hope – for the persistent and talented – that rose-coloured carpets might be theirs.

But whether the new post-war world of the 1920s offered them genuine freedom is another matter. These were the pioneers, it is true. But wage-earning women still had a long bumpy road to travel, a journey hampered by inequalities, discriminative practices, lack of opportunity and prejudice. Over the course of the last century many of these have, in this country, been surmounted: unions have backed women's rights and put pressure on the government; laws have been passed regarding pay, discrimination and conditions. Today a young woman can set out to be a railway driver or a doctor without encountering obstacles in her path. But no legislation can bypass the predicament that remains integral to the life of any single working woman: you can't have it all.

# 5. Caring, Sharing . . .

## Lonely days

'Nature did not construct human beings to stand alone . . .' wrote Bertrand Russell in 1929. 'Those who have never known the deep intimacy and the intense companionship of happy mutual love have missed the best thing that life has to give.' Russell himself, who went through no fewer than three acrimonious divorces, was not the best advertisement for conjugal happiness, but he was expressing a view that the happily married, at any rate, would find it hard to argue with. The impulse of each human heart is to seek closeness with another. With Russell's case in mind, it might be argued that such intimacy is rare in marriage, but his statement does not define 'happy mutual love' as being necessarily that of husband and wife, nor even that of man and woman. 'Love is something far more than desire for sexual intercourse; it is the principal means of escape from the loneliness which afflicts most men and women throughout the greater part of their lives . . .' wrote Russell. The human being needs sex, but more than that he or she needs companionship, understanding, sympathy and just someone to talk to. Perhaps these were, for the single woman, more fundamentally necessary than heterosexual love, romance, motherhood and wifely status. Lonely individuals reach in the dark for whoever may alleviate solitude. Unless that need could be met, the alternative, for many women denied the solace of marriage, was undeniably tough.

The loneliness could indeed be annihilating. Programmed for centuries to nurture and love, a woman deprived of human contact felt its lack more acutely perhaps than her aggressive male counterpart out there in the jungle, killing, pursuing, making money and running the world. As the author of *The Single Woman and Her Emotional Problems* (1935), Laura Hutton, wrote:

The basic problem of the single woman is loneliness . . . To a man love is but one factor in his life. To a woman it tends to be her whole life.

May Wedderburn Cannan, whose fiancé had died at the end of the war, braved day after day the anguish of disappointment and depleted hope. But it was no use struggling to leave the past behind; the regrets kept coming, and with the regrets the feelings of emptiness:

It was lonely. It was lonely because I went to work and came home again alone; and to a house which dear as it was to me, and God knew how dear, could never be one to which he would come; never his and mine. We had planned to live in Hampstead and I had thought of coming home to a small house on the slope of Downshire Hill . . . a small house with a small garden with a magnolia and a lilac: a small house in which you could still write poetry and toast crumpets by the fire on Winter Saturday afternoons . . .

Well that was all gone now. It is not only the Beloved that death takes. It is all the bright hopes.

The Oxford scholar Enid Starkie lived all her life in hopes of a permanent and all-consuming relationship, but it was never to be. Needy and temperamental, this wild Irishwoman never found the satisfaction she craved, as one relationship after another (some with men, others with women) crashed and burned. 'I have been lonely since I was a small child,' she confessed to a friend:

Few people have penetrated into complete intimacy with me . . . I have always been lonely – very very lonely – in Oxford where no-one really knows me . . . My last intimate relationship was one in which my friend penetrated more deeply into the inner core of my loneliness than anyone before, and I now feel a chill emptiness. I feel a weariness towards everything – a distaste. I know this will not last, but at the moment it makes me very unhappy.

And whereas today's single woman frequently proclaims her self-sufficiency, her satisfaction with solitude and freedom, for women of the inter-war generation isolation was all too often equated with being ridiculous. To loneliness were added the burdens of poverty and eccentricity.

*Poor Caroline* (1931), by Winifred Holtby, is a relentlessly uncomforting novel, its heroine a preposterous figure. It seems likely that in her portrayal of this sad spinster, Holtby was bravely and unflinchingly confronting her own fears of an unloved and lonely old age. The eponymous heroine, Miss Caroline Denton-Smyth, is brought low by her own ludicrous fantasies. 'Artistic', she is first seen draped in beads and lorgnettes, in an antique green coat trimmed with moth-eaten fur, her fringe in a frizz, topped with a feathered and ribboned red hat. In this guise she puts on a brave face, lunching with a financier at Boulestin's. But in reality Caroline lives up three flights of stairs in a bedsitting-room in West Kensington, eating bread, margarine and stale seed-cake, reduced to borrowing money. Her life is a struggle against despair and solitude. At nights, driven by her frantic need for companionship, she seeks out her landlady for a cup of tea and a chat – 'Not so lonely as going up to that room alone, night after night . . .' – but even that becomes impossible when she finds herself owing £7 8s 6d for the rent: '. . . I *can't* speak to her when I'm in debt like this.' Over the course of the novel, Holtby systematically demolishes the props that have underpinned Caroline's dignity and will to survive; her hopes of love, fortune and status disintegrate, until eventually her world collapses around her. A motor-car runs her over in Westbourne Grove, and she ends her days abandoned in a bleak public infirmary, her faith only intact. Poor Caroline indeed.

Winifred Holtby died too young to endure her heroine's fate, but single women who lived into old age had the all too real prospect of facing death alone. Norah Elliott was born in 1903. Her working life appears to have been spent as a schoolteacher, but as it drew to a close she seems to have been consumed with regret and pain. A brief memoir she wrote in old age gives little away, but there are clues that in her childhood her family was forced by poverty into the workhouse, leaving her to be adopted. But only remnants are now left to tell the world of Miss Elliott's sadness as she contemplated her final lonely days on earth and wondered whether oblivion or rest with her creator awaited her. One gusty September day, when she was eighty, she picked up pen and paper to try to express in blank verse her sense of the suffering that threatened to engulf her:

> Another dark, cold, rainy day,
> So I am truanting from chapel
> And will spend my time alone
> Whilst the slow hours drag on relentlessly.
> Death seems like a long-awaited friend
> When the future holds no hope of joy . . .
>
> Neglect and loneliness waiting to attend
> My last hours, when soon I'll expect to know . . .
>
> To discover how my unconscious choices
> Led to arthritic pains and suffering,
> To virginity that fled from love,
> Longings for love buried by fear,

So that they died and left me feeling
That I have thwarted my destiny.

Another teacher, Miss Ethel Wragg, wrestled to come to terms with her enforced lack of companionship. She wrote a diary in which she weighed up her enjoyment of privacy against the deprivation of solitude. Miss Wragg, who was forty-five, worked in Wirral, and Sunday 12 September 1937 found her happily giving herself the treat of breakfast in bed alone. Small comforts like this seemed to her extra special. A once-a-week luxury, the relaxation allowed her to think uninterrupted, and she indulged in the mental pleasure, for her, of attempting to solve some mathematical problems. Somewhere in the background, barely heard, a door opened and closed:

Suddenly, I cry a halt to this wandering, because I am feeling sorry that there is no one here with whom to talk . . .

Miss Wragg stopped herself at this point because she realised that she was at risk of sliding into an abyss of self-pity. She had caught the sound of Miss J., her fellow-lodger, leaving the house. The distant clatter recalled her to the fact that she was alone, and that her cogitations could have no interest to Miss J. There was a friend with whom she could have discussed her interest in mathematics, '. . . but she is miles away'.

While I was retracing my thoughts, I suddenly realised that at the bottom of my mind was a want for a friend – & this desire was working up into consciousness through a whole lot of extraneous thoughts – as it were . . .
Conscious finally that I want a friend to talk to – I ask myself why? The answer: – to lose myself in the friendship – to enter into the unconsciousness of friendship. The answer was a shock. Do I crave friendships then in order to escape from life as it is? There is aloneness today. I want to think about friendship. What is it? . . . I realise that on Sunday there is time to think.

With awareness came reconciliation. By evening Miss Wragg was able to look back with satisfaction over her day and pass over that moment's fear of the abyss. It had gone.

9.30 I realise that I have been quietly happy and content to be alone.

In the same year Harriet Warrack, a thirty-three-year-old single laboratory worker, was surveyed about her social life. She listed her friends and acquaintances. Out of forty-eight people, twenty-eight were women friends, and of these twenty-one were spinsters, whose average age was thirty. (Of all her male acquaintance, only one was a bachelor.) The brief descriptions of her friends given by Miss Warrack are enlightening:

Female. Known about 20 years. Spinster aged 30 years. Studied music. Shorthand typist. She has a small private income and does not have to earn her own living but does so because she is bored at home and does not get on with her mother who thinks she should be married.
Social circle.

Female. Known 6 years. Spinster, age 26 years. Insurance clerk . . . Would like to have a man friend and get married but is not very attractive to men which gives her a rather aggressive attitude to those she meets.
Lives at my digs. Social circle.

Female. Spinster aged 35 – Shorthand typist . . . Takes very little interest in politics or world affairs – occasionally reads the newspaper and a novel. Whole life is rather unhappy as feels she is a failure because she has not got married although very attractive and good-looking; still hopes to meet a wealthy man who will supply her with a handsome home.
Social and work.

Female. Known 7 yrs, age 45. Spinster, clerk, very conservative – lived with invalid mother for many years and looked after her entirely. Mother has now died so she is beginning to go out more. Rather frightened of losing her job as has made no provision for old age. Reads daily newspaper and very little else.
Work circle.

Evidently, as a working woman, Harriet Warrack was thrown among others of her kind. She may not have deliberately sought to make friendships among other single women, but it is surely likely that she made common cause with their predicament.

Not surprisingly, single women often look to each other for attachments. Then, as now, the feeling of being demonised and excluded from the 'smug married' world led to the pairing-up of women who shared household expenses and found companionship, understanding and closeness. In some cases such relationships often came close to the Russell definition of happy mutual love, but where they did not they were still, for many, the best thing that life could give.

## Companions, consolations

Just as it drove people apart, the war united people, sometimes with indissoluble bonds. In Essex, two little girls were growing up in the early 1900s; they went to school together. In their teens they courted two young men who were friends, and together they both agreed to marry their sweethearts. Then their boys went off to fight in the war. They were both killed. Miss Prior told this story in her eighties to the attendant who was looking after her in a home for the elderly. Miss Patch, her friend, and she were still together, sixty years later. They had never married, and though Miss Patch suffered from dementia, the two of them still chose to share a bedroom. Through thick and thin Miss Patch and Miss Prior had never parted. 'After our sweethearts died we set up home together, to share our grief. Of course, we would never have looked at anyone else.'

Vera Brittain's war had left her beached and bereft; and yet it was inconceivable to her that she return home to her parents in provincial Buxton, where their narrow-minded social circle continually tut-tutted about her failure to get a husband. Self-sufficiency was all, but self-sufficiency shared made for a less lonely independence. She and Winifred Holtby determined to survive on their scanty allowances, coaching, teaching, writing and part-time lecturing. They rented a partitioned studio in Bloomsbury. It was freezing cold, sunless and cramped. Her relatives were astounded that she could endure the discomfort – 'but to me it was Paradise'.

She and Winifred 'revell[ed] in the uninterrupted companionship of those crowded days, so busy and yet so free . . .' It was a complicated, fruitful partnership. Both were driven by literary and political ambitions, both had lived through the dark days of the war, loving and losing. Both were courageous, independent-minded feminists. For Vera, this friendship, with its intellectual guidance and practical support, went some way to replace the beloved brother Edward whom she had lost. For Winifred, it saved her from the fate of poor Caroline. Together they wrote, lectured, travelled, admired each other's clothes, cleaned the studio and cooked their dinners. Together they praised, rejoiced, commiserated and remembered.

It would be easy to cite more examples of supportive females setting up home together like this in the post-war world. The novelist Irene Rathbone, whose fiancé was killed in Iraq in 1920, just after the war had ended, set up home in Chelsea with a group of like-minded women friends. Though she was living in an emotional vacuum, the parties and cultured conversation kept her from despair, if not indifference. Ivy Compton-Burnett's world was shattered by war. She was later to excuse her lack of literary productivity between 1911 and 1925 with the consummate understatement: 'One was a good deal cut up by the war; one's brother was killed, and one had family troubles.' Noël Compton-Burnett's death, she would add, 'quite smashed my life up, it quite smashed my life up'. In 1919 Ivy moved in with the writer Margaret Jourdain, whose humour and vitality gradually restored her drained nerves.

As most women know, female friendships have the capacity to provide compatibility and love of an entirely different order to the love of a wife for a husband. In her friendship with Gwyneth Wansbrough Jones, the formidable social reformer Geraldine Aves discovered an emotional attachment which brought a deep level of fulfilment to both their lives. Gwyneth shared Geraldine's devout faith; they were fellow pilgrims. 'It is good to be able to travel together . . .' wrote Gwyneth, '. . . and although we have different obstacles to climb over, I expect we can help each other with them, and that there will sometimes be a rainbow that we see all the more clearly because there are two of us.' Love could be expressed in practical ways too; at the age of forty the pianist Myra Hess was rescued from crushing loneliness and despair after the death of her mother by the devoted ministrations of her new secretary, Anita Gunn. Anita, known as 'Saz', was to remain at Myra Hess's side for more than thirty years. There was nothing she would not do for her. On tour she packed, took phone calls, pacified impresarios and agents, got them in and out of hotels and concert halls, shopped, ironed, and played double solitaire between fixtures. According to Saz they had 'high old times' and 'roared with laughter from morning till night'.

★

Such relationships were the 'shining threads in my life', 'golden cords, strong and untarnishable', or simply 'a real insurance for old age'. Whether or not one chose to share a roof, single women cite friendship more than any other factor as contributing to their happiness and fulfilment. The psychologist Esther Harding stressed that one of the results of women forced to seek each other's company was the evolution of female friendships into something of unprecedented value.

But if friendship offered solace and companionship to the single woman, how much more might the ready-made relationship between sisters provide an anchorage for women adrift? Many without husbands gratefully accepted the consolation and continuity offered by that closest of confidantes. As Irving Berlin famously wrote:

Sisters, sisters,
There were never such devoted sisters,
Never had to have a chaperone, no sir,
I'm there to keep my eye on her –
Caring, sharing,
Every little thing that we are wearing . . .

If they ever performed it, no song could have been more appropriate to Elsie and Doris Waters, musicians and comedians who lived, sang and entertained the nation together for over forty years. They were East Enders, Elsie born in 1893, her sister six years later. Show business was in their blood; Edward Waters, their father, ran his family like the von Trapps, as a performing troupe comprising himself, his wife and their six children Art, Jack, Bill, Sam, Elsie and Doll. Blacked up as minstrels and dubbed E. W. Winter and his Bijou Orchestra, they appeared at church bazaars and seaside concerts at Clacton-on-Sea. Elsie and Doris never married, but always lived together, and such was their success that no man could have provided for them better. Moreover, they were completely interdependent.

It was after the war that Elsie and Doll's duo career took off, and soon they were being paid £8 a week for their stage double act. Wireless broadcasts followed, and the sisters got up a comedy turn combining jokes and crosstalk with musical numbers; in character Elsie was Gert and Doris was Daisy, two gossipy old charladies dissecting their sweethearts, and other people's, or commenting on births, marriages and deaths from the sidelines. Their Cockney accents breathed life into the stuffy atmosphere of the pre-war BBC, which in those days tended to be grandiloquent in tone. By the late 1930s Gert and Daisy were already firm favourites with Queen Elizabeth (later the Queen Mother), and were being booked to appear in royal variety performances. After the Second World War they were both made OBE, starred in three major cinema films, and had two elephants at London zoo named after them. Elsie outlived her younger sister by twelve years, but for two talented girls from Poplar, life could have had little more to offer.

Talent and resourcefulness gave women like this the possibility of making their own way in life; with the love and support of a sister setbacks could be overcome and ambitions realised. Tess, Una and Carmen Dillon set out to succeed, survived in a man's world, and all became prominent in their fields.

The girls were the three youngest of six children. Strict Catholics, the Dillon parents were not rich but, determined that all their offspring should have the opportunity to attain success in life, they made the necessary sacrifices to educate them well. None of the three sisters married; all three were high-flyers.

Tess took a first-class science degree and became head of physics at Queen Elizabeth College, London. Una was drawn into the world of publishing, bought a dilapidated bookshop in Store Street, Bloomsbury, and exerted considerable energies into turning it around. Dressed in a tweed suit, she bicycled round London delivering orders to her customers. Dillon's Bookshop thrived, attracting an academic and literary clientèle, and by the time of her retirement in 1967 Una had expanded into large new premises, cornered the market in teacher training manuals and educational texts, and entered into partnership with London University.

Carmen Dillon meanwhile developed into a talented artist, whose initial leaning was towards architecture. Friendship with the film art director Ralph Brinton led to a career in films – not, in those days, an easy option. The British film industry found it hard to accept the presence of a woman on set, and Carmen was forced to endure reproaches from all sides: women shouldn't be taking men's jobs, women can't work within budgets, women must not give orders to men or step on to the studio floor. She stuck it out and in 1937 was made chief art director at Wembley Studios. She worked with Sir Laurence Olivier, and her résumé was to include such notable films as his *Henry V* (1944) and Joseph Losey's *The Go-Between* (1970). For twenty-five years of her thirty-five-year career she was the only woman art director in Britain.

For forty-four years Tess, Una and Carmen shared a mansion flat in Kensington High Street. Religion, science, travel, art, books and music enriched their lives. Could marriage or children have given them more, without also detracting from such abundance?

Gert and Daisy were two halves of a whole; the three Dillon sisters, while taking quite separate paths in life, were inseparably joined. But the equation for arriving at such geometry doesn't always balance. Take Florence and Annie White.

Florence White had a mission. In April 1935 she set up the National Spinsters Pensions Association to fight for the right to pensions of unmarried working women. And she struck a chord: 600 women attended the first meeting of the NSPA; four months later nearly 8,000 had joined, and by December the Association had sixteen branches spread across the north of England. Florence, who was now nearly fifty, had found her life's work, and it was full-time. She was determined to make the nation 'spinster conscious'. Campaigning, organising petitions and speaking at rallies left no time for dressmaking and piano lessons, which all through the 20s had kept the wolf from Florence and Annie's door. She could never have kept going had it not been for her sister's practical turn of mind.

Annie had been a keen amateur playwright, with several local successes to her name, but now there was a need for a more reliable income. Back home in south Bradford, she had been attending night classes in confectionery. In 1929 the sisters opened a confectioner's and baker's in Lidget Green, where to begin with – inevitably – Annie did all the baking and Florence iced the cakes and served the customers. They lived over the shop. Somehow, Florence combined her political activities with decorating iced fancies and slicing up parkin. But when the NSPA took off, the buns and flapjacks were handed back to Annie. Florence slept at the shop, but that was all.

Annie was back-up. She baked the cakes and ran the business. Not only that, she turned her literary talent to writing Florence's speeches and acted as her secretary. Help had to be brought in. Imperious as ever, Florence leant on her niece Dorothy to leave her job at the mill and come into the shop, and another local girl, Bertha, was hired to bake. Joe Wells, an elderly and mild-mannered uncle who had settled into cosy retirement, was cajoled out again and prevailed upon to do part-time clerical work for the movement. Then they got a delivery boy with a bicycle.

Every day, while Annie and Bertha toiled in the bake house, Florence was out on the campaign trail – Manchester, Stockport, Leeds, Leicester. Her return was an anxious moment at the Lidget Green shop. Had her day gone well? Interfering and bossy, she was much given to smashing crockery and throwing things, and when she was on the premises tension could mount. The bicycle boy would spot her first. 'Florrie's back,' he would call, and the household would hold its breath. If Florence found things not to her liking there would be hell to pay.

One day in the busy run-up to Christmas Bertha blundered over a tricky cake recipe; a whole batch went wrong, and though Annie was sympathetic she agreed that the cakes were unsaleable. Best to pop them down in the cellar for now and get on with making a new batch; the spoilt ones could be got rid of later. That same day Florence got home earlier than expected. Powerless to prevent her, Annie followed horrified as her sister went down to the cellar and discovered the spoilt cakes. Upstairs, the nieces cowered as battle ensued, descending some time later to find the cellar strewn with crumbs and currants, the debris of their frenzied bombardment.

Rows between the sisters erupted with terrifying frequency, and Annie could give as good as she got. If you walked into the middle of one you took the consequences. Uncle Joe appeared one day bearing a well-meaning treat, some prime steak – a rare luxury in that stretched household. Unluckily he walked in exactly as Florence and Annie were deep into a stormy exchange – no missiles this time – and Florence was winning. Annie, in a rage, stomped off to bed. Uncle Joe put the steak on a plate and tiptoed up to her room, where he gingerly placed it on her bedside table. The peace offering could not have been more misjudged. Annie leapt out of bed in her bloomers and vest, yelled at poor Joe in her broadest Bradford to get out of the house and pretty quick too, and hurled the steak down the stairs after his retreating form with all her might. It wouldn't do to waste good food. Joe picked it up and washed it and put it in the pantry. Then he went home.

But Annie was always there for her sister. She was secretary, editor, speech-writer, companion, political hostess, cook, home-maker. Neither ever considered for a moment leaving the other; neither doubted the other's worth. Through triumphs and crises they were shoulder to shoulder, working to the same end. The things that mattered to them were taken for granted, unspoken and unquestioned, as such things are in families – their cat Ginger, for instance. During the Second World War the White sisters offered refuge to a spinster who had been evacuated from Bethnal Green. This lady had the misfortune to step backwards off a chair and accidentally land on Ginger. At the time Florence was addressing a combined meeting of the NSPA London branches at the Bonnington Hotel. In the middle of this she got an urgent telegram from Annie: 'Come home at once. Ginger ill.' Florence was on the next train back to Bradford. Sadly there was no hope for the cat, who had suffered internal injuries. Both the sisters were prostrated with grief. 'Auntie Florence was crying for days,' remembered Dorothy. 'We dared not mention his name for weeks and his collar had to be kept safely in a drawer.'

In 1940 Florence White's campaign bore fruit. Insured spinsters over sixty would get ten shillings a week. It was not as good as she had hoped for, and she was to continue fighting for a better deal, but it was a major concession by the government, and a personal triumph. The tributes poured in from her supporters. In the words of a Bradford factory worker: 'All the spinsters in England should rise today and salute her.' And the following couplets were sent in from a schoolchild admirer:

> God made each maid a husband
> But men on earth must fight,
> So just in case there aren't enough
> He made Miss Florence White.

In 1946 Florence herself started receiving her old age pension. By then the shop was getting too much, and the years of campaigning had taken their toll on her health; one day, after spending seven hours in the lobby at the House of Commons, she suffered a mild heart attack. In 1955 she and Annie turned their backs on Bradford and retired to a two-bedroom bungalow in Morecambe. They were still quarrelsome, still affectionate, still inseparable. But now it was Annie's turn to be looked after, payback time, and she made the most of it. Querulously complaining of a series of ailments, she languished in bed while Florence devotedly ran around cooking and keeping house. It was all a front. Florence would go to great lengths to smooth counterpanes and bring her sister dainty meals before she left the house, but no sooner was the door closed behind her than Annie was out of bed and buttoning her blouse ready for a walk or an outing. By the time Florence got home, there was Annie back in bed again, surrounded by pills and patent medicines. In the event, Florence died first, in 1961, when she was seventy-five, collapsing suddenly as she prepared to go out and deliver an address to the Yorkshire Society Ladies' Section.

★

Florence White's campaign to get financial help for spinsters grew not only out of her awareness of the poverty of lower-paid single women, but from the reality of such women's lives, whose scanty incomes often had to stretch to support their relatives. Today it is unlikely that an unmarried daughter would accept meekly that her lot in life was to live with and look after her parents. But in the nineteenth and early twentieth centuries that duty was taken for granted. Women were, above all else, carers. If they had no husband to care for, they must care for their nearest and dearest, and so it fell to the spinsters to take on this often thankless task. Jobless, or on low wages, keeping elderly, often invalid dependants out of the workhouse could be a desperate, hand-to-mouth business.

Florence had first-hand experience of this situation. She herself had little in common with her mother, but there was never any question of leaving her to fend for herself. James White, their feckless father, had been mostly absent when she and Annie were growing up, and had died when they were in their late teens. Caroline White lived with her spinster daughters for the rest of her life. She had her uses in fact, for, while practically illiterate, she did the housework, but Florence had no intention of making sacrifices. Mother shared a bedroom with Annie, and was finally moved up to the attic, while Florence occupied the 'best' room. Nevertheless, there

Caroline remained until her death in the early 1930s, by which time her daughters were well into middle age.

And this situation was entirely typical, entirely accepted. At the turn of the century an estimated 300,000 women were at home looking after their elderly parents.

Doris Smith had been a primary school teacher all her working life. In her hundred-and-first year Miss Smith – very frail, very deaf, at times confused – was living in a residential home in Ascot. I went there to ask her about her memories.

The extremely old often seem to look back on their past as on a landscape blotted out by heavy snowfall. All is white and drifting, save for the few distinct landmarks that interrupt the muffled scenery: a steeple, a tree, a tower. For Doris Smith, that tower was her mother. Marriage 'wasn't to be'. Sometimes she regretted it. But Doris's mother was an invalid and this fact, as she said, 'planned my life'. Mother couldn't be left. There was a sister who cared for her during the day while Doris was at work; then when Doris came home, it was her turn. It left no time for anything else, '. . . and if I had got married, what would have happened to Mother?' What had been the high point of her life? I asked her. The drifts cleared; Doris's reply was faint but unhesitating: 'It was when I got my college certificate, which meant I could earn more money to look after Mother. The extra salary meant I was able to help more.' Nothing was more prominent in this woman's century-long life than the attachment and sense of responsibility she felt towards her ailing parent.

In such relationships, devotion was assumed on both sides, but daughters, willing and loving as they might be, often found themselves imprisoned by their sense of filial duty. There were cases where young women who might have married felt unable to leave because of family responsibility. If they worked, they did so in order to contribute to the family budget. And consciously or not, the older generation often leant on unmarried daughters to stay that way, on the assumption that their place was the parental home. Radclyffe Hall's novel *The Unlit Lamp* (1928) explores the tug of love that left Joan Ogden a spinster, shackled to her needy mother. The claims of Elizabeth, her closest female friend, and Richard, who wants to marry her, fail to weigh beside those of the traditional mother-daughter bond. But Richard is appalled:

'How long is it to go on,' he cried, 'This preying of the weak on the strong, the old on the young; this hideous, unnatural injustice that one sees all around one, this incredibly wicked thing that tradition sanctifies? . . . She's like an octopus who's drained you dry . . . a thing that preys on the finest instincts of others, and sucks the very soul out of them.'

Margaret Howes, another resident of a care home in the west of England, now in her late nineties, might not have described her mother as an octopus, but she was like Joan Ogden in feeling unable to put her own needs first. A matter-of-fact and intelligent woman, Miss Howes was stoical about the raw deal life had dealt her; for there was something tragic, if unsensational, about her situation. Imperceptibly, over time, Margaret's mother robbed her of the ability to love.

As a young woman Margaret had ambitions to be a teacher or a nurse, but she was persuaded out of them. The training would have meant residence in a hostel, and Mrs Howes needed her daughter at home. Instead, she lowered her sights and got a job as a dressmaker. Margaret's mother also was a semi-invalid (is it uncharitable to speculate that these weakly women might perhaps have recovered if left to their own devices?). In any case, it was particularly impressed upon Margaret that as a girl her place was at home, looking after her mother. The job at a West End garment wholesaler's was designed to help contribute towards her mother's hospital bills, which would otherwise have completely drained her father's earnings as a railway boiler-maker.

Any thoughts Margaret might have had of marriage, or even of a better career, were ruled out by her circumstances. 'I would have liked to have trained as a nurse, but my parents couldn't afford it. My mother's attitude was that it was all right for my brother to leave home, but if I wanted to that was different. According to Mother, what was wrong with home?'

Escape via marriage was simply impractical. For a start, according to Mrs Howes, it was impossible to 'throw yourself' at a man. '*He* will find *you* . . . and I never had time, or any money. Women did not go out to work, and if a girl married she expected her husband to keep her. It was just not the thing for married women to go to work. My mother was in and out of hospital so many times, and I was never free. I think, looking back, there was possibly a bit of moral blackmail. My brother could do what he liked, he got married and had children, but a girl's function was to stay at home . . .'.

Both Margaret's parents died when she was in her thirties, and she was overwhelmed with relief at finally finding freedom. But by then the loving impulse had, in her view, atrophied in her. 'I wouldn't describe myself as a very emotional person. Over the years, not having any emotional stimulus when I was at the right age for it, it hasn't been fostered . . . and then it dies. Love isn't everything in life . . .'

Suffocated by her mother's needs, Margaret Howes turned her back on intimacy, looked solitude in the face, and learnt over the years not to pity herself. 'Lonely? Well, I've lived alone for many, many years, and it's gone on so long now that one doesn't feel it so much. It's what one has become accustomed to. The difficulties that occurred were my own difficulties, not someone else's difficulties.' During the Blitz she and her mother had sheltered from bombs in the coal-cellar together, and after her death the fear and loneliness of the air-raids so crushed her that she could almost have wished her mother back; but it was never so bad again. She got a place at Bedford College to study social sciences, acquired a dog, developed a thirst for education, travel, walking and agriculture, and ended up working in local government. 'Life's a gamble, but it's also what you make it. If you ask me who the most important person is in my life, it's myself,' she said.

★

Synonymous with home, mothers at the turn of the century were established as the gravitational centre of a child's universe. The novelist Phyllis Bentley described her mother Eleanor (always known by her husband as Nellie) in terms of the very architecture that sheltered them: she was 'the queen of the house, the pillar, the roof-tree . . . we were all attached to her . . . with every fibre of our being'. When Phyllis's own dreams of marriage receded, the pull of home drew her inexorably to her mother's side; with few intervals, she remained there until her mother's death at the age of ninety-one, by which time Phyllis herself was fifty-five.

Nellie was widowed in 1926. There were three sons, but Phyllis, as unmarried daughter, now became responsible for her mother. This responsibility invaded every aspect of her life for the next twenty-three years. She now dealt with all the household bills and business matters, with travel and holidays; her money, and above all her time, were not her own, and when her mother fell ill she nursed her. Even when she was away from home Phyllis wrote to Nellie every day. In the gaps she was struggling to write novels. She was endlessly patient.

For Nellie could be a monster, terrifyingly unpredictable. Impetuous and wilful, she could not understand her children's feelings, enraging and distressing them. On a good day she would happily spend hours reminiscing, vividly drawing on her fascinatingly detailed memories of Huddersfield history, which Phyllis then used to embroider her own narratives. But all too often, particularly when the Depression of the early 1930s hit the family textiles business, Nellie would allow rage, fear and impatience to get the better of her: 'If you don't finish that novel soon, I shall leave you and go away!' she would cry.

As her health deteriorated Nellie's demands grew while her patience dwindled yet more. It fell to Phyllis to keep her petulant mother entertained, and taking the frail invalid shopping, on outings, or to the theatre was an ordeal. Too proud to be helped, but too weak to walk far, she would fight every offer of assistance. Risking the wrath of policemen, Phyllis would park the car in front of a theatre in the pouring rain, settle her mother into the auditorium, before dashing back to re-park and return soaked and dishevelled to her own seat just in time for the curtain to rise – only to have her mother complain peevishly, 'Where have you been all this time? Your hair's very untidy . . .' When she could no longer leave the house, Nellie became increasingly difficult and eccentric. She developed an obsession with wanting to warm and air clothes. Phyllis would go out for half an hour and return to find underwear, sheets or even mattresses strewn around the open hearth; 'I was terrified lest something catch fire.' Nellie endlessly scolded her daughter for her inadequacies; she was late, messy, neglectful. ' "I hope you never write another novel!" she exclaimed once angrily when I did not run fast enough to answer her bell. "Every time *you* write a novel *I* age ten years." '

But Phyllis never wavered in her care and love. Nellie always came first. Only when work made inescapable demands did she leave her mother; for nothing else would she abandon her. 'For though I sometimes felt a frustration, a bitterness, a resentment almost amounting to hatred of my mother, I also loved her, and could not break her heart.' On the rare occasions when Nellie was quiescent, she would lay her head on her daughter's breast and, one evening, when Phyllis had washed her, combed her and tucked her up, she settled on her pillows, looked up lovingly, and said, 'I hope when you grow old you'll have somebody as nice as you to look after you.' It was reward enough.

Resolute and saintly, Phyllis would have given up writing to look after her mother, if they had not needed that income to help pay for her care. The novels and articles were a necessity, not a luxury, but she was beset with difficulties in getting them written. She had to cook, serve and clear meals, dust and clean, dress and nurse the invalid. Getting a few hours to herself was incredibly hard. Her work suffered, she fell ill, and for the last five years of her mother's life she was almost unable to write.

At last in 1949 Nellie died, quietly, in her daughter's arms. What kind of love was this, that consumed and almost destroyed the bestower? Phyllis Bentley's feelings for her mother were a stressful and complicated mix of love, rage, tenderness, pity, resentment. Nellie's needs replaced those of husband, child and, almost, career. No marriage could have asked more of her. Their relationship drained Phyllis of all her emotional resources; she gave it all she had to give. And when it was over:

I am fully aware how ungrateful, how cruel, how tragic for my mother it sounds when I say that the five years after her death were a period of great personal happiness for me. But so it was.

Uncomplicated delight in simple things now returned to her life. The weather, cups of tea, the sea, walks on the Pennines, train journeys, friendships:

After April 1949 I was free to enjoy all these ordinary pleasures of humanity without a sense of guilt. I was no longer neglecting my duty if I indulged in them. Free, and without a sense of guilt – those are the operative words . . . I crammed my life joyously with activities.

Phyllis's literary career continued to flourish, and her belief in the brother-hood of man sustained her enterprise. Recognition and admiration came to her in her lifetime. Anyone pitying the spinster for her loveless life might well consider how depleting and exhausting love can be, and how its converse – solitude, independence and the freedom to work – can liberate and fulfil.

★

It was Angela du Maurier's view that spinster daughters never quite flew free. Never having a husband, the gold standard for all their relationships and achievements was a parental one. She confessed that in her own case, even years after their deaths, her parents' influence continued to cramp her vision. 'Daddy' always wore a tie; he would never have worn shorts, even in summer. What a deplorable fashion! And nobody's housekeeping measured up to Mummie's.

The writer Elizabeth Goudge, born in 1900, was another of these uncriti-cal spinster daughters. As an only child, she revered her parents. Her father, an ordained academic, was a pious, hard-working man, a vigorous, manly scholar of monk-like simplicity. Her mother was intrepid, charming, vivaci-ous and something of a grande dame. But she too was ill. When Elizabeth was quite a small child, Ida Goudge collapsed with terrible pains in her head; some form of poisoning appeared to have nearly paralysed her and she could barely move. Ida's youth was over, and from that time on, with periodic remissions, she was never well again. For her daughter, from then on, everything outside caring for her took second place.

Elizabeth, a much-loved child, grew up surrounded by beauty, in Wells, Ely, Oxford and Hampshire. But her schooling was inadequate, and her memoirs reveal a kind of passive helplessness in the face of fate. In Ely straight after the war she fell in love. 'It ended in tears, of course. Does not every first love end in tears?' What then was to become of her?

Parents of that era realised that unless their daughters had exceptional beauty and charm they would not marry. The First World War left few young men alive. The phrase used at that time, 'the lost generation', sounds poetical but it was the truth . . . And so at that time there were millions more women than men in England.

Elizabeth had learnt to write passably, but that didn't seem to offer prospects of earning a living. Nursing? It turned out that she had a heart complaint and the arduous training would kill her. 'So we had to think again.' Ida now decided to have her daughter trained as a handicrafts teacher, but though she attempted for a while to instruct children in embroidery and leatherwork, Elizabeth found she missed home. As an invalid, Ida was living a confined life with one devoted servant on the Hampshire coast, her beloved husband joining her whenever he could be released from his work as Professor of Divinity in Oxford. And it was here at Barton-on-Sea that Elizabeth found herself as a writer. 'My handicraft training was not now providing me with what I wanted, a home-based career so that I could be with my mother as much as possible . . .' she recalled. *Island Magic* was written in a corner of her mother's bedroom at Barton. The novel was acclaimed and her career as a writer blossomed, but at that period little else in her life proved fertile. At Barton her mother continued to be racked with pain and illness. Operations succeeded each other; after each one she nearly died. Elizabeth herself now fell into a pit of depression in which she doubted her faith and ultimately her own identity. This was followed by a terrifying nervous breakdown. Then in 1939 her father died. 'Between my father and my mother the closeness had been lifelong. They had been almost one person. What the parting meant to her she allowed no one to know.'

Ida and Elizabeth now clung to each other like shipwrecked passengers; on their raft they were joined by the family nanny. The three of them moved to Devon. Here through the air raids of the 1940s mother and daughter shared a bed – 'determined to be together whatever happened'.

With the night-time bombers booming over nearby Plymouth, each super-stitiously clutched the object most precious to her: Ida, her jewel-case, and Elizabeth, the manuscript of what was to become her best-seller, *Green Dolphin Country*. After its publication in 1944 financial anxiety was at an end.

For six devoted years after the war Elizabeth nursed her mother: a long, hard struggle, made worse by Ida's mental collapse. She died at last in 1951. And now Elizabeth, in her fifties, was finally alone.

★

But not quite alone. The index of Elizabeth Goudge's autobiography includes an entry under 'Dogs'. It lists the following: Brownie, Coach, Froda, Max, Randa, Swankie and Tiki – in total twenty-two pages cover a lifetime of fox terriers, half-breeds, spaniels, chows and Dandie-Dinmonts. Here, undoubtedly, Elizabeth found love. Brownie had a noble forehead and paced beside her with dignity on their walks. A 'perfect being . . .', he '. . . had no faults . . . [and] he loved deeply'. What human being could measure up to Brownie?

Not quite so anthropomorphised, the three Dandies – Tiki, Randa and Froda – became known as the Hobbits. Like Tolkien's sub-humans, they had 'the art of disappearing swiftly and silently', 'and like the Hobbits they have large furry feet'. Each was loved in its own special way. Tiki, like a witch's familiar, had special perceptions, and could always tell in advance when her mistress was coming home. Randa was 'a beautiful film-star . . . a fine lady who liked to pose on silken cushions'. Froda was 'a fairy creature who . . . [appears and disappears] like a gleam of sunshine, aloof and mysterious in her fantasy world'.

[I believe] that the love we have for our animals insures their immortality for as long as the love lasts . . .

wrote Elizabeth.

This was perhaps the kind of thing that the psychologists were warning against. Maude Royden, the feminist and preacher, felt compassionate pity for the countless maiden ladies whose sentimental attachments to their pets inspired ridicule. 'I think of the imbecilities in which the repressed instinct has sought its pitiful baffled release, of the adulation lavished on a parrot, a cat, a lap-dog . . .' And Laura Hutton, in her appraisal of single solitude, *The Single Woman and Her Emotional Problems* (1935), also remarked on how frequently the middle-aged and lonely found outlets for their emotional life in exaggerated and doting affection for animals: '. . . a love which is so often made fun of, but is so real to the lover . . .'

Angela du Maurier was under no illusion about the fact that her adulation of dogs was a replacement for other loves. At twenty-two Angela had met 'a god-like individual' while on holiday on the Riviera. 'This was IT at last . . . for two months life was at its most blissful.' For that brief span she indulged her fantasies to the full; there were to be blue delphiniums as she walked up the aisle; her best friends would all be there . . . and then he jilted her. Nursing a broken heart, Angela walked into Selfridges . . .

. . . and there found the person who was my one true love for fourteen years. She cost me six guineas only, and she was Chinese. I called her Wendy. Wendy Pansy Posy Lollypop Stone-Martin . . . She was a *tiny Pekinese*. Just three months old.

But she would not concede that the Pekinese was limited by her animal nature. 'Wendy . . . was a Person.' She was astoundingly intelligent, wilful, musical ('she would roll over in ecstasy when she heard the Fire Music of the *Walküre*'); she was also an intrepid traveller, talented rat-catcher, and all-round terrific sport. For Angela, there was 'something fundamentally lacking in the type of person who does not believe that animals have souls':

If you have a dog you need never feel alone. Their companionship is one of the most precious things in life . . . Their very silence can show affection, and the expression in a dog's eyes will give its heart away. I have cried with them and blasphemed in their company, and they have quietly looked up, and perhaps licked one's hand, or even put their paws on one's lap. The dog that loves its owner and who is loved in turn always knows when something is amiss.

Maude Royden and Laura Hutton were both understanding of the need to be needed by small powerless creatures; they could see how strong was the impulse which drove such women to discharge their emotional energies on an animal. The energies were normal. It was all a question of finding balance, self-knowledge and adjustment to the 'rich resources of life in our present age'. Each woman had her own personal contribution to make, married or unmarried.

Cicely Hamilton lived with a cat called Peterkin, and she was clear-sighted about Peterkin's role in her life. She herself contributed greatly over the years. As a writer, campaigner for women's rights, teacher and journalist, she was a committed and lifelong feminist. Early on she had come to recognise that frittering her life away trying to be attractive to the opposite

sex was a waste of her valuable time, and that her ambitions would be
unachievable with a husband in tow. Choosing not to marry was for her a
cool-headed decision. Cicely was emphatically not uncomfortable about
living alone, '. . . like the traditional spinster, with a cat for company'. In
her sixties, after a busy life, she found solitude brought contentment. But
the cat helped. Cicely was as absorbed by the qualities of her beloved
Peterkin, with whom she poses on the frontispiece of her autobiography
(*Life Errant*, 1935), as Elizabeth Goudge and Angela du Maurier were by
their dogs. Cats, Cicely claimed, made better companions in a solitary
household than dogs. Dogs were too apt to give 'persistent, uncritical
worship . . .', whereas cats did not suffer fools. With a cat around, you
didn't need a human companion to tell you your faults. Though fond of
her, Peterkin was, like all his species, selfish and lazy, and Cicely felt that
his presence was a salutary rebuke to her own tendencies to moral turpitude.

With a cat there is no need of the human antidote; the cat is not given to worship.
It is affectionate – that I can testify – but without any element of fawning; rather
is it balefully authoritative. However humble its immediate ancestry, it remembers
its divine descent; born in the gutter it will enter a drawing-room and take the
best chair for itself!

## Other people's babies

In truth, such pets were the babies these women never had; little, needy
and lovable, they drew out the caring, protective nature of their owners.
But many childless women found careers looking after real babies. For them
the deep emotions of motherhood could in some measure be echoed, if
not replicated, in the intimacy between a nursemaid or nanny and her
charges.

Pretty Nell Naylor was a typical case, a labourer's daughter from Lincolnshire who met her fiancé when she was fresh out of nanny training college
in 1912. Nursemaiding might have seen her through till their marriage, but
the young man was killed, and Nell never got her own babies to look after.
From the age of twenty-four she appears to have given up hope of love. 'She
never bothered with that sort of thing from then on . . .' her great-niece
remembered. While the war lasted she helped nurse injured soldiers, from
a sense, perhaps, that further needless deaths could be prevented. After the
war was over she joined the exodus to the Dominions, finding a job
nannying in Canada. In 1921 she returned to England. For the rest of her
life she nurtured, loved and cared for a succession of fortunate upper-

middle-class boys and girls. 'We adored her; she was in every sense a member of the family . . .' one of these remembered.

The children's nurse Miss Olive Wakeham was another; 'I loved those children – all of them!' Her babies were as well looked after by her, as cuddled and cared for as they were by their own mothers, and perhaps better. Lady's maid Rose Harrison's relationship with young Michael Cranborne is another instance of mutually adoring companions. It would not be hard to produce more cases where lower-class nannies were indeed far more loved, trusted and confided in by the children of the often remote and uncaring upper classes. The children, when they grew up and wrote their memoirs, were eloquent about these carers, who soothed their fears, kept their secrets, protected and loved them; from Winston Churchill to Edward Sackville-West, Frances Partridge to the Marquis of Bath, they paid them ample tribute.

But the nannies themselves rarely committed their emotions to paper. It is hard to find accounts that illustrate how the abundant love felt by these working-class women for their privileged charges to some extent compensated for its shortfall in their own lives. One can only conjecture. But that the children's love was reciprocated is beyond doubt.

Nanny Robertson joined the Eyre family in 1935 when she was forty, and stayed twenty years. She was smiley and plain, with wild hair that she liked to brush into buoyant and uncontrolled coiffures. Completely calm, simple, and somehow heroic, she dedicated herself to her surrogate family of seven children. Their lives were hers. For eight years she never took a day off; her generosity was boundless. Peter, the second boy, recalled: 'She was very demonstrative. She hugged us all a lot. She never got angry . . . Her own life and concerns did not seem to interest her . . .' (perhaps she had none?) and '. . . she was always bringing us presents'. Peter once asked Nanny Robertson whether she had ever had a boyfriend, but she wasn't forthcoming. ' "I knew a young man who tried to be cheeky to me on a bridge. I gave him a good hiding." The feeling was that she had had a hairbrush handy.'

Nanny Robertson left when Peter was fifteen. She settled in the south of England with her sisters, wrote to the Eyres all the time, and continued to send them presents on any excuse. They would visit her, and there was always a huge nursery tea, with masses of cake. Peter bought her a dog. 'She died when I was abroad. I cried for days. Her life seemed somehow so pathetic in retrospect, devoted to us.'

That sense of pathos is most piquantly captured in A. P. Herbert's 1930 ballad, 'Other People's Babies – A Song of Kensington Gardens':

Babies? It's a gift, my dear; and I should say I know,
For I've been pushing prams about for forty years or so;
Thirty-seven babies – or is it thirty-nine?
No, I'm wrong; it's thirty-six – but none of them was mine.

*Other people's babies*
*That's my life!*
*Mother to dozens*
*And nobody's wife.*
*But then, it isn't everyone can say*
*They used to bath the Honourable Hay,*
*Lord James Montague, Sir Richard Twistle-Thynnes,*
*Captain Cartlet and the Ramrod twins.*
*Other people's babies,*
*Other people's prams,*
*Such little terrors,*
*Such little lambs!*
*Sixty-one today,*
*And ought to be a granny;*
*Sixty-one today*
*And nothing but a Nanny!*
*There, ducky, there,*
*Did the lady stare?*
*Don't cry! Oh, my!*
*Other people's babies!*

In the absence of first-hand evidence from the nannies themselves, A. P.
Herbert's Nanny offers a voice from the past – but one that is, perhaps,
rather a construction than a reality. Jonathan Gathorne-Hardy wrote a book
about nannies,★ and although he agrees that there was 'a tragic side to a
Nanny's life . . . a melancholy note of renounced happiness . . .', he also
suggests a more complex state of affairs. According to him, some of these
women were in truth relieved that the children were not their own, and
feared being burdened with the deeper level of responsibility carried by a
mother. 'They instinctively knew that they could never marry and have
children because of their fear and dislike of sex and their reluctance to
assume the burdens of family life.' Did women take up nannying because
they didn't want husbands, or couldn't get them, or did nannying make

★ *The Rise and Fall of the British Nanny*, Hodder & Stoughton, 1972.

them unmarriageable? Whatever the case, the single nanny generally remained single. And if she did not find that bathing the Honourable Hay satisfied the profound instincts of womanhood, there were compensations. Every summer afternoon throughout the mid-century she might have revelled in the joys of human contact to be discovered amid the baby-carriages and balloons bobbing across the lawns of Hyde Park as upon a vast sea. Gathorne-Hardy pictured the scene:

For many, the richest moments of their lives passed there. Nannies were going to it before the First World War, but it was during the 1920s and '30s that it seems to have reached the zenith of its popularity . . . What a sight! A vast concourse of Nannies, thronging, drifting, sitting, rocking, more numerous than the buffalo upon the plain, more talkative than starlings at a moot. Here the gossip seethed and flowed . . .

As an image of the two million Surplus Women, set those happy Hyde Park afternoons against the popular representation of the barren British spinster. Here were babies, ducks, hoops and balls, bruised knees and daisy-chains, boasts and memories, joy and drama, kissing and consoling. This was a family.

Lady Astor's personal maid Rose Harrison was one of the few unmarried servants of that generation to publish a memoir, and in all probability many of her kind – nannies as much as anyone – would have felt as she did towards the end of her life:

. . . The family were still there and have been to this day. 'You will never want for anything, Rose,' her ladyship often said to me. The children have seen to it that their mother's word has been honoured. I was given a pension and instructed to ask for help if ever I wanted it . . . There is something else they have given me which has made my retirement the richer: their continued affection and interest. I visit them, they visit me. I am still one of the tribe.

★

For nannies to seek outlets for their love among their charges is no more surprising than that their charges should find the nannies themselves replacing mother, husband, lover or dependant. Elizabeth Goudge's nanny was so devoted to the family that 'she would never have got married however many men had asked her', or so Elizabeth claimed. Ida Goudge was utterly reliant on her; as an infant Elizabeth was with her far more than she was with her own mother, and loved her more. Nanny never deserted them, and when she was killed in a Second World War air raid the little family felt broken by her loss.

A nanny might be friend, companion and mother all in one. When war left disappointment in its wake, these steadfast women had soothing words to comfort, cradling arms to caress. They loved with generosity and compassion, and often with far greater wholeheartedness than the parents they substituted for.

A stock character throughout Noël Streatfeild's children's books, the orphaned Fossil girls' nanny in *Ballet Shoes* was reliably large, strict and comforting

Joan Evans's parents didn't really want her. Her father, Sir John Evans, was seventy when she was born; her mother was his third wife, and was in her late thirties. Both were scholars and intellectuals, and Joan's arrival in 1893 was an unwelcome distraction from her mother's elevated interests. The baby was nothing but a nuisance, and soon after the birth Lady Evans went on holiday for six weeks without her. When Joan was nearly a year old, nanny Caroline Hancock was employed to look after her – and stayed for the next sixty-seven years. On her arrival, Lady Evans asked her as a matter of form whether she would promise to love her infant daughter, to which Nannie Hancock responded that she really couldn't make such a commitment until she had got to know the child. Nobody, however, could have been more committed.

Without her love, Joan's childhood in an imposing Hertfordshire residence would have been sad and solitary indeed. Sir John and Lady Evans were often away from home and, though rich, grudged money for toys and amusements. Plasticine, for example, was prohibited, and drawing presented difficulties '. . . for I was not allowed an india-rubber, for fear crumbs should fall on the carpet'. Friendships were discouraged. One day her mother unluckily discovered that Joan had saved for months to buy Nannie a modest present, and gave her a most serious scolding. Her elderly father, though often absent, was more benign: scholarly yet playful. He wrote Latin verses to her puppy, taught her whist and showed her how to label his collection of rare coins. But when she was fifteen he died. All Joan's stifled passions as she grew up were poured into Nannie's welcoming embrace: '[She] was so much part of my life that I cannot easily write of her. Neat of figure, nimble of movement, fresh of colour, dark of hair, with a soft face that never hurt when she kissed one, and beautiful hands that could soothe or caress, she was a woman that many men found lovable.' Nevertheless, she stayed. For Joan, Nannie's kindness, sincerity and liberality were a firm foundation, and they were always together – for even when Nannie took her yearly holiday at her parents' rural cottage in Buckinghamshire, Joan went too. 'My mother . . . was not willing to undertake any responsibility for me while Nannie was away.' It was here, rather than in her parents' home, nurtured by the warm, thrifty and old-fashioned way of life of the Hancock family, that Joan put down deep and stable roots.

In 1909, when she was sixteen, the widowed Lady Evans decided to take her daughter to Florence, and while there Joan fell in love. Perhaps to relieve herself of the tedious duty of entertaining a schoolgirl, Lady Evans permitted Joan to spend time with the eighteen-year-old son of some old Hertfordshire friends who were also visiting Florence and, thrown together, the two young people soon had eyes only for each other. It was a delicate, innocent romance. The beauties of the Certosa and San Miniato were enhanced by the pleasure they took in seeing them together. Yet despite the mutually unexpressed love that animated every moment of that brief Italian springtime for them, it wasn't all solemn. Joan still wore pigtails and a pinafore. Unsophisticated and unpretentious, at Gilli's they ate their way through no fewer than sixteen little cakes at a sitting. They laughed and were happy. It was more a healthy comradeship than a dreamy yearning.

In her autobiography the young man is not named, so it is hard to tell whether this was the one and only romance in Joan's life, or indeed whether he was even the same man to whom she refers some twenty pages later. By then five years had passed and the world was opening up for her. Joan had put her hair up and lengthened her skirts; she boasted a nineteen-inch waist. A winter in Rome exploring the mosaics and Cosmati work of early Christian churches had awakened in her a passion for medieval culture and architecture. But war had broken out. Joan had now escaped from the meaningless claustrophobia of life with her widowed mother in Hertfordshire, and in October 1914 went up to St Hugh's College, Oxford, to read for a Diploma in Anthropology and Religious History. The trenches had emptied the colleges of men, and though not officially admitted as members of the university, the undergraduates to be seen around Oxford at this time were mostly women students like Joan:

. . . Inevitably we lived in the shadow of war; the telegram we saw upon the hall table when we came in from a lecture was almost certain to mean grievous anxiety or loss for one of our number . . . over everything hung a fog of rumour.

Nannie came to visit. But autumn 1914 was a time of sorrow for all, and Joan was not exempt. Her bereavement, at twenty-one, though referred to for the first and last time buttressed between more generalised bereavements, must have been acute:

The friendliest of my nephews . . . was killed early in the term; a friend whom I might well have married was killed a few days later; and I felt the senseless destruction of Reims as an acute personal loss.

She never mentioned him again.

In 1915 Joan mused in her diary on what the future held in store for her. She was rich, and she could choose what to do. Should she become a critic, an archaeologist, a writer of some sort, or would she be better suited to a dilettante life '. . . in which I may see beautiful things and have the pleasure of idle days and beautiful surroundings . . .'? She no longer even posed to herself the option of marriage at some unforeseeable time, and it appears that any hopes she may have had in that direction were now forever buried. When the Armistice came she and a friend stood at her window to hear the pealing of the Oxford bells: 'They seemed to be ringing a dirge for our youth that was gone with little to show for it but loss.'

Joan Evans became a collector and a scholar, with many publications and honours to her name. France was her lifelong passion. Her sense of beauty was communicated through her profound love and knowledge of medieval French life and art. And she shared it, until that lady died at the great age of ninety-seven, with Caroline Hancock: Nannie.

They lived together, and from 1928 Nannie travelled with Joan every year to France. She developed a taste for Romanesque architecture. While Joan examined each village church they stopped at in scholarly fashion, conscientiously photographing details of vaults and ambulatories, Nannie, in old age not so nimble, was to be seen before the statue of the local Virgin, those deft beloved hands busily tidying up the banks of candles. The churches may have been Catholic, but '. . . [she] liked to leave them neater than she found them'. Three years after Nannie's death, Joan wrote her autobiography *Prelude and Fugue* (1964) and dedicated it to the memory of the only human being who had, throughout her life, given her trust, belief and unconditional love.

## Lonely nights

Close friends, loving relatives, intimate carers: who would dispute their role in giving and returning love and alleviating loneliness? The soft smoothness of a female kiss that didn't hurt or rasp, beloved hands that comforted and soothed . . . The mute adoration of a faithful pet, content to be fondled and stroked, also allowed single women to express that part of themselves that sought physical contact; though if we are talking the language of substitution, Ginger, Peterkin, Brownie and the Hobbits took the place rather of their mistresses' children than of their lovers.

In her memoirs, Elizabeth Goudge is voluble about love. She loved richly and profoundly, whether it was her family, her friends, her dogs or her Creator. But she never talks about sex. Are we to assume that she felt no deprivation, that she didn't have needs in that respect? Were passion and desire strangers to her? A generation before, a woman's sexuality would have been ignored, denied. But Elizabeth Goudge was born in 1900; can she, an intelligent, well-read woman, have been entirely oblivious of Freud, of D. H. Lawrence, of Marie Stopes and the psychologists? One thing is sure, whatever privations in this respect Miss Goudge may have learnt to live with, she felt no need to share them with her readers. The nearest she got to betraying any sense of physical shortfall was in describing the nervous breakdown she suffered when she was in her thirties. This followed on both her parents, and then she herself, undergoing surgery. Elizabeth endured guilt and misery at her mother's illnesses, seeing Ida dealing with terrible pain and knowing how sorely that struggle tested her faith; but her own faith never wavered until she herself was called upon to endure:

'It is when it touches your *own* flesh,' my mother said once, 'it is then that you know.' It did not touch my flesh so badly as it touched my mind for after the little succession of family disasters I fell headlong into what is called a nervous breakdown, a state which as all its victims know can be terrifying.

Depression, fear, confusion and suicidal tendencies engulfed an otherwise serene and rational woman. Perhaps it is far-fetched to suggest that a series of operations are an inadequate explanation for such a descent into mental illness. Whatever the case, a religious woman like Elizabeth Goudge certainly found it impossible to do anything other than hint at some indefinable blankness in her life. And any attempt to disinter the realities of living without sex in the first half of the twentieth century is liable to meet with the same obliqueness and avoidance.

How hard it was to admit feelings of frustration emerges in Freya Stark's memoir of her early life, *Traveller's Prelude* (1950); she struggled with her single state until eventually – in desperation perhaps at her sense of failure – marrying the homosexual diplomat Stewart Perowne in her mid-fifties. But already in her mid-twenties Freya – who had been disfigured by an accident in early childhood – was suffering acutely from feelings of humiliation and physical deprivation, made worse by her mother's all too obvious attempts to get her married off. Freya squirmed at Flora Stark's indiscriminate promotion of entirely ineligible suitors, yet she wanted what marriage could bring:

My mother longed to see me engaged . . . and felt it her own failure if I failed to become so . . .

However this may be, my failure to find a husband made me frustrated and unhappy, for I felt it must be due to some invincible inferiority in myself. And what is worse, I thought my natural desires in this direction so extremely indelicate as to be hardly admissible, even to myself.

And this – in the public domain at least – is about the nearest we get to a spinster's confession of unrequited lust.

It may have been easy for a minority of Bloomsberries and Bohemians to discuss nymphomania, copulation and the clitoris with impunity; D. H. Lawrence may have got away with describing how the gipsy's body 'rippled with shuddering as an electric current . . .' as he held the virgin in his arms. But then people like that weren't respectable. Virtuous virgins may have known about these subjects, but they simply didn't feel able to discuss them.

So we find ourselves in swampy territory, walking uncertain pathways. Beyond, the land lies submerged, unknown, forbidden. For the most part the biographical phrase 'she never married . . .' represents a warning sign inscribed with the words DON'T ASK.

But sex was in the air, and this at a time when more women than ever were doomed to celibacy. From being censored and avoided, marital relations were emerging as a legitimate topic of discussion, so long as they remained marital. Surplus Women were left out of that debate. Marie

---

# MARRIED LOVE

## A NEW CONTRIBUTION TO THE
## SOLUTION OF SEX DIFFICULTIES

*A BOOK FOR*
*MARRIED COUPLES*

BY

# MARIE STOPES, D.Sc., Ph.D.

With a Preface by
Dr. JESSIE MURRAY

*Fourteenth Edition.    Revised and Enlarged*

*Six Shillings Net*

TO the married and to those about to marry, provided they are normal in mind and body and not afraid of facing facts, this should prove a most helpful book.—
*British Medical Journal.*

---

Though ground-breaking, Marie Stopes's sex advice books signally failed to embrace the unmarried

Stopes's books on birth control and sexual love were addressed firmly to married women and working mothers. Unsympathetic to the unmarried she may have been, but that didn't stop the singles from throwing themselves on her mercy. For of course, they had sex feelings too:

From Miss D. E. Knight, April 1919:

Dear Dr Stopes . . .

I am 34 years of age, am not married, & have never been engaged; but for
years now I have been troubled by intensely strong sexual feelings which
have never been satisfied, sometimes the craving has been so strong that it
has almost amounted to bodily pain. I . . . have been brought up in a middle
class conventional life, where to mention such feelings & to ask questions
about the principal thing in life was considered most improper &
degrading . . .

From Miss Hilda Winstanley, April 1920

For the sake of a friend I am venturing to ask your advice . . .

Absolutely by chance – she is very highly sexed – it appears she produced in
herself the sexual orgasm to which you referred in your book. At the 'tides'
explained by you, she tells me she cannot resist bringing this sensation of the
nerves to herself by friction. I am wondering if she is acting in a way that is
harmful to herself, or as she is so terribly highly sexed and is in the very best
of health, is it doing her good to give way? She says she simply has to do it . . .

From Miss NN, September 1922

I am unmarried but the sex instinct is tremendously strong in me . . .

   I feel that desire is absolutely right and natural and the normal heritage of
every healthy woman whether married or not.

   But I am not quite sure whether even under strong sexual desire it is ever
*right* to induce excitation of the clitoris and the wonderful thrill which is the
outcome of such an action? . . . Do you think that an occasional indulgence
viz two or three times a month is detrimental to health – or disloyal to the
highest and best we know? . . .

   It may interest you to know that I am 41 years of age and only realized the
possibility of self satisfaction at 32 . . .

From Miss Nancy C. Thorn, October 1931

Dear Doctor,

I am writing to you to see whether you can help me at all. I am feeling rather
worried over myself at present, and have done for some time.

   When I was eight years old or perhaps a little younger I stumbled by
accident on what I have since learnt is called 'Masturbation'. I thought I was
the only person who did such a thing until a few years ago (I am now 25)
and it did not strike me as being wrong. Now it has become such a habit that
I find it very difficult to break myself of it . . .

   I do not do it so frequently as I used to and I feel I am very weak in not

being able to stop. Ought I to stop at once or try gradually or 'carry on'? I
do not feel I want to do the latter.

I went two months once without performing, but felt wretched.

. . . Apologising for troubling you

Marie Stopes kept every single one of the multitudes of letters sent to her
in strictest confidence by women and men, married and single alike – an
extraordinary archive of fear, ignorance, doubt and unhappiness. She also
answered them, though not all the replies survive. In the numerous cases
of single women who put their desperate cases before her, Marie Stopes
inclined towards a brisk, no-nonsense response. It was more than her
reputation was worth to be seen to encourage immorality, and she was very
cautious about recommending masturbation, advising Miss NN that, since
she was over the age of thirty, it might be beneficial to indulge twice a
month, but only so long as she acknowledged that it was dangerous.
Generally she advised her frustrated correspondents to find something else
to fill their time, work or an absorbing occupation (knitting, perhaps?), before earnestly expressing the hope that they might marry at some unspecified
point in the future:

I do not know how the sex instinct can be legitimately fulfilled, except by deflecting
it into sound work.

At the time of conscious need of sex, really hot baths are good in dissipating the
electric energy which accumulates.

The problem you raise is, of course, one of an increasingly urgent nature since
the cruel devastation of the War, and it is one which I fear individuals must solve
for themselves at present.

Yours very truly . . .

This was a typical reply to an unmarried woman who wrote to her asking
how she could satisfy her sex instincts.

Evidently, single women did endure frustration, but it is hard to discover
what proportion allowed it to get the better of them. A psychological study
of 500 single women conducted in America in the early 1930s revealed that
a third of them had had 'a love interest'. Of these, under a third had had
sexual intercourse – or one woman in every nine. Four hundred and forty
of those women were virgins. From the same sample, it was estimated that,
though only one third of the women actually admitted it, four out of five
of the women had masturbated.

None of this is surprising, and it is surely reasonable to assume that these statistics would apply equally to women in Great Britain. It would appear too that many women accepted the generally held view that sublimation of the sex instincts was easier for them than it was for men; 'I think a woman is different to a man. She doesn't get so frustrated,' remembered a spinster interviewed for the BBC in her nineties. 'It's more necessary for a man. A woman can divert her stream of energy elsewhere.' This lady, Irene Angell, did her best to divert her own energies into her job; after the war she was working as a secretary, but when her divorced boss and she fell in love the atmosphere became suffocating, and she fled, fearing scandal. In old age none of Miss Angell's regrets were for the sex she'd missed out on, they were all for the companionship, love and children.

Nevertheless, as the letters to Marie Stopes reveal, and as some of the quotations from the American case histories demonstrate, the attendant misery could be acute:

– She complains at thirty-seven that two doctors have told her she ought to get married, one a year ago. 'I've cried every night since.'

– 'Could you not introduce me to a man who would be a suitable husband?'

– 'About masturbation, it is my greatest comfort that the doctor does not know all; the shame, the sorrow, the never-ending struggle.'

Marie Stopes's postbag tells the same story. A lonely twenty-eight-year-old wrote to her as a last resort for advice on how to lose her virginity: 'I am craving for real love and affection. Every heart desires a mate! . . . I am unable to find a companion.' This woman had turned for help to a psychologist, who told her that being a virgin at her age was most unusual, and advised her to hurry up and get some sex at the earliest opportunity. But how? 'I was brought up that a girl must refuse having relations before marriage. I am in despair.'

Unhelpful exchanges, unsympathetic doctors – to whom could the single woman turn? As we have seen, there were a number of books aimed at singles, and these tried with the best of intentions to meet a crying need. In her *Sex Philosophy of a Bachelor Girl* (1920), Clara Amy Burgess urged her celibate readers to seek out the silver lining. Doing without sex meant doing without venereal disease, without gynaecological or obstetric complications, and without 'the nervous and mental disorders which follow on too frequent sex-indulgence'. Burgess adamantly maintained that succumbing to passion was more injurious than celibacy, for intense passion overwhelms, absorbs and harms; it is impure. The woman who gives in to the sex instinct becomes morbid, melancholy and rude. Somehow the bachelor girl must learn to disregard the prevailing obsession with the physical and animal. Modern novels, for example, were degenerate. Don't

Sex and the single woman: by the 1930s there was no shortage of literature on the subject (illustration from *Live Alone and Like It* by Marjorie Hillis)

read them, she urged. She also asserted that suppressed sex could in itself be a resource, channelled in the right way; far from becoming frigid and withered, the sexual energies would course through the bachelor girl's veins and find new outlets, causing her to glow with health and find a new spring in her step.

As far as possible, and she knew this was asking a lot, Burgess advised the bachelor girl to isolate and banish all her sexual feelings. 'Keep sex in a strong-box, with other interests sitting on the lid to hold it tight.' The other interests she recommended – among them cleaning up slums, organising neighbourhood clubs, learning a language and folk-dancing – were aimed at refreshing the mind and wearying the body, thus promoting healthy sleep. Anyone who still felt like a spot of exciting friction at bedtime after such an action-packed day surely wasn't doing her bit.

Nevertheless, Clara Amy Burgess had a point about looking on the bright side; society did not tolerate extra-marital sex, nor was the post-war world a propitious one for casual sexual relationships. A man could sow his wild oats, but a woman who did so was a slut, and risked pregnancy. Contraceptives were often faulty, and in any case not widely available, and chemists were disinclined to sell them to single people. Unmarried mothers got little sympathy or help; very few of them chose to battle on alone. The mothers were sometimes condemned to asylums, while their babies were put out for adoption or sent to reformatories. In 1937 the government estimated that up to 60,000 illegal abortions were being carried out yearly, a substantial minority on single women. It was also widely believed that one in five of the four million soldiers who had returned to England had brought back with them a venereal disease; syphilis was then incurable. There were indeed compensations for being a virgin.

Despite this, the stigma of being a spinster was so fearful that many women succumbed to sex, believing they'd get a husband that way. Betty Milton, who was in service as a kitchen-maid after the war, felt that at twenty-six her marriage prospects were receding. Life in service didn't offer many opportunities for meeting men, apart from the boy who delivered the groceries. She wasn't very keen on him, but she started seeing him and eventually agreed to have sex because he promised to marry her. 'I began to consider myself left on the shelf, an "old maid" . . . I hated it but at twenty-six I was dead scared of losing him.' Betty got caught by the man's mother, who abused her with every name in the book; she was lucky not to get pregnant, for the man was nowhere to be seen. Poorly paid and dependent, women of this class were particularly vulnerable: the 'superfluity' of women was even more pronounced in the world of Upstairs-Downstairs, where they outnumbered men by five to one, than it was in the wider world. Men could take their pick, and were often ruthless.

## The blessed fact of loving

For, as ever, double standards prevailed among the male population. Women were supposed to be pure, lovely brides in white, but they were sex objects too. A spinster offended on both counts. Often losing her looks as she pushed into middle age, she was also likely to be a virgin. The existence of the Surplus Women, and their huge numbers, challenged a man's most dearly held beliefs about his honour and his potency. And so, like Gallichan and Ludovici, the men fought back, vilifying the unhappy singles and blaming them for the blamelessness of their lives.

Small wonder, then, if the spinsters themselves sought what consolation they could among their own sex. Female friendships like that of Vera Brittain and Winifred Holtby, Geraldine Aves and Gwyneth Jones, or Miss Patch and Miss Prior were immensely common. But instead of being accepted, such necessary and desirable relationships were often accused of being deviant and perverted.

Few women could hope to live up to the virginal ideals of a generation of Englishmen, middle-aged spinsters least of all (*Strand Magazine*, December 1922)

Already the sight of corduroy-clad landgirls alongside women dressed in the uniforms of the auxiliary forces of the war, followed by the boyish fashions of the 1920s, had given the *bien-pensant* bourgeoisie some anxious moments. Now, with the vocabulary of homosexuality, inversion and Uranianism★ entering the language, the dividing line between friendship and lesbianism was becoming very fine indeed. Doreen Potts, who talked to me about her life as a single woman in the 1920s and 30s, was eager to point out at the very beginning of our interview that she had lots of good girlfriends – 'but that's all they were! I wasn't a lez!' Vera Brittain was also guarded. After Winifred Holtby's death, when she wrote and published her eulogy *Testament of Friendship*, she was careful to be unambiguous about the nature of that friendship. She had married; Winifred had not. She did not want anyone to think that Winifred had played the role of substitute husband.

The prosecution of Radclyffe Hall in 1928 for her lesbian romance *The Well of Loneliness* raised public consciousness of same-sex female relationships as nothing before, and many women innocent of anything more sinister

---

★ The word, though not in the *Oxford English Dictionary*, seems to have been coined by Edward Carpenter (1844–1929, author of *Love's Coming of Age* [1896] and *The Intermediate Sex* [1908]) to describe both male and female homosexuality.

than sharing a church pew found themselves the subjects of hostile insinu-
ation. Beatrice Gordon Holmes thought *The Well of Loneliness* a dreary book,
but having lived through a period when parents insisted that their daughters
were chaperoned by other women every minute of the day, she couldn't
help finding the resulting furore amusing:

Oh! The vicarages and country homes who felt their peace of mind forever
poisoned as they contemplated Daphne, Pamela, Joan, and Margery all living
together with unthinkable consequences . . .

Gordon was completely broad-minded. Tender, loving emotions, she rightly
claimed, 'know no barriers in the human heart'. A little psychoanalysis goes a
long way, was her view, and the attached jargon was too clumsy and inexact
a label for what were entirely natural, suitable and passionate friendships.

It is hard to do anything but guess at how many of such friendships
included an element of passion. The taboos against it were strong but, as
we have seen, so was the need for sexual release and the expression of
physical affection. Marie Stopes had her share of worried correspondents
agonising over their lesbian leanings. Miss L. Redcliffe wrote to her in 1922
begging for advice:

. . . I have a very strong tendency to be attracted by my own sex.

I have made great efforts to overcome this – but the force of it is so strong that
it seems to me most important that if there is anything I am ignorant of I should
have advice . . .

The reply was benevolent but dismissive:

Such a feeling as you describe is sometimes more or less normally developed in
late adolescence, and is a phase to pass through just as teething in a younger stage
. . . Keep your mind off the physical side of that aspect as much as possible and
lead as healthy and as busy a life as you can. Some good hard brain work on some
subject of study would probably be a very beneficial thing and I think you will
find the normal sex attraction will assert itself and this phase pass entirely away.

Sybil Neville-Rolfe,* the author of *Why Marry?* (1935), was less inclined
to view lesbian feelings as 'just a phase'. She stated her view that lesbians

---

* Founder of the Eugenics Society, later the British Social Hygiene Council, which promoted eugenics, sex education, marriage, and order and decency in public places.

should be looked on as sick and abnormal. But her condemnation was tempered by compassion. Poor dears, they couldn't help it: 'the war left behind it a generation of Eves in an Adamless Eden . . . Starving for love, deprived of homes and denied the joys of motherhood, many women found in friendship one with another some sort of substitute for these normal but lost relationships.'

Neville-Rolfe felt the need to clear up any ambiguity and educate her readers. She had had so many letters from women who didn't understand the difference between 'normal' crushes and dangerous, predatory relationships. One of her correspondents, a forty-year-old teacher, had gone to a lecture by a psychologist who had terrified her with dire warnings about the dreadful things women got up to if they were left alone together. What was she to do? She had been making plans to share a home with her best friend, a forty-five-year-old widowed postmistress. But what if it were harmful? Another young lady had written to her to bemoan the fact that her mother was interfering with her relationship with her greatest friend, Doris, whom she saw as 'undesirable'. This young lady couldn't see what all the fuss was about. Doris was clever, well-read and was planning to take her on holiday to Italy – what could possibly be the harm in that? After all, it wasn't as if Doris was some kind of temptress, on the contrary: 'Doris can't stand men and is never the least interested in them. I think she is much too like one herself! You've only got to see her to realise she isn't "fast" . . . she always dresses [plainly] . . . and looks awfully well in . . . the top part of a man's evening dress and a short black skirt. However, that is just to prove to you that she would look after me all right in Italy and wouldn't be dashing about after men.' This case was used to demonstrate how careful one should be; 'looking after' could mean all sorts of things. Forewarned is forearmed.

Not everyone was so portentous about the results of female 'friendship'. The sex advisers were well aware that when women cohabited one thing might lead to another. Laura Hutton, for example, delicately hinted at the unconscious forces at work when women's friendships progressed to intimacy. Hutton believed that the sex element in these friendships was far better recognised and accepted than repressed. Putting the lid on it was asking for trouble: guilt, resentment and tension were bound to result. For Hutton sex between women was 'a problem to be worked out with care'. Esther Harding, author of *The Way of All Women* (1933), was still more tolerant. For her, sex was subsidiary to love, and to women's particular genius for intimacy. Harding commented on the prevalence of pairs of women setting up house together, and noted that more and more women seemed to be adopting 'a somewhat masculinised dress and manner, as

<br>

well as certain masculine characteristics'. But instead of condemning these women as perverted predators waiting to pounce on innocent ingénues and carry them off to Italy, Harding saw them sympathetically as a sign of the times. Women in the post-war world were entering professions, rejecting domesticity and becoming independent; they were crossing into male territory and, to prove it, they put on men's clothes. Instinct will out, however: you could take the woman out of the home, but you couldn't take the home out of the woman. Deep down '. . . she wishes to have a home of her own'. And so these loving ménages grew up – comparable only to marriage in their richness, stability and permanence. But with a difference: empathy and harmonious relationships were the special sphere of women, and even the best heterosexual marriages could rarely provide the quality of emotional satisfaction and security to be found in many female friendships. And Harding went further:

Love between women friends may find its expression in a more specifically sexual fashion which, however, cannot be considered perverted if their actions are motivated by love.

Esther Harding's endorsement of sex between women would probably have fallen on stony ground with Elizabeth Goudge. She was a devout and obedient Christian; nevertheless Harding's emphasis on love would have struck an answering chord. Drained dry after her mother's death, the only thing that could replace that crucial relationship was a new and wonderful friendship:

Without my mother's vivid presence the place was dead . . .
    The weeks dragged by and kind friends came to visit me, but I lived in a dusty desert. Everything, I felt, had come to a dead end. There seemed no way out or through. Then the autumn came bringing with it what I suppose is the greatest miracle of every human life, the miracle of renewal . . .

Facing solitude was the hardest thing she had yet confronted. It was something of which she had no experience and, ignorant of her own inability to cope, she tried for a while to battle on. Friends saw that she was failing. One of these, determined to help, tried to persuade Elizabeth to write to a single woman she knew who she thought would keep her company, at least for a while. Doubtfully, she did so, receiving an equally doubtful reply, but a promise nonetheless to pass the winter in Devon. And in this way Jessie Monroe entered her life:

[I] went out into the garden and heard a very clear voice saying the words that are now so delightfully familiar. 'I'm sorry I'm late.' We looked at each other. I saw an upright, capable-looking young woman with a head of hair like a horse-chestnut on fire, and the white magnolia skin that goes with such hair. Her eyes were very direct. She looked young enough to be my daughter and I doubted if she would stand me for long, yet when I went to bed that night to my astonishment I found myself flooded with happiness, and slept deeply.

Jessie has stood me for twenty-one years and has been the most wonderful event that ever happened to me.

Thus in her final home near Oxford, together with Jessie and a succession of adored dogs, Elizabeth Goudge found peace in advancing age to write, to remember and to reflect on what she had gained and given to life.

Her autobiography, *The Joy of the Snow*, came out in 1974. In it she struggled honestly and scrupulously to balance out the joys and the sorrows. The realisation that she would not marry was mitigated for her by the sense that the women of her generation had value in the workforce; she would not have argued with Mrs Fawcett's view that war had liberated a generation – and surely the 'women's libbers' of the 1970s had missed the point? For people like her it had all happened fifty years earlier. And though it had taken many years and much regret – for above all she had found it hard to bear the thought that she would never have children – she had learned to 'recognise and deeply prize the blessings of a single life' and to feel grateful:

For the childless woman there is no lack of children in the world to love, even if they are not her own, and nothing to prevent a single woman experiencing the richness of falling in love now and again all her life. And indeed it *is* richness, for to every human being the pain of perhaps not having love returned is less important than the blessed fact of loving.

Elizabeth Goudge loved bountifully: her mother and her father, her nanny, her friends, the many strangers who wrote to her about her books, her dear dogs, Jessie Monroe, and above all her God. There had been loss, grief and heartache, but as the title of her autobiography suggests, in this woman's life joy tipped the scales.

★

It is perhaps too easy to describe a single woman's religious feelings as a substitute for a real relationship. For many their religion was entirely real, their faith built on a rock of certainty. In the 1950s the social researcher

F. Zweig interviewed an elderly unmarried factory cleaner in Lancashire. After this woman's mother died she had looked after her invalid and mentally retarded sister for twenty-two years. 'I stayed single because of her. What husband would want her in his house? Mine was a wasted life but in a way it wasn't, because I have done my duty . . . I am religiously inclined. I believe God picks out certain jobs and gives them to those people who will do them. Nowadays people are fond of pleasures. They are out for all they can get but not out for work . . . I am not lonely. I believe in the Divine Presence. When my sister died, I felt panicky at first, but I prayed and after that I was quite calm. I know when I die I won't be alone.' The isolation had been dreadful but for this woman, unlike poor Norah Elliott with her 'longings for love buried by fear', the terror that her life had indeed been wasted gave way to the certainty of comfort and reward in heaven.

Elizabeth Goudge looked at life through a more complex lens. Her soul's journey was a matter of fundamental importance to her; she believed that she was made to love God, and that God loved her. Her life, imperfect as it was, consisted of a quest to deserve God's infinite love, and she gave these matters much profound thought. Elizabeth's love of her Maker was, in her cosmology, an affirmation of her lesser, human loves, never a replacement for them. Geraldine Aves's faith too was foremost in drawing her close to her friend Gwyneth Jones: 'This year you have given me a new, very dear friend: one of Thy loving servants, may we help one another to serve Thee more nearly; and may our love for one another be hallowed by our love of Thee,' she wrote.

★

In *The Art of Loving* (1957), the social psychologist Erich Fromm wrote:

If I am attached to another person because I cannot stand on my own feet, he or she may be a life saver, but the relationship is not one of love. Paradoxically, the ability to be alone is the condition for the ability to love.

Fromm's wonderful essay stresses the active nature of love, and its inclusiveness: 'Love is not primarily a relationship to a specific person; it is an *attitude*, an *orientation of character* which determines the relatedness of a person to the world as a whole, not towards one "object" of love,' he asserts. To lower one's loving horizons to the hunt for a husband was a denial of loving.

Elizabeth Goudge, with her emphasis on 'the blessed fact of loving', would surely have agreed. And so would Maude Royden, who, speaking to a generation of women who had lost their hopes of finding a loving mate, preached: 'Love alone can build. Love alone creates . . .' She implored the women of the post-1918 world not to let their maternal and loving impulses shrivel unused:

There is no power to create but love. We know this, we women [because] we are old in the work of making homes . . . for lack of this conception, the world perishes . . . the world needs it more than you dream.

In 1920, still reeling from international cataclysm, those urgent words could not have been wasted on her hearers.

# 6. A Grand Feeling

## A cause, a purpose and a passion

War taught the people of Britain to lower their expectations of happiness. In the 1920s our country was a nation mutilated by loss. Much of what Winifred Holtby wrote wrestles with the predicament of the young women, buoyant and optimistic by nature, forced to come to terms with the disappointment of being single. In her 1934 essay 'Are Spinsters Frustrated?' she looked deep into the needs of unmarried women who, like her, sought fulfilment where it appeared to be lacking. Winifred Holtby was in no doubt that human contact was vital: 'We need intimacy; we need tenderness; we need love. But tenderness is not enough. We must have passion. We must at least once in life have burned to the white heat of ecstasy.' But she was not just talking about sexual fulfilment:

We must have achievement. We must feel the pleasure of creation . . . [And] we can know no ultimate peace unless we have worshipped some purpose larger than ourselves – a God, a cause, a leader, an idea, even another human person. Without that reverence we walk crippled, our human stature maimed. We are frustrated.

So how did the Surplus Women find happiness?

★

In 1918 Gertrude Caton-Thompson's life seemed to her an emotional blank. 'Carlyon's death had left me with the feeling that nothing much mattered . . .' she remembered. Gertrude was thirty. The man she had loved lay in a British war grave, and it seemed pointless to think of replacing him. It was absolutely clear to her that she would never love anyone again.

When Gertrude wrote her book *Mixed Memoirs* (1983), she did so in a genial and factual style; she was also, as one might expect from her archaeological methods, meticulously chronological. She does not elaborate in them on how she emerged from this state of insensibility. We are simply asked to accept that she did. But the hints are there. After the Armistice was declared Arthur Salter, her employer at the Ministry of Shipping, asked her to accompany him to the Versailles Peace Conference. In preparation for her Parisian sojourn she went shopping with her mother and bought 'spring suiting, a ravishing evening dress, and a hat or two'. She was comfortably billeted in Rue Bassano. On weekends out from Paris she went for walks in the woods at Compiègne and picked lilies-of-the-valley. Salter and she dined with friends in the Bois de Boulogne and relished a superb meal 'which included cold salmon mayonnaise and bowlfuls of fraises-du-bois with lashings of cream'. When the Conference was over there was a holiday with friends in Ireland – 'a happy time, doing nothing in particular except golf and exercising dogs'.

Though Carlyon had died, Gertrude's appetite for pleasure had not.

And then there was archaeology – a purpose larger than herself. On 23 November 1921 Gertrude set off for Abydos in Upper Egypt with her teacher and mentor, the great Egyptologist Professor Flinders Petrie. Before the war she and her mother had travelled in first-class cabins and stayed in luxury hotels. This journey was rather different, but Gertrude was so excited that spending two days stranded by a seamen's strike in an insanitary and disreputable inn in Marseilles did nothing to dampen her spirits. A week later she was in Cairo; a day's journey took them on to Luxor. She rode out to Abydos on donkey-back.

For four months Gertrude slept in a tent. She and the other students lived frugally off tinned herring; the Petries were famous for their abstemious lack of interest in food and comfort. Gertrude worked hard under the dictatorial and painstaking 'Prof', brushing the sand from tombs 5,000 years old, and unearthing skulls, amphorae, implements and artefacts, all to a background rattle of machine-guns at Assiut, where the British were now defending themselves against a mutinous native mob. This turbulent region was only about 150 miles across the desert from Baharia, where Carlyon had met his dreadful death five years earlier. Gertrude's memoirs pass over this, dwelling instead on the project in hand:

From first to last I revelled in the work done in that glorious sunshine . . . I had minded not at all the poor food and unnecessary discomfort of camp life . . .

She was drinking it in, hungry to learn, excited, thrilled by the landscape, the people, the companionship of camp life, and by her own pioneering ambitions.

And so began a pattern in Gertrude Caton-Thompson's life. The year 1922 saw her excavating Neolithic tombs in Malta. In 1923 she started a lifelong association with Newnham College, Cambridge, where she met her closest friend, Dorothy Hoare. In 1924 she was back with Petrie in Egypt again. Until the Second World War Gertrude's life alternated between the rigours and excitement of fieldwork, and the more decorous pleasures of scholarship, friendship, walks, culture, golf and motor-car outings. (Economically she was self-sufficient, largely through skilful management of her own portfolio.)

In Qau in Egypt Gertrude lodged in a ninth-dynasty tomb which she shared with a family of cobras: 'the cook offered to kill them, but I would have none of it: they had priority of occupation and their forebears had probably used it since it had been hewn from the rock 4000 years ago.' She was more anxious about hyenas, however, and took the precaution of sleeping with a pistol under her pillow.

Later in Malta she spent her days excavating a Neolithic temple, and her evenings and weekends picnicking under the megaliths and enjoying the gaieties of colonial military society.

In 1925 Gertrude set out on her own dig in the Fayum desert with one other British woman to take charge of the camp, and five of Petrie's best Qufti workmen. Egypt was in a state of insurrection but, though advised to leave, she was quite sure that the upheavals would not affect her in her distant desert location, and determined to press on. She bought a box Ford, piled on her equipment, hired a Nubian chauffeur, and got safely to Medinet-el-Fayum. There the Governor earnestly recommended that she abandon her car and take camels. 'I ignored advice and proved that with care and avoidance of certain types of ground the car was an unqualified success.' They arrived without incident and spent the next two months making a detailed reconnaissance of Neolithic flints. It was a time of 'utter bliss without an anxiety in the world'. She was to return twice more, making important discoveries about unknown Neolithic civilisations in that area of north-western Egypt, and in 1934 published her findings in *The Desert Fayum*. Over the years Gertrude Caton-Thompson was to earn a prominent place in the annals of twentieth-century archaeologists; her methods of scientific sequence dating were revolutionary, and her conviction that occupied settlements could teach us as much about the past as cemeteries and tombs was endorsed by successive researchers. Her site work in the Egyptian desert was acclaimed by the Egyptologist Gerald Wainwright, who declared that in importance it rivalled Carter's discovery of the tomb of Tutankhamen.

In later expeditions Gertrude Caton-Thompson excavated the monumental ruins at Zimbabwe in southern Africa, the Palaeolithic remains at the Kharga Oasis in the Egyptian Sahara, and the Moon Temple of Hadhramaut in southern Arabia. Leopards, fevers, fleas, swamps and preci-

pices, storms at sea, floods, cyclones and crocodiles beset her under-
takings, but Gertrude's stoical upper-class upbringing and military cor-
rectness stood her everywhere in good stead: 'Mercifully I am not easily
alarmed,' she wrote. But at the beginning of the Second World War her
usual robustness began to ebb away with spells of weakness and giddiness;
after the age of fifty there were to be no more field trips, though she
revisited excavations in East Africa. Her academic work and her friendships
flourished, however; in Britain she made her home with her dear friend
Dorothy, who had married a fellow archaeologist, Toty de Navarro. Gertrude
loved them both equally; she described Dorothy as 'the mainspring of my
life', while rejoicing in Toty's wit, intellect and generosity. Toty had
no difficulty in making his wife's closest friend welcome in their Worcester-
shire home. 'To this unique gesture I owe some 39 years of unclouded
happiness.'

Gertrude Caton-Thompson was twenty-eight when Carlyon Mason-
MacFarlane died; she lived nearly another seventy years: they were years of
intrepid adventure, intellectual purpose, deep friendship and simple, intense
pleasure. She was admired, loved and widely honoured. A life bled of
meaning had been reanimated. Could anyone describe such a woman as
unfulfilled?

★

It should not be assumed that for lack of husbands the unmarried women
of the 1920s and 30s were universally celibate, nor that they conformed to
the expected model of frumpy, thwarted spinster. As Winifred Holtby
pointed out, '[the spinster] may have known that rare light of ecstasy. In
certain sections of society, it is possible that she will have had lovers.' And
it is true that one doesn't have to look far to find unwed and childless
women finding fun and fulfilment in ways often barred to the conventional
wives and mothers of early twentieth-century Britain.

The war had subverted all the old rules. Young women released from
their parlours and sculleries to join the war effort found opportunities for
sex and romance with men of all backgrounds. When a soldier whose life
expectancy was perhaps only a few weeks asked you to sleep with him, it
seemed somehow cruel to say no. 'Life was very gay,' remembered one
young woman. 'It was only when someone you knew well or with whom
you were in love was killed that you minded really dreadfully. Men used
to come to dine and dance one night, and go out the next morning and be
killed. And someone used to say, "Did you see poor Bobbie was killed?"
It went on all the time you see.' After the war some wag suggested fixing

a plaque to the wall of a famous London hotel: 'to the women who fell here during the Great War'.

The legacy of loss would never be forgotten by the young women of Britain – the memorials on every village green were there to remind them – but now they wanted to turn their backs on grief. Barbara Cartland was of that generation. She remembered the courage of many of her contemporaries who, though crushed by bereavement, 'reddened their lips and [went] out to dance when all they loved most [had] been lost . . . They accepted death with a shrug of the shoulders.' Their elders expected them to sit at home and cry, and condemned them as hard and callous, but the new generation was, according to her, 'out to conquer'. The 1920s saw a release of pent-up energy. In reaction to four years of crippling conflict, and bedevilled by fear of the future, they simply wanted, like Gertrude Caton-Thompson, to pick lilies-of-the-valley, and wear ravishing evening dresses, and eat strawberries with lashings of cream. They wanted to charleston, shingle their hair, wear short skirts, join the Women's League of Health and Beauty, even buy rose-coloured carpets.

Set free from the shadow of death, many of these young women now recognised the new decade as offering deliverance from another noose, that of convention. And contraception was a reality. The use of birth-control devices increased hugely after the war. For a liberated minority that meant they were free to spurn the prevalent sexual Puritanism and patriarchal standards of Edwardian Britain. Not entirely with impunity perhaps, but the liberated single woman of the 1920s was no longer spoken of as 'fallen'. She was no longer expected to flee the country in disgrace, as her equivalent only twenty years earlier might have been.

Eastbourne might seem an unlikely place to come across an unrepentant flapper from the twenties. Indeed, meeting Mary Cocker, now in her late nineties and living in a rather characterless old people's home in that dispiriting seaside resort, it was hard to visualise the old lady with bent spine, straggly hair and missing teeth as a saucy bachelor girl. When she spoke, however, Miss Cocker was sprightly and decisive. No nonsense.

I might not have found out so much from my meeting with Miss Cocker had it not been for a mix-up with her visitor appointments that afternoon. When I was shown into her room I was greeted with a cross 'Who on earth are you?' She was clearly expecting somebody else. After some excuses and explanations we proceeded with the interview, but ten minutes later there was a knock on the door. It was Olive, the middle-aged friend she had been expecting, so I excused myself and left them to chat. About forty-five minutes later I went back to see whether we could resume the interview and, as Olive was still there, she sat in while we talked.

The conversation ranged over Miss Cocker's family and upbringing; her mother died when she was four, and she was brought up by her father, who worked in Customs and Excise, and her grandmother. She was a Londoner. After she left school she trained as a shorthand-typist and learnt commercial French; she worked as a salesgirl at Harrods, had various jobs as one of the 'business girls', and did secretarial work in an advertising firm. But it soon emerged that her real love was travel. Over a long life Miss Cocker had been to America three times, to Germany, Austria, France, Italy, Switzerland, and made a memorable trip to Iceland. She'd been to Japan, and had also flown over Mount Everest en route to China, where she'd seen the Great Wall and the terracotta army. Settling down simply couldn't compete. 'All I was doing was thinking of the next holiday abroad. I just liked to travel. That was much more interesting to me than any men. I used to be saving up for the next holiday . . .'

I couldn't help wondering how she could afford to see the world on such a scale. The clue came in her approach to the opposite sex: 'I was an awful flirt. I was quite attractive I suppose, but I didn't want to get married, and I never particularly wanted to have children. I had boyfriends – thousands of them. And I didn't have to work, I could work if I wanted to. Financially I was lucky. As a single person you're responsible for yourself. I think you've got to work it out – you've got to have a brain and use it. That's my advice.

'A lot of women are so stupid. They are absolutely stupid. The feminists are barmy – you know, they either know it all, or they try to be cleverer than the men. I never knew it all, I was never cleverer; I'd say, "How marvellous of you! Oh yes, aren't you wonderful" and purr just like a pussy-cat. Play the helpless little woman. What's the good of being a woman if you don't get what you want? I like being waited on and having people do things, especially men. Not that I fancied them anyway. I didn't want to sleep with them. I don't think that going to bed is a great achievement. I didn't do that much; and if I did, I knew exactly what I was doing. Next question!'

Later, on my way back from Eastbourne, the questions I had felt prevented from asking were answered when I unexpectedly ran into Olive in the station car park. She too was on her way home. 'I couldn't help laughing,' she said, 'listening to you talking to Mary about her boyfriends. You know, there's only one word that would ever spring to my mind if you asked me to describe her: Mary was like a courtesan. You see, she knew exactly how to give men what they liked. Mary told me she never had to pay for a thing in her life. She got men to do whatever she wanted. She could twist them round her finger.'

There were business girls working long hours for cranky bosses, strap-hanging on the underground, shivering in lodgings, eating buns in lonely tea-rooms, dreaming of romance; and there were business girls like Mary Cocker. Mary Cocker had no time for the other sort. 'There's no point in being miserable. If you are then you've brought it on yourself. I went to all the places I wanted to go to, and that was the thing that gave me the most pleasure in my life. I've been very lucky. I've had some very good friends – of *both* sexes. I certainly didn't miss out on the man front. And it never, ever, *ever* crossed my mind to envy women who were married.' Determination, drive and a certain artfulness got Mary Cocker what she wanted out of life, and she very clearly had no regrets. 'I believe there's a God. I believe if you do something bad you get paid out. It's good to get into the habit of being nice to people, and it's easier to be like that, isn't it? Things like that, they count to me.'

★

Mary Cocker may not have rated going to bed with men as a great achieve-ment but, like many others of her generation, she was not plagued by guilty feelings at doing so. For fearless and free-spirited women who knew, as recommended, how to use their brains, the risks were much reduced from a few decades earlier. Winifred Holtby's essay didn't specify London's Bohemia as fertile territory for lovers, but she undoubtedly had the Café Royal crowd in mind when she referred to 'certain sections of society'. Straight after the war, Fitzrovia, Bloomsbury and Chelsea were full of single women tasting the joys of uncommitted sex – like Kathleen Hale, who escaped from her repressive family, sold her bicycle for the price of a one-way railway ticket, and set off to be an artist in Soho. At the bar of the Studio Club she met the painter Frank Potter, recently demobilized. Having already previously decided to fall in love with him, she was struck dumb with emotion. Frank 'teased me out of my priggishness and the false values that I had absorbed from my suburban background . . .' Their love affair lasted several years, and though the subject of marriage came up, it 'seemed to be something that happened to other people . . .' and so she never took it seriously. During that time Kathleen was working as secretary to the famously lecherous painter Augustus John. Eventually, 'out of curiosity', she slept with him too. With the sex element out of the way, their friendship increased.

Augustus's seductions were legendary. This was a world of illicit entanglements, *ménages à trois*, pick-ups and infidelities, labyrinthine

1. *Private View* (1937) by Gladys Hynes. Unmistakable in the centre of the picture, Radclyffe Hall and her lover Una Troubridge saw no need to conceal their sexual orientation in such tolerant milieux.

22. A Universal Aunt.

23. 'Other people's babies …'; but there were compensations to be had in the rich social life led by nannies between the wars.

24. Mary Milne, Matron of St Mary's Hospital, Paddington. Her fiancé was killed in the war.

25. Tea, sympathy and iron discipline; in the 1920s nursing was one of the few professions seen as respectable for decent young ladies.

27. Rowena Cade, founder of the Minack Theatre, Cornwall.

26. After her mother's death, Phyllis Bentley rediscovered a guiltless freedom.

28. Winifred Haward and Louis Hodgkiss: 'a great love that survives the night and climbs the stars'.

29. 'I would live my life over again': lady's maid Rose Harrison.

30. Post-war, women replenished the ranks of white-collar workers killed in the trenches.

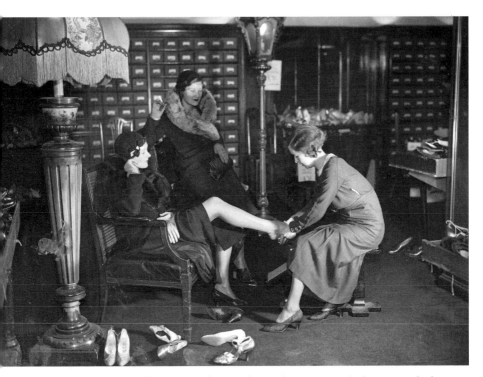

31. In 1921 ninety per cent of women working in the retail sector were single; even at the luxury end, they often worked twelve-hour days in atrocious conditions.

32. Margery Perham's eminence as an expert on African affairs was recognised by the British government. Margery with Masai warriors in Kenya, 1930.

33. The archaeologist Gertrud Caton-Thompson.

34. Women working in the laboratory at Girton College, Cambridge.

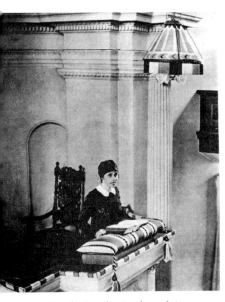

35. Maude Royden in the pulpit.

36. Preacher, journalist and charity worker Rosamund Essex with her adopted son, David.

37. Picnics and prayer meetings: members of the Christian Alliance of Women and Girls on holiday in Scarborough, 1929.

38. Campaigning for spinsters: on the right, Florence White.

relationships.\* 'Spinster' might not be the first word that springs to mind when describing such women as his partner Dorelia, or Dora Carrington, or Brenda Dean Paul, or Gwen John, or Stella Bowen, or Kathleen Garman, or Viva King, or Dorothy Brett, or Irene Rathbone. These women were not wives in the first instance, but they had sex with men, and in some cases children, and in many cases rich emotional lives with their lovers. They didn't have the security of a husband, but neither did they have the duties of a wife. And for the first time in history the sexually liberated single woman became possessed of a certain enviable glamour.

★

The writer Irene Rathbone is now largely forgotten, though the Feminist Press has reprinted her most successful novel, *We That Were Young* (1932), an account of the war and its aftermath. Here, as in so much of her fiction, Irene Rathbone's own life story is thinly disguised, and the voice is that of an adventurous and liberated woman, passionate and politically *engagée*.

Irene was born into a middle-class Liverpool family in 1892. She was sent to a south of England boarding school, and in the immediate pre-war years flat-shared with a female cousin in 'New Woman' style in London. Acting, and women's suffrage, absorbed her energies; she played several Shakespearean roles, and appeared in a Noël Coward play. In 1915 she fell in love. Between 1914 and 1918 Irene threw herself into the war effort, both in France, volunteering for the YMCA, and as a VAD in London. Her beloved younger brother died in Germany in 1919. Mansfield Priestley Evans, her fiancé, survived the war, but went out to serve with the English military government in Iraq. In 1920, two whole years after the Armistice was signed – by which time it must have seemed safe to assume a happy outcome – the news came that he had been killed there in a village uprising. By a cruel twist of fate Irene Rathbone joined the Surplus Women.

Post-war, Irene lived a semi-Bohemian life in Chelsea with a group of women friends, financing herself with office work and occasional stage roles. Dorothy Wadham of PEN and the writer Storm Jameson were among her friends. Joan, her heroine in *We That Were Young*, leads a life that mirrored her own at that time:

By night she danced, and went to studio parties up and down London, and was in all sorts of 'swims'. There were so many people who were interesting, so

\* See Virginia Nicholson, *Among the Bohemians – Experiments in Living*, Viking, 2002, Chapter 2: All for Love.

many new books to be read and discussed. And there were occasional trips abroad.
    . . . But in spite of her many activities, in spite of her genuine capacity for
enjoyment, if Joan had been told, by someone who knew, that to-morrow she
would have to leave all this and die, she would simply have said, 'Oh!'
    At the roots of her being there lay a vast indifference.

So her thirtieth birthday came and went; nobody of any significance came
to agitate her heart. But among the 'many books to be read and discussed',
one of the most talked-about of the late 1920s was *Death of a Hero* (1929).
Born in the same year as Irene, its author, Richard Aldington, was the
angry young man of his day; endowed with smouldering good looks and
brilliant talent, he was a glamorous figure in the literary world. Aldington
had already made a name as a poet and co-founder of the Imagist movement,
but *Death of a Hero* made him a celebrity. Irene must have read this
excoriating anti-war satire when it first came out, admired it, and then
sought out his poetry, but they did not meet until two years later in 1931.
When they did, her world was turned upside down.
    Six years after her affair with Richard Aldington ended, Irene set out her
recollections of their short idyll in a little book, *Was There a Summer?* (1943).
By the time the book was published Richard himself had moved on;
he was living in America with Nellie McCulloch, his second wife and
daughter-in-law of a previous mistress, Brigit Patmore. For him the affair
with Irene had been a transient pleasure, one among many. But for her it
had been a sacrament; she never loved anyone else.
    The prose-poem *Was There a Summer?* is not finely written, but every
line is saturated with emotion, dwelling on the detail of the relationship,
draining the draught of memory to its last, blushful, bubble-beaded drop.
From her park seat in misty London Irene conjures the warm south and
sunburnt mirth of their Provençal interlude with thirsty nostalgia:

> So fade out, London trees!
> Fade, fur-wrapped ladies
> Hurrying with small reluctant dogs back down dim paths
> To teas in Kensington,
> Fade . . .
> And shine Provence!

So we learn their story. In 1931 Richard was living in the south of France;
Irene had written him fan-mail about his work. For over a year they
corresponded, and finally he suggested she visit him at Le Lavandou, where

he had gone to write. He booked her into a hotel not far from the villa he had taken and here, among the pines and sudden sunlit sea of the Côte d'Azur, she found herself that summer. Of course she was already in love with him, from reading his poetry, but even so she was unprepared for the *coup de foudre* which struck her when they eventually met:

> He stood in front of me, sunbeams about his head
> And smiled through the midst of them.
> I thought a god was there.

Slowly she took in his appearance. Richard's smile and rather quizzical eyebrows gave him an irresistible charm; he was wearing a sleeveless blue shirt, red-brown fishermen's trousers and old espadrilles; his shoulders were broad and flat, his body slender, tanned and taut from swimming. This was more than a meeting of minds; Irene felt hollow with love and desire, for as they talked it appeared that he liked her too. They would write, he said, and walk, and go for drives to sleepy hill villages in his battered car. 'We can work, swim, talk or be silent together.' Then as the sky turned rose-colour, he strolled back with her towards the hotel; twilight was gathering. As they parted Irene could not suppress the urge she felt to raise her hand to his breast; he intercepted her gesture and held it in his – 'Then quick and light he put a kiss on it;/ Turned; went.' Was it a salutation, a gift, or a promise? Faint with emotion, Irene walked on suffused with the sweetness of that moment, sure now of her feelings, though unsure of his.

It was only a fortnight, but the memories were to last her lifetime. They became lovers. The hot, jewelled days succeeded each other. The mornings she spent reading, idling or exploring the vineyards, then the hour came when she walked to the villa and in the heat of the day they both flung themselves near-naked across the bright sand and into the translucent sea, to swim and float dreamily, then bake their salty bodies on the sun-struck beach. Then back to the villa for bread, chicken, salad, fruit, dawdling over their red wine till desire overcame languor and they moved to the cool shadowed bedroom. Expert, tender, sexy, imaginative, Richard's love-making left Irene brimful and replete with consummation:

> . . . I thank him for ever (looking back)
> Thank my perfect lover
> For the sheer beauty he brought to those hours:
> Tears stand in the eyes at it.

Nothing tainted their idyll. Even the small discolorations – the 'bruised blossom marks' – she later found on her skin were to her evidence of their fierce desire for each other, and she smiled secretly to herself when she saw how he had marked her body with his passion, knowing too how fiercely she had responded.

For her the happiness was entire and perfect. The battered car took them up to a mountain *auberge* with a sunset view where they drank *vin du pays* under a vine canopy and slept deeply in a huge bed. Wakened early by goat-bells, they relaxed back into warm contentment till the girl came to bring 'Monsieur et Madame' their coffee.

Richard was rare, as Irene said, in combining a graceful body with a lively and learned mind, and so they talked on history, and literature, discussing mankind and civilisation, peace, war, philosophy, sex, power and religion. Pink roses and oleander scented their moonlit terrace as she recited poetry to him, Milton, Carew and Ronsard. Sometimes the song of the nightingales drowned their conversation and they fell silent to listen. And sometimes she cried in his arms at the beauty of it all: 'Now, now, *now* I am happy.'

But it could never have lasted. Richard's complicated love life ruled out anything beyond this temporary affair. Not yet divorced from his first wife, he was at this time heavily involved with Brigit Patmore. He was disinclined to waste the opportunity of making love to his attractive admirer, but nothing more permanent was ever on the horizon. Richard asked Irene to stay longer, but what was such an invitation? It was not the invitation she wanted, the invitation to become Madame to his Monsieur. 'I adore you' was always on his lips, but never 'I love you':

> It was death in life to say no.
> But unless I stayed for always
> (And that was not asked)
> 'Longer' was impossible.

He declared that he would come to see her, after the summer. He couldn't do without seeing his friends, and libraries, and her, he said . . . but they were empty assurances, and he did not return to England. Finally a letter came that ended it all for her, 'Then no more ever.'

Lynn Knight's introduction to the 1989 edition of *We That Were Young* reports that Irene Rathbone's affair with Richard Aldington continued on and off until he left Brigit Patmore for his next lover, Nellie McCulloch, in 1937 – the year that Irene wrote *Was There a Summer?* The poetic version of her affair would seem to have been a dramatisation of events; things weren't in reality so cut and dried. In her essay Knight hints at the messy, clandestine nature of their relationship, with Irene in the role of the 'other woman', snatching what time Richard could spare her from Brigit, living for his brief visits to London, and the final shock of that last letter, finishing things for ever between them.

Whatever the case, Irene's searing affair with Richard Aldington continued to possess her. It surfaces with regularity in her fiction. In *October* (1934) the warm south of her idyll is represented by two Frenchmen, Gilbert and Henri. Gilbert wrote novels – Jenny had read them, and loved him for them, even before she met him. Jenny and Gilbert loved tempestuously, but Gilbert left her – 'full of promises, full of smiles' – and never wrote to her again. Henri and Rose too have loved each other with heartbreaking passion among the perfumed, moonlit Provençal nights; she writes to him, but he never replies . . . After *October* Irene wrote *They Call It Peace* (1936), in which the sensual side of her affair is achingly resurrected; here Joan and Paul's love is consummated over a London summer of hot city pavements, 'great still shadows in the breathless parks', the air filled with the drugged scent of honeysuckle, and roses blowing and scattering their petals in Kew Gardens. Joan, dreamy and desirable in briefs and camisole, blooms too – 'not [with] the bloom brought by fresh air, but that other, more subtle, brought by a physical love-life delighted in'. Paul drives her out to a riverside inn, where they swim, dine on the terrace and he makes love to her in a bedroom with a window opening on to trees. But their affair has no future; Paul is married:

Now she knew that Paul had a wife, had a child, had a house. Knew it. Domesticity had smiled its smug smile at her . . . she had seen . . . a pair of toothbrushes in the bathroom . . .

The cost had been very dear. Envy of wifehood – not of house, not of child, but just of wifehood – shook her. The female in her forlornly raged.

Lynn Knight comments sparingly: 'There were other love affairs, but Aldington remained significant . . .' Irene Rathbone never married. It is probable that in 1946, when she was in her fifties, she met Richard once again. He was back in Paris. Their views on that occasion seem to have collided over the question of France's suffering during the recent conflict, for Aldington, now married to Nellie McCulloch, had spent the years of the Second World War in America. It is hard not to wonder whether he had read *Was There a Summer?* 'I loved him once,' Irene wrote to her friend Nancy Cunard.

Aldington and Nellie parted in 1950, and he suffered a nervous breakdown. Soon after, his literary reputation received a major setback when he published a debunking biography of T. E. Lawrence. He lived the rest of his life in poverty in France, and died in the Burgundian village of Sury-en-Vaux in 1962. Irene read of his death in *The Times*. 'For years & years, as you know,' she wrote to Nancy, 'R. & I had not met, not written. Therefore my sorrow may be considered foolish. But I can't somehow bear him not to be in this world.' In 1964, after a visit to Nancy in the south-west of France, Irene returned home via Burgundy, where she sought out Richard's grave. There she placed flowers on the black commemorative slab and, for a while, remembered. 'It was very clear that she had never wavered in her love for Richard,' wrote a friend who knew them both.

If the abiding impression of Irene Rathbone's love affair with Richard Aldington is one of waste and melancholy – of the emptiness of a barren life – then perhaps the last word on it should be given to the author herself, who, despite being deserted and betrayed, despite all the heartbroken tears and forlorn rage, rejected the pity of others, and refused to pity herself:

Hear this, you tired fat-shouldered London trees,
You smug furred women,
And you, my other self in me who bleeds!
I hold this truth, at this moment –
Even if I lose or deride it later –
The heaven of Happiness-in-Love once entered
Is there for always.

I have been blind with pain
But then
Blind almost with bliss too . . .

For how many of the smug, furred, married women had ever had such a summer, or could ever have such memories?

★

Perhaps the definition of spinster needs to stretch to accommodate women like Irene Rathbone who saw no reason to conform to the expectations of that term, who were open about their erotic needs and refused to deny them. The 'female in her' may have envied wifehood and coveted that symbolic wedding ring, but for her such a love needed nothing so banal to sanctify it. Blessed by sun and sex, 'We knew, my love and I,/That this life of ours here was a sacrament . . .' She had burned to that white heat. Irene Rathbone, and others like her, were pioneers, ahead of their time, and perhaps today's general acceptance of their expanded morality is one of the reasons that the word spinster has so little relevance in the twenty-first century. Bohemianism had unlocked the door.

## The Well

Bohemianism also unlocked the door for lesbians. During the war women who didn't marry because they loved women had a brief sense of having found a purposeful identity. Writing about the women's ambulance unit on the Western Front in *The Well of Loneliness* (1928), Radclyffe Hall recalled:

. . . a battalion was formed in those terrible years that would never again be completely disbanded. War and death had given them a right to life, and life tasted sweet, very sweet to their palates. Later on would come bitterness, disillusion, but never again would such women submit to being driven back to their holes and corners.

Their relationships brought them the tenderness and intimacy – the passion too – which as human beings they craved. Nevertheless many lesbians left out on the margins still felt a mixture of shame and confusion, alongside a deep-rooted belief that a sexual orientation which brought them happiness and fulfilment must be blameless. Lesbianism (unlike male homosexuality) was not illegal, but it was not sanctioned either. In 1920, even before the highly public court case surrounding the publication of *The Well of Loneli-ness*, Radclyffe Hall had gone to court to defend herself against accusations that she was 'a grossly immoral woman'. The jury, manoeuvred by the skill of a shrewd counsel, acquitted her, as did her own conscience, but she knew that if her sexual behaviour had come under real scrutiny she might not have got off so readily.

At that time lesbian women had no public champion, and another ten years were to pass before Hall was to stand in the witness-box on their behalf. After the war lesbians looked in vain for someone to speak out on their behalf. In 1918 one of them wrote pleadingly to Marie Stopes. She was forty-eight years old, she said, and having always been highly-sexed had been driven to relieve herself by masturbation. She wanted advice, but she also wanted Dr Stopes to take up her cause and that of other 'Uranians':

I write, hoping you will not think me impertinent in doing so, to ask you quite frankly if you will not come forward as the champion of woman Uranians, and explain our position to the public in a way they can understand; they must not go on thinking the silly cruel things about us they do at present . . .

What I feel so strongly is that the girls must be helped. I have suffered so much in my life (and so have some of my women friends who are also inverts) because my temperament was neither recognized nor understood; so much of my suffering was so entirely unnecessary. Until parents and teachers are instructed in the matter this endless mishandling of such girls will continue. *Someone* must instruct them, and it is essentially a woman's job. Won't you be the woman to help us through?

. . . We want a champion badly, and would be only too willing to welcome her.

Marie Stopes was not sympathetic. Her reply was brief – she would be happy one day to attempt a short book on the 'disease of Uranianism'. She could see herself as the doctor, or saviour perhaps, of such women – but never their champion. They must fend for themselves.

Not surprisingly in this climate the voices that did speak out for lesbian women were cautious ones. In 1924, four years before *The Well of Loneliness* was published, a minor writer called Sylvia Stevenson set down her painful meditations on the theme of lesbian orientation in a novel whose heroine, Sally Wraith, struggles for recognition of her forbidden emotions. The novel, mostly forgotten now, was entitled *Surplus*.

*Surplus* was not prosecuted, perhaps because its author, in insistently stressing that her heroine was virtually asexual, was very careful not to stick her head over the parapet. But despite itself, Sally Wraith's yearning to demonstrate her love persistently surfaces, barely articulated. The book is in fact a rather wearying example of confessional literature, which asks the reader to follow the meandering and ultimately unsatisfying relationship between Sally, who works as a garage hand, and her artist friend Averil Kennion, charming in paint-smeared overalls. Nevertheless the novel, as it ploughs its way through the ups and downs of their relationship – the loneliness, the jealousies, the cross-purposes and the brief ecstasies – makes an unambiguous plea on behalf of all the misunderstood women for whom 'friendship' – as Stevenson terms it – meant more than marriage ever could.

*Surplus* reads very like autobiography, as it traces its heroine's life and love story. Sally (Sylvia?) knows from the outset that she will never pair off with a man: '. . . she had a perverse and ridiculous objection to being kissed.' She's as much of a misfit when it comes to work too, refusing to get a job as a lady's companion. To her father she's a failure, with no qualifications, no job and no husband. Then she meets Averil. For Sally it is love at first sight, but though Averil adores her their friendship has, for her, no baggage of commitment. Agonisingly for Sally, Averil likes men, and she even enjoys kissing them. More angst is in store when a third woman appears on the scene, and Sally is consumed with jealousy, followed by stricken disbelief when Averil then announces she wants to get married. Married!

'. . . What's the idea? Are you getting tired of me, or what?'

'Of course not' – Averil put out a weary hand – 'But we couldn't expect to go on living together all our lives, surely?'

She said it as if it were quite an ordinary statement, and it was too much for Sally.

'We are going on together – I thought it was to be for always and so did you,' she cried. 'We belong together. Promise you won't leave me, promise! You're the only creature I really care for in the world, you can't leave me alone. I want you too much.'

'But, my dear old thing, Barry wants me too,' said Averil.

Almost to the last breath, terrified of being left alone, Sally fights to keep Averil. Life is cruel. Already the war had robbed so many women; her failure to find a job or to be married had outlawed and condemned her. Then Averil came along and seemed to offer the sweet surety of love; and now, mercilessly, ironically, marriage comes like a thief to steal the one companion she would live or die for. Sally feels like a freak, a 'scapegoat, cast out from the herd', a frustrated spinster:

'It's unfair!' she cried. 'I love a woman with all the strength of my heart, and I'm sneered at, laughed at, condemned to solitude as if I'd committed a crime.'

How could she live, alone for ever? *Surplus* ends, however, with hope. Was Sally really a freak? – a misfit? Maybe not. Maybe there were 'others like her . . .'? Maybe there were even great numbers of 'unmated women' out there, looking for 'friendship'? And if there were, and they were to find it, surely they would discover that they had not, after all, missed out on the greatest thing the world has to offer: love – 'the only human attribute that is indestructible by time, that is certain to survive time, if humanity itself survives'.

As the aggrieved heroine of a rather tedious novel Stevenson's Sally Wraith is not a character worth following for 300-odd pages; however, as the archetype of a misfit – a suffering, denying, unhappy, misunderstood

example of what many, many women at that period must have undergone
– her plight is pitiable. Just how many there were is impossible to say.
Crushed by the respectable world, this love dared not speak its name.

Luckily for those misfits daring enough to venture beyond the confines
of respectability, there was a joyful alternative. In 1920s Britain – above all
in London – artists and subversives made up a recognisable Bohemian
sub-culture. At the Café Royal homosexual woman felt accepted among
like-minded comrades: modernist poets, exhibitionists, cross-dressers,
abstract expressionists, models and nightclub dancers. The Ham Bone Club
and the Cave of Harmony too were full of them. Here they could dance
together, unafraid, knowing that the shortage of men had made this a
common sight. In *The Long Week-End* (1941), a social history of Great
Britain between the wars, Robert Graves and Alan Hodge noted the
increase of homosexuality following the German example: 'In certain Berlin
dance-halls, it was pointed out, women danced only with women and men
with men. Germany land of the free! The Lesbians took heart and followed
suit, first in Chelsea and St John's Wood, and then in the less exotic suburbs
of London . . . [They] were more quiet about their aberrations at first; but,
if pressed, they justified themselves . . . by pointing out that there were not
enough men to go round in a monogamous system . . .'

Like Marie Stopes, Graves and Hodge appear to have viewed 'The
Lesbians' as deviant. The psychologist Esther Harding was more apologetic;
she felt that the 'rise' in lesbianism was attributable to career women
who reached their thirties only to find 'all the men of their age already
married . . .', the implication being that such 'deviancy' was forgivable in
the circumstances. Even so, Harding's attitude betrays her sense that if they
couldn't get a man, the Surplus Women would have to get their fun where
they could.

The lesbians themselves had their own charmed circles, however; and
they saw themselves as the last word in modernity and emancipation. In
the early 20s Radclyffe Hall (known to her friends as John) was at the centre
of an exuberant crowd of artistic and theatre types. There was the cellist
Gwen Farrar, with her basso profundo voice, her horn-rimmed glasses and
her on- (and off-) stage partner, the pianist Norah Blaney. There was the
American revue star Teddie Gerard, who stunned audiences in 1915 with
her appearance in a backless gown while behind her a chorus of male
crooners sang, 'Glad to see You're Back, Dear Lady'. The defection of
Teddie's lover Etheline to Eileen Bliss got everyone gossiping, but Teddie
herself seemed unperturbed. She was a hard-drinking, promiscuous adven-
turess with a drug habit. They were joined by the spendthrift Alabama-born

*First Lady Pipe-smoker.* "I SAY, ISN'T YOUR PIPE A BIT LARGE?"
*Second ditto.* "NOT A BIT. I WOULDN'T BE SEEN DEAD WITH AN EFFEMINATE LITTLE THING LIKE YOURS."

According to *Punch*, size mattered to certain women as much as to men (June 1921)

actress Tallulah Bankhead, the eccentric millionairess and speedboat racer Jo Carstairs, and the widowed but lesbian playwright, Gabrielle Enthoven. Then there was 'Toupie' Lowther, divorced daughter of the Earl of Lonsdale, and Enid Elliot and the Honourable Eileen Plunkett, all ex-wartime ambulance drivers. The *Daily Mail* fashion correspondent, Evelyn Irons, and her partner Olive Rinder both provided the intrigue of their tortuous *ménage à trois* with Vita Sackville-West, while 'Poppy' and 'Honey' were a pair of drunk-and-disorderlies known only by their first names. Escaped from her marriage of convenience, the artist Romaine Brooks (of a slightly older generation) sometimes put in an impressive appearance with her lover, the American poet Natalie Barney. Romaine Brooks, like Radclyffe Hall and many of the others, preferred to wear severe, masculine attire; her self-portrait shows a crop-haired wraith with feverish eyes and funereal garb. In *The Forge* (1924), Radclyffe Hall described her as 'beautiful with an elusive, inward kind of beauty difficult to describe'. This crowd rode motorcycles, cropped their hair, smoked jewelled pipes and danced jazz. Hall herself wrote all day, talked, smoked and partied all night.

If like Radclyffe Hall you were 'in' with them, the social whirl was an intoxicating cocktail. In Bohemia, 'Sapphism' was just another life-enhancing eccentricity. If you wanted to call yourself Dickie, Jo or Billie, wear double-breasted jackets and wing collars and crop your hair, nobody felt threatened. At Goldenhurst, his house on Romney Marsh, Noël

Coward kept open house for the *beau monde*, which included the Radclyffe Hall circle. The dinner parties there rang with howls of laughter.

But when the storm broke over *The Well of Loneliness* in 1928 Radclyffe Hall's privacy was at an end. By the time it was published she was already an acclaimed writer, with a best-selling novel and two prestigious literary prizes behind her. As such she was positioned to attract both notice and censure. For the editor of the *Sunday Express* no abuse was too strong: 'I would rather give a healthy boy or a healthy girl a phial of prussic acid than this novel,' he raged. *The Well* had gone as far as any book could in depicting lesbian relationships, although the nearest it came to being explicit was some rather hot kissing. Probably the righteous anger of the *Sunday Express* was directed against the euphemistic phrase which ends Chapter 38: '. . . that night they were not divided'. There is nothing stronger than that, unless one takes exception to some fuzzy emotional passages referring to ardent fulfilment, turbulent rivers and dim golden hazes.

Recently, it has emerged that the storm over *The Well* made waves even in political circles. The male establishment had strenuously discouraged any mention of lesbianism, to the extent of actively denying its existence. In 1921 a bill making lesbianism illegal failed to pass into law because MPs considered that it was wiser to sweep the whole issue under the carpet than to risk dignifying such a disturbing and repellent practice with legal endorsement. Plainly, they feared 'the oxygen of publicity'. When the *Well* storm broke, the Prime Minister, the Chancellor and the Home Secretary went to great lengths to suppress Hall's book, and the Director of Public Prosecutions made clear his fear that an increase in female homosexuality would exacerbate the man shortage: 'I am afraid [that] curiosity may lead to imitation and indulgence in practices which are believed to be somewhat extensive having regard to the very large excess in numbers of women over men,' he wrote. In other words, the powers-that-be were persuaded that the book's lesbian content threatened the wellbeing of the entire nation.

But now Radclyffe Hall was on the warpath. Conspicuous in the court in a Spanish riding-hat and a long leather coat, she became the public and political face of lesbianism. Her stand was for all those 'inverts' and 'deviants' abused by a hostile world; she stood up for the unlucky, 'the weak and the hopeless'; she wanted to bring the rest of the world to understanding. In the event Sir Chartres Biron, the Chief Magistrate, condemned *The Well of Loneliness* to be burnt as an obscene libel.

There is of course nothing like banning a book to guarantee that it will be obtained, read and discussed in the most public way possible. *The Well* found publishers and translators abroad and sold millions of copies; in 1949 the Falcon Press bravely tested the law again and the book was published in Britain. By a certain satisfying justice, the case achieved the exact result that the politicians had most feared, and to the fury of those who wanted the novel extinguished, the Radclyffe Hall trial fanned the lesbian flames into a bonfire. Homosexual women had found their champion – one they had long been waiting for. *The Well of Loneliness* is still in print.

★

Dancing to jazz bands, smoking jewelled pipes, and confronting the might of the law weren't everyone's notion of a contented emotional life. From the outset Angela du Maurier had hankered for marriage, but her lack of success with men may well have turned her towards her own sex. Angela was a serial faller-in-love. In the summer of 1929, when she was twenty-five, she fell madly in love with 'X', a man whom she described as Mr Right; unfortunately nobody else agreed, including X's wife. The affair, like all the others, ended in tears. The following year she met her 'twin', Angela Halliday. It was as if their identities had become blended from the outset, for they were both born on the same day, 1 March 1904; both their mothers were named Muriel, and both their fathers went to Harrow. Their nurses were both called Nurse Pierce, and as babies both were wheeled in their perambulators around Regent's Park. However, they differed by being ten inches apart in height. In her autobiography du Maurier is cryptic, but the clues are there; she appears to have found her true orientation.

From that point on, there is little talk of relationships with men; instead she sits down to write her first novel, *The Little Less*, the story of a lesbian love affair. (After *The Well of Loneliness* no publisher would touch it, and Angela had to bowdlerise it for eventual publication in 1941.) Later in life, when she came to write a second volume of memoirs, *Old Maids Remember* (1966), Angela took good care to remind her readers that the Bible – in the story of Ruth and Naomi – acknowledged female love. In the memoir du Maurier persisted in claiming that her relationships were innocent, and it may well be that they were. It infuriated her to think that a same-sex ménage was always immediately assumed to be debauched. Living on your own was the only way to ensure an unsullied reputation, and who in their right minds would settle for that? So what could a middle-aged old maid possibly tell anyone about love? More than you might think, was the implication of her defended reply. Sex was a justifiable pleasure in life, and after all, in her words, 'to be white as the driven snow at thirty is just damn silly'.

For Angela du Maurier discretion was the key, and there are plenty of examples of lesbian women who quietly and discreetly settled down with their chosen partner for a lifetime of tender intimacy and rewarding hard work. Paul Fussell, an historian who grew up after the First World War, recalled a clichéd folk-memory of such women:

A common sight in the thirties – to be seen, for some reason, especially on railway trains – was the standard middle-aged Lesbian couple in tweeds, who had come together as girls after each had lost a fiancé, lover or husband . . .

This type was often to be found among the educational community, among those who had read the more broad-minded psychological literature on women's sexuality and spinsterhood. So long as women like this maintained a façade of utter probity, it was possible to have a full emotional life. Alice Skillicorn, principal of Homerton Teacher Training College in Cambridge from 1935, first met Dorothy Sergeant in the early 1930s. They were both working in the school inspectorate at that time. But Alice's appointment as the leader of a premier educational institution, responsible for several hundred young unmarried women, made it impossible for her to risk scandal, so Dorothy remained in the background. Thus during the week Alice lived in college and played out her headmistressy role to perfection: gruff, forceful and bossy, she didn't waste words and could be austerely unapproachable.

The weekends and vacations were a different story. The couple shared a house, where Dorothy's abundant domestic skills came into their own, and where her warm, easy-going, gregarious character melted Alice's repressed emotions. Alice and Dorothy remained together for nearly forty happy years, until Dorothy died in 1969. Alice was broken-hearted. Ten years later she too was laid to rest in the same grave, whose tombstone records their 'dear and devoted friendship'. Everyone knew, but no one was offended.

Relationships like this offered real and lasting happiness. Love, achievement and creativity were part of their lives, and many others'. The textile designers Phyllis Barron and Dorothy Larcher found equal happiness together. This pair of talented artists worked and lived together in a lovely Georgian house in the Cotswolds from 1930. A friend described it as 'a marriage of true minds'. Besides being a subtle and distinctive designer, Barron (as she was always known) was a pillar of the community; she was chairman of the Parish Council and a member of numerous local committees.

Another devoted partnership was that of Dr Helen Mackay and the scientist Lorel Goodfellow. Also known by her surname, Mackay was an eminent paediatrician, committed to finding the cause and cure of infant anaemia; together she and Goodfellow published research into this important topic. They also shared a passion for bird-watching. Mary Renault met her lifelong companion Julie Mullard while both were training as nurses at the Radcliffe Infirmary in Oxford. The pair settled in South Africa, where Renault devoted herself to literature. Female (and male) homosexuality were to become dominant themes in her novels.

The novelist Sylvia Townsend Warner's relationship with the poet Valentine Ackland is a great love story. Valentine's early life was unhappy, confused and promiscuous (with both sexes); her attachment to Sylvia brought much-needed stability and domestic contentment, and they too stayed together until death parted them after nearly forty years. On New Year's Eve 1950 Sylvia wrote to a friend from the Norfolk coast where they were staying, conjuring a picture of cosy matrimonial bliss, tinged with romance:

We have been snow-bound and ice-bound for days at a time . . . A devoted baker brought us bread twice a week; we had our woodpile, and the sea kept on adding to it with driftwood; once, when all the water froze, we melted snow . . . I have not seen Valentine so happy nor so much herself for years, and all her beauty has come back to her, and she walks about like a solitary sea nymph . . . a sea nymph who can split logs with an axe and manage a most capricious petrol pump, and cut up large frozen fish with a cleaver.

It was a brilliant idea to come here . . .

## The urge

The new freedom wasn't just a question of sexual licence, or the expression of sexual orientation. The rewards were great for women of energy and initiative like Winifred Holtby, or the stockbroker Beatrice Gordon Holmes, or the campaigner Florence White. They fully justified their claims to self-sufficient, contented lives. Marjorie Hillis summed it up in her manual *Live Alone and Like It* (1936): 'You will soon find out that independence, more truthfully than virtue, is its own reward. It gives you a grand feeling. Standing on your own feet is extraordinarily exhilarating.'

After the war a single, economically self-sufficient woman without family responsibilities had the world at her feet, at a time when conditions abroad encouraged her to look beyond Bradford or Basingstoke for freedom and fulfilment. A journalist writing in *The Times* in 1922 urged unmarried women to take advantage of a new climate of post-war tolerance to be found in France. The French respected initiative, seriousness and English good manners, and in their country to be a spinster was 'no longer a disgrace; . . . merely a misfortune'. Nobody would ask awkward questions if a single woman wanted to sit in a café alone; and she might visit whom she chose:

She goes unquestioned and unprotected to studios, restaurants, and places of amusement. Whatever her means or her place in society, the unmarried English-woman in France has opportunities of seeing and knowing French home life which are rarely offered to the married woman.

A spinster with an income no longer needed to feel imprisoned.

In 1922 a young woman named Etta Close found herself in exactly this position. Her family's demands were not compelling, but they were tiresome. Luncheons with lady-friends had limited attractions, tea-parties even fewer. She was sick of being treated by her relatives as a useful aunt endlessly available to accompany her nieces to have their teeth pulled at the dentist, or to pick up her nephews from railway stations, feed them and tip them before seeing them off again on the next train to Harrow. It galled her to think of her married brothers and sisters saying to each other: 'A single woman, you know, with nothing in the world to do, of course she ought to be glad to be of use to others.' Their attitude set her to pondering how somebody with 'nothing to do' should be spending their time, if not servicing their nearest and dearest. It seemed to her that all too often such women, even when blessed with health and money, created fetters for themselves:

Looking with a disinterested spinster eye on the world, I notice that even . . . those who do not marry a man seem invariably to marry themselves to a garden, or a house, or a dog, and then having forged their own chains say pathetically, 'If only I were free, how I would love to travel and see the world.'

Etta was determined not to fall into that trap. She was free, and realised it, and without further ado she made up her mind to go travelling.

There were a couple of false starts, however. Her stockbroker advised her to go to Monte Carlo and, persuaded that a spell of dissipation might be just the right antidote to life as a maiden aunt, she set off there. But the Casino and the Café de Paris left her cold. She drifted down the coast to Cannes for some tennis, then on to Menton. Everyone there seemed obsessed with talking about their ailments. The bright grass seemed fake, and even the flowers seemed varnished, over-bright. 'I felt sick, everything artificial . . .' France wasn't living up to its early promise. Then a friend said, 'Go to Kenya.' ' "If there is a ship going to Mombasa soon and there is an empty cabin on her I will go," I answered, being a believer in fate.' Ten days later Etta set sail.

Via Port Said and the Seychelles the steamer eventually docked at Mombasa, where, within hours of her arrival, the monsoon struck. Etta sat in a railway carriage with an umbrella over her head as the rain bucketed in from both sides, forming a lake on the floor. Next day the line climbed through mango trees and cocoa palms, then on uphill through thorn scrub inhabited by lions, zebras and antelopes. Her adventure had begun.

Two years after her African journey Etta Close wrote her account of it in *A Woman Alone, in Kenya, Uganda and the Belgian Congo* (1924). She had seen Kilimanjaro, encountered tarantulas over breakfast, eaten antelope, fungus, mealies and rotten fish, seen hippopotami, crocodiles and lions. There had been mountains, banana forests, big-game hunts and tribes with poisoned arrows. Etta had also caught malaria and heard herself described as the first woman to go out 'on her own' into the game country. 'On her own' was relative – she was accompanied by a Dutchman named Mr Trout – but he forbore to help her:

I scrambled up and down the most horrible places, getting along alone as best I could . . .

Altogether I would say to a woman going to a wild country to learn never to be hungry unless there is something to eat, never to be thirsty unless there is something to drink, and never be sleepy or tired unless you know your bed is ready for you. When you have mastered these three simple rules go out on safari and you will enjoy yourself.

Etta went to Africa intending to stay three months; she stayed eighteen.

The question to ask is – was it worth it? And I reply – a thousand times yes.

Etta Close's safari had its challenges, and she nearly died of malaria, but she was doing nothing unprecedented. The world had opened up since the nineteenth century when Isabella Bishop and Marianne North had penetrated the Kurdistani desert and the jungles of Sarawak. Travel was getting easier. All it took to see the world was determination. Large numbers of maiden ladies packed their portmanteaux and set out undaunted – as missionaries, mountaineers, archaeologists, explorers, soldiers, nurses and naturalists.

The spinsters spread far and wide. Entomologist Evelyn Cheesman described her passion for exploration as 'the Urge'. In 1924 she travelled to the Galápagos Islands with her specimen boxes and butterfly nets. Subsequent trips took her to the remotest jungles and mountains of Papua New Guinea. There the indigenous population knew her as 'the woman who walks' and 'the lady of the mountains'. But Evelyn was not ladylike: dressed in voluminous bloomers and canvas shoes, she was independent, brave and strong-minded. Una May Cameron, heiress to the Dewar whisky fortune, educated at Cheltenham Ladies' College, used her wealth to indulge her passion for mountaineering. By 1938 she had scaled peaks not only in the Lake District and the Alps, but also in the Rockies, the Caucasus and East Africa. She was the first woman to climb Nelion and Batian, the two peaks of Mount Kenya. Standing on those summits, it is unlikely she ever wished she were in Kensington.

The Gamwell sisters, Hope ('the thick one') and Marian ('the thin one'), had been brought up by their mother to treat life as an adventure. Both were wartime members of the First Aid Nursing Yeomanry, or FANY, driving a vast Daimler fitted out with portable baths to wash and disinfect the Belgian army. After the war they set out together – by car – to prospect for farming land in East Africa, and hacked a coffee plantation out of 1,000 acres of virgin bush south of Lake Tanganyika. When not battling off hyenas or contending with tsetse fly, they were training as pilots.

The London parlourmaid Gladys Aylward★ was determined to worship a purpose larger than herself by becoming a missionary; she saved up her wages and set out for China on the Trans-Siberian Railway. The endless journey took her through Eastern Europe, across the Steppes and into the immense grandeur of Siberia. On the Manchurian border a small war meant the train could go no further. Gladys picked up her cases and walked down the railway line. It was perishing cold and she heard wolves howling. In Vladivostok she was arrested by Soviet officials, but escaped on a Japanese ship; finally, famished and weary, she arrived at her destination of Yangsheng, Shansi province. There, for the next twenty years, Gladys put her simple and fervent Christianity into action, tending lepers, helping refugees, caring for sick children, and always preaching the stories of the Testaments

---

★ Aylward became a household name when she was portrayed by the actress Ingrid Bergman in the 1959 film version of her life, *The Inn of the Sixth Happiness*. In fact, Miss Aylward strongly objected to the casting of Bergman in the role, since she was a divorced woman.

that inspired and guided her at every turn. She adopted five Chinese children, and watched them grow up. They called her Ai Weh-te – 'the virtuous one'.

★

The broadening of horizons helped to put personal unhappiness in perspective. At the age of seventy-seven Dame Margery Perham looked back on her youth in a BBC talk entitled 'The Time of My Life'. The year she chose to recall was 1921; the journey she took then fulfilled a childhood dream, and provided a guiding purpose for the rest of her life. But at the time the decision to travel to Africa was taken under doctor's orders. Margery had suffered a complete nervous breakdown and was firmly advised to take a year's convalescence.

The breakdown was the result of a pile-up of troubles both during and after the war. Margery's catastrophe was not the man shortage, nor even the death of a sweetheart, but the loss of the person she loved most in the world, her brother Edgar, killed in the awful slaughter of Delville Wood on the Somme in 1916. Edgar and she had been inseparable as children. They had invented a private world, written each other long letters when he was away at boarding school, composed a joint opera and studied at Oxford together. She found it almost unbearable to live without him. In her 1927 novel *Josie Vine*★ Margery struggled to describe the depths of grief which afflicted her during that terrible time:

. . . After twenty-five years of vigorous life, his body lay, a disfigured and useless thing, already touched, perhaps, by the decay that would soon crumble it into the earth on which it was lying. She felt the sword-like severing that had cut away her comrade from her side and put an end to his music, his learning, and laughter . . . She dared not look upon the years during which she would live on without him; to be alive now – to be strong – to breathe and eat, seemed a treachery to him.

'. . . Why were we born at all, or allowed to love each other so? Oh God, God, how could You let it happen?'

Then she sank into that silent realization of loss in which human nature reaches the utmost limit of suffering.

After the war Margery took her degree, and got a job in the history faculty of Sheffield University. She was utterly miserable, barely clinging

★ Margery Perham denied that the novel was autobiographical, but it contains too many parallels with her own life for this claim to be convincing.

to existence. Female academic staff were exiled to a freezing and comfortless dungeon called the 'Ladies Common Room'; her salary was inadequate. Nightly she travelled on a clanging tram to her nasty cheap rooms on the edge of the city and consumed her meagre meat and pudding 'which I had cut up into four portions to last for four days'. When demobilisation came, bringing with it a torrent of students needing tuition, she was crushed with overwork. 'My one recreation was to walk out on to the rather grim moorland and sit down amongst the wiry inhospitable heather which was grimed with soot, and contemplate, physically and mentally, the dark bare horizon.'

Grief and exhaustion took their toll. Margery was sliding into the abyss. When her doctor issued his command some self-preserving instinct drove her to reach into her childhood and fulfil a secret dream of travel. Her early reading had been Kipling and Rider Haggard. From a very young age, when the grown-ups had asked her what she wanted to be when she grew up, Margery's invariable answer had been 'a big-game hunter in Africa'. By luck her older sister Ethel was married to a colonial administrator who had recently been posted to Hargeisa, British Somaliland. Now Ethel was due to join her husband, so in 1921 she and Margery set sail together in a P & O liner from Tilbury. The adventure, and the healing, had begun.

They travelled via Aden and then took a cattle-boat across the gulf. At Aden Margery was overwhelmed for the first and last time with a night-marish recoil of fear and revulsion at the thought of her own vulnerability as a white female among savages: 'I was about to commit myself to that black continent across the water; one, almost alone, among tens of thousands of strange, dark, fierce, uncomprehending people, and live away on that far frontier, utterly cut off from my own race.' But the feeling passed and, despite many real dangers, never returned. At Berbera on the coast of Somaliland the ladies were eventually met by the District Commissioner, Margery's brother-in-law Major Rayne. Accompanied now, they travelled 200 miles on camel-back, through the inhospitable wasteland of north-east Africa, to the distant outpost of Hargeisa.

. . . Hargeisa. It is still a magic word to me. Yet there wasn't much to see – sand, thorn-trees, aloes, a few stony hills, a *tug* or dry water-course . . .

You might well ask how such a place could give me the 'time of my life'. Yet it did. Whatever my later travels in more beautiful and dramatic parts of the continent, this was my *first* Africa.

In her own words, Margery Perham was 'gloriously happy' in Hargeisa. She was transfixed by the beauty of the Somali people, by the burnished bloom of their dark skins, by their vigour and proud carriage. The Raynes lived in a reasonably comfortable compound; colonial life, even in the middle of nowhere, held to its traditions of Britishness. Tennis, steeple-chasing and shooting were all available. Margery and her sister donned evening dress before mounting camels to join the handful of British officers living in tents on the other side of the *tug* for pre-dinner drinks, though out in the bush she delighted in her costume of high leather boots, khaki breeches and wide-brimmed terai hat. But above all Africa itself bewitched her. On moonlit nights ghostly hyenas prowled around the compound; from the roof where Margery slept under the stars she heard their unearthly howls and felt a quiver of exhilarated fear. When the rains finally fell on that desiccated landscape the unforgettably acrid scent of dust and water filled her nostrils.

There was danger all around. Between their tribes the Somali people could be as fierce and ruthless as they were often gentle and loyal. There was strife between Christian and Muslim, and Margery never forgot the fearful day when the Major found a document pinned to a thorn tree calling upon their loyal soldiers to cut the throats of their white masters and join with the Muslim uprising to overthrow the infidel. Fortunately for them the soldiers ignored this diktat, and their throats were not cut.

Most of all a trek with her brother-in-law to reconnoitre the Abyssinian frontier sated Margery's thirst for adventure. On the map the border area was blank, with the word 'Unexplored' printed tantalisingly across it. 'As far as I know no Europeans had ever followed our route . . .' They set off with a party of resplendent Somali police in uniform, travelling sometimes on camel-back, sometimes by pony, winding their way through the thorn-scrub. Every day they rose at first light, and started out through the mysterious silence of the African dawn; in the heat of the day they rested. They camped out in beautifully decorated Indian tents.

Night was the zenith of adventure. I slept on a camp-bed in the open with large fires on each side of me to scare potential carnivores – lions, hyenas or leopards. The police built a high *zareba* of thorn branches round our camp. They would sing themselves gutturally to sleep. Then that miracle of the tropical night of stars! If the moon was up the sand turned the colour of milk. These nights utterly fulfilled the heart's desire of my childhood for adventure in Africa.

But more was to come, for one night a lion jumped the defences of a neighbouring Somali camp and killed a man. Margery accompanied Major Rayne tracking the pack across the bush; after a day's pursuit she became

separated from her brother-in-law and found herself face to face with an
exhausted, angry lion. Fortunately the animal uttered a snarl and, hearing
it, the experienced Major fired his gun into the air, scaring it back into the
bush: for Margery, this incident was the climax of the entire expedition.

The year ended. Margery Perham went back to Sheffield, back to the
sooty heather and the clanging trams. And somehow this time it was
different. Her experience of Africa had dislodged the cloying misery which
had clamped down over her hopes and ambitions. She found friends, bought
a motor-bike, wrote a play and acted in it, and had two novels published.
But Africa never loosed its hold on her; her fascination with the country,
and the issue of our own responsibility for it as colonisers, took root in her
brain. By chance in 1924 a post came up at her old Oxford college; her
scanty experience of the colonial administration was by then sufficient
for her to be asked to instruct foreign service probationers. And that was
the beginning of a lifetime of travel and research, of teaching, advising,
publishing and journeying. Margery went to the Pacific islands, to the
Antipodes, to America, the Caribbean, and made many return visits to
Africa. When Major Rayne died in the 1940s Margery and her sister set up
home together in Surrey, which became her base for writing when not
abroad. Her academic eminence as an expert on African affairs was recognised by governments at home and overseas and in 1948 she was honoured
with a CBE.

'And what about my beloved Somaliland?' In 1960 the new government
invited Margery to attend the independence celebrations as its guest – 'so I
could see again that harsh land and those handsome, high-spirited people
rejoicing in their freedom and unity'. The occasion had personal echoes
for her. She remembered the days of tribal strife; conflict had brought
tragedy for her too, but her life's work had been to attain peace between
peoples. Certainly, their ecstasy now mingled with her own, for in that
stony unexplored desert, forty years earlier, she had found a passion, a
purpose and, after terrible anguish, peace of mind.

## Finding happiness as a 'bach'

But it was no good pretending. A lot of the Surplus Women still found it
tough being surplus. Independence could be isolating. Urges didn't come
to everyone. Closer to home, for the average Surplus Woman confined to
office, classroom, scullery or bedside, what silver linings could enable them
to look on the bright side? How did the single woman deal with the black
times, the natural feelings of forlorn rage, loneliness and disappointment

that crowded in upon them? The anti-feminist Charlotte Cowdroy cited a women's magazine article describing a new disease: 'one-room-itis', from which many of the bachelor girls were suffering. 'One-room-itis' afflicted hostel-dwellers in big cities, living on inadequate wages, condemned by lack of resources to spend cheerless evenings washing and mending stockings, with never any fun, never any games. Miss Cowdroy's unrealistic (and somewhat hypocritical) solution was to discourage women from ever entering the workplace. They should all get married and have babies. Some hope.

There were advice-givers who adopted a more optimistic and practical line when addressing the Bachelor Girl. Many of their suggestions have already been outlined in Chapter 3; they ranged from taking up callisthenics to astrology, home decorating to football, learning German to good works.

'One-room-itis' as seen by *Woman's
Weekly*, 1920

But, as was so often the case, it was the women's magazines that seemed, somehow, to understand best what it was like for the bachelor girl with 'one-room-itis'. 'Little City Girl All Alone' was the title of 'a little article for the Business Girl who Lives in Digs, and Feels Rather Lonely', published in *Woman's Weekly* in March 1920. The drawing that illustrates it shows the young thing in a nightie with a quilt wrapped around her shoulders to keep off the chill, perched on the edge of her iron bed with its inadequate light; she probably had no chair. The uncurtained window looks on to the empty blackness of night, and the walls are bare. The book she is reading may be the Bible or Ethel M. Dell – we don't know.

'There are some advantages, I suppose, in being out in the world on your own,' said a business girl rather wistfully to me. 'And all the stay-at-home girls I know envy me my latch-key and complete independence – but, do you know, sometimes I'm frightfully lonely.

'You see, I'm out at business all day, and I don't have many chances of making friends . . .'

*Woman's Weekly* to the rescue. Take the initiative, urged the author of the article. There were office friendships to be made, contacts to be made through churches, and for goodness' sake, JOIN something. There were simply endless clubs: the YWCA, amateur dramatics, debating clubs and cycling clubs. 'Don't shut the door in the evenings and sit alone, when you are pining for a friend. Go out instead . . .'

If you did, there were open arms to greet you. So manifest was the issue of the Surplus Women that concerned bodies started to look at ways to assuage their needs. The Christian Alliance of Women and Girls was an outreach group set up in 1920 to offer friendship and religion specifically to women living in cities who suffered from 'one-room-itis'. Covertly, they feared that the girls would find their way from their 'one-rooms' and on to the streets if not steered towards more virtuous paths. The CAWG aimed at lifelong membership (unlike the YWCA), so was also particularly sympathetic to the older spinster who 'had once again got relegated to Cinderella's part behind the scenes'. For these ladies the CAWG offered clubs, hostels and, importantly, a solution for single women anxious about where to spend their annual holiday. Great efforts were made in fundraising to provide cheap, comfortable, seaside hostels in such pretty spots as Keswick or Llandudno, where singles were able to spend a happy fortnight together enjoying rambles, picnics and prayer meetings.

Networking was the key to curing 'one-room-itis'. Even before Florence White achieved her goal of pensions for spinsters aged sixty, her National Spinsters Pensions Association had not only given many single women a cause to rally behind, it had also provided a social amenity for the lonely. The Bradford branch of the NSPA started a Spinsters' Club, laying on all kinds of diversions and outings. 'I find real pleasure, and comfort, in our Spinsters' Club,' declared Miss Ethel Curtis, who at seventy-four was their oldest member. 'It is not only the concerts which are so kindly given to us, or in the little rambles; it is deeper than that. It is in meeting ladies of age and circumstances that are like my own, and in extending to each other sympathy and kindness, which will always make any gathering into a real club.'

Trade unions for working women did more than support their cause as employees; they were also a social outlet. For example, the female-dominated teaching profession saw the National Union of Women Teachers' conference as the high spot of their annual calendar – an excuse for a party. Alongside the debates members drank toasts, and entertained the delegates with orchestral recitals and community singing. At branch level NUWT members could attend their local HQ for weekly evening classes in Esperanto, ballroom dancing or to participate in amateur dramatics. And when in 1928 the Vote was granted to all women over twenty-one, members celebrated with a party at the Restaurant Frascati in London, where they ate and drank to the music of the NUWT choir.

Women's clubs also provided pleasure and comfort to career women making their way in the precarious and often hostile male professional world. The Soroptimist Clubs were for them: started in America, they got a toehold in Britain from 1923, and offered membership on the same basis as the Rotary Clubs for men – each business or profession was represented by one member. The stockbroker Beatrice Gordon Holmes was approached to join on behalf of women in finance. After years fighting a lone corner in a male-dominated world, it was a happy surprise to find that there were other pioneers who, like her, had broken through into trade and commerce:

I rediscovered women after years of daily living in a world of men. I was delighted with the discovery, because I had not encountered women of that calibre and distinction in numbers before. I like women, I have always liked women, but circumstances and, above all, my fundamental social shyness had kept me out of touch with other women of my generation.

Organising on behalf of professional women gave Gordon a new lease of life. In 1938 she went on to become first President of the British Federation of Business and Professional Women; the dynamic social atmosphere of Gordon's salon of professionals was described by one of its members:

Gordon Holmes, having changed her white suit for a colourful loose robe, reclined on a sofa propped up by cushions, smoking a cigarette in a fantastically long holder, whilst the others gathered in a circle round a large and cheerful fire. Ideas flew back and forth – some to be rejected instantly by the President, others to be seized on and eagerly developed . . .

★

In such ways, the Surplus Women offered each other support, guidance, intimacy, love and fun. Gradually and fearfully, the young women were recovering. Their natural appetites were reviving. Women like Vera Brittain who thought they had lost everyone they ever cared about confessed that there were things worth going on for: 'I love my uninterrupted independence . . . At long last I had achieved the way of living that I had always desired; I rejoiced in my work.'

Life had to go on for the Surplus Women. It took a particular kind of vitality and fearlessness to survive the blow of loss, and some never did. It was probably harder in some ways for the women who had never loved and lost, women like Winifred Haward who simply hoped in vain for a husband, for a 'great love that survives the night and climbs the stars'. Winifred Holtby confessed to the same desire for a passion that would one day come along and thrill her to the core: 'I really shall be disappointed if I go through life without once being properly in love.' Vera Brittain had no further wishes in this respect; she never reckoned on meeting anyone to replace Roland Leighton in her heart. Though she moved on, stoical, valiant, she owned later – despite having married and had children – that for years she had 'thought about little else but the war and the men I lost in it'.

But that conflict had claimed so many victims already. On the whole, Britain's single women had no intention of adding their own names to the casualty lists. There were many unlucky women, many poor and lonely spinsters, but victim mentality, defeatism, self-pity were not, in those still patriotic days, acceptable mindsets. Faint-heartedness was equated with cowardice in the public mind, and to succumb would be to betray the bravery of those who had died.

Thus one is more likely to come across stoical silence in the face of misfortune than a death-wish, and more likely still to find faith, fortitude and a sense of purpose. Life at the age of twenty, or even thirty, still stretched ahead. This was a vision which counted blessings, made the best of a bad job or, like Winifred Holtby, protested loudly against the notion that failure in marriage was the equivalent of failure in life. There was no excuse, she declared, for one in four women feeling cursed by their spinsterhood, and society must take the blame for making husbandless women feel that they were, of necessity, unfulfilled.

In May 1920 *Woman's Weekly* ran 'An Understanding Little Article', entitled 'Finding Happiness as a "Bach"'. The writer 'eavesdropped' on six single young women – Alicia, Mollie, Mona, Josephine, Janet and Frances – toasting their toes round the snuggery fire and talking about whether a woman could find true happiness without marriage.

Alicia was a schoolmistress:

'I mean to be happy in my career,' she said. 'I don't think for a moment that I shall marry.' We all knew that Alicia had once been engaged, and that she had lost her lover 'out there.'

Mollie was a doctor:

'I don't think an ambitious woman should marry . . . You can't run a career and a home too . . . As there seems to be a surplus of women I suggest careers as a substitute for a man. Like Alicia, I think a career can bring great happiness.'

Josephine spoke next:

'Well . . . I haven't a career, yet I have a jolly time as a "bach" . . . In fact, I get more invitations out than I want. I think a "bach" can be happy if she doesn't get selfish.'

Mona:

'Living alone does incline one towards selfishness . . .'

'That's what you have to guard against,' said Josephine.

'Jo's right,' chimed in Janet. 'She knows another thing, too, and that is never to let herself grow stodgy . . . I think others want you when you keep bright and merry. I mean to keep in touch with all the modern movements, read the latest books, see the plays and listen to the lectures . . . No single woman leads a lonely life when she keeps herself up to concert pitch.'

And Frances:

'Once . . . I thought I should marry because I so badly wanted a home of my own and kiddies to play with. But I found out that it is possible to have a home without a man, and that there were always other folk's kiddies to play with . . . I get a good many of the joys of motherhood without any of the responsibilities.'

. . . 'I think we're all on the right track,' said Mollie.

How genuinely representative of the post-war generation were the voices of Alicia, Mollie and their chums? Real women's voices echo the fictional ones. Here is a single teacher, Margaret Miles, remembering her life in the 1930s:

I worked hard, but I lived in a fairly carefree way. I read a lot . . . I played tennis at the local club, I went to dances, and I went to London to the theatre . . . I was interested in the League of Nations Union, and helped with the Nansen pioneer camps in Devon during the holidays.

My proudest possession was a second-hand Baby Austin . . . which I bought for £25 and drove recklessly and often, I regret to say, brakelessly, to all sorts of places. I could not really afford it and I suppose I should have saved my money, but it gave me a great deal of fun and a sense of adventure.

Caroline Haslett, a single woman who trained as an engineer and was to become the founder of the Electrical Association for Women, poured her energies into championing the cause of women in the electrical industry. Life could be wonderful for singles, she maintained. 'The world is hers for the winning . . . What can the time of our aunts offer in comparison?' At the age of forty-three, her own appetite for life was intense:

Gardening gives me great pleasure and the delights of driving are such that I have used a car for many years in London . . . I find myself heartened and invigorated by visits to the theatre . . .

I play golf, and swim, and row with great zest and some competence, and I even play tennis at times. Though I thoroughly enjoy skating, I am far from the competition stage! I revel in the public forum . . . Books still have an irresistible appeal for me.

Both these women highlight the pleasure of having cars. They were at this time relative novelties, and for women to be seen in the driving seat still had a certain shock value. But cars were all the more a wonderful release and an enhancer of status for the single woman. For Phyllis Bentley the £175 she paid for a car made her feel 'agreeably dashing and independent, indeed let out of prison again into the free world'. After stifling years spent tied to the home she felt rejuvenated.

But it took reserves of honesty and good cheer for spinsters to come to terms with the encroaching years, and in the face of visible wrinkles the euphoria sometimes faltered noticeably. The 'bach' couldn't go on being girlish past her thirties, and women in the first half of the twentieth century were almost as absorbed in keeping age at bay as we are today. Even Winifred Holtby (who died at the age of thirty-eight) was not impervious to the deluge of books and advertisements aimed at selling beauty aids to the not-so-young. An 'apocalyptic and terrifying' corset catalogue sent her scurrying for the tape measure to check her hip measurement (forty-two inches). Her resolve to improve with age wavered when confronted by the persuasions of copywriters to nourish her fading skin with almond oil, and stave off waning desire with patent medicines and slimming systems. Middle life could be a testing time as diminishing attractiveness reinforced the greater disappointments of life.

Old age was even harder. The children's author Noël Streatfeild reconciled herself to its onset by writing herself a list of sensible rules, including:

Never willingly mention your health. People may ask how you are but they don't want to know . . .

Never, never criticize those younger than yourself. If tempted remember yourself at their age and blush.

Go to church regularly even if you don't feel like it. God understands it's tough growing old and will help you to be pleasant about it.

Make your motto 'Keep right on to the end of the road.'

Streatfeild made a point of keeping up appearances. She loved clothes and, determined not to conform to the frumpy spinster stereotype, she would cut a dashing figure in public swathed in minks, her hands beautifully manicured in blood-red nail polish.

Angela du Maurier didn't pretend that she liked it; sixty seemed to her a dreadful age to be. It conjured up 'a stout, high-busted party with woollen stockings and golf-shoes, hair in a bun, clothes too tight, a jolly laugh, ever so hearty . . . And, of course, a spinster.' The contrast with her youth both appalled and amused her. Privileged, pretty, prim, but always, always in love, the young Angela's life had been a stream of romances, parties and dreamt-of kisses. She recalled her tiny wardrobe stuffed with evening dresses, and how after every ball she used to toss aside her silk stockings to be darned by the housemaid . . . in those days she had taken for granted a fairytale future, married to a viscount with six children. Forty years later Angela was an English maiden lady in tweeds, a bit down on her luck, eating kitchen suppers and doing her own ironing. 'I laugh to myself as I realise that such a future as it conjured up to me at twenty-odd would have brought me almost to the verge of suicide.' And yet the simple compensations amounted to true happiness: 'The joy of early bed and a good book to read. The bliss of saying on the telephone, "I don't go out at night any more".' It was worth anything not to be such a gauche flapper.

And it could be even better than that. On the isle of Seil, overlooking Mull and Jura, among the sheep bells and the scent of peat, Angela du Maurier experienced moments of unequalled spiritual peace:

It was there . . . one afternoon in solitude, that I found that Peace which Passeth Understanding. If IT comes to one in one's lifetime and one recognises it there is no joy to equal it. It has not the fiery joy of passion, not the glory of happiness which comes to one with great love for another human being; it is a quiet God-given moment of such tranquillity that you can hear the precious stillness of extreme quiet and want nothing else at all.

The human appetite for joy finds satisfaction where it can. In *The Single Woman* (1953), Margery Fry drew on a lifetime of experience as a spinster to address the question of how to find happiness outside the expected wifely and motherly roles. At the age of nearly eighty, enjoying the moment, living in the present and grasping beauty seemed to her more than ever fundamental:

It seems to me that a pleasure in small things does come back to one; the beauty of the outward world and of people, the satisfaction of warmth in sunlight or fire or even in a hot bottle, the friendly gesture of a child or the ripe juiciness of a plum – it is good to savour these things as they come. Shall I admit to you that sometimes as I wait for a bus on a wet, London winter's night . . . when no very obvious gratifications are present, I say to myself, 'Well, anyhow I'm alive and I can see the other people and the play of lights reflected from the pavements and even the posters.'

★

'Once you get over the disgrace, it's the best life!' was Anne McAllister's view of spinsterhood. She was an academic psychologist and expert on phonetics who spent over sixty years helping children with speech and learning difficulties. She never married.

William Brown's maiden aunt re-
discovers pleasure (illustration from
*William the Fourth* by Richmal
Crompton)

Perhaps the generation who lived through the horrors of the 1914–18 war was less disposed than our own to expect large-scale gratifications from life. Likewise, deep disappointment can engender equally profound gratitude for small mercies, for wet pavements, hill walks and good books, for the pleasures of the mind and fleeting loves, for the joys of friendship, and the grand feeling of independence.

Winifred Holtby paid tribute to the women who bravely faced out disappointment and made fulfilled lives for themselves:

It is impossible . . . to call such women frustrated; most of them live lives as full, satisfied and happy as any human lives can be. Ecstasy, power and devotion have enriched them; they have served a cause greater than their own personal advantage.

You didn't have to drag out the rest of your days in a state of blighted hope. Being single could be better than that. Like Caroline Haslett, the feminist writer Cicely Hamilton believed that the world had adjusted its view of spinsters. Writing in 1940, she looked at her society and her country and concluded, '. . . there are, I imagine, few parts of the world where the once traditional contempt for the spinster is more thoroughly a thing of the past'.

Moreover, she simply rejected the love-centric view of the world. As a young woman she had been, briefly, broken-hearted when a man she loved left her. But barely a fortnight later she was astonished, and a little shocked, to find herself merry, carefree and heart-whole. She was somewhat ashamed at her inconstancy, but drew the conclusion that dying for love would have been an error. 'The realization . . . [cured] me, once for all, of the idea that love was woman's whole existence.' And she learnt too, to bless her 'single star':

If I had married and been fortunate in husband and children, I should have known happiness of a kind that is strange to me; but on the other hand – not a doubt of it – I should have had to pay for that special form of happiness with some of the keenest of my interests, and with some of the best among my pleasures.

The writer Elizabeth Jenkins felt blessed too that she clearly lacked the powerful personal desires that appeared to motivate most women. 'It's remarkable really that, when I lacked so many things that other women seem to want, I never pined to be married or have children. I feel I have been undeservedly lucky.'

Feelings like these weren't reserved for the privileged and educated. Just a few years after she had gone into service with Nancy Astor, lady's maid Rose Harrison was asked by her employer's son what her ambition was. 'And I replied, after a moment's hesitation, "To live my life over again." Today my answer, without any hesitation, would be the same.'

## Surviving the night

And yet Winifred Haward still felt incomplete. The 'great love that survives the night and climbs the stars' for which she longed continued to elude her. When she came back from her second, disastrous stay in New Zealand, she drifted, feeling like a failure. She had been badly bitten in her twenties, with hopes raised and dashed. She had thought George would marry her, but he had rejected her on the grounds that she was too 'high class'. Now, though she had a couple of 'mild affairs', she looked in vain among her social group for anybody who could offer 'great love'. At her age – thirty-five – it seemed increasingly unlikely that she would find him. Despite her Cambridge degree Winifred couldn't get an academic post, so she boned up on north-country history and found work in Lincolnshire teaching evening classes. The income was inadequate, and in the summer months she moved to York and took guided tours round Fountains Abbey and Brontë country. Her father lent her the money to buy a rather feeble shop in Lincoln selling teak elephants, papier-mâché trays and Indian crafts. Then in 1939 she persuaded BBC North to try her out writing and presenting a fifteen-minute wireless talk about an Elizabethan noblewoman from Skipton. They liked it, and more talks followed. As war broke out Winifred applied for, and got, the job of her dreams: she was appointed programme assistant in Manchester, on £450 a year, researching and producing talks for transmission around the region. 'All those years in the wilderness were over! I was just forty-two.'

Winifred was a year into her new career when she first met Louis Hodgkiss. Louis was a couple of years younger than Winifred, born in 1900. Two more unlikely routes coinciding in happiness could scarcely be imagined. Their backgrounds and expectations were entirely dissimilar. The country solicitor's daughter from Suffolk who had won a top history scholarship to Girton was now in her forties; she was short and plump, with the reputation of being 'rather formidable'. Her youthful hopes of romance had all converged on the officer class of her youth, that lost generation mowed down in their thousands at Mons and Ypres and on the Somme. The war, she now felt, had denied her all chance of happiness.

Louis was emphatically not officer class. He had grown up in great hardship in Wigan. Mary, his mother, had been a kitchen-maid; Edward Hodgkiss, her husband, was an alcoholic and ne'er-do-well who beat his wife and children. Mary Hodgkiss ran away and took work at a hotel patronised by theatre folk. Though she returned to her husband, Louis was probably her illegitimate son by one of them.

The boy was stubborn and pugnacious, but he was an eager learner and loved reading. On his fourteenth birthday he started work down the pit. Twelve months later, in 1915, he signed up for the navy. Protected in the gun turrets, Louis didn't see much action; he survived the Battle of Jutland and the attack on Zeebrugge. He was tough as wire and when his ship moved south he became featherweight boxing champion of the Mediterranean fleet.

After the Armistice Louis determined to get out of the navy; not so easy, as it turned out. After a series of escapades he deserted and made his way to Glasgow, where he was saved from starvation by a gang of criminals and prostitutes. The police finally caught up with him and he was court-martialled and sentenced to ninety days' hard labour before being put back on board a ship bound for the Middle East. Finally, at the age of nineteen, he was given a dishonourable discharge.

It was back to the pits for Louis, and back to a new sea of troubles. Before he was twenty-two Louis had married a pretty, ignorant and un-scrupulous young woman named Nellie Walsh. She already had convictions for theft and street-walking, and she lied to Louis that she was pregnant. The marriage was a disaster from the start.

The Labour cause beckoned, and life seemed to be taking a new direction. Louis joined the Left Book Club, and tried his hand at writing. In 1935 Louis Hodgkiss's first mining novel made it into print; he got £25 for it. A certain glamour attached to him as a published author. Women were attracted by his gritty charm; though small, he was sinewy and muscular, with dark hair and strong, open features. His renown grew; BBC North Region scheduled three plays by him for production in autumn 1939, but with the outbreak of the Second World War they were all cancelled.

It was an unlikely chance that brought Winifred and Louis together in September 1940. As talks producer Winifred had been asked to find a speaker who could broadcast an appeal to the public for wartime economy in the use of fuel. Who better than a coalminer, someone who had to dig that fuel out of the ground? But where would she find one with the ability to give a broadcast? A colleague of Winifred's remembered the miner whose plays had been cancelled. 'Try Louis Hodgkiss,' he suggested. She wrote to him, and they met; they 'got on well'. To him she seemed pleasant but a bit formidable. Together they sat down and rewrote the draft script, which had obviously been worded by someone who knew nothing about mining. A few days later he successfully gave the broadcast, and afterwards they chatted in the canteen. In Winifred's words:

She said she would get in touch with him if there was any other material he could provide. He rather hoped they would meet again.

So, as it happened, did she.

Winifred and Louis continued to meet intermittently over the next nine years. They did more broadcasts together, they went on moorland walks. He told her about his writing and hinted at his unhappy marriage; she asked him to the theatre. But after the war ended he became deeply depressed; the writing didn't seem to be going anywhere. Nellie and he were both unfaithful to each other. There were violent rows, and he began to drink heavily. Somehow his life had lost all its meaning; he considered walking out on Nellie, emigrating, or perhaps just getting lost one day out on the moors and never coming back. There were mine shafts out there where a body could lie undiscovered for a long time . . . The only thing that deterred him was the thought of his friendship with 'the lady from the BBC'. But where could that go? He was nearly fifty, working-class, broke and battle-scarred. She was a dumpy, bookish, fifty-two-year-old middle-class spinster.

In 1949 Winifred's boss died; her new boss was hostile and obstructive. She considered moving to London, but '. . . it meant parting from Louis'. That stopped her in her tracks. She decided to give it a chance.

I asked him to my flat. I told him about the proposed transfer to London and said that I would much rather stay in the North. I wondered if he would guess why. He did. He said, almost with a sob, 'I can't bear to lose you.' Then he took what must have been a colossal risk. He took me in his arms and kissed me. He said afterwards that he half-expected I would slap his face, or say something sarcastic. I responded with all my heart: he knew and I knew that come wind and high water, there wasn't anything for us except one another.

★

Nellie refused to give Louis a divorce, and promptly went to earth. For the next twenty-five years he and Winifred lived 'in sin'. The 'quality' snubbed them, but they didn't care. They were profoundly happy, 'united by the deepest trust and affection'. Finally, divorce law reform enabled Lewis to obtain a decree nisi from the elusive Nellie, and in 1972, when she was seventy-four years old, Winifred Haward married Louis Hodgkiss.

The story of Winifred Haward up till her mid-forties is a typical one. Though the country's losses were universal, women of her class were particularly afflicted by the casualties of the Great War. Without disre-garding the fact that for every officer killed, twenty 'Tommies' fell, it is worth looking at the implications of the real inequality in the casualties based on class. Simply put, the chances of dying were higher if you were an officer than if you were a private. Statistically, for example, the death rate of Balliol graduates who joined the army was exactly twice the national average; 31 per cent of the generation who matriculated from Oxford in 1913 were killed.

Why was this? Historians looking at the statistics of the Great War have demonstrated various reasons: for a start, it seems that a higher proportion of middle- and upper-class men enlisted in the army. Certainly the public schools and universities so instilled the patriotic ethos into their pupils that only a few stubborn dissidents braved the accusation of cowardice that met their perceived dereliction of duty. 'Dulce et decorum est pro patria mori' was their mantra. Also, the privileged public-school boys could be more easily spared from their peacetime occupations than workers in industry and agriculture, and they were healthier too. Rickets and asthma saved the lives of thousands of working-class boys who did not get through the medical tests for military service. But the reality of the front line also ensured that, proportionally, officers took more of a beating than their men. When the lads went over the top, the captains and subalterns were in front. Privilege had its price.

Thus when Winifred Haward wrote, 'I knew that [marriage] was almost impossible because hardly any men of my own age had survived,' what she meant was: 'I knew marriage was almost impossible because hardly any men of my own age and *class* had survived.' Winifred was not a snob, but she only learnt, finally, to be flexible when all other avenues had closed. Falling in love with a married working-class miner and naval deserter had not been on her mental map. In the end Winifred had the courage to outface social disapproval and the broad-mindedness to accept love when it offered, even from the most unlikely quarter. To the end of her days she gave thanks for the happiness that had, finally, come her way. Her memoir ends with the words:

There is love and there is sorrow, but the gain outweighs the loss, if you will make it so.

★

As a coda, the story of Miss Amy Langley bears out Winifred Haward's affirmation. Like Winifred's, her life saved its surprises till the last. And she too was overwhelmingly thankful. Miss Langley was living in an old people's residential home when she wrote her autobiography in 1978. Born in 1896, she was one of the thousands who had never found a husband. Profoundly shy and inhibited, a childhood experience with a friend's father who had tried to abuse her had left her 'dried up'. Imprisoned by fear, she had never been able to talk about it.

Despite this, romance had briefly flickered into life during the First World War when, under a 'pen-friendship' scheme, she started up a correspondence with an Australian soldier serving in France. One day she got a letter from him saying he was going on leave and asking to visit. 'Of course I was all of a flutter!' The details of that day were imprinted indelibly on her memory. An inexperienced cook, Amy was preoccupied with the anxiety of what to make her unknown guest for dinner. All went well with her beef-steak pie until it came to the pastry, which would not roll out but fell apart in crumbs. In despair she did her best to press the dough together to make dumplings:

O the fuss and worry of that pie-cum-dumplings. I can see and feel myself tense and nervous waiting for the door knock to come. When the knock did come what a flurry it put me in! I had never seen this boy friend – he was only a 'pen-friend'.

It all went off very happily and after the meal we went for a ride on the top of a bus. How excited I was! I wore a lavender check cotton summer dress which I had made . . . We had a happy day and he went back to France and our correspondence went on as before, but then a blank and no more letters from him.

Wounded, killed . . . ? Nobody ever thought to inform the soldier's pen-friend of his fate, whatever it was.

Humble and industrious, Miss Langley spent her long working life as a dressmaker, pinning and altering lavender check frocks and taffeta gowns for other people. Years passed. After the soldier disappeared, there were to be no more flutters or flurries. Her capacity for feeling seemed to have atrophied; emotional lives were something other people had. In old age she found refuge in Avenue House, a home for the elderly in Bristol.

Miss Langley was eighty-two when a new resident arrived who upset the equilibrium of her calm old age. This was an elderly gentleman who at first got on her nerves by being familiar and telling jokes. But his presence grew on her. In some indefinable way he reminded her of George, a much-loved brother, now dead. To her astonishment it turned out that he and George had been born on the same day. When this 'friend' began to call her 'Dear' she was agitated in the extreme. 'Never in my life had anyone called me "Dear", not in my home, never!' The thaw had begun. 'This was the first emotional moment in my life.'

Gently and unobtrusively, this man became Miss Langley's closest friend. They spent hours together watching tits and robins feeding from the bird-table in the garden of Avenue House and gradually, with much trepidation, she began to realise how much he meant to her. 'Finding oneself in an emotional situation at the age of eighty-two is both surprising and difficult! This is the experience one expects to go through when one is young . . .' Yet the inhibitions still ran deep.

One day over coffee with the residents the subject of a recent newsworthy child-abuse case came up. Amy listened as her friend expressed his dismay at the squalid story, and as he did so she suddenly and unexpectedly found the barriers lifting. Buried fears and doubts began to rise to the surface; she was engulfed by powerful emotions of love and liberation:

What an experience to fall in love at eighty-two! . . . I trembled all over . . . Falling in love had destroyed that which had held me back. [He] did not know what he had freed me from . . . I came out of that room shocked but with a wonderful feeling of release and gratitude . . . [I was] ready to fall in love, [he had] given me peace at last . . . Now at last I was free.

On that note of reconciliation and hope, Miss Langley typed the last lines of her autobiography. She does not tell us what was the outcome of her release, but she concludes with a fervent prayer of recognition to her Maker: 'I offer up my gratitude to the Power that guides our ways. A Divine adjustment is being made in all our affairs according to infinite wisdom and love.' God may well have intervened, or perhaps it really was a miracle, but without question Amy's story challenges despair, and records a small victory for the human spirit.

# 7. The Magnificent Regiment of Women

## The challenge of loss

Two years after the Great War ended, the preacher Maude Royden, then at the height of her fame, stood before the delegates at the International Alliance for Women's Suffrage in Geneva and pleaded with them to help prevent another war:

Women whose husbands or lovers the war has slain, mothers now childless, women who have not borne and now may never bear a child, to you above all belongs the service of the world . . . [Bring] to birth a new world . . . make the nations a family – and of the world a home.

Maude Royden, and many inspired by her, set out in those post-war decades to make a better job of things than the incompetents who had brought them war in the first place. Royden was in her forties when she preached this message. Disabled – she was born lame – and unmarried, she knew what it meant to be alone in the world. Until her death in 1956 Maude Royden directed her own considerable energies to the service of the world, employing her God-given gift of eloquence to campaign for ideals she saw as emphatically feminine: suffrage, women's priesthood and pacifism. She wrote too with indignation and deep sympathy of the plight of the millions deprived of sex, marriage, motherhood and home-making. Why, she later wrote, must an entire generation of 'normal' women be required to accept perpetual virginity in the interests of conventional morality? Why must the cost of war be borne by unmarried women forced to endure imposed chastity? Celibacy could be glorious, but only if it was not imposed but embraced:

Where chastity has been accepted with ardour as a thing noble in itself or necessary for the attainment of some noble end, there is no repression: there is a wide and spacious freedom . . . Are not the great celibates of history among the greatest and most universal lovers of mankind?
 . . . It is the ideal realized that is the best defence of the ideal.

First and last a visionary, both through her oratory and by her own example Maude Royden was an advocate for the single women of her generation, and a prophet of the generation to follow.

In the first volume of her autobiography (*Under My Skin*, 1994), Doris Lessing angrily reminded her readers of the disaster that was the First World War:

Unlived lives. Unborn children. How thoroughly we have all forgotten the damage that war did Europe, but we are still living with it. Perhaps if 'The Flower of Europe' (as they used to be called) had not been killed, and those children and grandchildren had been born, we would not now in Europe be living with such second-rateness, such muddle and incompetence?

Lessing writes powerfully, and many male commentators have endorsed her view that contemporary failings were the result of that 'Lost Generation'. Our traditional ruling classes had been wiped out, and with them had gone Empire, top-nation status and European supremacy: all the glittering prizes whose lustre had irradiated that sunny prelapsarian Edwardian world. 'Nobody, nothing,' wrote J. B. Priestley, 'will shift me from the belief, which I shall take to the grave, that the generation to which I belong, destroyed between 1914 and 1918, was a great generation, marvellous in its promise.' All those beautiful Balliol boys became enshrined forever in a 'Gone-with-the-Wind' myth of lives cut short and blighted hopes.

But there is another way, a less bitter, and also less romanticised way of construing the world we live in. Rather than wringing our hands over the loss of our ruling elite, we should perhaps focus on the lives of those left behind. The surplus two million had much to wring their hands over, but if such women – declared redundant in a maimed society – had weakly submitted to being unjustly marginalised, we might still be living in a patriarchy. Despite their many talents, the class of empire-building classicists running this country were not renowned for their impartiality towards women – and what if the Flower of Europe had turned out to be as bigoted and sexist as some of their fathers? Women might still lack the professional, political and social status that they have today. Instead, in the twenty-first century, women feel empowered by history to expect the equality, respect and rights accorded to them by law and justice.

From the perspective of two generations, the single women of the 1920s and 30s would appear to have precipitated the already vibrant feminist movement of the pre-war period into perhaps the most significant social change of the twentieth century. A cohort of stay-at-home wives and mothers could never have achieved for women what this generation of spinsters did in meeting the challenge of grief and loss. For them, being denied marriage was a liberation and a launching pad.

They were not in the first rank of suffragettes and pioneers, but, on foundations laid by those earlier women – education, opportunity, equality – and through sheer force of numbers, they steered women's concerns to the top of the agenda, and there they have remained.

★

In 1921 a delicately beautiful and immaculately well-dressed spinster named Gertrude Maclean sat down over dinner with her relatives to try to decide the matter of her future. She was thirty-seven. Seventh of nine children, Gertie belonged to a privileged Victorian military family; there were ponies and picnics, long sunny days and a beloved nanny. Nothing could be more conventional, more idyllic than such a childhood. Like her friends in the same social set, she grew up conforming to the expectations of her class: church bazaars and dress fittings by day, dinner parties and dances by night. One by one Gertie's brothers and sisters got married. But Gertie didn't, despite dalliances, and despite offers. Why she remained so implacably single is hard to say; did she really, as her chronicler suggests, love clothes much more than men? Unquestionably, she loved children, but seemed to want none of her own. By the time war broke out she was already thirty, and had stepped decisively into the role of perfect aunt to her numerous nieces and nephews. 'She was a rock and a sport.' Forever absent on some tour of duty in foreign parts or stranded in the shires, the mothers and fathers came to rely on her. A sort of down-to-earth Mary Poppins, Gertie was always on hand to solve the logistical problems of conveying their children from port to station to school and back again, taking in the zoo, Harrods' schoolwear department, and Gunter's on the way. She told them stories, packed their tuckboxes, and smelt subtly delicious. They all adored her.

But after the war Gertie began to feel redundant, surplus to requirements. Being needed as an aunt had fulfilled her just as for other women being needed as a wife gave meaning to their lives. Now the absent mothers and fathers had come home, and the children had begun to grow up. Gertie had energy and imagination. What was she to do with the rest of her life? Her uncle had no doubt that Gertie's talent for aunting should not be wasted:

'Why not, my darling gel, do for others what you have been doing for your own family?'

Gertie gave a quick reply.

'And be a Universal Aunt?'

Second thoughts and maybes were not part of Gertie's nature. She stayed up late, composing her letter to the family solicitor. Before putting it into the morning post, she read it through and realized she had found her need and her answer.

Gertie set up the first office of Universal Aunts in the back room of a bootmaker's at 181 Sloane Street. She immediately advertised for a helper. Miss Emily Faulder responded. 'Why don't you apply?' her widowed mother suggested to her, adding dismissively, 'After all, you are not fitted for anything else.' Miss Faulder was also in her mid-thirties; marriage had passed her by, and with the post-war husband shortage she had no prospect of it. But she had been her military brother's hostess in Hyderabad; she had helped to bring up five younger siblings and loved children and animals, and she was a lady. She was perfect Aunt material. Gertie and Emmie referred to each other as Miss Maclean and Miss Faulder for the rest of their working lives together.

Now that Gertie had an office, an assistant, a table, a chair and a notebook, it only remained to advertise her company's services, and the following notice duly appeared in *The Times*:

UNIVERSAL AUNTS
(LADIES OF IRREPROACHABLE BACKGROUND)
CARE OF CHILDREN
CHAPERONAGE
HOUSE FURNISHING
SHOPPING FOR THE COLONIES
RESEARCH WORK

The timing was perfect, and soon the telephone line was buzzing with enquiries from clients and applicants. This was not the opening women with business, professional or academic qualifications were looking for, but it was the perfect outlet for intelligent, capable ladies with all the aunty virtues: good health, time to spare, maturity and a can-do attitude. Though not all the Aunts were single, a large number of Surplus Women fitted that description. Emmie took interview notes on her applicants and filed them in a card index. They make revealing reading:

MISS PHYLLIS BECKETT
Age 30.
Young and sporty. Knows all about 'footer' and white mice. Guaranteed not to

nag. Can slide down banisters at a push. This lady will be one of our most popular Aunts and be in great demand.

## MISS PANSY TRUBSHAWE
Age 32 (verging middle)
Understands cricket and foreign stamps as she has five brothers. Not much else. There will be a waiting list of preparatory school boys.

## MISS HYACINTH PLUMMER
Thirties (late)
Can play Halma, Snakes & Ladders and tell moral stories. No doubt has a selection of modesty vests or chiffon roses for the front of her lower necklines.

Universal Aunts now established the reputation that it has never since lost, for '*Anything on a business basis*'. The Aunts were superb child-carers, and soon became a common sight at railway stations, clutching the hands of small, labelled children in blazers and caps as they escorted them to the right school train. But the Aunts were also unfazed by requests to buy Christmas presents, organise manicures, find flats, entertain at children's parties, catalogue libraries, pack for trips abroad, obtain theatre tickets and shop for everything 'from a hair-pin to a Moth aeroplane'. One Aunt was sent to meet the 3.15 at Paddington and escort a monkey to its new home in Kent. Another one had a mongoose to lodge with her for a week while its owner was abroad. Aunts were employed to make up fourths at bridge, purchase corsets and organise fire extinguisher tests. Aunts who could speak foreign languages took guided tours up the Rhine or rescued stranded travellers. Upper-class Aunts stood guarantor for American debutantes who wanted to be presented at Court. The agency gave advice too: How did you join the Freemasons? How did you sue your solicitor? When you had to pay off your gambling debts, how did you sell your diamond brooch? Universal Aunts knew the answers to all such questions; they were the lifestyle consultants of the 1920s.

By the end of the decade Gertrude Maclean had transformed herself into a successful businesswoman, but she had also transformed the lives of large numbers of 'irreproachable' spinsters. These were the single women who, in a previous life, might have been condemned to what Osbert Sitwell described as 'the most degrading profession in the world', that of lady help, paid to devote herself with dumb patience to the caprices of some cantankerous old party in a seaside town. Women of this type were too energetic to do nothing, but too unqualified and too class-conscious to make their unaided way on the competitive coalface of modern commerce.

Many of them found their need and their answer with Universal Aunts. They won the love of children and the gratitude of grown-ups. The unmarried ones among them were valued and respected in a way many of them had never expected to be. War had broken down the drawing-room doors; and the genteel spinster who found a role outside them was not easily tempted back inside.

Unquestionably, life for a single middle-class woman in the 1920s had more to offer than at any previous time, and those women were eager to grasp at opportunity. In *The Prime of Miss Jean Brodie*, Muriel Spark celebrates the energy, idealism and sheer zeal of the Surplus Woman:

There were legions of her kind during the nineteen-thirties, women from the age of thirty and upward, who crowded their war-bereaved spinsterhood with voyages of discovery into new ideas and energetic practices in art or social welfare, education or religion . . . They went to lectures, tried living on honey and nuts, took lessons in German and then went walking in Germany; they bought caravans and went off with them into the hills among the lochs; they played the guitar, they supported all the new little theatre companies; they took lodgings in the slums and, distributing pots of paint, taught their neighbours the arts of simple interior decoration; they preached the inventions of Marie Stopes; they attended the meetings of the Oxford Group and put Spiritualism to their hawk-eyed test.

For the middle-class single with some money, self-sufficiency and feelings of usefulness were often their own reward.

## We are not downhearted

'Nothing is impracticable for a single, middle-aged woman with an income of her own,' wrote Sylvia Townsend Warner. Living in caravans on honey and nuts was a luxury available to women with incomes. The campaigner Florence White, however, spoke for the poor spinster, dispossessed and inarticulate. She spoke for women like Miss Cox, a forty-eight-year-old cook in a factory, whose mother had died when she was sixteen and who had brought up her family of seven, then gone out to work herself. She spoke for Miss Barlow, a fifty-six-year-old print-worker who had been made redundant and was then told she was too old to apply for another job. She spoke for the thousands of factory workers and mill-girls, growing older in northern towns, whose drudgery supported our industry, but whose unjust plight remained disregarded by the government. There were women who lived in back-to-back houses and had worked for the same mill or factory from dawn to dusk for fifty years. And at the end of those decades of servitude they won the right to a fifteen-shilling pension. There were sick women in their forties and fifties who dared not visit the doctor in case they lost their jobs, women made redundant refused employment because they were too old, single women with dependent families to look after, women weary, hungry, lonely and broken in health who had to keep working without holidays year after year, unable to retire and collect their pension before they were too careworn to enjoy it. Florence White spoke for these women, and she wanted their voices to be heard.

At 9.40 on the morning of 5 June 1937 a train drew in to Keighley station. Gathered waiting on the platform, the excited crowd poured into its coaches. In every window posters had been pasted: RESERVED: SPECIAL TRAIN FOR SPINSTERS. The Keighley Branch of the National Spinsters Pensions Association soon settled in for the six-and-a-half-hour journey to Kings Cross, a slow progress as it stopped en route to fill up further with Branch members from across the North of England. At Shipley, Bradford, Leeds, Wakefield and Sheffield they piled on, laden with bags and banners, the slogan 'Spinsters Pensions' or 'Pensions at 55' conspicuous on badges and sashes decorating their collars and sleeves. The mood was exhilarating. On arrival in London, Miss Florence White was met by a police escort, and led her army of spinsters en masse to the Kingsway Hall in Covent Garden. There programmes of the day's events were on sale, 3d each. As every Branch arrived, they were applauded, until the auditorium was full to bursting with thousands of spinsters. Florence White rose and went to the podium.

Sir Kingsley Wood, Conservative Minister of Health, was Florence's target. Despite deputations from the NSPA, Sir Kingsley still refused to make any concessions to their demands for pensions for spinsters at the age of fifty-five. The cost would be prohibitive, he said. 'Sir Kingsley says No, we say Yes!', 'We are not downhearted, but determined', 'A Fair Share for All', read the banners. An eloquent speaker, Florence also directed her anger at the unfairly privileged war widow. Those who had had the luck to be married – even if only for a day, as in some cases she was able to cite, before their husbands went back to the Front and were killed – could find themselves comfortably off for the rest of their lives. How unjust was that to the millions of women who, but for the war, might also have been married, and were now left unprovided for by the state?

After speeches in Kingsway Hall a uniformed brass band assembled and accompanied the spinsters in a four-abreast procession to Hyde Park. To the tune of 'God Bless the Prince of Wales' they marched through the London streets singing:

> Come Spinsters, All Attention
>     And show that You're alive,
> Arise demand your pension
>     When you are fifty-five.
> There is no earthly reason
>     To wait another day,
> If you will get together
>     Unitedly and say
>         We Spinsters call attention
>         To show that we're alive.
>         Demand we all our pension
>         When we are fifty-five.

No detail of organisation had been left to chance by the meticulous Miss White. The capital knew they were coming. 'No matter where we went on streets or around corners,' remembered one of the Keighley branch members, 'we had everyone's applause, old and young. We passed a few hospitals and at each window the nurses would be cheering and waving and groups of maids would be on the doorsteps.' At Hyde Park the press cameras were waiting and the movement's top orators took the platform, followed by celebrity star Norah Blaney, who performed a ditty specially composed by her partner Gwen Farrar:

> We spinsters are a happy lot
> And do the things we should,
> We should be far happier
> If only Kingsley Wood.

Till late that night the northerners were free to roam London; for many of them it was their first time in the capital, and they made the most of it, sight-seeing, glorying in the pubs and restaurants and the bright lights. The train back to Bradford left at 12.50 a.m., and many had to travel yet further before getting back home in time for a weary breakfast. It had been a grand day for the Cause.

★

Well before the war the early feminists had shown it could be done. The struggle for the vote had started in 1897, when Millicent Fawcett founded the National Union of Women's Suffrage Societies. This was succeeded in 1903 by the Women's Social and Political Union, started by Mrs Pankhurst and her daughters, who set a precedent for activism in pursuit of the vote. The leaders of the suffragette movement and their followers campaigned by fair means and foul to gain recognition for their cause; to this end windows were broken and stones thrown, churches and politicians' homes were fire-bombed, works of art vandalised; most famously Emily Wilding Davison became a martyr when she died from her injuries after throwing herself under the King's horse on Derby Day, 1913. Other militants were cut free from the railings to which they had chained themselves, imprisoned and, in a number of cases, aggressively force-fed.

When war broke out in 1914 Emmeline and Christabel Pankhurst called on their supporters to repudiate violence, and patriotically to support the government in every possible way. This proved a winning card. The politicians who in February 1918 passed the Representation of the People Act, giving the vote to property-owning women over thirty, did so partly in recognition of the vital role played by women workers in munitions factories and on farms, but also partly because after four years of war the last thing they wanted was a return to militancy on their doorstep. The events of the 1917 Russian revolution offered a fearsome precedent. As it happened, the Act failed to enfranchise most working-class women – the munitions workers and landgirls who had done such sterling service – and they had to wait another ten years before being accorded equal voting rights with men; but in 1918 all the campaigners knew that a barricade had been demolished which could never be rebuilt. The status of women was irrevocably altered.

When the suffrage movements were founded before the war, centuries of patriarchy presented a monolithic structure, a resistant edifice made up of hardened convictions: convictions of male superiority, of a natural sexual hierarchy in which women were subordinate in every way to men, in short, of the inequality of the sexes.

The First World War dealt a blow to that entrenched male position from which it has never recovered. The damaged soldiers who crept back home from their dugouts after demobilisation were victors only in name. There was massive unemployment. One young woman described the all too common sight in 1920 of 'patient queues of hollow-eyed men outside factories hoping to be taken on ... who, by a nervous movement, a twitching muscle, or a too rigid tension, would betray the fact that they were all in some greater or lesser degree suffering from shell-shock'. Set alongside these unfortunates, the young women of the post-war period were the gainers. Among some more broad-minded commentators the view was that men were in fact less able to endure mental strain than women. War had tested the men and found them wanting. 'Women are accustomed to nervous shocks and stand them better,' stated the eminent psychiatrist Sir Robert Armstrong-Jones. And that same whirlwind of war which had traumatised and depleted the male population had also raged through masculine institutions, flattening obstacles in the way of women's emancipation. Though decades had yet to pass before even a semblance of true equality prevailed, still, in those early days ambitious and talented women had reason to feel victorious.

When women got the vote in 1918 it was only the first in a series of male defences which started to tumble after hostilities ceased. In 1919 the Sex Disqualification Removal Act changed the law which barred women's entry to the professions. For the first time women could stand for Parliament, become vets, architects, civil servants, lawyers or sit on juries. In

A 1930s careers manual recommended aviation for girls: by then, life for the single woman seemed to be brimming over with adventurous opportunities

1920 Oxford University allowed women to take degrees;* in 1928 the Equal Franchise Act finally permitted women over twenty-one to hold equal voting rights with men. The 1920s was a decade of firsts. 1920: the first women were permitted to perform jury service. 1921: Victoria Drummond became the first woman to join the Institute of Marine Engineers. 1922: Aileen Cust became the first woman member of the Royal College of Veterinary Surgeons. 1923: Evelyn Cheesman became the first woman curator at London Zoo. 1924: Margaret Bondfield became the first

---

* Cambridge lagged behind in this for another twenty-eight years, withholding full university membership from women until 1948.

woman minister in Parliament. 1926: Hilda Matheson was appointed the BBC's first-ever Director of Talks. 1928: Eleanor Lodge became the first woman to gain a doctorate from Oxford University. 1929: Margaret Bondfield became the first woman cabinet member and privy councillor. In government departments, legal chambers and financial houses, in the army and the police forces, in hospitals and dental surgeries, laboratories and universities, in Fleet Street and on farms, on racetracks and golf courses, in the air, on water and in the remote islands of the Pacific, unmarried women whose lives only thirty or forty years earlier would have been confined to parlour and parish were starting to compete with men for authority, enterprise and glory. Though not all of them could be 'firsts', they shared the same pioneering spirit. For many of these single women, life now seemed to be brimming over with opportunities for adventure. For every disappointed spinster gnawed at by poverty and blighted hopes, there was another who looked into a future full of bright possibilities – for personal satisfaction, for social value, for the betterment of her world.

One lady who wrote to me about her spinster aunt, whose fiancé had died as a result of the war, concluded her letter: 'How I miss her! There was only one Bessie Webster, but there must be many similar stories.' Miss Bessie Webster's life might well stand for the multitude of those maiden aunts who resolutely made lives for themselves in the liberating world of the 1920s. Jimmy Brown, Bessie Webster's fiancé, had been a talented linguist and academic; they met at Glasgow University where Bessie was studying Modern Languages, and they fell in love. Jimmy was a jewel among men, and Bessie and he were besotted with each other. His death when it came must have knocked the bottom out of her world.

But Bessie wasn't the type to mourn the rest of her life away. She was twenty-four; she was devoted to her family, she was a fluent linguist, a talented pianist, and was characterised by a streak of irrepressibility that both delighted and maddened those who knew her. After a spell learning secretarial skills and working in an office (where she had an affair with her married boss), she joined ICI and began a lifelong career in industry. Her niece described how Bessie '. . . gave the company a verve and excitement that galvanised the Central Labour Department into actions they would never have dreamed of without her. "Bessie" was everywhere, on intimate personal terms with everyone, from the various Chairmen, to the cleaners and porters. And she was known and welcomed at every factory she visited, over the length and breadth of Britain.'

Vivacious and approachable, Bessie Webster remained a magnet for men – some of whom tried and failed to persuade her to go to bed with them

– but she never married. Her sister was convinced that Bessie could never have dwindled into domesticity. She was in her element at the annual ICI conferences, where, as a passionate music-lover, her job was to organise the entertainment, and she was soon on close terms with many of the celebrity artistes of her day. A celebrity herself, she held court on these occasions in the midst of a throng of captains of industry where she was often the only professional woman. 'ICI gave her a freedom she would otherwise not have known . . . None of this would have come her way if she had "dwindled into a wife". [Marriage] would have bored her to distraction,' wrote her niece.

Bessie unrepentantly ran her own life, and such was her humour and directness that her colleagues, though occasionally driven wild, let her get away with doing things her way. In the thick of a crisis it would be discovered that she'd gone to have her hair done; policemen waved her on through red lights, and shop assistants gave her priority. In later years she drove an open-top Sunbeam which she would park recklessly as near as possible to Knightsbridge, before swanning into Harvey Nichols for lingerie or Harrods for library books (though well-read, her particular taste was for lurid and violent murder fiction, which the librarian took care to reserve in advance of her visits).

Bessie's speciality was personnel, and nominally she was employed to report to the Central Labour Department on working conditions in the various ICI factories, but the reality was much more diverse. She 'collected' jobs, serving on all the Company's committees that related to employee welfare. Her work took her abroad, gave her status in a big organisation, and offered endless variety. She was, she confessed, not good at detail and routine, but she brought an unprecedented energy and élan to Board meetings, to the Amenities Committee and the ICI Clothing Panel which surprised and delighted her colleagues at Head Office. 'I have always enjoyed what I had to do . . .' she remembered, '. . . but some of my more candid friends might say it is because I don't worry enough.'

Deep down, Bessie kept faith with Jimmy, and never considered marriage with anyone else after he died; every year on the anniversary of his death she wrote to his parents. They had given her, in his memory, a Blüthner piano which was her most treasured possession. His ring was on her finger till the day she died. 'If she had regrets about how her life had turned out, she never said so.' Bessie Webster turned her face to the sun. 'She was a great life-giver, who made friends everywhere she went . . . She was a wonderful aunt. I loved her dearly.'

Miss Bessie Webster never achieved fame; like many of the women whose stories I have told in this book, hers was a life encompassing private grief and limited recognition. Who can ever know the depths of anguish she endured when she lost the man she loved? What road did she have to travel in order, eventually, to arrive at that unpretentious assessment of her own life, that really she didn't worry enough? Let the love and admiration she inspired testify to a journey completed.

## A good strong character

Now that women's history is on the syllabus, and has expanded to fill countless shelves in countless libraries, the achievements of the women's movement over the two inter-war decades have received their due. The historians have documented how in the last century the doors for women were slowly but surely creaking open. We can read about the campaign of the Six Point Group, about *Time and Tide* and its crusading journalists, about reform of the divorce laws, about the various fights for equal education, equal pay and equal opportunities (not all of those fights yet won . . .). But we have to look in the Biography sections to find out what it felt like to live through those momentous times.

Take Rosamund Essex, who wrote her memoir *Woman in a Man's World* (1977) when she was in her late seventies. Rosamund was born in 1900, 'when girls were still accounted for not very much more than for marriage in later life'. Though much loved, she was, from her earliest years, the butt of family jokes that she was unlikely to amount to anything. Disabled by a deplorable stutter – she could not even say her own name – Rosamund meekly accepted her parents' estimation of her general incapacity: 'We know you haven't any brains, darling. But you have a good strong character and that will carry you through life.' That was before the senior mistress at Bournemouth High School for Girls decided to set matters straight for the entire sixth form by pointing out to them – as 'a statistical fact' – that only one in ten was ever likely to find a husband. With her destiny thus blighted, it is remarkable that Rosamund was able to recover her self-esteem and make a fulfilling life for herself. But she achieved this, and more.

Her family's low expectations spurred Rosamund to prove herself, 'even if I was inferior'. Classics had always held her enraptured from childhood, and her father's decision to take orders as a High Church priest when she was only five meant that family mealtimes were dominated by theological discussion. This stimulating intellectual climate gave her confidence. By the age of eighteen Rosamund was head girl at Bournemouth and felt able to compete for an Oxford scholarship in Classics. Like so many other young women who knew they would have to make their own way in the world, Rosamund was among the 'sudden rush of post-war women who wanted a university education'. In 1919 she went up to St Hilda's College. The following year Oxford made the liberal gesture of admitting women as members of the university:

So I was matriculated, became an undergraduate, bought a commoner's gown, was fitted with a floppy Latimer cap, and felt the exhilaration of belonging to an old and honourable community. It is probably difficult for emancipated women now to understand our small triumph then. I said to myself at the time – I remember it well – 'This is something that can never be taken away from me. It has happened. It is a little bit of glory.'

But Oxford was still a man's world. Many of the dons hated having women in their lectures; one made the women sit behind him so that he could not see them. Another addressed the undergraduates as 'Gentlemen – and others who attend my lectures'. Rosamund took up rowing, but the women's eights were not allowed to practise when men's eights were on the river, so they had to squeeze in their sessions early in the morning; and, because wearing shorts for this activity would have been unthinkably unfeminine, the girls had to row dressed in their cumbersome skirts, so billowy that they had to be anchored at the knee with loops of elastic. Rowing in these conditions wasn't easy. 'But it was another bit of glory that we did it at all.' Despite the apparent opportunities for female under- graduates to meet men at this time, none of them came Rosamund's way. She was, like her contemporary Winifred Haward, on a tight budget, which barred her from a glamorous social life. Convention demanded rigorous chaperonage, and one could only meet men in the common-rooms, not in one's bed-sitter. In any case, '. . . men seldom came, frightened off by too large a flood of young females'.

One evening, as college tradition required from time to time, Rosamund took dinner at high table and found herself seated next to the college principal, who asked her what her future plans were. Well aware that her options were not vast, Rosamund was nevertheless dead set against becom- ing a teacher. The principal was sympathetic. 'Teaching has rather an old-maidish image, hasn't it?' she agreed.

'I should hate to grow into an acidulated old spinster,' I said, and went on without ever having thought of it before, 'I think I shall adopt a child when I am earning enough money.' The idea came right out of the blue. It was said lightly and casually. The principal laughed and said that I should probably forget such a fantastic idea soon enough. But I did not. It stuck at the back of my mind for many years to come, till the right time arrived.

Meanwhile, Oxford's intellectualism sapped her childhood faith. By her third year Rosamund was quite convinced that there was no God, and took to walking round the college garden fiercely proclaiming her new-found atheism: 'There is no God. The whole thing is rubbish.' Her parents wisely tolerated this lapse; probably they saw that their immature daughter would see the light in her own good time. Which she did, one evening at home in her final vacation, when God Himself in person appeared to her quite unexpectedly in a dark passage. After that, faith returned little by little; it was to guide the rest of her life.

One day, soon after she was twenty, Rosamund's stutter suddenly ceased – 'I do not know why . . .' From then on her confidence in her abilities soared. She came down from Oxford in 1922, with a vague ambition to get 'a really good job' – in politics perhaps? Secretarial skills seemed like a must, so she enrolled at Mrs Hoster's training school and found a room in a hostel near Sloane Square. The hostel was nicknamed 'The Catteries' – appropriately, as it seemed to her, for it was full of 'lots of old cats . . . very acidulated spinsters'. With a degree in Classics, plus shorthand and commercial Spanish, Rosamund landed a job as political secretary to the formidable Margaret Haig, Viscountess Rhondda, who had been a militant suffragette and was, arguably, the leading feminist of the inter-war period. Rosamund soon found herself out of sympathy with Lady Rhondda, whom she regarded as a battleaxe. 'She treated me like dirt. I began to hate rampant feminism, and I still do.' For a while she assisted Lady Astor with her 1922 election campaign, but she had had enough of politics, and instead found herself a post in the archaic and other-worldly offices of the Society for the Propagation of the Gospel.

In her own memoirs, Rosamund herself was quite unable to explain why she took the next step in her life. Perhaps working for the Gospel Society had directed her thoughts inwards towards her own burgeoning religious impulses, or perhaps it had something to do with relinquishing any vestigial hopes she may have had of marriage. Maybe she shared Maude Royden's view that supernatural love exceeded earthly passions. Whatever it was that caused her to offer herself as a postulant nun to a small Franciscan Order in Dalston, it was a disaster from the start. 'Never could there have been so unsuitable . . . a candidate.' The tyranny, harassment and pettiness of convent life caused her to boil with rage; the lack of common sympathy and kindness baffled her and shook her convictions. Austerity – cold, hunger, discomfort, hard work and exhaustion – she could cope with, but inhumanity, verbal abuse, intellectual starvation, pettiness and unreasoning obedience were asking too much. Her rebellious posture caught up with her when the Reverend Mother took her aside to criticise her pronunciation of the word 'refectory' (the convent's dining-room). Rosamund, a highly educated Latinist, pronounced this word 'reféctory', from the Latin *reficere* (*reféctum*). Reverend Mother insisted that it should be pronounced as she did, 'réfectory', with the emphasis on the first 'e':

'And', she went on, 'you must not only say what I say, *but you must believe that it is right.*' I could not think a thing true which was not. I said so. I was very soon dismissed from the community. And a good thing too. I was far too individualistic, far too independent, far too disinclined to blind obedience to fit into the Religious Life.

Afterwards, Rosamund came to believe that the twentieth-century decrease in religious vocations reflected the fact that spinsters of the pre-First-World-War era, who retreated into nunneries because they had no other choices, were used to being pushed around. Modern women like her were better educated, less submissive. They had been taught to stand up for themselves, and were not prepared to be bossed about by men, Mother Superiors or anyone else.

Practically penniless when she left the convent, Rosamund had difficulty adjusting to a world where it was now essential for her to earn a living. Her father, whose sacrifices had paid for her education, had become priest of the poverty-stricken East End parish of All Saints, Poplar. Though living under his roof, she was determined not to be a financial burden to him, and decided to try for journalism. The slump was at its height when she went for an interview at the *Church Times*, and she was pessimistic about her chances. But luck was with her, and the editor offered her some temporary reporting work. She was told not to expect more. 'I was a woman. They did not want a woman on a staff where all the senior journalists were men.'

But Rosamund Essex had found her life's work; she remained on the *Church Times* from 1929 until her retirement in 1960, after ten years as its editor. She learnt on the job, though her colleagues were often unhelpful and misogynistic. At every step of her promotion she was told that this was an unprecedented concession for a woman, and that she would go no further.

Early on she quite deliberately appropriated the sphere of interest which was to become her own special field: poverty. In Poplar, the raw material for her articles was on her doorstep. There, whole families lived in rat-infested squalor; despair was endemic. Out-of-work men were known to cut their own throats when they could no longer support their children. The Church opened its doors to meetings of the angry unemployed, risking a barrage of scornful Cockneys: ''Ow would you parsons like to live on 33s 7d a week with seven children?' 'We are living a life of misery, but it's no bleeding good taking it to the Lord in prayer.' Rosamund was there to report it all. 'I had chosen poverty; so if I was to write about it, I must understand it to the full.' She was nearly cudgelled by a policeman at the unemployment rallies in Hyde Park, and narrowly escaped flying bottles at the Waterloo out-of-work riots. Her pieces were endorsed by the paper, and her status rose, along with her salary. Nor had she forgotten the wish expressed to her college principal years earlier: 'I think I shall adopt a child when I am earning enough money.' With no prospects of partnership or marriage, at the age of thirty-nine, Miss Rosamund Essex became a mother.

Rosamund found David in a 'home' in South Croydon. She was methodical about her selection, seeking out one of many unwanted children from an institution which made no stipulations about access by the natural mother or the adoption society. Knowing that as a working woman she would have to employ a nanny, she wanted to be sure that the child could let her know that all was well while she was out of the home, so she chose one aged two and a half who could already talk. Her willingness to take a boy amazed the official at the institution, who assumed that a childless spinster like her would be craving a substitute doll to dress in frocks and adorn with hair ribbons. David took a while to settle. He was fearful and had difficulty walking, having spent a large portion of his infancy strapped into a pram. But from the beginning Rosamund loved her blond boy; it was almost an effort for her to remember that he was not hers by nature. Gradually her happiness and pride instilled trust and an indissoluble bond grew between them.

Rosamund Essex continued to break through barriers. In 1950 she became editor of the *Church Times*, the first woman to hold such a post for a London journal which was not aimed exclusively at a female readership; on retirement in 1960 she joined Christian Aid as a speaker and fund-raiser, and in 1969 she became the first woman lay reader in her diocese, and one of the first in the country. Guided always by a powerful humanitarianism, her work brought her into contact with royalty, archbishops and politicians; into her late seventies she travelled widely for Christian Aid, and she continued to preach in pulpits across the country. For this woman, the causes of her life were manifold – poverty, injustice, torture and racism cried out to her for redress, but her heart was stirred equally by the need to witness the gospel and defend her faith in Christ. Across the misogynistic and conservative territory of the Anglican church she blazed a fiery trail. In looking back over her life, there were no regrets about things left undone, only ambitions for things left still to do, and gratitude:

I am concerned in living [life] *now*, for whatever time I have left. I have so much, and want still to do so much. I have a son of whom I am intensely proud – he is a lay reader just as I am – a daughter-in-law who is my dear friend (can every mother-in-law say that?) and two grandchildren, a boy and a girl, who are the crowning joy of the original adoption. How many spinsters have had the chance of such happiness? . . . I have a home and friends and work and impossible aims, which means I have a great deal of struggle to come.

## Doing things that matter

War and the franchise changed the nature of women's ambitions, giving them new complexity and diversity. Fulfilment through marriage was still the general expectation, but the image of wedded bliss that once seemed so graven on female consciousness began to be blurred and effaced by new dreams. The dream of political power, the dream of economic self-sufficiency, the dream of the boardroom, of public life, of professional achievement and personal affluence, of creativity, exploration and self-expression all took on reality, as more and more women showed them coming true. Mrs Pankhurst's followers grew up in an age intoxicated with self-belief:

What a time those early suffragette days were to a young girl! The joy of marching and carrying a banner, the frenzy of great speeches, the defiance of unjust laws, the opposition to anything that prevented the coming of the great new world – no thrill of soldierly music could equal their appeal. The end of an outworn age was at hand, I believed, and the great to-morrow was being ushered in.

This woman was the young Caroline Haslett, aged eighteen at the time she was writing about, fervent with grand but barely formed ambitions for a future that would take her away from her restrictive Victorian upbringing.

Caroline was born in 1895 and grew up on the Sussex Weald; her parents were devoutly religious, with a deep sense of social responsibility which they passed on to their children. Mr Haslett, a railway engineer, believed that duty to one's neighbour was duty to God; and as it turned out his eldest daughter took after him in ways he could never have foreseen. Caroline was a dreamer, and though she was a voracious reader her teachers at Haywards Heath High School were disappointed in her: 'Caroline! You'll never be any good if you can't make a buttonhole!' lamented her needlework mistress. Back home in her father's workshop the girl's unladylike absorption with tools and mechanisms left Mr Haslett baffled. How could she become a teacher, as he and her mother wished her to be, if she could not learn feminine accomplishments?

And what else was she fitted for? For as a girl Caroline was not strong. She suffered from a weak spine, for which the accepted treatment was enforced bed-rest. Condemned to lengthy periods of inactivity, she lay on her couch observing with mounting frustration and anger the prodigal expenditure of female energies on what seemed to her an endless round of pointless tasks. Were human beings fit for no more than carrying buckets of coal from the outhouse to heat the stove, before emptying the ashes and carrying them all back out again? Why toil all day to heat water so that a mountain of dirty linen might be washed, then starched and laboriously ironed, only for the whole proceeding to be repeated again the following week, and so on and on till the crack of doom? 'I did not want to spend my life like that. It seemed a waste of time.' At this stage Caroline had not yet made the connection between electricity and domestic labour-saving, but deep down she railed at the injustice of woman's lot, and her interest in emancipation grew. She joined the Suffragettes. At the same time something inside her determined never to be a housewife.

If marriage was ever on the agenda, Caroline Haslett put it firmly where, to her, it belonged: well below her personal ambitions and ideals. The only young man who got close to her was eliminated when he turned out to have entirely unreconstructed views over the matter of a village scandal. Caroline had taken the side of a young unmarried mother who had been thrown out of her home. She intervened and persuaded the angry parents to take the girl back. Her own young man was horrified, and informed Caroline that he could not continue to walk out with her if she made such an unladylike spectacle of herself; she must choose between him and the girl. Caroline's principles prevailed, 'and that was the end of that romance'.

Caroline must have known that she would never be a teacher or a wife. The evidence suggests that for her remaining single was a conscious choice; aware that her unusual gifts would be eclipsed within marriage, she opted to express them to the full in the interests of her sex. But in 1913 she was still uncertain of what direction to take next, and complied submissively with the suggestion of a family friend that she enrol at a commercial college in London, before taking up employment in the clerical department of this friend's boiler company. Boilers made sense to Caroline. She was soon familiar with all the company's products, made herself invaluable to her surprised bosses, and met with no opposition when, towards the end of the war, she asked to be transferred to the factory in Scotland for some hands-on experience in boiler-making. 'As soon as I got into the works, I knew this was my world,' she later remembered. 'In this new and exciting atmosphere of men and machines, she found her spiritual home,' wrote Caroline's biographer.

Caroline Haslett was far from alone among women who got their hands dirty during the war and by so doing learnt the value of industrial method and mechanisation. But she was rare in her determination to use that knowledge to try to better the lot of her entire sex. Machines, she felt sure, could help women to escape from the endless round of coal-scuttles and washing-baskets, and give them a life as exciting and rewarding as they deserved. The more she pondered this, the more it became her mission to emancipate women from domesticity by the use of machinery.

When after the war women workers were driven back to the kitchen by the returning menfolk, a door seemed to have closed. But not on everyone. The Surplus Women were free to make their own way in that 'great new world' that the war had opened up for them, and Caroline was one. For her, the wives were the losers; she saw herself as among the lucky few.

At the age of twenty-four she picked up an advertisement which read: 'Required: Lady with some experience in Engineering works as Organizing Secretary for a Woman's Engineering Society.' Such a post was made in heaven for Caroline Haslett; she applied, got the job, and started out on the pioneer path that was eventually to make her a prominent public figure. The Engineering Society was a forum for 'technical women'; women like her who found satisfaction among the oil and dirt of a noisy workshop were still very rare. The society offered these lonely few the resource of a professional organisation. It was also a campaigning body and, braving masculine resistance, Caroline became extremely effective at persuading colleges and institutes to open their doors to women trainees. As editor of the Society's Journal, *Woman Engineer*, she also used its pages to pursue her personal mission to release women from drudgery and allow them to lead fuller lives. She held a competition in which the contestants had to place imaginary home improvements in order of preference. Top of the winning list was a dishwasher, operated by a hand-pump. Runner-up was a thermostatic oven which doubled as a food-warmer. Other entries included a hydro-powered knife-cleaner, a floor-polisher operated from a standing position, and a hostess trolley that doubled as a coalbox on wheels. 'In the early days of these women pioneers they were dreams that seemed as unattainable as the crock of gold at the foot of the rainbow.' In 1925 Caroline organised a Society conference at the British Empire Exhibition, attended by the great and the good of royalty, politics, science and feminism. The Women's Engineering Society was on the map.

It was a small step from the advancement of engineering to the promotion of electricity in the home. In 1924 it was already clear to Caroline that electrical power offered extraordinary potential for liberating women; this scintillating force was for her a means to the realization of a dream. She aspired to the day when by its miraculous power every household in the land would be cleaned, dusted, washed, heated, lit and fed. When that day came women might rest from their labours, lay down their mops and their dustpans and, like men, turn to the great causes of human advancement. In November that year the Electrical Association for Women was born, with Caroline Haslett as its first director. 'I see in this new world a great opportunity for women to free themselves from the shackles of the past and to enter into a new heritage made possible by the gifts of nature which Science has opened up to us,' she wrote.

Caroline practised what she preached. A journalist who came to interview her in 1925 found her in buoyant mood in her attic flat; with help from a friend she had entirely rewired it and installed cunning gadgets such as a square kettle and saucepan which fitted together over a single hotplate, thus using half the power. A woman's need for economy, home planning and independence guided her every step. Caroline herself was a woman whose ardent sense of purpose never clouded her charm, mischievous humour and appetite for life. She inspired intense loyalty. Never without a scribbling pad to jot down the ideas with which her mind teemed, she was also a careful listener, a devout Christian and an eager enjoyer of the good things in life. She loved her garden (the flowerbed of her Kentish cottage was cut to the shape of an electric light-bulb) and she loved good food, so much so that she was soon fighting a losing battle with her weight. Spells at health farms became part of her calendar; she would go off for a week at a time to be hosed with mud, fed on prunes and tortured in the gymnasium. It never made much difference. 'I think she was a woman who loved life and made the most of what she had to offer to anyone she came in contact with. I don't think personal gain ever occurred to her,' recalled her niece.

Caroline held the post of director of the EAW for the next thirty-two years. When in 1947 she was honoured with a DBE she knew her life's work really had made a difference. It was a life of campaigning and writing, managing and delegating, travelling and speech-making. Her qualities of

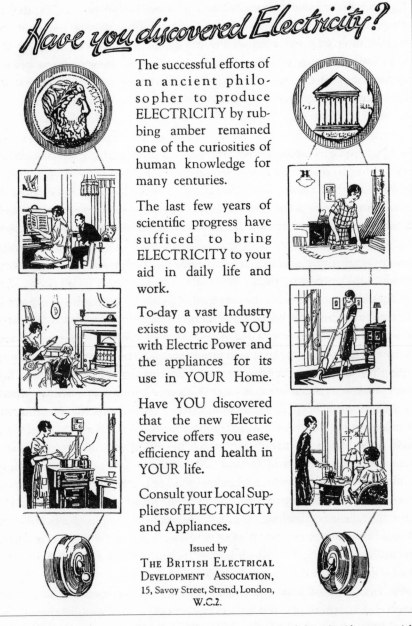

An advertisement in a 1926 issue of *The Electrical Journal* visualised the miraculous potential of electricity to transform women's lives

integrity and practicality made her invaluable to the many other public bodies and committees on which she served. She lived to see the EAW with a 14,000-strong membership, though not long enough to see the association disbanded when by 1986 it became clear that its aims had been so fully achieved that it was no longer necessary. By then electric ovens, refrigerators and dishwashers were commonplace. Women worked for wages. Some men even shared the housework, compliantly flicking the simple switches that operated the automatic washing-machine or multi-function vacuum cleaner. Dame Caroline Haslett died in 1957 and was, at her express wish, cremated by electricity.

★

Not being married allowed Florence White, Rosamund Essex and Caroline Haslett to play to their formidable strengths. They were pioneers. Single women like this changed the world they lived in. And there were so many of them: scientists, teachers, doctors, politicians, lawyers, artists and explorers. The vicissitudes of life – ridicule, prejudice, disappointment – had not subdued this parade of indomitable ladies. A thread of determined ambition ran through them. They would fly, they would discover, they would build, educate, help, cure, protest, transform. This book has attempted to tell the stories of some of them, both famous and forgotten. To highlight only a few is to do an injustice to the extraordinary numbers of single women between the wars whose confidence, energy and courage still inspire; fortunately there are encyclopedias-full of them.

Today the organic farming movement honours Miss Eve Balfour for work done at a time when holistic agriculture was regarded as cranky if not downright mad. Lady Eve, daughter of the 2nd Earl of Balfour, used her privileged background to pursue her own passionate interest in farming. In 1918 nobody noticed that the vigorous young woman in charge of training a gang of landgirls on a Monmouthshire farm was not twenty-five, as she claimed, but only nineteen. After the war she and her sister purchased a Suffolk farm where in the 30s, having discovered that eating compost-grown vegetables cured her rheumatism, she began her experiments with organic cultivation. Her book *The Living Soil* (1943) was the influential text behind the formation of the Soil Association, which she co-founded in 1946. Not content with her role in this (literally) ground-breaking project, Lady Eve played saxophone in her own dance band, passed her pilot's licence in 1931, crewed sailing ships and wrote successful detective novels. 'I am just surprised to see that what I stood for all my life is no longer derided but more or less accepted,' she remarked at the age of ninety.

The drive to reconstruct the ground beneath her feet consumed Miss Rowena Cade for over fifty years; in her case it was the granite headland which suggested a natural amphitheatre overlooking the sea at Porthcurno in Cornwall that inspired her to build the Minack Theatre. Miss Cade had loved theatricals since she had played a childhood Alice in *Through the Looking Glass* at home in Derbyshire. After the war she settled in Cornwall, bought the headland for £100 and had Minack House built. The cliff-face theatre project was the irresistible outcome of her desire to put on plays. From 1928 she devoted her energies to its creation, and with the help of her devoted gardener and a local craftsman set out to smooth the crags into a stage and seating. Craggy, silver and gaunt herself, she is still remembered by villagers hauling bags of sand on her back up the steep cliff path from the beach. The first production at the Minack was *The Tempest*, with lighting provided by car headlights. Over ensuing years a proper auditorium was created, followed by pathways, walls, parking space, an access road – all painstakingly hewn out of the rocky cliffs, and financed by Miss Cade, who gradually saw the magic spell of the Minack growing in reputation. She herself worked on, in sun and in rain, until her mid-eighties; her elaborate sketches for weather protection at the theatre have still not been accomplished.

Miss Ellen Wilkinson was elected Labour MP for Middlesbrough East in 1924, while still lacking the household qualification that entitled women over thirty to vote. Ellen had grown up in a grimy terrace house with an outside privy; though her parents were uneducated she gained a university scholarship. 'I learned all too early that a clear decisive voice and a confident manner could get one through 90 per cent of the difficulties of life,' she remembered. The only proper boyfriend she ever had introduced her to Marxism. She broke off the engagement, but socialism was in her blood. 'If a girl has not shown an overwhelming desire for public life by the time she is eighteen . . . really [she] had better teach, or become a secretary, or get married.' For her there was simply no time to be married (though she squeezed in a couple of affairs with politicians). In 1936 'Red Ellen' was at the head of the famous Jarrow crusade with the jobless of the north-east; as an international socialist her anti-fascism brought her prominence. In the 1945 Labour government she triumphantly managed to raise the school-leaving age to fifteen while finding resources for free milk and free school meals. 'The thrill of leadership . . . being in the battle with the workers . . . doing things that matter . . .' were what drove her, and though tiny – she was only four feet ten inches tall – she didn't allow herself to be intimidated. Her instincts were those of the rebel. In manner she was outspoken and emotional, in style exhibitionist: hatless, crop-headed, she caused gasps of astonishment when she walked into the House of Commons in an emerald green dress. Miss Ellen Wilkinson made both enemies and loyal friends; and she made a difference.

The sure march of women into male-held territory continued throughout the inter-war period, though in those days the House of Commons made few compromises for them – in 1923 the women MPs had to walk a quarter of a mile from their cramped office to get to the nearest ladies' lavatory. For the Liberal party Megan Lloyd George energetically represented her constituents in Anglesey and opposed appeasement, while from the other side of the House Miss Irene Ward campaigned for women's economic rights and was to become the longest-serving woman MP. The issues of women's rights and employment were the lifelong passions of Nancy Seear, who was raised to the peerage in 1971, and whose sponsorship of the Sex Discrimination Act of 1973 ensured her legacy to the nation. 'Let me put it like this,' she explained, looking back over her remarkable career, 'I'm a single woman. There is no doubt that it is very, very much easier if you are single than if you are married.'

The trade union movement – in particular the poorly-paid garment workers whom she spoke for – benefited from the ferocious energies of Miss Anne Loughlin, tiny, stylish and bossy, who by the age of thirty-five had fought her own way from the sweatshops of Leeds on to the TUC general council, and was made DBE in 1943. The upper echelons of the Civil Service also gained the formidable abilities of spinsters like Dame Evelyn Sharp and Dame Mary Smieton, the two first women to head government departments in this country. Dame Evelyn, who was honoured for her key role in the framing of important planning laws, confessed that she regretted remaining single: 'I should prefer to have been a man: then I could have had a career and marriage too.' Dame Mary rose in her career to become director of personnel of the United Nations. She shared a home with her sister, and lived to the great age of 102.

The fortress of politics was a clear target for the regiments of advancing women, but Surplus Women had lots of surplus energy, and they expended it on almost everything hitherto regarded as 'male'. In 1910 Miss Cecil Leitch had given the suffrage movement a welcome publicity boost by defeating the leading amateur golfer Harold Hilton. After the war Miss Leitch went on to win championship after championship: the British Open twice, the French five times, the Canadian once. In 1929 the mountaineer Dorothy Thompson became the first woman to climb Mont Blanc by the Brouillard Ridge. The following year Miss Marjorie Foster confounded no fewer than 861 men competing against her by carrying off the sovereign's prize for target rifle shooting – in 140 years the only woman to achieve such success. The oarswoman Amy Gentry was undefeated sculls champion until 1934; and in 1935 the virtuoso wicket-keeper Betty Snowball became a member of the first women's cricket team to tour Australia. All were unmarried.

As in so many cases of women who invaded male strongholds, it was the war that gave them their opportunity. Military enlistment caused the gradual dislocation of public services. Women police officers like Mary Allen were first recruited (on an unpaid and voluntary basis) in 1915, largely to control prostitution which had escalated in the proximity of army recruitment camps. The war also gave Mary Baxter Ellis her chance to join the armed forces. She defied her parents, trained as a chauffeur, and immediately joined FANY as a driver; her service won her medals for gallantry. By 1932 she had become corps commander of the unit – an inspirational leader renowned for her probity and valour.

On the home front Miss Verena Holmes profited by the wartime absence of men to gain a formal apprenticeship in the field which had fascinated her since childhood: engineering. She learnt to work everything from a diesel engine to a torpedo, and employed her skills to create a range of useful inventions – assorted medical apparatus, safety paper cutters and rotary valves. In 1931 her versatile talent earned her admission to the Institution of Locomotive Engineers: the first woman to gain such entry. Verena Holmes's contemporary, Victoria Drummond (whose early career is described in Chapter 4) also seized the chance offered by the war to pursue her ambition of becoming a marine engineer. The struggle was a severe one; despite demonstrable experience she continued to fail her chief engineer's exam through no fewer than thirty-seven attempts. 'After some years even Mr Martin [her tutor] had become convinced that it was because I was a woman they would not pass me. Of course I was not deterred. It even became quite a joke between us.' Her determination paid off. In 1940 Victoria's ship SS *Bonita* was attacked by a bomber. 'My duty was to keep the engines going as long as they would turn.' She took charge, dismissed all the engine-room staff, and for nearly half an hour battled single-handedly in scalding steam and deafening noise to keep the ship's speed up. Miraculously they were not hit. When the ship made land Victoria was greeted with a heroine's welcome, and awarded the Lloyd's war medal for bravery at sea.

As Victoria Drummond found out, getting acceptance and professional recognition was an uphill struggle. Among the lists of eminent female medical workers who dedicated their lives to patient care in the first half of the twentieth century, nearly all were nurses. A few determined women managed to train as doctors. This was easier during the war because of the shortage of male doctors, but in the 1920s the big teaching hospitals, unable to stomach the thought of mixed gynaecology classes, closed their doors to women again. In her bid to become a doctor, Octavia Wilberforce was thwarted at every turn by her parents, who told her that medicine was 'unsexing' for women. Though well-to-do, her father cut off all financial support. Octavia failed her exams seven times before managing to pass in all subjects. Supported by friends, Dr Wilberforce eventually became a highly regarded diagnostician and, perhaps out of fellow-feeling for them, founded her own convalescent home for stressed and exhausted women. A few more names – Diana Beck, Dorothy Russell, Esther Rickards, Letitia Fairfield – stand out from their generation as exceptional women doctors. But women neurosurgeons, pathologists, even gynaecologists or paediatricians like them were hard to find in those days. And because marriage seemingly barred the way to hospital appointments or posts with administrative responsibilities, those that there were tended, as a result, to be unmarried.

Women lawyers – known as 'Portias' in the popular press – had a slightly easier time of it than the doctors. So many young lawyers had joined up and been killed in the war that there was a serious shortage of barristers and solicitors, particularly in family firms. With a son dead, blind or shell-shocked, the father of a family practice would be grateful to see his clever daughter step into her brother's shoes. The first female solicitor, Carrie Morrison, qualified in 1923. Even so, by 1938 only an average of fifteen women a year were qualifying as solicitors. One of these, Miss Eulalie Spicer, was to become one of the most prominent divorce lawyers of her day; though the clues given by her emphatically masculine appearance – complete with Eton crop, suit, tie and cigarette holder – suggest that her own unmarried state was no great cause for regret. Among the first women barristers was Miss Elsie Bowerman, an active suffragette who at the age of twenty-three had survived the sinking of the *Titanic*. After this nothing seemed impossible to her. As a hospital orderly she joined the Allied retreat from Russia in 1917 and witnessed the February revolution in St Petersburg. In 1918 she joined Christabel Pankhurst on the hustings, and was called to the bar in 1924. Later she founded the Women's Voluntary Service and represented women at the United Nations. The first British woman judge was Miss Sybil Campbell, who became a barrister in 1922 and was appointed to the judiciary in 1945. Miss Campbell immediately gained a reputation for the severity of her sentencing, when she handed out six weeks to a man who had stolen three bars of soap. But the protests stemmed in part from specious outrage by petty, and sexist, criminals who saw pilfering as their right. By the time she retired Miss Campbell had won a reputation for fairness and humanity.

Typical of the public-spirited women who entered the law at this time was Miss Mary Freeman, who grew up in Slathwaite, at the smart end of Huddersfield. She and her sister Margaret, a teacher, lived all their lives together in the same house. Mary read law at Manchester University, and qualified as a solicitor in 1929. She was articled to her father, and after his death took over the practice. She pursued her chosen career for the next thirty-five years. The Misses Freeman jointly personified spinsterly respectability. They never drank in pubs, and on Saturday nights were to be found working at home until their ten o'clock bedtime. Guided by their strong protestant ethic, they supported the local church, the Girl Guides, local music and drama, and gave unstintingly to their community:

Remember that it was the spinsters that kept the country going. It was not only us. You're to remember that the men were killed in the First World War – there weren't any men to go round. All my friends are 'Miss'. We had a family of four neighbours here – all unmarried. There's Miss Roberts there, and ourselves, and next door here, and I think that the Sugdens had a spinster in the family hadn't they? – and the Webbs – Dorrie was a spinster. It's not a bad life. There's a lot to be said for it. The important thing is to enjoy and be enthusiastic. And take everything that comes.

In science women often had to twist and dive to find outlets for their talents, often in less mainstream disciplines. We find women marine zoologists like Sheina Marshall, women bacteriologists like Muriel Robertson, women biochemists like Dorothy Lloyd or Marjory Stephenson (all unmarried) taking advantage of those then relatively undefined fields; for them too, gaining posts was problematic, and they often had to exist from one grant to another. For the forty years that she ran the Strangeways Research Laboratory in Cambridge, Miss Honor Fell was not paid a salary, but survived on a research grant from the Royal Society – which, although it did not admit women scientists, supported them financially. Under her directorship the laboratory became world-famous (gaining her a DBE in 1963), while remaining homely and hospitable. At teatime Miss Fell would gather her staff together to talk over their work; this had an added advantage. Steam from the boiling kettle helped to humidify the laboratory environment, which in turn helped to moisten culture dishes containing embryonic tissues awaiting dissection. Honor Fell's joy in her work kindled the enthusiasm of her colleagues, and not having the commitments of home or family released her: 'I had a lovely Saturday afternoon, with the whole lab to myself,' she wrote to a fellow scientist; and, 'On Sunday I shall have an orgy of staining slides.'

On the whole academia offered a haven for the ambitious and educated spinster of the period. Gertrude Caton-Thompson's story is not untypical; the satisfactions of archaeology seem to have offered profound consolations. Dorothy Garrod was born a couple of years later than her, in 1892; her early life was convulsed by tragedy when two of her brothers were killed at the Front, and the third died in the 1919 flu epidemic. Her studies took her to Oxford after the war, and she developed a passion for Neanderthal caves. On site Miss Garrod was rigorous and imperious, but could also delight her colleagues by her witty conversation and skill with the flute. In 1939 she became the first woman professor at Cambridge University, and in her lifetime was garlanded with honorary degrees, a CBE, and fellowship of the British Academy. Miss Margaret Read was also a Cambridge history graduate when she lost her husband-to-be in the First World War. In 1919 she went to live with her brother in India, and turned her formidable talents to the study of anthropology. Colonial education was to become her speciality; tenacious and implacable, she gained a PhD, worked as a government adviser, was appointed Professor at the London Institute of Education, travelled for the UN, and was made CBE in 1949.

'One of the most comfortable jobs, and one of the most sheltered lives open to an unmarried woman, is that of a don on the staff of one of the women's colleges in Oxford or Cambridge,' remembered Professor Barbara Wootton. (She herself was still a student at Girton when her husband, with whom she had spent only thirty-six hours of married life, died of wounds in France.) Many a harassed mother or overworked housewife might well have envied the bookish, studious lives led in those tranquil quadrangles. True, such women often had public and private turmoil to contend with. Margery Fry, principal of Somerville College, Oxford, battled unsuccessfully to persuade the university authorities not to restrict the numbers of entrants to women's colleges. Julia Mann, the economic historian and head of St Hilda's, Oxford, sacrificed her own comfort to fund provision for scholarships and facilities at her college. Before she became an Oxford don, Margery Perham suffered a nervous breakdown when her beloved brother died in the First World War.

But their contributions too were magnificent. Enid Starkie, Doctor of

French literature at Somerville College, Oxford, brought all her passionate understanding of the works of Baudelaire, Rimbaud and Flaubert to bear on advocating their works, while the study of Russian at Cambridge was immeasurably advanced by the persuasive powers of Elizabeth Hill, Professor of Slavonic Studies at Cambridge University. The government turned to Margery Perham for advice on colonial administration when formulating post-imperial policy, and Enid Russell-Smith had an entire career as an enlightened civil servant, deeply committed to social reform, before taking up her university post as Principal of St Aidan's College, Durham. As an academic, Margery Fry also poured her civic energies into penal reform; she was made a magistrate in 1921 and was the first education adviser to Holloway prison. After her retirement she wrote her illuminating and compassionate short book *The Single Woman* (1953), in which she paid tribute to all the spinsters upon whom the smooth running of society depended.

---

Ladies seeking
**SCHOLASTIC APPOINTMENTS**
can be assured of prompt and efficient assistance by placing their requirements in the hands of
**Truman & Knightley,** Ltd.
**SCHOLASTIC AGENTS.**

who introduce Assistant Mistresses and Matrons to nearly all the leading Public and Private Schools at home and in the Colonies.

No Registration Fee.    Terms on application.

OFFICE:
**61, CONDUIT STREET, W. 1.**
Phone : Gerrard 3272.          Telegrams : Tutoress
(2 lines).                              Phone : London.

**MISS KERR-SANDER'S**
**Secretarial Training College**
175, Piccadilly, W.1.
Gerrard 2130

Well-educated women desirous of fitting themselves for the higher branches of the Secretarial profession will receive a thorough course of training in English Shorthand and Typewriting, Book-keeping, Foreign Languages and Foreign Shorthand, etc.

Positions found for pupils when efficient.

Pupils can join at any time provided there is a vacancy.

---

Classified advertisements in *Women's Employment* (January 1925), a new magazine targeting the expanding female labour market

The opening up of education to women gave many of them undreamed-of career openings. Elizabeth Denby studied social sciences at the London School of Economics during the First World War; it led her into the voluntary sector, where she experienced at first hand the implications of bad housing. Working alongside architects and local authorities, Miss Denby was to become a leading urban reformer, and tireless campaigner for better housing solutions in inner cities. 'My life, my interest, enjoyment and heart, [now] lay with new building, with construction and everything it meant,' she wrote. Brenda Colvin was another young woman whose early teaching inspired her to set out in a new direction – in her case that of landscape architecture, an undervalued branch of design at that time. From planting and landscaping gardens she moved to the design of industrial and urban landscape.

Humanitarian instincts, moral courage, conscience and kindliness are qualities which distinguish many of the women whose huge range of activities I have been describing, but the circumstances of the post-war world demanded, and received, a surge of new and fervent commitment to righting the wrongs of a dangerous century. In the nineteenth century idealistic women might have meekly set out to convert the heathen in Nigeria. They now found more vital causes in the twentieth. Hard to define as a group, they were best described in Keats's *Hyperion* – quoted by women's historian Sybil Oldfield in her compendium of women humanitarians – as '. . . those to whom the miseries of the world are misery and will not let them rest'. Out of 150 entries in Oldfield's book, two-thirds were single women or childless. But at the end of a long career working to alleviate tropical diseases among children from Ghana to Japan, Dr Cicely Williams felt that she was '. . . mother to millions of babies'. Dr Williams was one of the first women to train at Oxford University's medical school; it was her observations in the field that led to the identification of *kwashiorkor* – childhood malnutrition. In Singapore in 1941 Cicely Williams heroically cared for a hundred sick infants dumped in the city's dental hospital. She commandeered milk and boiled it for them on Bunsen burners; when the Japanese ordered her to move on she despairingly handed as many of them as she could over for adoption, before herself being interned in Changi prisoner-of-war camp, where for two years she endured malnutrition, disease and the constant fear of torture. Nevertheless she continued after her release at the end of the war to work in child health for another forty years.

Doreen Warriner was another supremely brave and intelligent woman who abandoned a brilliant academic career to go to the rescue of the thousands of Jews and socialists in Prague threatened by Nazism in 1938. The British government's betrayal of Czechoslovakia filled her with shame, and she took personal responsibility for getting huge numbers of these desperate refugees into hiding, providing them with passports and, when Hitler's army marched in, helping them to escape. Her contemporary Evelyn Bark's amazing gift for foreign languages – she was fluent in at least six – was the foundation of her work for the British Red Cross. Having set up a tracing service for people with missing relatives, in 1945 she found herself in charge of the horrifying and heart-breaking task of reuniting survivors from Belsen concentration camp. She was foremost among the

British liberators who endured terrible conditions to feed and medicate the emaciated survivors and remove the unburied dead.

The injustice and oppression of the twentieth century offered ample scope for such gifted, courageous and selfless women to dedicate their lives to famine relief, interracial integration, fighting oppression, helping refugees, healing, educating, rescuing and cherishing. But the conditions of that century also enabled women to give the very best of themselves. As Cicely Hamilton wrote:

> Teach me to need no aid of men,
> That I may aid such men as need.

The male business world defended its inner strongholds as tenaciously as it could, but with a vast army of 'business girls' camped outside in the typing pool it was only a matter of time before a few of them began to break in. Elsie M. Lang, author of an assessment entitled *British Women in the Twentieth Century* (1929), commented on the number of women holding well-paid posts and directorships in commercial firms, from wholesale druggists to rubber manufacturers, produce agents to publishers. 'The majority of the great business women of to-day,' she wrote, 'have climbed into positions of £1,000 a year and even more by means of shorthand and typing.' Chapter 4 described how by sheer determination Beatrice Gordon Holmes learnt to be a stockbroker and became director of the leading 'outside house' in the City of London; by 1930 she was making up to £5,000 a year (equivalent to over £200,000 today). But even her affluence did not match that of Alice Head, editor and managing director of *Good Housekeeping* magazine, who by the time she was in her thirties was said to be earning more than any other woman in Britain. Like Gordon Holmes, Miss Head had started out training as a shorthand typist. By 1933 enough women were employed in the broadly defined field of business and the professions for a British branch to be formed of the International Federation of Business and Professional Women. Three years later Gordon Holmes was invited to Paris to speak to their Congress on 'Women in Finance':

There in Paris, in July, 1936, I saw a brilliant platform of public women of all nations. To me as an old suffragette it was thrilling . . . in 1904 we [had been] told that although women might get the vote . . . not in our lifetime could we expect to see women in Parliaments and Governments, women in public office, women in all the professions. Such progress would not be possible for our generation – if ever.

And there in front of me on that Paris platform in July, 1936, were contingents of women parliamentarians from all countries . . . distinguished women doctors, lawyers, teachers, writers, artists . . . It had the effect on me of a revelation: I felt like Rip Van Winkle. Since 1912 I had been absorbed in earning my living, making my way in the business world . . . Only there in Paris, listening to speeches and reports covering every form of human endeavour, did I realise the immense amount of public work that women were doing in every section of society all over the world, by means of organised groups working through definite national and international programmes.

The magnificent regiment of women! Yes, I suddenly seemed to blink my eyes open into and on to a new world at that Paris Congress in July 1936.

Gordon Holmes was justified in feeling part of that magnificence. Her reputation was made. Elsie M. Lang's book credited her as the first woman stockbroker. A decade after the war, Lang catalogued the inroads made by women into the male domain. Despite being temporarily interrupted by the return of male employees after demobilisation, their onward march was steady. And it is impossible not to be struck – as Lang respectfully refers to the ladies by their titles – by how many of them were single. Just some of them, extracted from her list, are as follows:

Miss Ellen McArthur – the first woman to be awarded the degree of DLitt by the University of Dublin
Miss Nairn – winner of the gold medal and first woman to obtain Classical Tripos at Cambridge University
Miss Gertrude Tuckwell, first woman JP to be sworn in in London
Miss Faithfull, Principal of Cheltenham Ladies' College
Miss Margaret Beavan, Liverpool's first Lady Mayor
Miss Edith Beesley, manager of the West End branch of the Southern Life Association
Miss Reynolds, head of one of the largest publicity firms in England
Miss Kathleen Britter, the first woman conveyancer
Miss Harris Smith, in 1920 made a fellow of the Institute of Chartered Accountants
Miss E. D. Clarke, estate agent and auctioneer
Miss Robert of Liverpool, awarded Williams' memorial prize at the Royal Veterinary College
Miss Dicker, film production technician
The two Misses Banks, the first two women to run a second-hand bookshop
Miss Gladys Burlton, Principal of the Burlton Business Institute
Miss Irvine, the only professional tea-taster appointed by HM Government

Miss Gertrude Mann, manufacturer of mosaics
Miss Lorimer, buyer in the Oriental Department of one of the big London stores
Miss Gwen Nally, pageant producer
Miss Maud West, detective

If the idea of a woman detective would have been unthinkable in, say, 1890, men had fewer problems with the idea of a woman artist. The arts have never been the exclusive preserve of men, and music and watercolours were deemed sufficiently dainty and useless for the fairer sex to be allowed to participate, so long as they were amateur. By the turn of the century even a woman novelist was no longer expected to write under a male pseudonym, though eyebrows might still be raised when daughters went on the stage, and much brow-beating took place when women abandoned all for the easel. But Virginia Woolf's battle-cry for writers in *A Room of One's Own* (1928) – 'A woman must have money and a room of her own if she is to write fiction' – carried with it the imperative of no-strings professionalism. As Woolf pointed out, women had, since time began, been too busy giving birth to and bringing up the human race to have time for serious writing. Their talent could only thrive if that ceased to be expected of them. In other words, there must be no babies, no housework and no demanding husbands. Extend that to musicians, painters, performers, poets, and it is easy to see why, in a world where babies and husbands were denied, professional women artists flourished. Without the contribution of unmarried women the British cultural scene would have been notably poorer.

The preceding chapters have already discussed some of the writers who remained unmarried – women like Elizabeth Goudge, Phyllis Bentley, Winifred Holtby, Ivy Compton-Burnett, Elizabeth Jenkins, Sylvia Townsend Warner, F. M. Mayor, Richmal Crompton and Irene Rathbone. And there were more: Rachel Ferguson, Mary Renault, Noël Streatfeild, Edith Sitwell, Valentine Ackland, Rhoda Power, Lettice Cooper, Muriel Jaeger . . .

Recruitment to art schools was higher in the inter-war period than it had ever been before, and it was estimated that of the 200,000 self-styled artists working in Britain up to 1939, the majority were women, though it appeared that a minority of these actually lived by their art. Gwen John and Dora Carrington are perhaps the best-known single women artists of the early part of the twentieth century, but there were others: Margaret Pilkington, one of the finest wood-engravers of that generation, the textile designer and illustrator Enid Marx, her friend the potter Norah Braden, the figure painter and landscape artist Nano Reid . . .

The stage and screen too were lit up by the talents of a clutch of formidable spinsters: the grand comic Irene Handl made batty old ladies her speciality, perhaps feeling herself to be one. Doris Speed and Margot Bryant both became familiar faces throughout the land with their roles in *Coronation Street*. Miss Speed played Annie Walker, the withering landlady of the Rover's Return, for twenty-three years, and Miss Bryant played Minnie Caldwell, the naïve little old lady often to be seen with her glass of stout gossiping in the pub snug. Dame Gwen Ffrangcon-Davies made her name in the leading role of Shaw's *Back to Methuselah* in 1923, and went on to star as Juliet to John Gielgud's Romeo; their stage partnership was to last half a century. Dame Flora Robson's personal life was as dramatic as that of the many heroines she played. In the early 20s she too worked with Gielgud, but fell madly in love with his contemporary, the director Tyrone Guthrie. Her yearning to have children by him drove him away; ten years later Guthrie married a cousin. Flora had a knack of falling for unavailable men, like Robert Donat and Paul Robeson. Her anxiety was that she would inevitably find herself typecast as a tortured spinster, and ironically enough it was her final role, at the age of seventy-three, as the quaint Miss Prism in Wilde's *The Importance of Being Earnest*, that was to bring her immortality. In the light of Flora Robson's longing for the children she was never to have, perhaps she did indeed have special insight into this character; but it must have taken self-command to give the 'handbag' scene with Jack Worthington its full comic impact:

JACK: Miss Prism, more is restored to you than this hand-bag. I was the baby you
    placed in it.
MISS PRISM [*amazed*]: You?
JACK [*embracing her*]: Yes . . . mother!
MISS PRISM [*recoiling in indignant astonishment*]: Mr Worthing. I am unmarried!
JACK: Unmarried! I do not deny that is a serious blow. But after all, who has the
    right to cast a stone against one who has suffered? Cannot repentance wipe out
    an act of folly? Why should there be one law for men and another for women?
    Mother, I forgive you.

The reality was that the practice of a professional art itself often ruled out marriage. Myra Hess's luminous talent as a pianist was obvious from early childhood. By her early twenties she was becoming successful, and her fame steadily increased after her American debut in 1922. It was to be a career of constant touring and performances, often lonely, exhausting and uncomfortable. Her mother, to whom she was devoted, lived in hope that her daughter would marry, but Myra was committed to her music. In an interview she explained that she took both music and marriage too seriously to be able to do both. 'I couldn't. I'm afraid I would be too earnest about marriage, and in this business there is only one thing one can be really earnest about. That is playing the piano. One sacrifices a great deal, but there are compensations.' It was a question of priorities, and she had to choose. The cellist Beatrice Harrison and the singer Dame Eva Turner remained unmarried for similar reasons.

## 'You loved him'

How many of these talented and successful single women could have acquired their qualifications, consequent positions and fame while conforming to the expectations of wifehood? It may be that their skill, professionalism and leadership merely displaced the more decorous gifts employed by their married sisters in dropping off visiting cards, shopping and flower-arranging. It may be that their achievements cost them dear in disappointed hopes.

But if they were sometimes envious, sometimes sad, sometimes lonely, at least now they could no longer be regarded as superfluous. Thirty years earlier society would have treated them as rejects. Now in their flourishing second-hand bookshops, their busy veterinary practices and auction houses, their offices, courts, boardrooms and cutting-rooms, on the stage and in the studio, in the operating theatre and the laboratory, the lecture-hall and the drill ground, spinsters found self-respect and the respect of society. Like Muriel Spark's spinsters in *The Prime of Miss Jean Brodie*, they channelled their considerable energies into social welfare, religion, vegetarianism, slum improvement and theatre companies. They flew over Mount Everest, kept pigs and chickens, saved up and bought their own houses, learnt German.

Feelings of social usefulness compensated for a lot, though when retirement came it could be hard. When Mary Grieve handed over the editorship of *Woman* magazine after twenty-five years she had to contend with a crisis of identity which shook her to the core. Her personality had been bound up with an entire working life spent on the magazine. At the age of fifty-six she no longer knew who or what she was. Forced on to her own company, it was only the realization that a new journey was beginning that made her able to come to terms with the 'stranger' that she now encountered. Miss Grieve picked up the pieces, turned to writing, and started a company cooking and supplying home-made pâté to the shops and restaurants near her home in Hertfordshire. Her autobiography ended with the words: 'Well, the journey is begun.'

★

Comparing the contribution of educated working women in the mid twentieth century to those of our own times, the writer and educationist Professor Alison Wolf has concluded that society as a whole was the beneficiary: 'The period . . . was a golden age for the "caring" sector in one major respect. It had the pick of the country's most brilliant, energetic and ambitious women, who worked in it as paid employees, but who also gave enormous amounts of time for free. Now, increasingly, they do neither.'

In 1940 the feminist writer Cicely Hamilton – herself single – took stock of the state of British spinsterhood:

Time was – and not so very long ago – when the middle-aged Englishwoman who had not found a husband was considered fair game for the jester; by the humorists of the Victorian age she was always depicted as a figure of fun – an unattractive creature who, in spite of all her efforts, had failed to induce a man to marry her. That was the old maid as a past generation saw her – and as we do not see her today; we have too many unmarried women successful in business or professional life, distinguished in literature, science, and art, to be able to keep up that joke.

Cicely Hamilton was perhaps unusual, if admirable, in seeing singleness as a win-win situation. Typically clear-sighted, she weighed the pros of spinsterhood against the cons of marriage, and concluded that marriage required more sacrifice than she was prepared to make. Her friendships, her interests and her pleasures, her independence and lack of fear for the future, must have been jeopardised with a husband and children to encroach on her time and prey on her anxieties. 'When I ask myself, do I regret my single blessedness? The answer is quite easily, No!'

As the author of *Marriage as a Trade* (1909) and *Just to Get Married* (1911), Cicely Hamilton was a self-confessed feminist who gave much of her life for her commitments. These included votes for women, equal pay, abortion law reform, birth control and rights for unmarried mothers. In partnership with the composer Ethel Smyth she wrote the lyrics for the suffragette anthem 'March of the Women':

Life, strife, these two are one,
Nought can ye win but by faith and daring:

On, on, that ye have done
   But for the work of today preparing.
Firm in reliance, laugh a defiance,
   (Laugh in hope, for sure is the end)
March, march, many as one,
   Shoulder to shoulder and friend to friend.

And as she marched, firmly relying, bravely defying, banner aloft, with her bold comrades beside her, surely Cicely Hamilton never cast a backward glance at the kitchen, the nursery or even the drawing-room, or sighed for a married life that was never to be. Didn't that sense of a cause greater than herself, a glorious mission, suffuse her with idealistic passions every bit as heated as the ardour that burns between two lovers?

The writings of brave honest women like Cicely Hamilton and Margery Fry, Winifred Holtby and Phyllis Bentley, Florence White, Caroline Haslett and Rosamund Essex, Gertrude Caton-Thompson and Winifred Haward are imbued with a stoicism and dignity that is hard to find today. These women had lived through disaster. The world they had been brought up to expect as their birthright had been taken away from them and destroyed. Instead of complaining, they bravely faced the future. 'Anyone can get married,' argued one of the NSPA branch members, 'but it takes a good valiant woman to remain unmarried.' In many cases such women were rewarded with abundant and fulfilling lives.

One could generalise that not having husbands gave the spinsters opportunities they could never otherwise have had – just as today one might also generalise that marriage and children reduce women's competitiveness with men. Beatrice Gordon Holmes believed that success was the 'most satisfying thing in the world – there is no champagne like success'. Though it would obviously be simplistic to claim that spinsterhood guaranteed success, the inter-war decades saw the single woman's emergence from the twilight zone of maiden aunthood into an altogether sunnier realm. The women in this chapter understood that marriage was only one kind of fulfilment. And by the time the Second World War broke out, the idea that marriage was 'the crown and joy of woman's life – what we were born for . . .' was starting to appear very outdated.

The women whose lives I have traced in this book each had their own mountain to climb. Whether or not our lives are engulfed by great historical events, we all try to make the best of the muddled, incompetent, second-rate world this is. And as death approaches it's a matter of chance whether each of us can look back on the past with more pleasure than pain, more pride than regret. In her ninety-fifth year Gertrude Caton-Thompson sat down to assemble a narrative from eighty-four years' worth of diaries. It was the final creative undertaking of an immensely hard-working and productive life.

★

Although she barely ever spoke of her love for Carlyon Mason-MacFarlane again, the distinguished archaeologist never forgot him, nor how passionately she had loved him as a young woman. She kept in intermittent touch with his brother and parents, who had been family friends. Twenty-four years after his brutal death in the Libyan desert, when Gertrude herself was in her fifties, she received a letter from Carlyon's elderly widowed mother, who was still living at Craigdarroch in the Scottish Highlands. Would she be kind enough to visit whenever she was next in Scotland?

The opportunity arose in September 1940. Newnham College, Cambridge, like everywhere else in the country, was preparing for the Blitz by blacking out its windows and digging bunkers in its garden. Gertrude took a brief holiday from her academic work and her air-raid warden duties to travel to Craigdarroch. There she found Mrs MacFarlane living alone in the isolated manse, cared for by two elderly servants and a kitchen-maid. She was frail and had greatly aged. For the five days she spent there Gertrude was left to entertain herself. The factor took her round the home farm and showed her the Highland cattle, and he organised her a day's trout fishing on the loch. In the silence and solitude of the glens it must have been hard for Gertrude not to remember how in July 1914 she and Carlyon had set up their rods side by side on the banks of the Conan, and how they had fished together in the peaceful waters while down on the Cromarty Firth the warships lay at anchor. Surely she also remembered Derby Day 1914, the carefree young man with his grey topper pushed back, munching his game pie on the roof of the brake . . . With a second world war looming, how could she have prevented the memories crowding back – of that tense summer just before the outbreak of the last war, when she and Carlyon walked those same purple moors in the pouring rain, knowing that hostilities would mean his departure for the Front? And how could she forget that she had never told him of her love, and that he had died horribly, never knowing what he meant to her? None of these thoughts are expressed in her memoirs, but her stay at Craigdarroch could not have failed to prompt reflections on the past with Carlyon. Her departure, when it came, must have left her with many more.

When she left, Gertrude went upstairs to bid Mrs MacFarlane good-bye. The old lady was in bed, and she bent to embrace her. As she was about to leave she noticed for the first time a table which stood beside Mrs MacFarlane's bed. It was spread over with fresh flowering heather, like a tablecloth. On the heather lay a sword, and medals. Gertrude stopped and, looking at Mrs MacFarlane, saw that they understood one another. 'It's been beside me for twenty-four years,' said the old lady. There was no need to acknowledge what, as a mother, she felt, and Gertrude was silent. Mrs MacFarlane was the next to speak: 'You loved him.'

It was a statement, not a question. But this time it needed a reply. What did it cost Gertrude to answer? For half a lifetime her secret had lain masked by scars. To surrender now would be to rupture a wound long healed over. It wasn't in Gertrude's character to do it.

'He was loved by everyone who knew him,' she said.

The generalisation, with its tacit confession, would suffice. There was nothing to be gained by self-indulgent histrionics. He was dead, and she had her life to get on with.

That was the last time she saw Mrs MacFarlane, who died not long afterwards.

After the Second World War Gertrude retired from fieldwork, but she made further visits to East Africa and continued to travel in Europe. She had many philanthropic interests and many friends. Into her eighties she served on the council of the British School of History and Archaeology in East Africa. Newnham made her an honorary fellow, in 1944 she was elected a fellow of the British Academy, and shortly before her death she was also honoured with a fellowship by University College, London. A fellow academic visited her in Wiltshire when she was in her late eighties: '. . . her pose was as upright and her mind as razor-sharp as ever, and she had that ethereal form of beauty, unrelated to good looks, sometimes manifested by very old people of exceptional character.'

Gertrude Caton-Thompson's memoirs were not written for publication, but were printed and distributed among her friends and colleagues. The act of setting down her memories, and her desire to share them, reveal her as a woman satisfied and grateful for the joys and rewards of a life well lived. Here too, in book form, she could finally tell the truth about the man she had loved so long ago, for the grief had passed. The wounds lay still undisturbed. Love, she had learnt, was not everything in life.

# Notes on Sources

The following notes give only principal sources consulted and are aimed – like the book itself – at the general reader rather than the academic. Where a particular work is used extensively, I have not repeated the source under the same chapter heading. Since in nearly all cases the text gives dates of any specific works mentioned I have not cited them in this section; for publication details and for further reading please turn to page 286 for a select bibliography.

## Introduction

**page xiii**. 'As the historian . . .': 'War, Death and Mourning in Modern Britain' by David Cannadine, in *Mirrors of Mortality – Studies in the Social History of Death*, ed. Joachim Whaley.

## 1. Where Have All the Young Men Gone?

### TWO WOMEN

**pages 1–4**. 'In 1978 . . .': May Jones's unpublished autobiography is held in the collection of working-class autobiographies at Brunel University.
**pages 4–10**. 'Silent obscurity . . .': *Mixed Memoirs* by Gertrude Caton-Thompson.

### DEEPLY LOVED AND SADLY MISSED

**page 13**. 'In 1911 . . .': Statistics on population and on the casualties of the First World War are readily available, and throughout this book I have used a broad range of sources, including the Equal Opportunities Commission website/research and statistics http://www.eoc.org.uk; www.firstworldwar.com/features/casualties.htm; *A War Imagined – The First World War and English Culture* by Samuel Hynes; *Women and the Popular Imagination in the Twenties – Flappers and Nymphs* by Billie Melman; *The Great War and the British People* by J. M. Winter; 'Britain's "Lost Generation" of the First World War' by J. M. Winter, essay in *Population Studies – A Journal of Demography*, Vol. 31.
**pages 14–15**. 'On Christmas Day . . .': *Testament of Youth* by Vera Brittain.
**page 16**. 'Lieutenant Will Martin . . .': The correspondence between Emily Chitticks and her fiancé Will Martin is held at the Imperial War Museum.

**page 17**. 'Another nurse . . .':*I Saw Them Die – Diary and Recollections* by Shirley Millard, ed. Adele Comandini.
**page 19**. 'Poor human beings . . .': Correspondence between Beatrice Webb and her sister quoted in *A Woman's Place* by Ruth Adam.

**page 20**. 'This fact had to be faced . . .': *Woman in a Man's World* by Rosamund Essex.
**pages 21–2**. 'Winifred Haward . . .': *Two Lives* by Winifred Haward Hodgkiss.

**page 23**. 'Poor May . . .': *Grey Ghosts and Voices* by May Wedderburn Cannan.

## 2. 'A world that doesn't want me'

**page 28**. 'Gradually, the majority . . .': *Hons and Rebels* by Jessica Mitford.
**page 29**. 'It was the general view . . .': *I Leap Over the Wall* by Monica Baldwin.
**page 29**. 'Robert Roberts . . .': *A Ragged Schooling – Growing up in the Classic Slum* by Robert Roberts.
**pages 30–31**. 'For Vera Brittain . . .': *Testament of Youth* by Vera Brittain.
**pages 31–3**. 'Winifred Holtby . . .': *Winifred Holtby as I Knew Her – A Study of the Author and Her Works* by Evelyne White; *The Clear Stream – A Life of Winifred* Holtby by Marion Shaw; *Selected Letters of Winifred Holtby and Vera Brittain 1920–1935*, ed. Vera Brittain and Geoffrey Handley-Taylor.

**page 41**. 'Not surprisingly . . .': *Life Errant* by Cicely Hamilton.
**page 41**. 'The war destroyed . . .': *Ivy When Young – The Early Life of Ivy Compton-Burnett 1884–1919* and *Secrets of a Woman's Heart – The Later Life of Ivy Compton-Burnett 1920–1969* by Hilary Spurling.
**page 42**. 'Enid Starkie . . .': *Enid Starkie* by Joanna Richardson.

**page 44**. 'All this helped . . .': *A Singular Woman – The Life of Geraldine Aves 1898–1986* by Phyllis Willmott.
**pages 44–6**. 'Victorian conventions . . .': 'Ladies in Restaurants', in *Testament of a Generation – The Journalism of Vera Brittain and Winifred Holtby*, ed. Paul Berry and Alan Bishop.

**pages 46–8.** 'When she was nearly ninety . . .': Amy Gomm's autobiography *Water Under the Bridge* is held in the collection of working-class autobiographies at Brunel University.

**page 48.** 'Bessie Webster . . .': Correspondence and details supplied to the author by Miss Webster's niece, Isabel Raphael.

**page 49.** 'Or take the writer . . .': Author interview with Miss Jenkins, 2004.

**page 49.** 'Similarly "Rani" Cartwright . . .': Author interview with Miss Cartwright, 2004.

**page 53.** 'When Vera Brittain . . .': *Testament of Youth* by Vera Brittain.

**pages 55–7.** 'In 1886 and 1889 . . .': *Biography of Florence White* (unpublished) by D. J. Prickett.

# 3. On the Shelf

**page 61.** 'When young Frances . . .': Quoted in *Out of the Dolls House – The Story of Women in the Twentieth Century* by Angela Holdsworth.

**page 62.** 'If the fire required poking . . .': *Youth at the Gate* by Ursula Bloom.

**page 62.** 'Henrietta (Etty) Litchfield . . .': *Period Piece – A Cambridge Childhood* by Gwen Raverat.

**page 62.** 'These women's husbands . . .': *Emma Darwin – The Inspirational Wife of a Genius* by Edna Healey.

**page 64.** 'There is nothing . . .': *Pedagogue Pie* by D. F. P. Hiley.

**page 64.** 'One of Ivy Compton-Burnett's . . .': *More Women than Men* by Ivy Compton-Burnett.

**page 65.** 'Thrilling to . . .': *A Life's Work* by Margaret Bondfield.

**page 66.** 'Rosamond Lehmann . . .': Quoted in *Rosamond Lehmann – An Appreciation* by Gillian Tindall.

**pages 66–8.** 'Winifred Haward . . .': *Two Lives* by Winifred Haward Hodgkiss.

**pages 68–71.** 'Phyllis Bentley . . .': *O Dreams, O Destinations* by Phyllis Bentley; statistics cited from *Women's Leisure in England 1920–60* by Claire Langhamer.

**page 71.** 'On her twenty-sixth birthday . . .': *Public Servant, Private Woman – An Autobiography* by Dame Alix Meynell.

### HEART-TO-HEART CHATS

**page 75**. 'After her brother . . .': *Testament of Youth* by Vera Brittain.

### A BUYERS' MARKET

**page 78**. 'Girls like Irene Angell . . .': Cited in *Out of the Dolls House – The Story of Women in the Twentieth Century* by Angela Holdsworth.

**page 79**. 'Postal worker Evelyn Symonds . . .': author interview with Miss Symonds, 2004.

**page 80**. 'Barbara Cartland . . .': *The Isthmus Years* by Barbara Cartland.

**pages 80–82**. 'Beatrice Brown . . .': *Southwards from Swiss Cottage* by Beatrice Curtis Brown.

**page 82**. 'Another of her contemporaries . . .': *Mount Up with Wings* by Mary de Bunsen.

**pages 84–5**. 'And sometimes it worked . . .': Cases and statistics cited in *New Horizons – A Hundred Years of Women's Migration* by U. Monk, and *Emigration from the British Isles* by W. A. Carrothers.

**page 87**. 'Dorothy Marshall . . .': Interview with Dorothy Marshall, 'Out of the Dolls House' archive, Women's Library.

**page 87**. 'Irene Angell's office boss . . .': Interview with Irene Angell, 'Out of the Dolls House' archive, Women's Library.

**page 87**. 'The sex psychologist . . .': *The Great Unmarried* by Walter Gallichan.

### 'BUT WHO WILL GIVE ME MY CHILDREN?'

**page 92**. 'This was surely true . . .': Held in the Marie Stopes papers, Wellcome Trust Library.

**page 92**. 'A survey of elderly spinsters . . .': *Old and Alone – A Sociological Study of Old People* by Jeremy Tunstall.

**page 93**. 'Never having thought . . .': Interview with Irene Angell, 'Out of the Dolls House' archive, Women's Library.

**page 95**. 'The short poem . . .': All efforts to trace the author of this poem have so far failed.

**page 96**. 'The preacher Maude Royden . . .': *The Moral Standards of the Rising Generation* by Maude Royden.

**pages 96–7**. 'Nobody would judge . . .': Author interview with Miss Wakeham, 2004.

**pages 98–9**. 'This appears to . . .': *Richmal Crompton – The Woman Behind William* by Mary Cadogan.

**page 99**. 'Winifred Holtby . . .': *The Clear Stream – A Life of Winifred Holtby* by Marion Shaw.

**page 100**. 'Angela du Maurier . . .': *Old Maids Remember* by Angela du Maurier.

**page 100**. 'Cicely Hamilton . . .': *Life Errant* by Cicely Hamilton.

**page 100**. 'Realistic and level-headed . . .': Author interview with Miss Cartwright, 2004.

**pages 100–101**. 'The author Elizabeth Jenkins . . .': Author interview with Miss Jenkins, 2004.

# 4. Business Girls

### WAR, WORK AND WIVES

**page 107**. 'At the beginning . . .': Statistics in this chapter have been drawn from a number of sources, including *Women Who Work* by Joan Beauchamp, *Back to Home and Duty – Women between the Wars 1918–1939* by Deirdre Beddoe, *Our Work, Our Lives, Our Words* by Leonore Davidoff and Belinda Westover, *Women Teachers and Feminist Politics 1900–1939* by Alison Oram, 'Britain's "Lost Generation" of the First World War' by J. M. Winter, essay in *Population Studies – A Journal of Demography*, Vol. 31; the BBC History website http://www.bbc.co.uk/history/: *Women and Employment on the Home Front During World War One*.

**pages 107–8**. 'Victoria Alexandrina Drummond . . .': *The Remarkable Life of Victoria Drummond, Marine Engineer* by Cherry Drummond.

### PALACES OF COMMERCE

**pages 111–12**. 'That was certainly . . .': Author interview with Miss Symonds, 2004.

**page 112**. 'Miss Doreen Potts . . .': Author interview with Miss Potts, 2004.

**page 113**. 'In 1930 . . .': *The Times*, 16 May 1930.

**pages 114–15**. 'Nineteen-year old Mary Margaret Grieve . . .': *Millions Made My Story* by Mary Grieve.

**page 115**. 'The free stews . . .': *Southwards from Swiss Cottage* by Beatrice Curtis Brown.

**pages 115–16**. 'Like Mary Grieve . . .': *All Experience* by Ethel Mannin.

**page 117**. 'Miss Skrine's short account . . .': From Mass Observation Archive, Day Surveys 1937, held at Sussex University Library.

**page 118**. 'The journalist Leonora Eyles . . .': *Careers for Women* by Leonora Eyles.

**page 118**. 'In *Lysistrata* . . .': *Lysistrata, or Woman's Future and Future Woman* by Anthony M. Ludovici.

### A ROTTEN HARD LIFE

**pages 121–2.** 'The average woman worker . . .': *Marriage Past and Present* by Margaret Cole.

**page 122.** 'There was shop work . . .': Cited in *Out of the Dolls House – The Story of Women in the Twentieth Century* by Angela Holdsworth.

**page 122.** 'Miss Doris Warburton . . .': British Library Millennium Memory Bank Oral History collection.

**page 123.** 'Marjorie Gardiner . . .': *The Other Side of the Counter – The Life of a Shop Girl 1925–1945* by Marjorie Gardiner.

**page 123.** 'In 1938 . . .': Cited in *Biography of Florence White* (unpublished) by D. J. Prickett.

**page 124.** 'One woman born . . .': Cited in *Women's Life and Labour* by F. Zweig.

**page 124.** 'Researchers looking . . .': *Women Who Work* by Joan Beauchamp.

### MISS ALL-ALONE IN THE CLASSROOM

**pages 126–7.** 'Education was the key . . .': Cited in *Out of the Dolls House – The Story of Women in the Twentieth Century* by Angela Holdsworth.

**page 128.** 'It would be a national disaster . . .': *The Times*, 21 April 1924.

**page 128.** 'Walter Gallichan . . .': *The Great Unmarried* by Walter Gallichan.

**page 128.** 'A. S. Neill . . .': *The Problem Teacher* by A. S. Neill.

**page 128.** 'A 1930 article . . .': Quoted in *Women Teachers and Feminist Politics 1900–1939* by Alison Oram.

**pages 129–32.** 'The sad case of Elizabeth Rignall . . .': Miss Rignall's unpublished autobiography *All So Long Ago* is held in the collection of working-class autobiographies at Brunel University.

**page 134.** 'Miss Hewson . . .': From Mass Observation Archive, Day Surveys 1937, Sussex University Library.

**page 135.** 'Miss Dudley's story . . .': Letter to the author from John Edge, Burnley.

**page 137.** 'author and documentary-maker . . .': Author interview with Dr Goodfield, 2004.

**page 137.** 'Another woman . . .': Letter to the author from Iris Graham, Birmingham.

**page 137.** 'Miss Lilian Faithfull . . .': *In the House of My Pilgrimage* by Lilian Faithfull.

### MISS ALL-ALONE ON THE WARDS

**pages 138–9.** 'When nineteen-year-old . . .': *A Victorian Son – An Autobiography* by Stuart Cloete.

**page 139.** 'One of them . . .': *Yes, Matron* by Gladys M. Hardy.

**pages 140–42**. 'Mary Milne . . .': Entry on Mary Milne in the *Oxford Dictionary of National Biography*.

## 5. Caring, Sharing . . .

### LONELY DAYS

**page 146**. 'Nature did not construct . . .': *Marriage and Morals* by Bertrand Russell.

**page 146**. 'May Wedderburn Cannan . . .': *Grey Ghosts and Voices* by May Wedderburn Cannan.

**page 147**. 'The Oxford scholar . . .': *Enid Starkie* by Joanna Richardson.

**page 148**. 'Norah Elliott . . .': Miss Elliott's autobiographical notes are held in the collection of working-class autobiographies at Brunel University.

**pages 149–50**. 'Another teacher . . .': Diaries by Ethel Wragg and Harriet Warrack, Mass Observation Archive, Day Surveys 1937, held in Sussex University Library.

### COMPANIONS, CONSOLATIONS

**page 151**. 'In Essex . . .': Letter to the author from Mrs L. Bryan.

**page 151**. 'Vera Brittain's war . . .': *Testament of Youth* by Vera Brittain.

**page 151**. 'The novelist Irene Rathbone . . .': From Lynn Knight's introduction to the Virago edition of *We That Were Young* by Irene Rathbone.

**page 151**. 'Ivy Compton-Burnett's world . . .': *Ivy When Young – The Early Life of Ivy Compton-Burnett 1884–1919* by Hilary Spurling.

**page 152**. 'In her friendship . . .': *A Singular Woman – The Life of Geraldine Aves 1898–1986* by Phyllis Willmott.

**page 152**. 'Love could be expressed . . .': *Myra Hess – A Portrait* by Marian C. McKenna.

**page 153**. 'If they ever . . .': Entry on Elsie Waters in the *Oxford Dictionary of National Biography*.

**pages 153–4**. 'Tess, Una and Carmen Dillon . . .': Entries on Agnes (Una) Dillon and Carmen Dillon in the *Oxford Dictionary of National Biography*.

**pages 154–7**. 'Florence White . . .': *Biography of Florence White* (unpublished) by D. J. Prickett.

**page 158**. 'Doris Smith . . .': Author interview with Miss Smith, 2004.

**page 159**. 'Margaret Howes . . .': Author interview with Miss Howes, 2004.

**pages 160–62**. 'The novelist Phyllis Bentley . . .': *O Dreams, O Destinations* by Phyllis Bentley.

**page 162**. 'It was Angela . . .': *It's Only the Sister* by Angela du Maurier.

**pages 162–4**. 'The writer Elizabeth Goudge . . .': *The Joy of the Snow* by Elizabeth Goudge.

**pages 165–6**. 'Cicely Hamilton . . .': *Life Errant* by Cicely Hamilton.

### OTHER PEOPLE'S BABIES

**pages 166–7**. 'Pretty Nell Naylor . . .': Information supplied to the author by Andrew Stewart-Roberts.

**page 167**. 'The children's nurse . . .': Author interview with Miss Wakeham, 2004.

**page 167**. 'Nanny Robertson . . .': Case cited in *The Rise and Fall of the British Nanny* by Jonathan Gathorne-Hardy.

**page 169**. 'Lady Astor's personal maid . . .': *Rose: My Life in Service* by Rosina Harrison.

**page 170**. 'Joan Evans's parents . . .': *Prelude and Fugue – An Autobiography* by Joan Evans.

### LONELY NIGHTS

**page 173**. 'D. H. Lawrence . . .': *The Virgin and the Gipsy* by D. H. Lawrence.

**pages 175–7**. 'Marie Stopes's books . . .': The Marie Stopes archive is held at the Wellcome Institute Library, London.

**pages 177–8**. 'A psychological study . . .': 'The Single Woman – A Medical Study in Sex Education' by Robert L. Dickinson and Lura Beam, in *Women and Children First*, ed. D. J. and S. M. Rothman.

**page 178**. 'I think a woman . . .': Interview with Irene Angell, 'Out of the Dolls House' archive, Women's Library.

**page 180**. 'Betty Milton . . .': Case and statistics cited in *A Secret World of Sex – Forbidden Fruit: The British Experience 1900–1950* by Steve Humphries.

### THE BLESSED FACT OF LOVING

**page 181**. 'Doreen Potts . . .': Author interview with Miss Potts, 2004.

**page 182**. 'Beatrice Gordon Holmes . . .': *In Love with Life* by Beatrice Gordon Holmes.

**page 183**. 'Laura Hutton . . .': *The Single Woman and Her Emotional Problems* by Laura Hutton.

**page 185**. 'In the 1950s . . .': *Women's Life and Labour* by F. Zweig.

**pages 186–7**. 'And so would Maude Royden . . .': *Women, the World and the Home*, sermon preached by Maude Royden quoted in *Women Against the Iron Fist* by Sybil Oldfield.

# 6. A Grand Feeling

### A CAUSE, A PURPOSE AND A PASSION

**pages 188–91.** 'In 1918 . . .': *Mixed Memoirs* by Gertrude Caton-Thompson.

**page 191.** 'When a soldier . . .': Quoted in *How We Lived Then – 1914–18 – A Sketch of Social and Domestic Life in England during the War* by Mrs C. S. Peel.

**page 192.** 'Barbara Cartland . . .': *The Isthmus Years* by Barbara Cartland.

**pages 192–4.** 'Eastbourne might seem . . .': Author interview with Miss Cocker, 2004.

**pages 194–5.** 'Straight after the war . . .': *A Slender Reputation – An Autobiography* by Kathleen Hale.

**pages 195–201.** 'The writer Irene Rathbone . . .': 'Irene Rathbone: The Great War and Its Aftermath', essay by Caroline Zilboorg in *Re-charting the Thirties*, ed. Patrick Quinn; also the introductory essay to *We That Were Young* by Lynn Knight.

### THE WELL

**page 201.** 'In 1920 . . .': *Radclyffe Hall – A Woman called John* by Sally Cline.

**page 201.** 'In 1918 . . .': The Marie Stopes archive is held at the Wellcome Institute Library, London.

**page 204.** 'The psychologist . . .': *The Way of All Women* by Esther Harding.

**page 207.** 'From the outset . . .': *It's Only the Sister* and *Old Maids Remember* by Angela du Maurier.

**page 208.** 'Paul Fussell . . .': Quoted in *The Generation of 1914* by Robert Wohl.

**page 208.** 'Alice Skillicorn . . .': 'Homoerotic Friendship and College Principals, 1880–1960' by Elizabeth Edwards, in *Women's History Review* Vol. 4, No. 2, 1995.

**page 208.** 'The textile designers . . .': Entries on Phyllis Barron and Dorothy Larcher in the *Oxford Dictionary of National Biography*.

**page 208.** 'Another devoted partnership . . .': Entry on Dr Helen Mackay in the *Oxford Dictionary of National Biography*.

**page 209.** 'Mary Renault . . .': *Mary Renault – A Biography* by David Sweetman.

**page 209.** 'The novelist Sylvia Townsend Warner's . . .': *Sylvia Townsend Warner – Letters*, ed. William Maxwell.

### THE URGE

**pages 210–11.** 'In 1922 . . .': *A Woman Alone, in Kenya, Uganda and the Belgian Congo* by Etta Close.

**page 212.** 'Entomologist . . .': *Time Well Spent* by Evelyn Cheesman.

**page 212.** 'The Gamwell sisters . . .': *An Adventurous Heart*, unpublished autobiography by Marion Gamwell, FANY archives.

**page 212**. 'The London parlourmaid . . .': *The Small Woman* by Alan Burgess.

**pages 213–16**. 'At the age of seventy-seven . . .': *African Apprenticeship – An Autobiographical Journey in Southern Africa 1929* by Margery Perham.

### FINDING HAPPINESS AS A 'BACH'

**page 217**. 'The anti-feminist . . .': *Wasted Womanhood* by Charlotte Cowdroy.

**page 219**. 'I find real pleasure . . .': *Biography of Florence White* (unpublished) by D. J. Prickett.

**page 219**. 'The stockbroker . . .': *In Love with Life* by Beatrice Gordon Holmes.

**page 220**. 'Women like Vera Brittain . . .': *Testament of Youth* by Vera Brittain.

**page 220**. 'Winifred Holtby . . .': *The Clear Stream – A Life of Winifred Holtby* by Marion Shaw.

**page 222**. 'Here is a single teacher . . .': Quoted in *Women Teachers and Feminist Politics 1900–1939* by Alison Oram.

**page 222**. 'Caroline Haslett . . .': *Myself When Young – by Famous Women of Today*, ed. the Countess of Oxford and Asquith.

**page 222**. 'For Phyllis Bentley . . .': *O Dreams, O Destinations* by Phyllis Bentley.

**page 223**. 'Even Winifred Holtby . . .': 'The Best of Life', in *Testament of a Generation – The Journalism of Vera Brittain and Winifred Holtby*, ed. Paul Berry and Alan Bishop.

**page 223**. 'The children's author . . .': *Beyond the Vicarage* by Noël Streatfeild.

**page 223**. 'Angela du Maurier . . .': *It's Only the Sister* and *Old Maids Remember* by Angela du Maurier.

**page 224**. 'Once you get over . . .': Entry on Anne McAllister in the *Oxford Dictionary of National Biography*.

**page 225**. 'Winifred Holtby paid tribute . . .': *Women and a Changing Civilization* by Winifred Holtby.

**page 225**. 'Like Caroline Haslett . . .': *The Englishwoman* and *Life Errant* by Cicely Hamilton.

**page 226**. 'The writer Elizabeth Jenkins . . .': Author interview with Miss Jenkins, 2004.

**page 226**. 'Just a few years . . .': *Rose: My Life in Service* by Rosina Harrison.

### SURVIVING THE NIGHT

**pages 226–9**. 'And yet Winifred Haward . . .': *Two Lives* by Winifred Haward Hodgkiss.

**pages 230–32**. 'As a coda . . .': Amy Langley's unpublished autobiography is held in the collection of working-class autobiographies at Brunel University.

# 7. The Magnificent Regiment of Women

## THE CHALLENGE OF LOSS

**pages 233–4.** 'Two years after . . .': *Women, the World and the Home*, sermon preached by Maude Royden quoted in *Women Against the Iron Fist* by Sybil Oldfield, and *Sex and Commonsense* by Maude Royden.

**page 234.** 'Nobody, nothing . . .': Quoted in 'War, Death and Mourning in Modern Britain' by David Cannadine, in *Mirrors of Mortality – Studies in the Social History of Death*, ed. Joachim Whaley.

**pages 235–8.** 'In 1921 . . .': *Universal Aunts* by Kate Herbert-Hunting.

## WE ARE NOT DOWNHEARTED

**page 238.** 'Nothing is impracticable . . .': *Lolly Willowes* by Sylvia Townsend-Warner.

**pages 238–40.** 'The campaigner Florence White . . .': *Biography of Florence White* (unpublished) by D. J. Prickett.

**page 241.** 'One young woman . . .': *The Isthmus Years* by Barbara Cartland.

**page 242.** 'Women are accustomed . . .' *British Women in the Twentieth Century* by Elsie M. Lang.

**pages 243–5.** 'One lady . . .': Correspondence and details supplied to the author by Miss Webster's niece, Isabel Raphael.

## DOING THINGS THAT MATTER

**pages 250–55.** 'Mrs Pankhurst's followers . . .': *Myself When Young – by Famous Women of Today*, ed. the Countess of Oxford and Asquith, and *The Doors of Opportunity – A Biography* by Rosalind Messenger (sister of Caroline Haslett).

**page 255.** 'Today the organic . . .': *The Daily Telegraph Book of Obituaries*, ed. H. Massingberd, and entry on Eve Balfour in the *Oxford Dictionary of National Biography*.

**page 256.** 'The drive . . .': Entry on Rowena Cade in the *Oxford Dictionary of National Biography*.

**pages 256–7.** 'Miss Ellen Wilkinson . . .': *Ellen Wilkinson 1891–1947* by Betty D. Vernon.

**pages 257–68.** 'The sure march . . .': Unless cited in the text or noted below, the principal source for the women described in this section is the *Oxford Dictionary of National Biography*.

**page 257.** Nancy Seear: Case cited in *Out of the Dolls House – The Story of Women in the Twentieth Century* by Angela Holdsworth.

**page 257.** Dame Mary Smieton: Obituary, *Guardian*, January 2005.

**page 258.** Mary Allen: *The Pioneer Policewoman* by Mary S. Allen.

**page 258**. Victoria Drummond: *The Remarkable Life of Victoria Drummond, Marine Engineer* by Cherry Drummond.

**page 260**. Mary Freeman: British Library Millennium Memory Bank Oral History collection.

**page 260**. Honor Fell (and others): 'Women in Medical and Biomedical Science', essay by Lesley A. Hall in *This Working-Day World – Women's Lives and Culture(s) in Britain 1914–1945*, ed. Sybil Oldfield.

**page 261**. Barbara Wootton: *In a World I Never Made – Autobiographical Reflections* by Barbara Wootton.

**page 261**. Margery Fry: *Margery Fry – The Essential Amateur* by Enid Huws Jones.

**page 261**. Enid Starkie: *Enid Starkie* by Joanna Richardson.

**page 263**. Cicely Williams, Doreen Warriner, Evelyn Bark: Cited in *Women Humanitarians – A Biographical Dictionary of British Women Active between 1900 and 1950* by Sybil Oldfield.

**page 264**. Cicely Hamilton: *Life Errant* by Cicely Hamilton.

**pages 264–5**. Beatrice Gordon Holmes: *In Love with Life* by Beatrice Gordon Holmes.

**page 264**. Alice Head: *It Could Never Have Happened* by Alice M. Head.

**page 266**. Margaret Pilkington: *Margaret Pilkington 1891–1974*, biographical essay by David Blamires.

**page 267**. Irene Handl, Doris Speed and Margot Bryant: *The Daily Telegraph Book of Obituaries*, ed. H. Massingberd.

**pages 267–8**. Myra Hess: *Myra Hess – A Portrait* by Marian C. McKenna.

'YOU LOVED HIM'

**page 268**. 'When Mary Grieve . . .': *Millions Made My Story* by Mary Grieve.

**page 269**. 'Comparing the contribution . . .': Alison Wolf, 'Working Girls', in *Prospect Magazine*, April 2006, No. 121.

**page 270**. 'Anyone can get married . . .': *Biography of Florence White* (unpublished) by D. J. Prickett.

**pages 271–2**. 'In her ninety-fifth year . . .': *Mixed Memoirs* by Gertrude Caton-Thompson.

**page 272**. 'A fellow academic . . .': 'Gertrude Caton-Thompson, 1888–1985' by Margaret S. Drower, in *Breaking Ground – Pioneering Women Archaeologists*, ed. Getzel M. Cohen and Martha Sharp Joukowsky.

# Select Bibliography

I consulted over 200 books while researching this one. The following list, while not comprehensive, credits the main works which I found indispensable to an understanding of the period and subject-matter.

## Biography, Memoirs, Autobiography

**Ackland, Valentine**, *For Sylvia: An Honest Account*, Hogarth Press, London, 1985.

**Allen, Mary S.**, *The Pioneer Policewoman*, Chatto & Windus, London, 1925.

**Asquith, The Countess of Oxford and (ed.)**, *Myself When Young – by Famous Women of Today*, Frederick Muller, London, 1938.

**Baldwin, Monica**, *I Leap Over the Wall*, Hamish Hamilton, London, 1949.

**Bentley, Phyllis**, *O Dreams, O Destinations – An Autobiography*, Gollancz, London, 1962.

**Blamires, David**, *Margaret Pilkington 1891–1974*, Hermit Press, Buxton, 1995.

**Bondfield, the Rt Hon. Margaret**, *A Life's Work – The Record of More than Half a Century of Public Life*, Hutchinson, London, 1949.

**Brittain, Vera**, *Testament of Youth*, Gollancz, London, 1933.

**Brittain, Vera**, *Testament of Experience*, Gollancz, London, 1957.

**Brittain, Vera, and Handley-Taylor, Geoffrey (eds.)**, *Selected Letters of Winifred Holtby and Vera Brittain 1920–1935*, A. Brown, London, 1960.

**Brown, Beatrice Curtis**, *Southwards from Swiss Cottage*, Home and Van Thal, London, 1947.

**Bull, Angela**, *Noel Streatfeild – A Biography*, Collins, London, 1984.

**Burgess, Alan**, *The Small Woman*, Evans Brothers, London, 1957.

**Cadogan, Mary**, *Richmal Crompton – The Woman Behind William*, Allen & Unwin, London, 1986.

**Cannan, May Wedderburn**, *Grey Ghosts and Voices*, Roundwood Press, 1976.

**Cartland, Barbara**, *The Isthmus Years*, Hutchinson, London, 1942.

**Caton-Thompson, Gertrude**, *Mixed Memoirs*, Paradigm Press, Gateshead, 1983.

**Cheesman, Evelyn**, *Time Well Spent*, Hutchinson, London, 1960.

**Clarke, Mary G.**, *A Short Life of Ninety Years*, A. & M. Huggins, Edinburgh, 1973.

**Cline, Sally**, *Radclyffe Hall – A Woman Called John*, John Murray, 1997.

**Cloete, Stuart**, *A Victorian Son – An Autobiography 1897–1922*, Collins, London, 1972.

**Close, Etta**, *A Woman Alone, in Kenya, Uganda and the Belgian Congo*, Constable, London, 1924.

**Cowdroy, Charlotte**, *Wasted Womanhood*, Allen & Unwin, 1933.

**De Bunsen, Mary**, *Mount Up with Wings*, Hutchinson, London, 1960.

**Drower, Margaret S.**, 'Gertrude Caton-Thompson, 1888–1985', in Getzel M. Cohen and Martha Sharp Joukowsky (eds.), *Breaking Ground – Pioneering Women Archaeologists*, University of Michigan Press, 2004.

**Drummond, Cherry**, *The Remarkable Life of Victoria Drummond, Marine Engineer*, Institute of Marine Engineers, London, 1994.

**Du Maurier, Angela**, *It's Only the Sister*, Peter Davies, London, 1951.

**Du Maurier, Angela**, *Old Maids Remember*, Peter Davies, London, 1966.

**Essex, Rosamund**, *Woman in a Man's World*, Sheldon Press, London, 1977.

**Evans, Dame Joan**, *Prelude and Fugue – An Autobiography*, Museum Press, London, 1964.

**Faithfull, Lilian**, *In the House of My Pilgrimage*, Chatto & Windus, London, 1924.

**Fyfe, Charlotte (ed.)**, *The Tears of War – the Love Story of a Young Poet and a War Hero – May Cannan and Bevil Quiller-Couch*, Cavalier Books, 2000.

**Gardiner, Marjorie**, *The Other Side of the Counter – The Life of a Shop Girl 1925–1945*, QueenSpark Books, Brighton, 1985.

**Goudge, Elizabeth**, *The Joy of the Snow – An Autobiography*, Hodder & Stoughton, London, 1974.

**Grieve, Mary**, *Millions Made My Story*, Victor Gollancz, London, 1964.

**Hale, Kathleen**, *A Slender Reputation – An Autobiography*, Frederick Warne, London, 1994.

**Hamilton, Cicely**, *Life Errant*, J. M. Dent, London, 1935.

**Hardy, Gladys M.**, *Yes, Matron*, Edward O. Beck, London, 1951.

**Harker, Cassy M., with Jack Glattbach**, *Call Me Matron*, Heinemann, London, 1980.

**Harrison, Rosina**, *Rose: My Life in Service*, Cassell & Co., London, 1975.

**Head, Alice M.**, *It Could Never Have Happened*, William Heinemann, London, 1939.

**Healey, Edna**, *Emma Darwin – The Inspirational Wife of a Genius*, Headline, London, 2001.

**Herbert-Hunting, Kate**, *Universal Aunts*, Constable, London, 1986.

**Hodgkiss, Winifred Haward**, *Two Lives*, Yorkshire Art Circus, Barnsley, 1984.

**Holmes, Beatrice Gordon**, *In Love with Life – A Pioneer Career Woman's Story*, Hollis & Carter, London, 1944.

**Huws Jones, Enid**, *Margery Fry – The Essential Amateur*, Oxford University Press, 1966.

**Mannin, Ethel**, *All Experience*, Beacon Library, 1937.

**Massingberd, Hugh (ed.)**, *The Daily Telegraph Book of Obituaries*, 5 vols., Macmillan, 1999.

**Maxwell, William (ed.)**, *Sylvia Townsend Warner – Letters*, Chatto & Windus, London, 1982.

**McKenna, Marian C.**, *Myra Hess – A Portrait*, Hamish Hamilton, London, 1976.

**Meynell, Dame Alix**, *Public Servant, Private Woman – An Autobiography*, Victor Gollancz, London, 1988.

**Millard, Shirley**, *I Saw Them Die – Diary and Recollections*, ed. Adele Comandini, Harrap, London, 1936.

**Mitford, Jessica**, *Hons and Rebels*, Gollancz, London, 1960.

**Perham, Margery**, *African Apprenticeship – An Autobiographical Journey in Southern Africa 1929*, Faber and Faber, London, 1974.

**Prickett, D. J.**, *Biography of Florence White*, n.d., unpublished (www.historytoher-story.org.uk Yorkshire Women's Lives on-line).

**Raverat, Gwen**, *Period Piece – A Cambridge Childhood*, Faber and Faber, London, 1952.

**Richardson, Joanna**, *Enid Starkie*, John Murray, London, 1973.

**Roberts, Robert**, *A Ragged Schooling – Growing up in the Classic Slum*, Manchester University Press, 1976.

**Shaw, Marion**, *The Clear Stream – A Life of Winifred Holtby*, Virago, London, 1999.

**Spurling, Hilary**, *Ivy When Young – The Early Life of Ivy Compton-Burnett 1884–1919*, London, Gollancz, 1974.

**Spurling, Hilary**, *Secrets of a Woman's Heart – The Later Life of Ivy Compton-Burnett 1920–1969*, Hodder & Stoughton, 1984.

**Stark, Dame Freya**, *Traveller's Prelude – Autobiography 1893–1927*, John Murray, London, 1950.

**Streatfeild, Noël**, *Beyond the Vicarage*, Collins, London, 1971.

**Sweetman, David**, *Mary Renault – A Biography*, London, 1993.

**Tindall, Gillian**, *Rosamond Lehmann – An Appreciation*, Hogarth Press, London, 1985.

**Troubridge, Una Lady**, *The Life and Death of Radclyffe Hall*, Hammond, London, 1961.

**Vernon, Betty D.**, *Ellen Wilkinson 1891–1947*, Croom Helm, London, 1982.

**White, Evelyne**, *Winifred Holtby as I Knew Her – A Study of the Author and Her Works*, Collins, London, 1938.

**Willmott, Phyllis**, *A Singular Woman – The Life of Geraldine Aves 1898–1986*, Whiting and Birch, London, 1992.

**Wootton, Barbara**, *In a World I Never Made – Autobiographical Reflections*, George Allen & Unwin, London, 1967.

# History, Psychology, Sociology, Advice

**Abbott, Elizabeth**, *A History of Celibacy*, Lutterworth Press, Cambridge, 2001.

**Adam, Ruth**, *A Woman's Place*, Chatto & Windus, 1975.

**Barron, Dana L.**, 'Sex and Single Girls in the Twentieth-century City', in *Journal of Urban History*, Vol. 25, No. 6, September 1999.

**Beauchamp, Joan**, *Women Who Work*, Lawrence & Wishart, London, 1937.

**Beauman, Nicola**, *A Very Great Profession – The Woman's Novel 1914–1939*, Virago, London, 1983.

**Beddoe, Deirdre**, *Back to Home and Duty – Women between the Wars 1918–1939*, Pandora Press, London, 1989.

**Berry, Paul, and Bishop, Alan (eds.)**, *Testament of a Generation – The Journalism of Vera Brittain and Winifred Holtby*, Virago, London, 1985.

**Birkett, Dea**, *Spinsters Abroad – Victorian Lady Explorers*, Blackwell, Oxford, 1989.

**Brookes, Pamela**, *Women at Westminster – An Account of Women in the British Parliament 1918–1966*, Peter Davies, London, 1967.

**Burgess, Clara Amy**, *The Sex Philosophy of a Bachelor Girl*, Advanced Thought Publishing, Chicago, 1920.

**Cannadine, David**, 'War, Death and Mourning in Modern Britain', in *Mirrors of Mortality – Studies in the Social History of Death*, ed. Joachim Whaley, Europa Publications, London, 1981.

**Carrothers, W. A.**, *Emigration from the British Isles*, P. S. King, London, 1929.

**Castle, Terry**, *Noël Coward and Radclyffe Hall*, Columbia University Press, New York, 1996.

**Chesser, Dr Eustace**, *The Sexual, Marital and Family Relationships of the English Woman*, Hutchinson's Medical Publications, London, 1956.

**Cole, Margaret**, *Marriage Past and Present*, J. M. Dent, London, 1938.

**Davidoff, Leonore, and Westover, Belinda**, *Our Work, Our Lives, Our Words – Women's History and Women's Work*, inc. contributions by Teresa Davy, Kay Sanderson, Macmillan Education, 1986.

**Dickinson, Robert L., and Beam, Lura**, 'The Single Woman – A Medical Study in Sex Education', in *Women and Children First*, ed. David J. and Sheila M. Rothman, first published 1934, Garland Publishing Inc., 1987.

**Doan, Laura L.**, *Old Maids to Radical Spinsters – Unmarried Women in the 20th Century Novel*, University of Illinois Press, Urbana and Chicago, 1991.

**Duquenin, Anthea**, 'Who Doesn't Marry and Why?', in *Oral History – The Journal of the Oral History Society*, Vol. 12, No. 1, Spring 1984.

**Edwards, Elizabeth**, 'Homoerotic Friendship and College Principals, 1880–1960', in *Women's History Review*, Vol. 4, No. 2, 1995.

**Eyles, Leonora**, *Careers for Women*, Elkins, Mathews & Marrot, London, 1930.

**Fry, Margery**, *The Single Woman*, Delisle, London, 1953.

**Fussell, Paul**, *The Great War and Modern Memory*, Oxford University Press, New York and London, 1975.

**Gallichan, Walter M.**, *Modern Woman and How to Manage Her*, T. Werner Laurie, London, 1913.

**Gallichan, Walter M.**, *The Great Unmarried*, T. Werner Laurie, London, 1916.

**Gathorne-Hardy, Jonathan**, *The Rise and Fall of the British Nanny*, Hodder & Stoughton, London, 1972.

**Graves, Robert, and Hodge, Alan**, *The Long Week-End: A Social History of Britain*, Faber and Faber, London, 1941.

**Hall, Ruth (ed.)**, *Dear Dr Stopes – Sex in the 1920s*, Andre Deutsch, 1978.

**Hamilton, Cicely**, *The Englishwoman*, British Council Publications, 1940.

**Harding, M. Esther**, *The Way of All Women*, Longmans, London and New York, 1933.

**Henry, May, and Halford, Jeanette**, *The Bachelor Girl's Cookery Book – Simplified Recipes for Amateurs*, Letchworth and London, 1931.

**Hiley, D. F. P.**, *Pedagogue Pie*, Ivor Nicholson & Watson, London, 1936.

**Hillis, Marjorie**, *Live Alone and Like It – A Guide for the Extra Woman*, Sun Dial Press, New York, 1936.

**Holden, Katherine**, *The Shadow of Marriage – Single Women in England 1919–1939*, thesis (Ph.D. University of Essex, unpublished).

**Holdsworth, Angela**, *Out of the Dolls House – The Story of Women in the Twentieth Century*, BBC Books, London, 1988.

**Holtby, Winifred**, *Women and a Changing Civilization*, London, 1934.

**Hutton, Laura**, *The Single Woman and Her Emotional Problems*, Bailliere, Tindall & Cox, London, 1935.

**Humphries, Steve**, *A Secret World of Sex – Forbidden Fruit: The British Experience 1900–1950*, Sidgwick & Jackson, London, 1988.

**Hynes, Samuel**, *A War Imagined – The First World War and English Culture*, Bodley Head, London, 1990.

**Jeffreys, Sheila**, *The Spinster and Her Enemies – Feminism and Sexuality 1880–1930*, 1985.

*Journal of Family History*, Vol. 9, No. 4, Winter 1984 – *Special Issue on Spinsterhood*; contributions by Susan Cotts Watkins, Michael Anderson, Ruth Freeman, Patricia Klaus.

**Kanner, Barbara Penny**, *Women in Context – Two Hundred Years of British Women Autobiographers*, G. K. Hall, New York, 1997.

**Lang, Elsie M.**, *British Women in the Twentieth Century*, T. Werner Laurie, London, 1929.

**Langhamer, Claire**, *Women's Leisure in England 1920–60*, Manchester University Press, 2000.

**Ludovici, Anthony M.**, *Lysistrata, or Woman's Future and Future Woman*, Kegan Paul, London, 1927.

**Melman, Billie**, *Women and the Popular Imagination in the Twenties – Flappers and Nymphs*, Macmillan, London, 1988.

**Miall, Agnes M.**, *The Bachelor Girl's Guide to Everything – or The Girl on Her Own*, London, 1916.

**Monk, U.**, *New Horizons – A Hundred Years of Women's Migration*, HMSO, London, 1963.

**Moore, Doris Langley [pseud: 'A Gentlewoman']**, *The Technique of the Love Affair*, Gerald Howe, London, 1928.

**Neill, A. S.**, *The Problem Teacher*, Herbert Jenkins, London, 1939.

**Neville-Rolfe, Sybil**, *Why Marry?*, Faber and Faber, London, 1935.

**Oldfield, Sybil**, *Women Against the Iron Fist – Alternatives to Militarism 1900–1989*, Blackwell, Oxford, 1989.

**Oldfield, Sybil (ed.)**, *This Working-Day World – Women's Lives and Culture(s) in Britain 1914–1945*, Taylor & Francis, London, 1994, includes essays by: **Elizabeth Edwards**, 'Women's Teacher Training Colleges'; **Maroula Joannou**, ' "Nothing is Impracticable for a Single, Middle-Aged Woman with an Income of her Own": The Spinster in Women's Fiction of the 1920s'; **Lesley A. Hall**, 'Women in Medicine and Biomedical Science'.

**Oldfield, Sybil**, *Women Humanitarians – A Biographical Dictionary of British Women Active between 1900 and 1950*, Continuum, London and New York, 2001.

**Oram, Alison**, *Women Teachers and Feminist Politics 1900–1939*, Manchester University Press, 1966.

**Oram, Alison**, 'Repressed and Thwarted or Bearer of the New World: the Spinster in Inter-War Feminist Discourses', in *Women's History Review*, Vol. 1, No. 3, 1992.

**Peel, Mrs C. S.**, *How We Lived Then – 1914–18 – A Sketch of Social and Domestic Life in England during the War*, Bodley Head, London, 1929.

**Quinn, Patrick (ed.)**, *Re-charting the Thirties*, London Associated University Presses, 1996, essay by Caroline Zilboorg, 'Irene Rathbone: The Great War and Its Aftermath'.

**Royden, Maude**, *Sex and Commonsense*, Hurst & Blackett, London, 1921.

**Royden, Maude**, *The Moral Standards of the Rising Generation* (pamphlet), League of the Church Militant, 1922.

**Russell, Bertrand**, *Marriage and Morals*, George Allen & Unwin, London, 1929.

**Scharlieb, Dame Mary**, *The Bachelor Woman and Her Problems*, 1929.

**Spring Rice, Margery**, *Working-Class Wives – Their Health and Conditions*, Virago, 1981.

**Tunstall, Jeremy**, *Old and Alone – A Sociological Study of Old People*, Routledge & Kegan Paul, London, 1966.

**Tweedy, Rosamund**, *Consider Her Palaces – A Study of the Housing Problem of Lower-paid Single Women Workers in London*, published by the Over Thirty Association, 1936.

**Vicinus, Martha**, *Independent Woman; Work and Community for Single Women 1850–1920*, Virago, 1985.

**Wallace, Diana**, *Sisters and Rivals in British Women's Fiction, 1914–39*, Macmillan, London, 2000.

**Winter, Denis**, *Death's Men – Soldiers of the Great War*, Allen Lane, London, 1978.

**Winter, Jay**, *Sites of Memory, Sites of Mourning – the Great War in European Cultural History*, Cambridge University Press, 1995.

**Winter, Jay, and Baggett, Blaine**, *1914–18: The Great War and the Shaping of the Twentieth Century*, BBC Books, 1996.

**Winter, J. M.**, *The Great War and the British People*, Harvard University Press, Cambridge, Mass., 1986.

**Winter, J. M.**, 'Britain's "Lost Generation" of the First World War', in *Population Studies – A Journal of Demography*, Vol. 31, No. 3, November 1977.

**Wohl, Robert**, *The Generation of 1914*, Weidenfeld & Nicolson, London, 1980.

**Zweig, F.**, *Women's Life and Labour*, Gollancz, London, 1952.

# Fiction/Poetry/Humour

**Adam, Ruth**, *I'm Not Complaining*, first published Chapman & Hall, London, 1938, new edition Virago, London, 1983.

**Arnold, Roxane, and Chandler, Olive (eds.)**, *Feminine Singular – Triumphs and Tribulations of the Single Woman, An Anthology*, Femina Books, 1974.

**Bowen, Elizabeth**, *A World of Love*, Jonathan Cape, London, 1955.

**Cannan, May Wedderburn**, *The Lonely Generation*, Hutchinson, London, 1934.

**Cannan, May Wedderburn**, *The Splendid Days*, Blackwell, Oxford, 1919.

**Compton-Burnett, Ivy**, *More Women than Men*, Eyre & Spottiswoode, London, 1951.

**Delafield, E. M.**, *Thank Heaven Fasting*, Macmillan, London, 1932.

**Fielding, Helen**, *Bridget Jones's Diary*, Picador, London, 1996.

**Hall, Radclyffe**, *The Unlit Lamp*, Cassell, London, 1928.

**Hall, Radclyffe**, *The Well of Loneliness*, first published 1928, Virago, London, 1982.

**Holland, Ruth**, *The Lost Generation*, Victor Gollancz, London, 1932.

**Holtby, Winifred**, *The Crowded Street*, John Lane, The Bodley Head, London, 1924.

**Holtby, Winifred**, *Poor Caroline*, Jonathan Cape, London, 1931.

**Holtby, Winifred**, *South Riding – An English Landscape*, Collins, 1947.

**Mayor, F. M.**, *The Rector's Daughter*, Hogarth Press, London, 1924.

**Perham, M. F.**, *Josie Vine*, Hutchinson, London, 1927.

**Rathbone, Irene**, *We That Were Young*, with an introduction by Lynn Knight, Feminist Press, 1989.

**Rathbone, Irene**, *Was There a Summer?*, Constable, London, 1943.

**Rathbone, Irene**, *October*, J. M. Dent & Sons, London, 1934.

**Rathbone, Irene**, *They Call It Peace*, J. M. Dent, London, 1936.

**Reilly, Catherine W. (ed.)**, *Scars upon my Heart – Women's Poetry and Verse of the First World War*, Virago, London, 1981.

**Spark, Muriel**, *The Prime of Miss Jean Brodie*, Macmillan, London, 1961.

**Stead, Christina**, *For Love Alone*, Peter Davies, London, 1945.

**Stevenson, Sylvia**, *Surplus*, T. Fisher Unwin, London, 1924.

**Townsend Warner, Sylvia**, *Lolly Willowes*, Chatto & Windus, London, 1926.

**Wade, Rosalind**, *Treasure in Heaven*, Collins, London, 1937.

## Archives, Websites, etc.

**The Stopes Papers**, Wellcome Trust Library.

**Collection of Working-Class Autobiographies**, Brunel University.

**Mass Observation Archive – Day Surveys 1937**, Sussex University Library.

**FANY** archive.

**The Institute of Electrical Engineers**, archive.

**The Imperial War Museum**.

**The Women's Library, London Metropolitan University,** 'Out of the Dolls House' archive.

**The Millennium Memory Bank Oral History Collection** at the British Library.

**Newspaper Collection**, British Library at Colindale.

**www.historytoherstory.org.uk** Yorkshire Women's Lives On-Line, 1100 to the present.

**www.firstworldwar.com**.

**www.oxforddnb.com**.

# Acknowledgements

My thanks go to the numerous people who have helped make this book possible; if precedence is due, then it must go above all to the members of my family, the friends and associates whose encouragement and help have been paramount. They are, in no particular order: my mother, Anne Olivier Bell, my agent, Caroline Dawnay, my editor at Viking, Eleo Gordon, and my husband, William Nicholson.

I would also like to make special acknowledgement to the following people who gave the idea for this book their blessing and helped in other ways too: Juliet Annan, A. S. Byatt, Rupert Christiansen, Richard Cohen, Margaret Drabble, Julian Fellowes, Victoria Glendinning, Valerie Grove, Selina Hastings, Lady Healey, Michael Holroyd, Hermione Lee, Kathy Robbins and Lynne Truss.

More specifically, I have had significant research assistance and time-consuming responses to my enquiries from the following: Max Arthur, Professor Norman Gates, Jonathan Gathorne-Hardy, Fiona Hackney, Rebecca John, Raynes Minns, Angela Neuberger, Anne Powell, Andrew and Phyllida Stewart-Roberts, Pat Utechin, Dr Caroline Zilboorg, and especially Sybil Oldfield.

I have particularly appreciated help from the many librarians, archivists and representatives of a number of organisations who took time to respond to my queries: Pauline Adams, Fiona Bourne, Deborah Bowles, Kevin Brown, Sarah Brydon, Ailsa Camm, Joy Cann, Adjutant Joan Drummond, Peter Forbes, Andrew George, Paula Gerrard, Jo Glanville, Sam Jones, Anne Locker, Janet Mann, Kate Perry, Dr Anne-Marie Rafferty, Dorothy Sheridan, Dr Roderick Suddaby, Lenore Symons and Miriam Valencia. Particular thanks to Penny Lyndon and Jane Vince, who helped me find my way through the invaluable archive of working-class autobiographies at Brunel University, and to Dr Lesley Hall at the Wellcome Trust Library for her guidance through the Marie Stopes archive. I am also grateful to Antonia Byatt, Teresa Doherty and Anna Kisby for arranging access to the 'Out of the Dolls House' archive in the Women's Library at London Metropolitan University. Others who kindly replied to my questions, letters and advertisements were Daphne Baston, Hugo Brunner, Mrs Lee Bryan, Canon John Edge, Dr Peter Estcourt, Jamie and Maggie Fergusson, Margaret Forster, Richard and Jane Garnett, Lady Gibson and the late Lord Gibson, H. V. Gilpin, Mrs Iris Graham, Miranda Grainger, Chloë Green, Lord Hutchinson, Lady Joanna Hylton, Michael Johnson, Sue Keighley, Lucinda Lambton, Philip Mayne, Susan McGann, Nick Milner-Gulland, Anne Morrison, Jane Mulvagh, the late Nigel Nicolson, Zoë Pagnamenta,

Isabel Raphael, Elizabeth Ray, Ged Robinson, Diane Spero and Simon Watney. Thanks too to Joanna Head, Emma Wakefield and Mary Cranitch of Lambent Productions.

I would not have been able to write this book without special help from Elizabeth Finn Care and their staff, whose excellent retirement homes give friendly and dignified care to the elderly (and who do much more too). Marian Flint most willingly and efficiently set up introductions to the ladies I interviewed: Rani Cartwright, the late Mary Cocker and her friend Olive Jefferies, Gertrude Foxley, Margaret Howes, the late Miss Mapp, Doreen Potts, the late Doris Smith, Evelyn Symonds, Olive Wakeham and Miss Willetts. Elizabeth Ray also effected my introduction to the staff and residents of Dresden House, Hove. I am grateful too to a number of other people who spared time to be interviewed: Dr June Goodfield, Ian Hamilton, Kate Herbert-Hunting and Angela Sinclair, Elizabeth Jenkins, Harry Patch and Joan Thornton.

Particular thanks to Douglas Matthews for his exemplary index; also to Stephanie Collie, Lesley Hodgson, Kathryn Laing, Annie Lee, Sophie Powell and all the publication team at Viking. Thanks too to Jeremy Crow of the Society of Authors, and to the staff of the London Library and the British Library.

Friends and family have helped in many ways, small and great. Thanks are due to Susannah Acworth, Russell Ash, Paul Beecham, Cressida and Julian Bell, Adam Curtis, Peter Grimsdale, Adam Low, Jamie Muir, Julia, Maria and Teddy Nicholson, Jane Salvage, Paul Spencer and Olivia Timbs.

★

In addition, the author gratefully acknowledges the kind permission of copyright holders to quote from the works of a number of authors and sources, as follows: Peters Fraser & Dunlop, on behalf of the Estate of Phyllis Bentley, for permission to quote from *O Dreams, O Destinations*; excerpts from *Thank Heaven Fasting* by E. M. Delafield (Copyright © Estate of E. M. Delafield 1989) also reproduced by permission of PFD (*www.pfd.co.uk*) on behalf of the Estate of E. M. Delafield; Gillon Aitken Associates Ltd on behalf of the Estate of Sir John Betjeman, for use of an excerpt from 'Business Girls' in *A Few Late Chrysanthemums*, also on behalf of the author for the use of a quotation from *Bridget Jones's Diary* by Helen Fielding; Constable & Robinson Ltd, for reproduction of excerpts from *A Woman Alone* by Etta Close, also from *Universal Aunts* by Kate Herbert-Hunting; A. P. Watt Ltd on behalf of the executors of the Estate of Jocelyn Herbert, M. T. Perkins and Molly M. V. R. Perkins for the excerpt from *Other People's Babies – A Song of Kensington Gardens*; A. M. Heath and Co. Ltd, for permission to quote an excerpt from *Beyond the Vicarage* by Noël Streatfeild (Copyright © Noël Streatfeild, 1971), and also for permission to quote excerpts from *The Well of Loneliness* and *The Unlit Lamp* by

Radclyffe Hall (both Copyright © Radclyffe Hall 1928); Macmillan & Co. for use of an excerpt from *The Prime of Miss Jean Brodie* (1961) by Muriel Spark; Virago, for excerpts from *I'm Not Complaining* by Ruth Adam, new edition (1983); Mark Bostridge and Rebecca Williams, Literary Executors for the Vera Brittain Estate, 1970, for the inclusion of quotations from Vera Brittain; Hodder & Stoughton for the use of excerpts from *The Joy of the Snow* by Elizabeth Goudge (1974); Jonathan Clowes Ltd, London, on behalf of the author, for the reprinting of an excerpt from *Under My Skin – Volume 1 of My Autobiography* by Doris Lessing, Copyright © 1995 Doris Lessing; the Sheldon Press for extracts from *Woman in a Man's World* by Rosamund Essex (1977); the Estate of Sylvia Townsend Warner for permission to quote from *Lolly Willowes* and *Letters*, ed. William Maxwell; the Bodleian Library, University of Oxford, for quotations from the writings of Enid Starkie; Faber and Faber Ltd for permission to quote from *The Waste Land* by T. S. Eliot; an excerpt from *Traveller's Prelude – Autobiography 1893–1927* by Dame Freya Stark reproduced by permission of John Murray (Publishers) Ltd. Grateful acknowledgements are also due to the BBC for use of extracts from the British Library Millennium Memory Bank Oral History Collection, and to Rosina Wood née Chitticks for use of unpublished excerpts from the writings of Miss Emily Chitticks now held in the Department of Documents of the Imperial War Museum. Quotations from the work of Elizabeth Bowen reproduced with permission of Curtis Brown Group Ltd, London on behalf of the Estate of Elizabeth Bowen, Copyright © Elizabeth Bowen 1955; quotations from U. Monk, *New Horizons – A Hundred Years of Women's Emigration* reproduced under the terms of the Click-Use Licence issued by the Office of Public Sector Information. Quotations from the Mass Observation Archive at Sussex University Library reproduced with permission of Curtis Brown Group Ltd, London on behalf of the Trustees of the Mass Observation Archive Copyright © Trustees of the Mass Observation Archive.

The author would also particularly like to thank the following: James Slater for permission to reprint excerpts from *Grey Ghosts and Voices* by May Wedderburn Cannan; Jean Faulks for permission to reprint excerpts from *All Experience* by Ethel Mannin (1937); Angela Holdsworth for use of material from *Out of the Dolls House*, BBC Books (1988); excerpts from *Josie Vine* and *African Apprenticeship* by kind permission of the Trustees of the will of the late Dame Margery Perham; Dr Alison Oram for use of material from her book *Women Teachers and Feminist Politics 1900–1939*, Manchester University Press (1996); Jonathan Gathorne-Hardy for permission to quote from *The Rise and Fall of the British Nanny*; Annabel Cole for permission to quote from *The Single Woman* by Margery Fry; the Estate of Irene Rathbone for permission to quote from her work. It should be mentioned that a large number of these copyright holders could not have been traced without the indispensable aid of the WATCH (Writers, Artists and Their Copyright Holders) database (*www.watchfile.com*), jointly run by the Universities of Reading and Texas, and supported by the Strachey Trust. While not quoting substantially from it, this book has also drawn from an unpublished biography of Florence White by Diana J. Prickett, written in 1986; the manuscript is accessible on-line via the website *www.historytoherstory.org.uk* Yorkshire Women's Lives On-Line.

Acknowledgements are also due to the following whose works have been quoted from: Ruth Adam, *A Woman's Place*; Gertrude Caton-Thompson, *Mixed Memoirs;* G. Phizackerley (ed.), *The Diaries of Maria Gyte*; Shirley Millard, *I Saw Them Die – Diary and Recollections*, ed. Adele Comandini; John MacArthur, *Shall Flappers Rule;* Anthony M. Ludovici, *Lysistrata, or Woman's Future and Future Woman;* Charlotte Cowdroy, *Wasted Womanhood*; Margery Spring Rice, *Working-Class Wives: Their Health and Conditions*; Christina Stead, *For Love Alone*; Rosamond Lehmann, *Invitation to the Waltz;* Beatrice Curtis Brown, *Southwards from Swiss Cottage*; Mary de Bunsen, *Mount Up with Wings*; Marjorie Hillis, *Live Alone and Like it*; Jeremy Tunstall, *Old and Alone – A Sociological Study of Old People*; Mary Grieve, *Millions Made My Story*; Rosamund Tweedy, *Consider Her Palaces*; D. F. P. Hiley, *Pedagogue Pie*; Gladys M. Hardy, *Yes, Matron*; Irving Berlin, *Sisters, Sisters*; Sybil Neville-Rolfe, *Why Marry?*; Esther Harding, *The Way of All Women*; F. Zweig, *Women's Life and Labour*; Erich Fromm, *The Art of Loving*; Sylvia Stevenson, *Surplus*; Dame Caroline Haslett, *Myself When Young – by Famous Women of Today*, ed. Countess Asquith; Rosalind Messenger, *The Doors of Opportunity – A Biography*; Maude Royden, *Sex and Commonsense, Sermon Preached in the Cathedral at Geneva on the Occasion of the Meeting of the International Women's Suffrage Alliance* and *The Moral Standards of the Rising Generation; The Lyrics of Noël Coward.*

While every effort has been made to trace the copyright holders of a number of other works quoted in this book, it has proved impossible in certain cases to obtain formal permission for their use. The publishers would be glad to hear from any copyright holders they have not been able to contact and to print due acknowledgement in future editions. Works whose copyright holders have so far proved untraceable are as follows: *Two Lives* by Winifred Haward Hodgkiss, published by Yorkshire Art Circus (1984); *Rose: My Life in Service* by Rosina Harrison, Cassell & Co. (1975); the poem 'Old Maid's Child', reprinted in *The Single Woman* by Margery Fry; *In Love with Life* by Beatrice Gordon Holmes, Hollis & Carter (1944); *A Victorian Son – An Autobiography* by Stuart Cloete, Collins (1972); *Prelude and Fugue* by Dame Joan Evans, Museum Press (1964); *Life Errant* by Cicely Hamilton, J. M. Dent (1935); *Call Me Matron* by Cassy Harker with Jack Glattbach, Heinemann, London (1980); *It's Only the Sister* and *Old Maids Remember*, Peter Davies (1951 and 1966), by Angela du Maurier.

The archive of working-class autobiographies at Brunel University has been an invaluable resource; the authors of these most poignant of unpublished works –

May Jones, Amy Gomm, Elizabeth Rignall, Norah Elliott and Amy Langley – and their hereditary copyright holders are lost in the mists of time, but should any of them emerge the publishers will be equally happy to give proper credit to them in any future editions.

# Index

abortions, 180
Ackland, Valentine, 209, 266
Adam, Ruth: *I'm Not Complaining*,
132–4; *A Woman's Place*, xii
advertisements: for matrimony, 88–9
Africa, 210–16
Aldington, Richard, 196–200;
*Death of a Hero*, 196
Allen, Grant, 65
Allen, Marian, 15
Allen, Mary, 258
Angell, Irene, 78, 87, 93, 145, 178
animals: love for, 164–6
Appleby Castle, Westmorland, 77
Aristophanes: *Lysistrata*, 38n
Armstrong-Jones, Sir Robert, 242
arts: women in, 266–8
Ashford, Daisy: *The Young Visiters*,
63
Asquith, Herbert Henry, 1st Earl,
24
Astor, Nancy, Viscountess, 78, 170,
226, 247
aunthood, 97–100, 235; *see also*
Universal Aunts
Austen, Jane, 33; *Sense and
Sensibility*, 72n
Australia: emigration to, 82–3
Aves, Geraldine, 44, 152, 180, 186
Aylward, Gladys, 212

bachelor girl: as term, 89–90; in
literature, 119; manuals and
guides for, 119–21; activities,

217–18; happiness and
fulfilment, 221–2; and ageing,
223–4; *see also* spinsters and
spinsterhood
Baldwin, Monica, 29
Balfour, Lady Eve, 255; *The Living
Soil*, 255
balls *see* dances and dancing
Bankhead, Tallulah, 205
Banks, Misses (bookshop owners),
265
Bark, Evelyn, 263
Barlow, Miss (print-worker), 238
Barney, Natalie, 205
Barron, Phyllis, 208
Bath, Alexander George Thynne,
7th Marquis of, 167
Beauchamp, Joan, 124
Beavan, Margaret, 265
Beck, Dr Diana, 259
Beckett, Phyllis, 236
Bedford College, London, 67
Beesley, Edith, 265
Belloc, Hilaire, 34–5
Benson, E.F., 35
Bentley, Eleanor (Nellie), 160–62
Bentley, Nicolas, 36
Bentley, Phyllis: background,
68–9; marriage hopes unfulfilled,
69–71, 101, 160, 266; writings,
71–2, 270; cares for mother,
160–62; owns car, 222;
*Inheritance*, 71; *O Dreams, O
Destinations*, 69

Holmes, Verena, 258
Holtby, Winifred: at Oxford,
30–31; friendship with Vera
Brittain, 30–31, 53, 151, 180–81;
background, 31; relations with
Harry Pearson, 31–2, 37; single
state, 31–3, 101; appearance, 37;
friendship with Cicely
Hamilton, 41; writings, 42, 266,
270; refused unaccompanied
access to hotel, 45–6; fictional
heroines, 51; character and
appearance, 53; death, 53, 181,
223; and children, 99; Vera
Brittain praises, 102; on
predicament of young women,
188; on knowing ecstasy, 191;
denies failure in marriage,
220–21; sense of ageing, 223; on
happiness, 225; 'Are Spinsters
Frustrated?', 32n, 54–6, 188,
194; *The Crowded Street*, 32, 51;
*Poor Caroline*, 147–8, 151; *South
Riding*, 32, 51, 54
homosexuality, 51, 181–5, 201–9
hostels, 113–14, 247
housework, 61–2
Howes, Margaret, 159–60
humanitarians, 263–4
Hutton, Laura, 44, 89, 91, 183; *The
Single Woman and Her Emotional
Problems*, 42, 146, 164–5

Ibsen, Henrik, 65
*Inn of the Sixth Happiness, The*
(film), 212n
Institution of Locomotive
Engineers, 258
International Alliance for Women's
Suffrage, 233

International Federation of
Business and Professional
Women, 264
Irons, Evelyn, 205
Irvine, Miss (tea-taster), 265

Jackson, Polly, Rose and Martha,
57
Jaeger, Muriel, 266
James, Henry, 33
Jameson, Storm, 195
Jenkins, Elizabeth, 49, 54,
100–101, 226, 266
John, Augustus, 194
John, Gwen, 195, 266
Jones, Gwyneth Wansbrough, 152,
180, 186
Jones, May (Margaret):
background, xiii, 1–2, 28, 44;
relations with Philip, 2–3; and
Philip's absence and death on
active service, 4, 15, 20; single
state, 101
Jourdain, Margaret, 152

Kenya, 211
Kilroy, Alix, 71
King, Viva, 195
Kingsley, Mary, 28
Knight, Miss D.E., 176
Knight, Lynn, 198–9

Lang, Elsie M.: *British Women in the
Twentieth Century*, 264–5
Langley, Amy, xiii, 230–32
Larcher, Dorothy, 208
Lawrence, D.H., 39, 173–4; *The
Fox*, 40
Lawrence, T.E., 200
lawyers: women as, 259–60